# ArtScroll Series®

**Rabbi Nosson Scherman / Rabbi Meir Zlotowitz**

*General Editors*

# UNDERSTANDING
# JUDAISM

Published by
Mesorah Publications, ltd

# A BASIC GUIDE
# TO JEWISH FAITH,
# HISTORY, AND PRACTICE

## RABBI MORDECHAI KATZ

A JEP / ROTHMAN FOUNDATION PUBLICATION

FIRST EDITION
*First Impression . . . November 2000*

*Published and Distributed by*
**MESORAH PUBLICATIONS, Ltd.**
4401 Second Avenue
Brooklyn, New York 11232

*Distributed in Europe by*
**LEHMANNS**
Unit E, Viking Industrial Park
Rolling Mill Road
Jarrow, Tyne & Wear NE32 3DP
*England*

*Distributed in Australia & Zew Zealand by*
**GOLDS WORLD OF JUDAICA**
3-13 William Street
Balaclava, Melbourne 3183
Victoria Australia

*Distributed in Israel by*
**SIFRIATI / A. GITLER — BOOKS**
6 Hayarkon Street
Bnei Brak 51127

*Distributed in South Africa by*
**KOLLEL BOOKSHOP**
Shop 8A Norwood Hypermarket
Norwood 2196, Johannesburg, South Africa

---

**THE ARTSCROLL SERIES**®
**UNDERSTANDING JUDAISM**
© *Copyright 2000, by* MESORAH PUBLICATIONS, Ltd.
*4401 Second Avenue / Brooklyn, N.Y. 11232 / (718) 921-9000 / www.artscroll.com*

---

*Typography by Compuscribe at ArtScroll Studios, Ltd.*

Printed in the United States of America by Noble Book Press
Bound by Sefercraft, Quality Bookbinders, Ltd. Brooklyn, N.Y.

In memory of

## EDWARD A. ROTHMAN ז"ל

נקי כפים ובר לבב

"who led his life with
honesty and integrity"

Published through the courtesy of the

**HENRY, BERTHA and EDWARD ROTHMAN FOUNDATION**

Rochester, N.Y. • Circleville, Ohio • Cleveland

*In appreciation to*

## DONALD TIRSCHWELL, ESQ.

*Together with his wife, Barbara,
he has fought for Jewish causes,
both here and in Israel.
They have raised two wonderful sons,
who have emerged as shining
lights in Torah Judaism.*

ℰ *and* ℰ

*In memory of*

## CHAYA PESSEL, a"h

### BAS

## R' YITZCHOK MOSHE

*whose life was imbued with Torah
and mitzvos, kindness and caring.*

תנצב'ה

# ᴇᴈ JEWISH EDUCATION PROGRAM (JEP)

The Jewish Education Program, a project of Agudath Israel of America, was organized in September 1972, and since its inception has become a well-known, active force in the field of Jewish education. Its guiding principle, "Reaching out to Jewish children whatever their background and wherever they may be found," was formulated in response to what has become a Jewish tragedy of massive proportions, namely assimilation and its tragic by-products.

Under the guidelines of prominent *roshei yeshivos* and leaders in the field of Jewish education, and staffed entirely by *bnei Torah* and yeshivah and Beis Yaakov graduates, JEP relies almost entirely on the talents and efforts voluntarily contributed by capable young Torah students.

Some of JEP's programs include: Shabbatons, in which hundreds of children from various communities in the United States and Canada experience the beauty of Shabbos in a Torah-true environment; Release Hour classes for spiritually starved public-school children; programs for needy Russian immigrants; *Ruach* and Seminar sessions for day-school students; *Chavrusa* Big-Brother programs; high-school encounter groups; Holiday rallies; yeshivah and camp placement; and the publication of educational material for thousands of young people.

Through these and various other programs, JEP hopes to ignite the spark of *Yiddishkeit* deep within the hearts of these individuals, and turn it into a blazing fire. It hopes to instill within these youngsters a love of Hashem and His Torah and an understanding of Torah-true Judaism.

The royalties from this book will go to benefit JEP's various *Kiruv* projects, which have been instrumental in the placement of over 2,000 children into yeshivos, Hebrew day schools, and summer camps.

# Table Of Contents

# APPENDIX

# ⋲ACKNOWLEDGMENTS

If history teaches us anything, it is that no person is solely responsible for notable achievements. There are always others whose major contributions helped see a project through to fruition, and if any credit results, they more than deserve to share in it.

Certainly, this *sefer* could never have been readied for publication without the selfless assistance of a number of very talented individuals, and I appreciate this chance to pay public tribute to the following:

Mrs. Chavie Aranoff, Tamar Frankael, and Chana Rochel Sommerstein, whose outstanding efforts in writing, editing, typing, and proofreading the manuscript played a very significant role in ensuring that it reached the highest possible standards.

Rabbi Eliezer Gevirtz, Rabbi Shimon Apisdorf, and Bezalel Lerner, who reviewed the entire manuscript and made helpful corrections and suggestions.

Rabbi Yosef Chaim Golding, Managing Editor of *The Jewish Observer,* whose editorial expertise and invaluable guidance was, as always, essential in the preparation of this volume.

A supreme expression of gratitude is due to Harav Yisroel Belsky, *shlita,* Rosh Yeshiva, Yeshiva Torah Vodaath; Rabbi Shlomo Frankel, *shlita,* and especially the eminent historian Rabbi Joseph Elias, *shlita,* dean of the Rika Breuer Teachers' Seminary. Their willingness to take time from their busy schedules to ascertain that the material in this volume meets with the high standards of *daas Torah* is most appreciated.

Special thanks to Ruchie Dachs, Sima Eichorn, and Gabriella Bachrach for their invaluable technical assistance.

I would like to express my thanks to the staff of Mesorah Publications, especially to Danny Kay who designed the magnificent cover, Mrs. Faigie Weinbaum who proofread, Avrohom Biderman and Mrs. Rivkah Hamaoui who helped organize and coordinate the work, Mrs. Esther Feierstein for her typing and her astute eye, and Chumie Zaidman who typeset the book. They have outdone themselves in making this book a work of beauty.

Many thanks to the members of the Henry, Bertha, and Edward Rothman Foundation, who have so graciously sponsored this and other JEP volumes. May Hashem enable them to continue their most worthy work on behalf of Jewish education for many years to come.

In addition, I would like to thank my parents, Mr. and Mrs. Moshe Katz; my in-laws, Mr. and Mrs. Yitzchok Berger; my dear children, and all the other members of my family.

My deepest esteem goes to my late wife, Chaya Pessel (Pessi) bas Yitzchok Moshe, who encouraged me, despite our busy schedules, to see this project through to fruition. Her life was imbued with Torah and *mitzvos,* kindness and caring. Her dedication to these ideals has given me the strength to incorporate these perspectives into the pages of this book. I hope I have done her justice.

And finally, my thanks to *Ha'Kadosh Baruch Hu* for enabling me to produce a work that, hopefully, will inspire others to take pride in their glorious heritage and strive, through *mitzvos* and *maasim tovim,* to help make the future even more auspicious for all *Klal Yisrael.*

Rabbi Mordechai Katz

Brooklyn, New York
Kislev 5761

# ᴗ§ INTRODUCTION

From the time of Abraham to the days of the Messiah, the Jewish nation has borne the responsibility to pursue an ongoing striving toward the ultimate goal of being a "kingdom of priests and a holy nation." The mere fact that a people was entrusted with a mission of such magnitude, and that the Jewish nation accepts this responsibility as their destiny, defines the character of the world, which is a manifestation of G-d's will. The history of mankind is shaped neither by accident nor happenstance. G-d ordained His will and we — the nation of priests — are here as an example to mankind to aspire to fulfill His will at all times.

At the very beginning of our history, the promise was given to our Patriarch Abraham that "all the nations of the earth shall be blessed in you." His descendants were entrusted with the charge of spreading the Divine blessing among all the nations of the world.

The Jewish people have not been promised military prowess or economic bliss but the sublime and often difficult role of being the kingdom of priests and to educate by example. The entire nation, serving as G-d's messenger, is to model reverence, righteousness, and compassion. Despite being a minority among the nations of the world, the Jewish people continue to survive. The study of the Torah and its laws, specifically, Shabbos, *Kashrus*, and Family Purity, create a strong spiritual, moral and ethical environment in which they are able to thrive. There is a fundamental difference between the Jewish nation and the others. They are the proud possessors of the Torah, which is the source of the uniqueness of Judaism.

Thus it is faith in G-d and His Torah which gave the Jewish people the will to withstand attacks of every kind, whether the brutal massacre of the mob, or the more subtle onslaught of various religions which sought to entice the "infidel" into its fold by any means. Who can deny, then, in the face of overwhelming historical evidence, extending over a period of nearly 4,000 years, that G-d and His Torah were the sole instruments which saved the Jewish nation from extinction?

Judaism is a living vibrant belief — and that is the secret of its survival. We are a chosen people — chosen by G-d to do His will — and we choose every day in every way to remain committed in thought, word, and action to G-d and His Torah.

In this volume we will explore the beliefs, practices, and history of Judaism.

# PART ONE

# 1

---
⊸⊸◌∽∾◌⊷
---

# Hear, O Israel ... G-d Is One!

---
⊸⊸◌∽∾◌⊷
---

## ↪§THE FOUNDATION OF JUDAISM

What is G-d? Is G-d the clockmaker deity of 18th century philosophers — the deists who believed that G-d created the world, set it in motion, and then left it to run of its own accord? Is He the "ineffable" of certain Eastern philosophies, sometimes described as "allness" and sometimes as "nothingness?" Is He (or She) the mysterious "force" of contemporary science fiction?

It is difficult to find the right descriptions for G-d, so it may be easier to begin by saying something about what G-d is *not*. Our ancestor Abraham set the pattern nearly four thousand years ago when he rejected idol-worship. G-d, Whoever He was, could not be identified with the sun, moon, stars, or other natural phenomena. The Divine cannot, in fact, be represented in physical form. This accords with the second of the Ten Commandments which states, "You shall not make for yourself a sculptured image." G-d cannot be reduced to human form either, as some religions have held. As the Torah states, "Take good heed of yourselves, for you saw no manner of form on that day when G-d spoke to you at Horeb ..." (*Deuteronomy* 4:15). [*Deuteronomy* is the last of the five books which comprise the Torah — G-d's words as dictated to Moses at Mt. Sinai.]

G-d has neither body, nor shape, nor form. Therefore He must be beyond space and time, which are the coordinates that define form. "He" must also be beyond gender. Use of the masculine pronoun is a convention with metaphorical meaning, but only a convention. Indeed, all the Bible's descriptions of G-d having physical form such as an "outstretched hand" are meant symbolically. G-d cannot be many Divine beings (not even a trinity), since more-than-oneness is a feature of physicality. He must be only One. "The Lord, He is G-d — there is none else beside him" (*Deuteronomy* 4:35). The great medieval philosopher Maimonides (known to Jews as the Rambam) went so far as to state in his code of law, "Whoever conceives G-d to be a corporeal being is a heretic and an apostate."[1]

To say that G-d is not anything in the world of space-time helps us expand our thinking. We can then say that G-d is both omnipresent and transcendental, two words that express the idea that G-d is not in space-time. Omnipresent means He fills all the universe, as Isaiah the prophet states in Prophets, "Holy, holy, holy is G-d of hosts — the whole world is filled with His Glory" (Prophets, *Isaiah* 6:3).

Further, since G-d has no physical properties and is beyond the laws of nature, He is transcendental, meaning that G-d must be prior to everything else, "outside" space-time, so to speak, such that G-d makes everything else possible. He has no beginning and no end. He always has been and always will be. This is difficult for our minds to comprehend, and is one among many wonders that we may never fully understand.

Since G-d is before and above all, we also affirm that He is Creator, and that His power in the universe is unlimited. We therefore speak of G-d as being omnipotent (all-powerful) and refer to Him in prayer as "King of the universe." He created space, time, and everything that is in it.

---

1. Rambam, *Mishneh Torah, Hilchos Teshuvah* 3:1. See also his discussion in *Guide for the Perplexed.*

# ~§ HOW IS G-D KNOWN?

The fact that G-d cannot be seen or pictured, touched or heard, is not proof that He does not exist. The human neurological system, however intricate it may be, operates within a limited pattern. In fact, the brain screens out many perceptions in order to give us a functional picture of reality, ensuring our ability to survive in the ordinary physical world.

In fact, we know from our everyday experience that there are nonphysical forces in the world. We cannot see love or touch hate, but they certainly exist. Even in what we call the physical world, there are some things that cannot be directly sensed with our physical form. We cannot, for example, hold onto an isolated electrical current or put it into a dish with our bare hands. Yet we know this current produces light and heat, and we can observe its effects even though the wire through which it passes looks no different from any other wire.

Invisible physical forces and emotional vibrations are analogous to Divine power in that they are beyond the physical senses but have results we can feel and observe. Similarly, we can prove G-d's existence through His creations and perceive through our higher intelligence His guiding of history, without being able to perceive G-d directly. To look at what is around us and deduce that there must have been an intelligence behind it is a classic proof of G-d's existence called the "argument from design." Although philosophers have offered challenges to this proof, it is still the strongest rational argument for G-d's existence, beginning with the observable physical world and appealing to everyone's natural reasoning ability.

> The emperor of Rome once chided Rabbi Yehoshua ben
> Chananya: "You call your G-d all-powerful? Why, I am
> much more of a god than He. Your G-d cannot be seen
> anywhere, and I am visible to all. If your G-d is so great,
> why can't I even see him?"
> The rabbi did not try to argue. He simply smiled and

*asked the emperor to join him outside. The emperor was puzzled, but he complied. Once they were out in the street, the rabbi asked the emperor to look up at the sky. The emperor stared up toward the blazing noontime sun for but a brief moment, and then was forced to look away.*

*"Is something wrong?" asked Rabbi Yehoshua.*

*"How can I look up?" complained the emperor. "The sun is blinding me. I can't see!"*

*The rabbi nodded knowingly. "I regret your discomfort, Your Majesty. I just wanted to point out that even so great a man as you cannot look at the sun for more than a moment. Yet the sun is only a creation of G-d, Who is the real source of all light, power, and energy. If man can hardly gaze at G-d's creation, how can he hope to see G-d Himself in all His Glory?"*

*The emperor smiled. He knew that he had been bested.*

*Talmud Chullin, 59b*

The argument from design states, in essence, that the complex laws of nature and living things are themselves proof that they could not have come about by sheer accident, but must have their source in an intelligent Creator. Indeed, they often seem to be deliberately planned. Even the simple structures of rocks and plants bear the signs of amazing symmetries and directionality. Cycles like the evaporation of water and the fall of rain, essential to life on earth, are extraordinarily complex. Scientists now know that if the historic temperature of earth varied only slightly, life would not have been possible.

If we look at the human being, it seems incredible that a person begins life as nothing more than a microscopic cell — a zygote formed by the union of two other minuscule cells, the sperm and the egg. From this tiny speck of matter emerges a being composed of billions upon billions of cells, diversified into many intricate organs.

Intricate chains of molecules structured in specific ways — dionucleic acid, or DNA — provide the "instructions" for the tiny cell to grow into a diversified human body. Each cell and group of cells seems to know what job it must do to make the whole organism work. The nerve cells convey sensations and communicate the necessary response to the environment. Cardiac cells work together to keep the heart beating so that blood can be pumped throughout the body. Other cells fight germs, digest food, or aid in reproduction. Glands secrete tiny amounts of hormones that regulate growth, maintain chemical equilibrium, and respond to our very thoughts. With every breath, an enormously complex process allows oxygen to move to each cell and removes carbon dioxide. If that oxygenating process stopped for just four minutes, the brain would begin to die.

Think of just one organ: the eye. Most of us take sight for granted, but consider for a moment how the pupil must open like a shutter to allow light in, and the lens must focus the light properly on the retina, which then relays the image via electrical sensations along the optic nerve. The rods and cones determine black-and-white and color vision. The brain receives the image upside down and must reverse it to orient us properly to the physical world. Meanwhile, the cornea protects the eye from damage and the tear ducts help remove foreign substances from the eye.

This color camera focuses automatically according to the object's distance, with the lens adjusting its degree of curvature as necessary. The iris controls the width of the entering light beam to admit the proper amount of light. The eye turns in the direction desired as the brain directs its musculature. The pressure of the fluid in the eye is calibrated to maintain the proper shape of the eyeball. The two eyes function as perfectly synchronized cameras to form one picture. In short, every component of the eye exhibits exquisite precision and is exactly suited for its specific function. Such a phenomenon points to an intelligent design behind it. Charles Darwin, the originator of evolutionary theory, the admitted, "The belief that an organ as perfect as the eye could have been formed by natural selection is more than enough to stagger anyone."[2]

The same is true, of course, of the processes of hearing,

---

2. Darwin quote.

thinking, smelling, tasting, touching, eating, breathing, ingesting and digesting food, and all the amazing processes of every human being, every animal, and every plant. The complexities of nature are eloquent witnesses to the fact that they must have been designed by a Superior Being.

Indeed, it no longer seems possible to deny the argument from design. In the heyday of extreme rationalism (known as positivism) in the early 20th century, scientists still hoped to be able to describe nature as a machine — an extremely complicated one, to be sure, but ultimately reducible to clearly formulated scientific laws. A reasonable thinker could then argue that the universe evolved in a mechanical way, somewhat like the "growth" of a crystal. Now, as the 21st century has come upon us, scientists seem to be finding that the universe can only be understood if we factor in the idea of something like "intelligence" that operates continuously in the patterns of existence, even down to the behavior of subatomic particles.[3]

If so, this means that it is no longer possible to say that the concept of G-d is being brought in to fill the gaps in areas that science does not yet understand, and that we will ultimately no longer need an idea of G-d. Rather, the concept of an Intelligence within and perhaps beyond the universe seems to be a necessary proposition.

## ເ§ THE CONCEPT OF CREATION AND SCIENTIFIC UNDERSTANDING

The Torah, in the first chapter of the Bible, states that in the beginning of the creation of what we know as "heaven" and "earth," G-d created the universe from nothing. Beginning with the creation of light, G-d then made and shaped everything in its position, resulting in the world as we perceive it. The events of this creation are presented as follows:

---

3. Scientists sometimes refer to this as "an intelligence behind creation."

| *First Day:* | Creation of light (and darkness). |
| *Second Day:* | Separation of the "waters," thereby making the upper and lower waters. |
| *Third Day:* | Accumulation of the lower waters, allowing dry land to emerge. |
| *Fourth Day:* | Creation and placement of sun, moon, and stars in the sky. |
| *Fifth Day:* | Creation of sea life and birds. |
| *Sixth Day:* | Creation of reptiles, animals, and finally man. |
| *Seventh Day:* | G-d "rested" from His work and sanctified the seventh day as the Shabbos, a day of rest. |

Several things are notable here. Before G-d acted, nothing existed, not even the basic elements or their energy particles. At G-d's command, things sprang into existence. This was the most spectacular of miracles, one far removed from our experience or imagination. The simple words in which it is described are an enormous understatement.

Second, the concept behind this description is enormously sophisticated. In contrast to the creation stories of many other cultures, the description given in the first chapter of *Genesis* is very abstract. A formless G-d manifests through the energy of sound ("and G-d spoke"), and His first creation is light. This is nothing like the humanoid deities of many other stories.

Third, the creation story moves forward in a precise order, from the energies of sound and light to the concept of atmospheres and fluids (upper and lower waters), then to the congealing of what we know as earth and into the regular motions of celestial bodies. Finally it moves to recognizable features of our planet's inhabitants — sea life, birds, reptiles, land animals, and human beings. While many questions can be raised about scientific theories of the origin of the universe and the evolution of life, what is remarkable here are not the differences, but the amazing similarities between the way the creation is portrayed in the Bible and the understandings of the most advanced branches of science — physics, quantum, physics, etc.

There are, of course, difficulties with most scientific hypotheses about the origin of life. Most problematic is the insistence of some scientific theorists that evolution occurred by chance. Many biologists have argued, on the contrary, that evolution by chance is mathematically impossible. Random mutation — the mechanism that supposedly resulted in billions of different species — could not produce the complexity of life on earth in the time span (four billion years of earth time) that science has allotted for it. J. W. Sullivan, one of the world's most brilliant physicists, has written that "the only possible conclusion so far as actual evidence goes is that the origin of life results from a supernatural, G-dly creative act."[4]

Another frequently mentioned problem is that the Bible describes creation as occurring in a matter of days, while science holds that the universe is fifteen billion years old. Interestingly, long before current scientific methods were invented, some of our sages discussed whether the time frame of "seven days of creation" in *Genesis* actually corresponds to seven days as we know them. They noted that the sun and moon, which were created "for [measuring] times and seasons," did not appear until the fourth "day," so what was the "day" like before then? Moreover, if we have to understand every later description of G-d as metaphorical, certainly the acts of creation that occurred before a human being was present to witness them can only dimly be understood in human terms. To support this point, they bring a number of statements elsewhere in the Bible suggesting that G-d's measure of time is not like ours: "A thousand years is but a day . . ." and "G-d's thoughts are not our thoughts."

We need not debate the time frame of creation with today's scientists, whose own theories are very much in flux. The crucial point is that Judaism insists that G-d authored the universe, created its orderly systems, and *continued to be involved* in every aspect of creation, phase by phase. The clockmaker deity who wound up the machine and left it alone is not the G-d of Judaism, Who cares for every element of creation, Who directs each plant

---

4. J. W. Sulllivan.

and animal in its growth and development, and Who planned the entire world as an arena in which human beings — the unique beings with free choice — could accomplish their destiny.

## ❧ WHY DON'T WE HAVE CLEARER PROOFS OF G-D'S EXISTENCE?

The argument from design is very persuasive on a common-sense level. But we often wonder why G-d does not speak even more clearly about His existence, to reassure us at least that He is present. In ancient times, it seems, people saw miracles and heard G-d's voice, or at least knew people who were clearly connected to the Divine force, like prophets. Why don't we have a few miracles in our day?

Humanity is, in a sense, an experiment. When G-d created Adam, He made a being who could decide whether to be like the rest of creation, acting on an animal level, or to be like G-d Himself. The crux of the human experiment, the one independent variable, was that we should have free choice. If miracles were commonplace and the Divine Presence was indisputable, humans would have no choice but to acknowledge G-d. It would be as if we were compelled to believe in G-d.

Miracles did happen long ago, because they were needed to demonstrate G-d's existence to a world that had no concept of G-d at all.[5] Once the Jews were launched as a chosen nation — as we will see below — manifest miracles were less necessary. Human beings were then free to make their own decisions on the evidence available.

Still, open miracles do occur at times. Interestingly, many people who say "Why don't we have miracles?" refuse to believe in them when they do occur. It is tempting to pass off miracles as coincidences or as something that science will eventually explain. This is, again, part of the test of our free choice.

---

5. Ramban, *Commentary on the Torah, Exodus,* end of *Parashas Bo.*

In fact, there is a completely different way to look at reality — namely, that everything is a miracle. If we accept the fact that G-d created the world and cares about it, then we can see G-d's contributions to the world as being continuous and ever flowing. We are surrounded by unrecognized miraculous events emanating from G-d. Indeed, we can see the continued existence of all things as dependent solely on G-d's will.[6] We live from one miracle to the next.

---

6. *Psalms* 119; *Midrash Rabbah.*

# 2

## The Grand Design

If G-d designed the universe in such a complex and intricate way that every element in it has a purpose, then surely the same is true of the creation of the human race. The human being alone among G-d's creations has the ability to be aware of and appreciate the Almighty's efforts. Therefore G-d must have put the human being on earth to play a part in the Divine plan and to fulfill a purpose.

But what is this purpose? What does G-d expect human beings to do with their lives?

## ᲛᏪ WHY DID G-D CREATE HUMANS?

Our sages tell us that the human being is nothing less than a miniature world, composed of the elements of earth and a Divine spirit.[1] Adam was G-d's final creation. Human beings are

---

1. *Nefesh HaChaim, Sha'ar* 1, Chapter 1, and *Sefer HaBris*.

uniquely able to recognize and relate to G-d because each person contains a spark of the Almighty within.

Humans were created with the specific purpose of emulating G-d's ways on earth.[2] As G-d's emissaries, our job is to ensure that justice and kindness predominate over violence and corruption. Judaism recognizes this in a framework of rules for all humanity, traditionally known as the Seven Noahide Laws. After the great Flood described in the book of *Genesis* in the Bible, Noah was sent forth into the world with a Divine teaching that, if followed, would prevent the world from degenerating into corruption as it had before. These seven principles are as follows:

1. Establish courts to preserve law and order.
2. Do not worship any idol or any deity other than G-d.
3. Do not blaspheme the Name of G-d.
4. Do not murder.
5. Do not commit adultery.
6. Do not steal.
7. Do not eat the flesh from a living animal (this prohibits cruelty to animals).

These laws are intended to help humans carry out their mission in the world and to serve as a basis for morality and ethics. The prohibitions against idolatry and blasphemy teach proper worship and respect for G-d, and remind humanity of the existence of a Divine Source. This in turn prompts human beings to respect their fellows who are also created in the image of G-d.

The prohibitions against murder, adultery, and robbery, together with the establishment of a system of justice, serve as the foundation for a social order where wrongs can be curbed and where evil is not allowed to have its way. The prohibition against eating living-animal flesh teaches man kindness toward lower creatures and respect for all of G-d's creation. In addition, because it is a limitation on one of our most fundamental desires, that of eating, it teaches that we must observe boundaries even when fulfilling our basic needs. We can and should control our animalistic desires.

---

2. Rabbi Samson Raphael Hirsch, *The Pentateuch,* commentary on *Genesis* 1:27.

A non-Jew who fulfills these seven commandments, under-standing that he or she comes from the One G-d, is called one of the *chassidei umos ha'olam* or "pious people of the world." Such a person, without becoming a Jew, earns life in the "World to Come." Judaism, unlike some other religions, does not reserve eternal life only for its members; the ultimate reward for living a righteous life is available to the conscientious non-Jew as well.[3]

Jews, nevertheless, were given a specific role in helping all of humankind achieve its mission, as we will discuss further below. Here we want to emphasize that, despite the fact that only seven laws are required to be observed by all of humanity, it has been very difficult for most people to keep them. To understand this, we will have to delve more deeply into our understanding of humankind, and the nature of free will.

## ✍ THE POWER AND DANGER OF FREE WILL

G-d favored Adam and all his descendants with a supreme gift: free will. Plants and animals are largely limited by their genetic programming to a life of pattern and instinct, reacting to stimuli along predictable lines. Humans alone can act in any number of ways. We are the only one of G-d's creations who have real choice as to how to conduct our lives.

We are created with free choice rather than as robots, because G-d wants us to achieve the potential of our creation, namely "in the image of G-d." G-d does not wish to force us to be righteous (almost a contradiction in terms), for that would frustrate the entire purpose of creation — to choose emulation of His ways and make the earth a dwelling-place for His G-dliness, and in doing so earning the greatest of rewards for eternity: closeness to Him.

Clearly, our goal should be to make positive use of our free will. But we are given challenges that make it difficult to choose

---

3. Rambam, *Mishneh Torah, Hilchos Melachim* 8:11.

correctly. We have strong emotions of envy, jealousy, and hatred that sometimes seem to overwhelm us. We have powerful desires that clamor to be satisfied. And we are finite — we exist within the limitations of time and space, and the powers of our own bodies.

In facing these challenges, the Bible tells us, humans fell time and again from their original Divine potential:

- Adam and Chava (Eve) in the Garden of Eden could have eaten anything they wanted, except the fruit of the Tree of Knowledge. Nevertheless they ate the fruit, and G-d sent them out of the Garden where they had to live a human life as we know it, with the hardships of toiling for sustenance and bringing children into the world.

- Cain and Abel were the first two sons of Adam and Chava. Cain was a farmer, Abel a shepherd. When they brought offerings to G-d, G-d preferred Abel's because Abel had brought his best, in great sincerity. Cain, in his embarrassment and anger, killed his brother. His punishment was to be a wanderer over the earth.

- In the ten generations from Adam to Noah, people became increasingly evil. (There were two righteous people in this period, Enoch and Methuselah.) The evil of the generation of Noah surpassed that of all previous generations in violence, robbery, and corruption. G-d had extended his patience over centuries, but He finally decided to destroy the world through a flood. Only the righteous Noah and his family would be saved.

Within a few hundred years, people had totally lost sight of the G-dly purpose for which they had been created. The sin of Adam and Chava was a misuse of their freedom of choice, following their personal desires in seeking to "know good and evil" rather than to obey G-d. In the very next generation, we find one of their sons murdering the other in a jealous rage.

By the time of Noah, people could not even be persuaded to consider that they might be following a wrong path. Our sages tell us that it took Noah 120 years to build the ark, and this was part of the Divine plan. G-d wanted to provide humankind with a chance to repent. Seeing Noah work so hard for such a long period, people would ask what he was doing. He would reply, "If we don't mend our ways, G-d will bring a flood to destroy the earth. Let's repent and change our behavior before it's too late.[4]" Unfortunately, Noah's contemporaries only scoffed, and the message went unheeded.

Exactly why G-d chose the kinds of punishments He imposed, and why He timed them as He did, is beyond human understanding. Nevertheless, it is clear that when human beings misused their freedom of choice, seeking their own egotistical pleasures instead of fulfilling their calling, consequences followed.

Nevertheless, G-d did not give up on the human race. The experiment on planet earth is not a cold, objective experiment run by someone who does not care about the results. G-d loves His creatures and wants them to succeed; He is involved with their grief as well as their happiness. When individuals appeared who honored G-d and who set their hearts to achieving His purposes — people like Noah and his family — G-d encouraged and rewarded them. This eventually set the stage for the emergence of others who would follow G-d's ways, and for the birth of the Jewish nation.

## ◆§ LOVE FOR G-D: THE EXAMPLE OF ABRAHAM

While everyone has an obligation to serve G-d as best he can in accordance with the laws G-d has given, the highest form of service comes from love of G-d. With our fellow human beings, when we truly love someone, we do things for that person without a sense of burden. So too, if we love G-d, we are able to do what He wants in a different frame of mind, with positive feelings and high motivation.

Love of G-d is not an inborn talent, however. It comes from our

---

4. *Rashi* on *Genesis* 3:4.

initiative and choice, nourished through our responses to the various events in our lives.

We can understand this by looking at the life of our ancestor Abraham, one who exhibited supreme love and devotion to G-d.[5] The *Midrash* tells us that he originally came from a family of idol-worshippers, and his own father, Terach, owned a shop where he sold idols. Abraham, while very young, came to the realization that man-made, lifeless statues could not be the rulers of the earth. He deduced that there had to be a superior force capable of creating the world and regulating all of nature.

Abraham transcended his pagan environment and recognized that the world is governed by one Supreme Being.[6] We can see him as one of the greatest thinkers of his time, able to see through the sham and false values of his generation, learning to understand the true purpose of life. He was willing to stand up and publicly proclaim his belief in the One Almighty G-d.[7] But for Abraham, this was not merely a philosophical supposition. His faith developed until it overshadowed everything else in his life. He dedicated his life to spreading the knowledge of G-d and was even willing to die for it. He became not just a believer in G-d but a lover of G-d, as the following story shows:

Terach once left his son Abraham in charge of the idol store, and Abraham succeeded in dissuading some potential customers from making purchases, describing to them the futility of idol-worship. Then a woman came in, bringing an offering of food for the idols. Abraham responded by breaking all the idols except for the largest. He placed a stick in its hand. When Terach returned, he was aghast at the wreckage in his shop and demanded an explanation. Abraham told him that the idols had fought over the woman's food offering, and the big one had smashed all the others. Terach did not believe him because, he said, idols cannot move or speak. Abraham then challenged him to stop worshipping mute stones.

---

5. Rambam, *Sefer HaMitzvos*, positive commandment #3.

6. Rambam, *Mishneh Torah, Hilchos Avodah Zarah*, 1.

7. *Midrash Rabbah* 39:1.14.

This act of heresy prompted Terach to bring his son to the mighty King Nimrod for judgment. Nimrod gave Abraham the choice of either worshipping Nimrod's idols or being thrown into a blazing furnace. Abraham promptly declared his allegiance to the one Almighty G-d and was hurled into the furnace. G-d protected him, and he was able to walk through the flames and emerge unscathed, to the wonderment of all.

Abraham's willingness to die demonstrated that his faith had penetrated his whole being. Moreover, his was not merely a private faith. His love of G-d was so strong that he desired to share it with others. He went out of his way to spread the belief in the One G-d and to impress upon everyone the love and kindness of G-d.

G-d rewarded Abraham by furthering his mission. Abraham received a prophetic call from G-d, to leave his father's country and birthplace, and go to another, as yet unnamed, land. Eventually, G-d revealed to Abraham that it was to be the land of Israel. G-d promised him that he would have a multitude of descendants and that this chosen land would ultimately be theirs. Abraham would be enabled to transmit his love of G-d to his son Isaac, and through him to all his descendants until they would become a self-sustaining group, faithful to G-d. As G-d said, "Abraham shall surely become a great and mighty nation, for I know that he will instruct his children and his household after him, that they keep G-d's way" (*Genesis* 18:18-19).

Abraham's life was not easy after he left his birthplace. G-d tested Abraham ten times to determine whether he was worthy of being the founder of the Chosen People according to G-d's plan. In the tenth test, known as the *Akedah* or "binding" of Isaac, G-d commanded Abraham to sacrifice his son, who was to perpetuate Abraham's heritage. The special difficulty in this task was that G-d was not asking Abraham to give up money, power, or status, but to sacrifice his greatest dream. If Abraham were to kill Isaac, his vision of becoming the ancestor of a people devoted to G-d would vanish. G-d had promised him a son, and Abraham had waited for the fulfillment of this promise till he was one hundred years old, almost past hope of receiving the right son. Now he was being asked not only to give him up, but to kill him with his own hands. This act was contrary to Abraham's kind, loving nature and to his understanding of G-d's benevolence. It reminded him of all he had fought against, since many idol-worshippers sacrificed their children to idols.

G-d knew that Abraham would make the right choice, that he would assent to performing this act, thereby elevating himself to a new level of faith. Abraham would set an example for future generations of total awe of G-d-even when this seemed to require going against what G-d was thought to be. In the end, G-d stopped Abraham at the last possible moment, with a heavenly Voice that told him not to kill Isaac. Abraham had demonstrated his perfect faith and sealed the covenant with G-d, ensuring that through Isaac the seed of G-d's own nation would be passed down. In reality G-d has never commanded a human sacrifice — nor will He.

Ultimately, the Holy Temple would be built on the spot where Abraham was willing to sacrifice his son — Mount Moriah — rather than on Mount Sinai where the Torah was given to the Jewish people. That was the level of Abraham's faith.

## ⊷§ THE MISSION CONTINUES

Abraham's mission was carried on in his family by his wife Sarah, and by his descendants Isaac and Jacob together with their wives, Rebecca, Leah, and Rachel. The Torah tells us many details of their lives to exemplify the way to love G-d and emulate His ways. Here are a few illustrations:

- When Abraham was recuperating after having obeyed G-d's command to circumcise himself, G-d appeared to comfort him. Abraham in turn provided hospitality to strangers, and his home was always open.
- Abraham bought a proper burial place for his wife Sarah when she passed away. This teaches us the importance of caring for the deceased. Her tomb, by the way, where Abraham, Isaac, Rebecca, Jacob, and Leah are also buried, has

always been a holy site for Jews in the town of Hebron in Israel.

- Isaac, Abraham's son, acquiesced in serving as a sacrifice to G-d when his father sought to fulfill G-d's command. He completely accepted his father's wishes that he not leave the land of Israel, and allowed a wife to be chosen for him. He also reinstated his father's claim on certain wells that had been filled in by the Philistines. Isaac thus illustrates awe and respect not only for G-d, but also for one's ancestors.

- Jacob, the son of Isaac who received the blessing to carry on the tradition, had to struggle a great deal in worldly affairs. He had to leave Israel because of a dispute with his twin brother Esau over the rights conferred upon the firstborn. He met Rachel, a cousin whom he wished to marry, but her father deceived him by substituting her sister Leah under the wedding canopy. He was allowed to marry Rachel also, but he had to work for twenty-one years for his uncle, a greedy, deceitful, and arrogant man. When Jacob returned to Israel, his beloved Rachel died, his only daughter was violated, and two of his sons drew him into a confrontation with a local tribe. Then ten of his sons sold the eleventh, his favorite Joseph, into slavery, and he did not see him for more than twenty years. Through all these trials, Jacob developed tremendous personal integrity and faith in G-d's direction.

- Sarah, Abraham's wife, devoted herself to her husband's cause, spreading the word of the One G-d. She was considered greater in prophecy than her husband, and advised him in sending away his son Ishmael (by his second wife, Hagar) to ensure the destiny of the family.

- Rebecca was chosen to be the wife of Isaac because of her extreme kindness. When Eliezer, Abraham's servant, came to her town seeking a wife for Isaac, he met Rebecca and asked her for a drink of water. She not only gave him water, but also drew water for all the camels in his entourage. She, like Sarah, had keen insight into her sons, Jacob and Esau, and saw that Esau did not deserve the birthright of the firstborn.

- Leah suffered from her status as the less-beloved wife of

Jacob. Nevertheless, she praised G-d for everything that came to her. She named her sons according to the good that G-d bestowed on her through each birth. Also, because of her devotion, she was privileged to bear six of the twelve sons of Jacob, as well as his one daughter.

■ Rachel went out of her way to protect her sister when their father was using them to practice deceit on Jacob. As her wedding day approached, Jacob, suspecting possible trickery, gave Rachel special codes to identify herself behind her veils. When Rachel learned of her father's scheme to substitute Leah in her place, she revealed the codes to her sister to save her any embarrassment. This selflessness was one of her special qualities. Rachel has been rewarded with a special place in the hearts of the Jewish people. Unlike the other patriarchs and matriarchs, she is buried in her own tomb in Beis-Lechem (Bethlehem), between Jerusalem and Hebron. There, it is said, she prays and cries to G-d that he will allow all the Jewish people to return from exile, to come back home to the Holy Land.

The examples of the patriarchs and matriarchs of the Bible teach us that each person has the potential to use his or her own personal qualities in love and devotion to G-d. It is noteworthy that they did not earn their place in history through holding high offices or orchestrating dramatic public events. It was in their own families and neighborhoods that they demonstrated the qualities that count for an elevated life.

The three patriarchs are said to represent the "three pillars" without which the world cannot stand: (1) acts of loving-kindness, (2) worship of G-d, and (3) Torah. Abraham's example of hospitality and caring for the deceased are illustrations of the first: acts of loving-kindness. Without this, human society would not be workable. Isaac, with his awe and respect for G-d and for his father, represents the second pillar: service and worship of G-d. Jacob, with all his struggles, represents the third pillar: Torah itself. Jacob was a person guided by G-d's directives and continually strived to apply them in daily life.

The examples of the women amplify and extend these qualities. Sarah with her gift of prophecy, and her sense for the needs of future generations, represents insight and clarity. Her helpfulness to and cooperation with Abraham demonstrate the essential qualities of partnership, particularly in marriage, that ensure the continuation of the human race. Rebecca represents, among other qualities, kindness that extends to all creatures in the world, through the act of watering the camels. Leah is an example of a life of gratitude, while Rachel demonstrates sensitivity to others that goes beyond the ordinary requirements of social propriety.

Through these examples and many more, the Torah teaches that it is possible to use our free will for the good of others and in service to G-d's great purposes. The family of Abraham demonstrated that it was possible to live a life of spirituality higher than is suggested by the Noahide commandments. The Noahide laws primarily tell us about the evil we must avoid; the patriarchs and matriarchs move to another dimension, telling us about the extraordinary good we can do.

# 3

## Seeing Beyond Suffering

We can admire the acts of righteous people of all times and places, from Abraham and Sarah's time down to the present, and see how their acts contribute to the building of the world along the lines that G-d wishes. Yet we often have questions about the difficulties that such people have in their lives. In a Divinely ordained world, one would expect the righteous to enjoy immediate happiness and the wicked to reap instant suffering. Yet experience often proves otherwise. In many cases, devout and saintly individuals seem to have led lives of misery, while corrupt people or atheists gain great material benefits. Clearly the world is not perfect, and part of our job is to improve it. And sometimes, Divine justice seems very far away.

If G-d is all-powerful and omniscient (all-knowing), as Judaism teaches, then G-d certainly does not inflict pain on individuals or on nations without reason. We humans cannot see the rationale, but this is only due to our limitations. We do not know what people really deserve, because we cannot see their innermost hearts, or know their struggles. We do not truly know that an event will really turn out to be "good" or "bad" for a person or group, because we cannot see the full flow of history.[1]

An example comes from the Bible, in the story of Jacob's return trip to his homeland in the Land of Israel. Jacob had fled his parents' home originally because his twin brother Esau wanted to kill him. After a difficult twenty years working for his uncle Lavan, being cheated and deceived, Jacob receives word that he can at last go home. But he learns that his brother Esau has been preparing to do battle with him. As it turns out, he does not fight Esau, but has to face a night battle alone with Esau's angelic messenger who permanently injures him.

Shortly after settling in the region of Shechem, the prince of Shechem kidnaps Jacob's daughter Dinah. Dinah's brothers, Simon and Levi, rescue her and punish the perpetrators as well as those who quietly allowed it, but this creates hostility and Jacob has to move on. Jacob's beloved wife Rachel dies after giving birth to her second son, Benjamin. She is buried on the road to Bethelem instead of in the family tomb. Finally, Jacob's favorite son Joseph (the older of Rachel's two sons) is kidnapped by his own brothers and sold as a slave. He ends up in Egypt, and Jacob has to endure twenty-two years of separation and grief.

Why did such a righteous person as Jacob have to suffer?

## ❧ WHY THE RIGHTEOUS SUFFER

Sometimes difficulties appear to be a punishment, when they are actually serving as tests sent by the Almighty. Often it is the righteous who are put to the sternest tests. If they are successful, they emerge with their faith and moral purity enhanced, and their behavior becomes a model for future generations.

The *Midrash Rabbah* explains the concept of a test with a parable. If you go to the marketplace, you will see the potter hitting his clay pots with a stick to demonstrate to his customers

---

1. Rambam, *Mishneh Torah, Hilchos Teshuvah* 3:1.

how strong and solid they are. But the wise potter hits only the pots he knows are strong, never the flawed ones. So too, G-d sends tests and afflictions only to people He knows are capable of handling them, so that they and others can learn the extent of the spiritual potential of a human being.[2] This applied first of all to the patriarchs and matriarchs.

As we see in the story of Jacob, he suffered a great deal in his life. Nevertheless he refused to lower his moral standards, did not give in to despair, and rarely complained. The final seventeen years of his life were ones of peace and contentment, surrounded by children and grandchildren, secure in the knowledge that from him would arise the future nation of Israel.[3] Thus, when G-d tests a person, it is to bring out his potential and allow him to express it through his actions. From our limited perspective, it may look like punishment of a righteous person, but it is actually preparing the person for a superior reward: to be a model for others.

Usually we think of goals as concrete, material things or social accomplishments. What if we set as our goal to become a model for all future generations? Could anyone hope to achieve anything greater in life?

## ◄§ MORE ON "REWARDS" AND "PUNISHMENTS"

Many people consider money to be the greatest reward. It can help a person live in great comfort. However, it can also prove to be a curse. It can invite thieves, evoke jealousy, and cause obsessions and unhappiness. Some people accumulate vast wealth and reach the height of prestige, but these achievements do not bring them satisfaction and contentment. They sometimes die drained, depressed, occasionally even without family or

---

2. *Midrash Bereishis Rabbah* 55:2.
3. *Daas Sofrim* on beginning of *Parashas Vayechi.*

friends. What appears on the surface to be a blessing may not turn out that way.

This can be explained with the following parable. When we look at a beautiful tapestry, we see on the front side an intricately woven, beautiful piece of art, drawing together threads of different lengths and colors to create an inspiring picture. But when we turn the tapestry over, we see a hodgepodge of many threads, some short and some long. Some are smooth, some are cut and knotted.

Similarly G-d has a pattern into which everyone's life fits. Some lives are knotted and twisted with suffering, some are cut short, some are extended beyond the average because the pattern of the Creator requires it.

Consider the story of Joseph, the favored son of Jacob. Joseph was his father's favorite son, yet he was thrown into a pit by his jealous brothers, seemingly doomed to die. The brothers had left the immediate area to avoid hearing his cries, but noticed a caravan of travelers who "just happened" to pick him up, and took him to Egypt. There, instead of becoming a menial slave toiling in the fields, he "just happened" to be sold to a person of importance in Egyptian society. His fate seemed to take a turn for the worse when he was unjustly accused of seducing his master's wife, then thrown into jail. Certainly this seemed to be random punishment. But he "just happened" to be in jail at the same time as Pharaoh's butler and baker, whose dreams he was able to interpret. This eventually led to his becoming second in command to Pharaoh, which in turn laid the groundwork for the immigration of Jacob's entire family to Egypt. There, Joseph was able to support his family through a terrible famine.

What seemed to be a series of unreasonable hardships and "punishments" for Joseph finally resulted in the establishment of the Jewish nation. From our viewpoint, G-d seems to have been rewarding and punishing arbitrarily, without any reason. As time passed, history proved otherwise. It turned out to be a far-sighted plan of the Almighty, giving benefit to the entire family of Jacob and establishing the foundation for all of

Jewish history. Likewise in our own lives: every twist and knot turns out to have its place in a great design that adds up to a work of art.

Whatever happens in this world is planned and controlled by G-d. We sometimes question this notion. "If G-d controls everything, why do terrible things happen? Why doesn't anyone seem to have an explanation for these events?" But we know from our own experience that hindsight is more accurate than foresight. What seemed tragic yesterday may prove to have been a wonderful coincidence tomorrow. All the more so when we think of events that interweave the lives of hundreds, thousands, even millions of people. We lack the total perspective that would explain things to us. Life is like a puzzle with the pieces scattered about, and each of us has only a few.

The story of Joseph is a biblical model for understanding this most important truth: G-d designed the puzzle and He will eventually link all the pieces into a perfectly comprehensible whole. Here is a story from much nearer our own times, which shows how deceiving appearances can be:

Two Russian friends decided to open neighboring stores in a Russian city in the early 1900s. One was ruthless in his business techniques and competed fiercely to win customers. His business prospered. His neighbor was scrupulously honest, never seeking to take an unearned *kopek*. Unfortunately, he was not able to make much profit, and he was forced to sell his store at a loss. Unable to make ends meet, he decided he would make the difficult and hazardous journey to America to start anew. As he struggled to rebuild his life, he bewailed his lot. Why had he, the honest man, suffered, while his less ethical friend had grown so successful?

Years later, after the honest man had finally established himself in the United States, he received news of his old friend in Russia. The new Communist leadership had confiscated all his property and exiled him to a slave-labor camp. The American now understood that his "punishment" had in reality been a blessing, and that by coming to the United States under duress, he had escaped a far worse fate.

# ✑ SUFFERING, SELF-EXAMINATION, AND TESHUVAH

G-d's great plan for the entire world is behind every act of suffering, but we still have the question as to the impact of suffering on individuals. In Judaism we have the concept of suffering as an opportunity for our personal spiritual refinement. Sometimes setbacks in our lives can prompt us to take stock of our actions. A door slamming in one's face may make that person question his or her path. Negative events can lead us to examine our deeds to inquire whether those events might be a consequence of our own inappropriate behavior. A temporary disappointment can result in a decision to improve oneself. This is what is involved in *teshuvah* (literally, "turning") or, as it is usually translated in English, repentance.[4]

Another aspect of the Joseph story brings out this point. When Joseph's brothers first came to Egypt to buy food during the famine, Joseph accused them falsely of being spies. Why was he causing them great anguish to no apparent purpose? Clearly, revenge was not his motive. With his power, he could have had one or more of them punished or killed to retaliate for what they had done to him years before.

The great biblical commentator known as the Ramban (Nachmanides) explains Joseph's actions as follows: Joseph's brothers (except for his younger brother, Benjamin) were collectively guilty of a grievous injustice toward him and toward their father. The spiritual honor of the whole family had been damaged by their act. The wrong had to be righted, and this could happen only if the brothers did complete *teshuvah*. Complete repentance occurs when a person is confronted with the same temptation to which he or she has previously succumbed. If the person withstands the test, resisting the temptation this time, then he or she has fully repented.[5]

---

4. Rambam, *Hilchos Taanis,* beginning of *perek* 1.
5. Rambam on Talmud *Yoma* 86a.

In the case of Joseph's brothers, the mere expression of regret would not have been enough. They may have been repenting out of fear for their lives. They had to demonstrate that faced again with the responsibility for the safety of their father's favorite son, they would not make the same mistake.

Joseph's accusation of spying was designed to force the brothers to bring Benjamin to Egypt, so that he could accuse Benjamin of theft and threaten him with imprisonment. Then the brothers would have a valid excuse to leave their youngest brother to his fate — for how could they confront the power of the rulers of Egypt? In facing this test, the brothers steadfastly refused to abandon Benjamin. If he were taken prisoner, they declared, all would go with him. When they showed their loyalty in this way, Joseph knew they were truly sorry for what they had done to him many years before, and they would never participate in such an act again. After they had completed their repentance, Joseph could reveal his true identity and reunite the family.

This teaches us that we should never say to ourselves that we are so deeply entrenched in sin that nothing can purify us. G-d's hand is always outstretched toward us, to receive us when we do *teshuvah,* no matter how far away we think we have been. With courage and conviction, we can move forward in repentance, knowing that G-d will help.[6]

The Rambam divides true repentance into three elementary stages:

- Recognition of and regret for the sin, and an inner desire to mend the wrong that was done. This is the first twinge of conscience.
- Abandonment of the old path of wrongdoing.
- Firm resolve to abstain from repeating the sin in the future.[7]

---

6. Rambam, *Mishneh Torah, Hilchos Teshuvah* 3:14.
7. Ibid. 2:2.

# ◈ INDIVIDUAL DIFFERENCES

E ven when we are able to understand how difficulties serve a good purpose in the end, we still may wonder at the amount of suffering that seems to be imposed on people who achieve great heights in spirituality or moral perfection. Why did Joseph suffer kidnapping, slavery, and imprisonment? Couldn't G-d have arranged some other way to get Jacob's family to Egypt?

The biblical commentators explain that Joseph's harsh treatment at the hands of his brothers, and his subsequent difficulties, come from the fact that he was not as careful as he could have been in speaking to and about them. When he told them his dreams predicting that he would someday stand over them, his words had the effect of arousing their jealousy. Moreover, the Midrash tells us, he mistakenly accused them to their father of eating meat from an animal that was still alive.

Although these were merely mistakes of judgment, they caused Joseph to go down to Egypt in more difficult circumstances than otherwise might have occurred. Joseph was being judged and "punished" precisely because he was a righteous person, of whom G-d expected more.[8]

Each of us is judged according to our level of understanding and ability. A person who has been a thief all his life might be rewarded simply for giving up stealing, even though he might not accomplish much else in life. On the other hand, a person raised in an honest, upstanding, and wealthy family might suffer because he did not take advantage of the opportunities for doing good which G-d had generously offered. Only G-d can know what is fair and just for each person.

# ◈ DELAYS IN PUNISHMENT

E ven when we see the wicked being punished, we sometimes wonder why it took so long for them to get their "just

---

8. *Bava Kamma* 56; Talmud *Yevamos* 121b.

deserts." This is because G-d is merciful and, rather than punishing a person immediately, prefers to wait and give the person a chance — many chances — to repent. This is part of G-d's plan. He does not wish to punish or see humans suffer. G-d wants human beings to recognize G-d's greatness and follow the Divine commandments.[9]

Sometimes the Almighty causes relatively minor difficulties and inconveniences, using lesser "punishments" to prod us. The Torah teaches us that this is to induce us to come back to our Divine source, and is a reminder to return to the path. Only when we ignore all the signs G-d is sending us does He mete out severe punishment.[10]

The concept of free will is central to the understanding of difficulties and suffering. Think about it. If G-d were to punish us immediately for every wrongdoing, we would be much like animals going through an obedience or behavioral-conditioning course. And, like the dog that responds to the sound of a bell by salivation, or to the sight of a fist by cringing, a person would choose his actions only from instincts of gratification and self-preservation — in effect, not choosing at all. The short of it is that immediate reward and punishment would signal the loss of free will.

Nor are humans rewarded or punished for actions over which they have no control; G-d's justice is implemented within the context of free choice. And He created the possibility of evil for us to overcome it and thus earn reward for such accomplishment. The greater the challenges, the greater the satisfaction in and reward for overcoming them. We see that since free will is primary in humanity's education and its movement towards its ultimate goal, immediate reward and punishment — the diminishment of our ability to choose — would utterly compromise the system.

---

9. *Exodus* 34:6 (the "Thirteen Attributes" of Mercy); Rabbi Moshe Chaim Luzzatto, "Introduction," *Path of Hashem.*

10. Cf. *Deuteronomy* 7:10.

# ←§ THE ULTIMATE REWARD

Another equally important reason we cannot understand why good and bad things happen to people is that we do not know what is in store in the "World to Come." G-d created two levels of existence. The present world is an environment of challenge and accomplishment, where a person is tested and refined. The World to Come is a second level, where the person's soul receives its ultimate reward, and we come to recognize the true nature of all our deeds. This world is actually an introduction to the world of the hereafter.[11] Rewards and punishments therefore are not completely visible to human beings in this world. We will only be able to understand them when we have the perspective of the World to Come.

An analogy can help us understand this concept. If a young child is offered the choice to go to either a jewelry store or a candy store, and is allowed to take anything inside, what would he select? The candy store, almost certainly. Does that mean the contents of the jewelry store have a lesser value than the candy store? Of course not. The child's comprehension is limited, so the candy, which he can enjoy immediately, appears more valuable. We are virtually children in understanding the world beyond this one.

Just as when a person matures and things that were once of vital importance pale into insignificance, the pleasures of this world have less importance as we strive to reach higher spiritual levels. The sages of the Talmud assured us that the pleasures of this world do not amount to a fraction of the pleasures of the hereafter.

Thus the World to Come is important to our understanding of reward and punishment, as is free choice. Our tendency is to look for evidence of enjoyment and suffering in this world. But our sages tell us that the righteous are often punished immediately for their errors in this world, in order that they fully

---

11. *Pirkei Avos* 4:21.

experience the superior pleasures in the next world with no diminishment. The other side of the coin is that the wicked may be rewarded in this world for their few good deeds, and will have to face the full consequences of their evil acts in the World to Come.[12]

> A PARABLE: *The mayor of a town wished to honor his most distinguished constituents with a party in their honor. In order not to insult the common folk, he first invited them to an informal social gathering with a few refreshments. One of the more illustrious residents happened to see the townsfolk enjoying themselves and asked the mayor why he had not been invited.*
>
> *"Don't worry," the mayor replied. "This is just a little party. It's nothing compared to the lavish feast I'm throwing for you and the other really deserving people. Be patient — your invitation to the gala celebration is on its way!"*
>
> *Likewise, what appear to be the rewards of the wicked in this world cannot compare to what the righteous will experience in the World to Come.*

There are those who wrongly assume that because our Bible does not speak much about the afterlife, it is not an important part of Judaism. This is far from the truth. The Bible is written primarily as a testimony for all future generations of humankind to understand what G-d promised to our ancestors, through His prophets, and how these prophecies have been fulfilled. The holy books tell the history of the Jewish nation on earth, and the stories and admonitions focus on matters that can be clearly demonstrated. The Bible does not explicitly promise the reward of the afterlife, for it cannot be demonstrated by events accessible or discernible to all. Our tradition clearly asserts, however, that there is an afterlife, and this is alluded to in a number of places in the Bible.

---

12. *Rashi* on *Deuteronomy* 7:10.

# ♔ IMMORTALITY IN HISTORY

When the Torah comes to describe the death of our ancestor Jacob, it does not say "Jacob died," but rather, "and he was gathered to his fathers." Why was the word "death" not used here?

A person can experience two deaths. One is a physical death, the cessation of bodily functions. This death comes to everyone, sooner or later. The other possible death is the end of one's influence and impact upon the world. For many people, both deaths occur simultaneously. If during his life a person accomplishes nothing of real value and leaves no descendants who remember him, neither his life's work nor his memory lingers on when he passes away. Others, however, live on in memory and their work influences generations to come.

Jacob no longer functioned physically after the age of 147. However, he achieved so much during his years of earthly existence that his influence and example are felt even today as though he were still alive.[13] He had wrestled with an "angel" that symbolized the forces of evil in the world, and had come out victorious, thus he bequeathed his descendants with the spiritual fortitude to overcome evil. Because he founded the still-thriving nation of Israel, his presence is eternal. His noble traits and his devotion to G-d are guides for us all. Jacob is actually more a part of this world than many people who are physically functioning today, but who are making no spiritual or moral impact.

Rav Yehudah ben Bava was also a person who realized his work could survive his death. He lived during the days of Roman oppression when the government decreed that the granting of *semichah,* rabbinical ordination, was forbidden under penalty of death. Nevertheless, Rav Yehudah ben Bava assembled five disciples and secretly ordained them. Just as he finished the ceremony, his disciples heard the footsteps of Roman soldiers coming after them. As they began to make their escape, they

---

13. Talmud *Taanis* 5b.

shouted to their mentor, "Quick, flee from the enemy! If you do not run, you will be killed!"

Rav Yehudah ben Bava refused. "I am an old man. Run and save yourselves, but I will stay. I have completed my life's work. Even if the Romans kill me, they cannot destroy my accomplishments. The words of G-d's Torah will live on!" Soon after, the soldiers captured him. They punctured his body with spears until, it was said, it resembled a sieve. However, his disciples and, in turn, their disciples transmitted Torah to others, and so it went through the generations, so that Rav Yehudah ben Bava lives with us to this day.[14]

Our goal can be to survive in this world even after death, even after our souls have gone to the World to Come. Although we must all die physically, if we accomplish something worthwhile during our lives, our achievements will live on.

## ⪻ REWARD AND PUNISHMENT FOR THE JEWISH NATION

What we have discussed thus far applies to every individual. Ideally, we should serve G-d out of devotion, as did Abraham and Sarah with their intense love for G-d. But we do not always do this. Since G-d put us here to accomplish a certain mission, He uses reward and punishment to help prod us along on the path so that we will listen to Him and follow His commandments.

This is a fundamental principle of justice in Judaism. Just as officers of the government can be censured by their peers, or even removed from office if they do not fulfill their assignments completely and with integrity, we, as G-d's ambassadors, are subject to correction. Similarly, the faithful government servant is rewarded with reappointment, more responsibility, and eventually a good retirement. If we are faithful and fulfill our assignments

---

14. Talmud *Sanhedrin* 13b-14a.

with integrity, we too will be given higher and higher responsibility in executing G-d's plans, and eventually enter the World to Come.

Now we want to consider how this concept applies to the Jewish nation as a whole. Isaac blessed Jacob with the promise that all nations would come to serve the people who would be his descendants (*Genesis* 27:29). He indicated, however, that this blessing would come to fruition only if the Jews adhered to G-d's Torah. If the Jews abandoned the ways of Torah, their enemies could gain superiority over them (*Leviticus* 26:14,15,16,17).

For example, when the family of Jacob first came to Egypt, their stay was intended to be temporary. Soon, however, their attitudes changed and, instead of remaining sojourners, they became settlers in a rich and flourishing nation. At first they lived in a secluded community in the region known as Goshen, but within a few decades moved and settled in various sections of Egypt. This put them in danger of losing their distinctive Jewish identity and forsaking the G-d of their ancestors. They were, in short, beginning to assimilate.

This was not true of all the Jews. The two sons of Joseph, Ephraim and Menashe, stayed true to G-d's principles even though they had been born in Egypt. As a result, parents even today bless their sons with the words, "May you be like Ephraim and Menashe." To their eternal credit, these brothers did not exhibit jealousy as had siblings in previous generations. Our tradition thus recognizes the extraordinary achievement of people who could rise above the corrupting influences of their environment.

The assimilation to Egyptian culture of the rest of Jacob's descendants bore dire results. Instead of accepting them, the Egyptians turned on them and enslaved them; the rulers initiated a policy of gradually increasing their oppression and set cruel taskmasters over them. This oppression was a direct punishment for the Hebrews' attempt to assimilate. Now they could not make the mistake of forgetting they were Jews, for the Egyptians would not let them.[15]

---

15. *Bais Halevi* on *Parashas Shemos.*

There have been many other times throughout history when the Jewish people have suffered tremendous catastrophes; in most of these cases, we find that a significant number of the Jewish population had been imitating the gentiles around them. It is true that there are also cases of anti-Semitism and persecution of Jews who were living steadfastly by the Torah. But from the times of slavery in Egypt, the succumbing to temptation to intermingle with other nations and adopt their ways has been a continuing theme in Jewish history. The consequences have been tragic.

This may seem harsh, but we must see that, especially when it comes to dealing with a large collective entity, it takes dramatic events to make people pay attention. If the Jewish people are to be reminded of their mission, it is not enough to send each Jew an e-mail message. When we fall asleep, we have to be awakened-sometimes with a disturbance. The biblical book of *Judges* illustrates this teaching well. Each time the Jews strayed from G-d's commands, their enemies gained the upper hand; their enemies were the medium through which G-d reminded the Jewish people that they were Jews. On the other hand, when the Jews remembered their Creator and cried out to Him in sincere repentance, they were ultimately saved from their enemies.

Yet we can also wake ourselves up — and thus avert potential disaster — by reconnecting to our tradition through study and action. The example of Moses himself is outstanding. Raised in Pharaoh's palace as the adopted son of Pharaoh's own daughter, Moses was given all that the Egyptian royalty could offer. Yet, when he grew to adulthood, he did not close himself off from his people. He went out and observed their suffering. As Rashi, the famous commentator of the 11th century, explains, Moses directed his heart and mind to share the experience of his fellow Hebrews.

When Moses saw an Egyptian taskmaster savagely beating one of the Hebrew slaves, Moses killed the Egyptian and buried him in the sand. The next day, Moses intervened in a quarrel between two Israelites. One of the two tauntingly asked Moses what right he had to judge others and would he kill them as he had done to the Egyptian. This comment revealed to Moses that his deed was known, and he knew he would be in danger when Pharaoh learned of it. He fled to Midian, where he stayed for many years until he was called to lead the Jewish people out of Egypt.

Thus Moses, our first and greatest prophet and national leader, had to fight assimilation. He knew in his heart that his first loyalty was to the Jewish people. He cultivated this loyalty and love until finally it led him to strike out against the oppressors, and caused him to leave his princely life to become a shepherd in a distant region. This was the foundation for G-d's call and for the Divine plan that would make the Jewish people into an eternal nation.

When we identify with our people, when we study our tradition, we can realign ourselves with the purpose to which we have been called. Our history is replete with "reminders," when we have abandoned our purpose, to come back to our collective mission.

Other nations are sometimes pressed into service to be the agents of this reminder. They have, at many times in our history, had the upper hand. Assyria, Babylonia, Greece, Rome, Byzantium, Spain have ruled large sections of the world where Jews lived, right down to the Soviet Union of the 20th century. But, like the empire of ancient Egypt, they flourished, and then they withered. The Jewish people still remain.

We may not understand why, at any given time, one group is castigated more severely than another. For example, in the Bible, we see that the generation of the Flood was destroyed and wiped off the earth. The generation of the Tower of Babel rebelled directly against G-d's authority, but their punishment was only that they be dispersed and scattered over the earth. Why these differences? Our sages explained that the generation of Babel, although defiant of G-d, did try to make peace among themselves and establish cooperative efforts. The generation of the Flood, however, committed heinous crimes against their fellow men, and ignored G-d's mandates as communicated through Noah.

We cannot always see clearly the merits and demerits of our fellows on the collective level any more than we can on the individual level. We can, however, try to learn from the lessons of history and from those who have deeply contemplated the meaning of events.

# ๙ MIRACLE, REWARD AND PUNISHMENT

Sometimes G-d deemed it necessary to use supernatural methods to impress upon humanity the benefits of good deeds and the futility of wickedness. G-d does not usually perform miracles, for they — like immediate rewards — can interfere with people's free will. However, at times it has been necessary. For example, at the time of our Exodus from Egypt, G-d heaped miraculous rewards upon the collective good, and stunning punishments upon the collective wrongdoers.

As mentioned above, the Jewish people had left their secure and separate life in Goshen and spread out among the Egyptians. The Egyptians enslaved them, and for 210 years the Jews suffered under their yoke. To some people at the time, the purpose of this slavery was unclear. Yet our sages have taught that the slavery was analogous to the production of steel: To produce steel, iron ore has to be smelted in a furnace at enormous temperatures, but when it comes out, it has amazing strength. Egypt was like a smelting furnace from which the children of Jacob emerged a tested but stronger nation. Despite the tragedy and hardships of slavery, they still retained their singular identity as Hebrews. They did not change their Hebrew names, their language,[16] or their style of clothing. They had merged into a unity of everlasting brotherhood.

Still, after so many torturous years, they did not have the moral fiber, nor were they at the spiritual level necessary, to become G-d's chosen nation and an example for the rest of humanity. G-d had to do something miraculous to take His people out of spiritual and physical bondage.

The miracles G-d wrought, which we celebrate at Passover time, were necessary to show the world, and especially the Jews themselves, that G-d does exist. G-d introduced himself to the

---

16. *Vayikra Rabbah* 32:5.

people of Israel, showing His power, His might, and His involvement with the world. This is what is referred to as G-d's "outstretched hand." In this way He taught the Jews to have faith in G-d. A central article of our faith, repeated frequently in the Torah and in many of our prayers, is "I am the Lord your G-d Who took you out of the land of Egypt, away from the house of bondage." This theme runs throughout the Bible and through our lives. The miraculous events of deliverance impressed themselves deeply in Jewish memory.

## ~§ ONE FAITH THROUGHOUT HISTORY

Yet miracle is also connected to faith. Since the Exodus from Egypt, people of faith have been leading us. When the Jews left Egypt, Pharaoh regretted having let them go. He assembled his charioteers and pursued the Israelites as far as the Red Sea. Soon the Jews were cornered, with the Egyptians at their backs and the sea before them. Watching their enemy draw closer by the minute, the Jews seemed petrified. Under specific orders from G-d, Moses stretched his rod toward the sea, and the people waited for something to happen.

A man by the name of Nachshon ben Aminadav, filled with faith in G-d, moved forward and began walking into the waters of the Red Sea, fully confident that G-d would save him. Just as the waters reached his neck, the sea parted and the Israelites were able to walk through on dry land (*Exodus* 13:3-7). Nachshon's unwavering faith led directly to the miracle that saved the whole people.

Ever since, whether in the wilderness, in the land of Israel, or in our long exile, faith in G-d has kept the Jewish people alive. The history of our people began with the faith of our ancestors in one G-d, Creator of the universe. That faith has carried us through all periods of history, whether peaceful or turbulent.

Today, people have many doubts. But a simple faith can undergird every action and every decision. Once a Jewish boy was asked how he knew that G-d existed. He replied, "I live near the seashore. If I go there and see footsteps in the sand, I know someone has been there. When I look up and see the sun, the moon, the stars, and the wonders of nature, that is like G-d's footprints — I know He is there." Likewise, when we see G-d's imprint on history, we can know that He is constantly with us.

Another child was told, "I will give you a gold coin if you can show me where G-d is." The clever child responded, "I'll give you two gold coins if you can show me where G-d is not!"

Such faith can work miracles.

# 4

Divine Teaching:
Revelation And Tradition

## ❧ THE IDEA OF REVELATION

Judaism teaches that our tradition derives directly from the word of G-d, revealed more than three thousand years ago. How do we know that this is true?

Historical proof is not like experimental proof, which is repeatable by other scientists. History is woven of unique events, which by definition happen only once. How do we know that any part of history is true — that Alexander the Great conquered India, or that George Washington crossed the Potomac? No one who is alive today witnessed these events, or spoke to any of the people who did. We rely on historical accounts, either recorded in some material form or transmitted by word of mouth.

The reliability of the biblical history, the recorded history of the Jewish people, is extraordinary. At one time historians wanted to believe that the early biblical books were mere legendary material, but this for the most part is no longer an acceptable position in scholarly circles. The more archaeological research is done, the more it supports even minor details of the accounts given in the Bible. In addition, the word-of-mouth history of our people is authentic and clearly traceable.

Part of our history is the record of events of revelation. Spectacular miracles were witnessed, recorded, and passed down by word of mouth from generation to generation, miracles that demonstrated G-d's existence to the Jewish nation. The redemption from Egyptian slavery, the splitting of the Red Sea, and finally the revelation of G-d's will on Mount Sinai were all accompanied by extraordinary events. In addition, the prophetic leadership of Moses for forty years established the precedent of a people being guided by the ongoing word of G-d, transmitted through a prophet.

These are not accounts of ordinary events, yet they are definitive of the Jewish people's experience. That experience has asserted, over and over again, that the people were given a Divine teaching — what we call the Torah — in a direct fashion, not from the hand of a mere mortal. Moses was the vehicle through which this teaching was handed down to the Jewish people, without changing a word or letter of what G-d revealed to him.[1]

The great philosopher Rav Sa'adia Gaon (8th century) once said, "Revelation is a process that gives us the truth at once by a direct method. The teaching of Judaism, besides coming through logic and reasoning, is based upon Revelation, which is a short and more direct road to truth."[2]

In medieval times, Judah HaLevi wrote a great philosophical work known as the *Kuzari,* which explained the basic teachings of Judaism to the king of a people known as the Khazars. This king was searching for the ultimate truth, and he invited representatives of the three major religions of his region — Judaism, Christianity, and Islam — to debate before him. Ultimately, he

---

1. *Kuzari;* Rambam, *Mishneh Torah, Hilchos Yesodei Torah* 8:10.
2. Rav Sa'adia Gaon, *Emunos V'Dei'os.*

chose Judaism for two primary reasons. First, the teachings of the other two religions stemmed from Judaism. Second, the other religions claimed that only their prophet or leader was inspired by G-d, but Judaism taught that every Jew saw G-d's miracles and heard His direct revelation on Mount Sinai.[3]

The miracles of the Torah were not performed privately or witnessed by only a few, who later persuaded the multitudes to believe. The entire people were eyewitnesses, as the Torah reiterates, "before the eyes of the people" (*Exodus* 19:11). Throughout Jewish history, Jews never questioned the fact that G-d had performed miracles in front of 600,000 men and their families. Despite the fact that the Jews were well known for being stubborn and unyielding ("stiff-necked," as the Torah itself says), and arguments were common among individuals and groups even in ancient times, no doubt was ever cast on the events of redemption and revelation and the basic truths these events communicated. G-d had indeed miraculously taken the people out of Egypt, kept them alive in the wilderness, and given them the Torah. The accounts were handed down through family traditions: "When your child asks you. . .you shall tell him" (ibid. 13:8).

*Pirkei Avos* (*Sayings of the Fathers*) begins with the words, "Moses received the Torah from Sinai and gave it over to Joshua" (1:1). This *mesorah* or "giving over" passed from generation to generation, reminding us of the words of G-d expressed in the tradition of the Torah and its commandments.

Only very recently — in the past two hundred years or so — have detractors within the camp of Israel begun to question everything that we have held dear. During the period of the *Haskalah* (Enlightenment) beginning in late 18th century Europe, such people began to claim that the Torah and tradition were man made, that they constitute an unnecessary burden on Jews, and that imposing a distinct way of life makes Jews the targets of anti-Semitism.[4] This led to the abandonment of age-old traditions.

---

3. *Kuzari.*

4. Rav Saadia Gaon, *Emunos V'Dei'os.*

The ideas promoted by the "enlightened" philosophers made it seem as though human beings could regard themselves as the center of the universe, and throw off the discipline of personal holiness and devotion to G-d that Judaism demanded. They claimed that, in the modern world, a person could have total freedom, and the Torah could be restructured to fit their definition of what was important and valuable. Tradition, in short, could be made to conform to modernity's standards. Those who objected to these claims were dismissed as fossils of a vanishing faith — as if the giving of the Torah was not a historical fact, and the word of G-d could die by human decree or be changed by majority vote.

What is it that parents have told their children, beginning with the generation that crossed the Red Sea more than 3300 years ago?

- After crossing the sea, we were led to Mount Sinai where G-d told Moses to have the Jews set up camp.
- G-d told Moses to remind people of their deliverance from Egypt, and to transmit His promise that if they obeyed Him, they would be transformed into a "kingdom of priests and a holy nation."
- The united nation responded, "All that the Lord has spoken we will do!"
- G-d told Moses that the people should prepare themselves for three days, carefully staying off the mountain itself.
- On the third day, thunder, lightning, and thick clouds covered the mountain, a trumpet call was heard, and Moses ascended Sinai.
- Then followed the supreme moment in the history of the world, one that has echoed down through all Western religions and profoundly affects everyone to this day. Every man, woman, and child heard the voice of G-d as He declared the foundations of religious and moral conduct for all time:

  1) *I am the Lord your G-d Who brought you out of the land of Egypt.*
  2) *You shall have no other gods before Me.*

3) *You shall not take the name of the Lord your G-d in vain.*

4) *Remember the Sabbath to keep it holy.*

5) *Honor your father and your mother.*

6) *You shall not murder.*

7) *You shall not commit adultery.*

8) *You shall not steal.*

9) *You shall not bear false witness against your neighbor.*

10) *You shall not covet your neighbor's house.*

■ The people were so awed that they withdrew from the mountain and pleaded with Moses to speak to them instead of having to hear G-d's own voice, for they feared they would die. Moses withdrew into the "thick darkness" and began receiving additional teachings.

This event, following on all the miracles that brought the Israelites out of Egypt, welded them into a unique people. Other world faiths have generally begun with a single individual who claimed to receive a special message and gradually gathered a following, and his followers gradually converted others. Not so in Judaism. To be sure, Moses was the leader who galvanized the Jews to risk leaving Egypt. But once they were brought to Sinai, G-d made sure that the entire nation was present to hear Him proclaim the Ten Commandments. The permanent bond that began with Abraham was now renewed and strengthened. It was a bond between G-d and the people of Israel.

## ∾§ THE COMMANDMENT AGAINST IDOLATRY

The second commandment, coming directly after faith in G-d ("I am the Lord your G-d. . ."), is, "You shall have no other gods before Me." On the simplest level, this commandment prohibits making idols and other images, actions contrary to the basic Jewish belief in a G-d Who has no physical form (see Chapter 1). Further, it prohibits believing in other gods because Judaism insists there is only one eternal G-d Who is all-powerful. In contrast to polytheistic religions, where different gods are thought to control different spheres of nature and different spiritual realms, we believe in One Source for everything, and One Ruler for the entire universe. Even though we also believe there are angels and lower spirits, they are all subject to the One G-d Who directs all their activities, and we pray only to the One.

When our forefathers proclaimed this principle to the world nearly 4000 years ago, it was indeed a revolutionary concept. Each natural phenomenon — sun, moon, fire, rain, etc. — was thought to be controlled by a separate deity. The world was an arena of chaos, full of struggle among the different gods and their natural forces. The idea of a harmonious pattern behind all events did not exist. In such a context, no general code of human conduct could be formulated either. Each group simply followed the customs of its ancestors and the requirements of survival.

In place of this, our ancestors proclaimed the idea of one G-d guiding all the varied aspects of the universe according to a unified Divine plan. Within this framework, a universal guide for human conduct also became possible. A moral code, rather than just a collection of ancestral customs, could be introduced.

Thus the commandment against idolatry is a fundamental aspect of the revelation that was brought into the world at Sinai. It is not merely an assertion of certain facts about G-d, but also an expression of faith in the unity of creation and an ultimate plan for the harmony of all life.

## ◄§ TORAH AS DIVINE TEACHING

Besides the basic commandments of belief in One G-d and refusing to worship idols, the revelation called "Torah" includes a great deal more. It includes information about the nature of the world and human beings, and an entire system of commandments known as *mitzvos*. This is all part of G-d's communication to human beings, and every part of it is significant. This Torah or Divine Teaching has never changed. To believe this is, as the Rambam wrote, one of the basic principles of the Jewish religion.[5] Our belief also includes the crucial idea that the Torah includes the necessary explanations of the Written Law, and that these too were given to Moses by G-d Himself. (These explanations are known as the Oral Law, and were written down 2000 years ago in the compendium we know as the Talmud.)

It only makes sense that there should be such teachings. Since there is a G-d Who created a world to be populated and directed by human beings, He had to provide humanity with directives that would enable them to live a proper life in G-d's world. Otherwise it would be like giving a child an expensive toy but with no directions as to how to put it together or use it. The revelations that came to Moses are the essence of these teachings. This is part of the faith that has been passed down from our ancestors to us for more than three thousand years.

Historically, other factors also support this belief (although one does not need to study history to have faith). Archaeologists have authenticated many of the places, people, and events described in the Torah. Moreover, the Torah itself testifies that the Jews did not accept authority easily. They often complained about G-d's actions and Moses' leadership, about having to go through the desert without meat and other civilized foods, without sufficient water, and the like. Some individuals directly challenged the leadership of Moses and Aaron. A "stiff-necked" people like the Jews would not have continued to follow them if they had not been certain of the miracles they had experienced, and particularly that Moses was the principal bearer of the Divine Revelation they had received at Sinai.

The fact that, despite the rebellion of a minority, such a people accepted and lived according to the Torah and never challenged its Divine origin, is itself evidence for the Torah's truth. Rational

---

5. Rambam, *Thirteen Principles, Perush HaMishnayos,* end of Talmud *Sanhedrin.*

explanations are not even supplied for many laws, such as *kashrus* (the dietary laws). Yet the people accepted them and taught them to their children. Parents would not deliberately lie to their children about such things, and surely not an entire nation of parents. Furthermore, over the generations many thousands of Jews were willing to sacrifice their lives for the Torah. They were certain, beyond the shadow of a doubt, that the tradition they had received was based on a true transmission. Our ancestors' devotion to their tradition is a guarantee of its faithfulness.

Also, certain facts and predictions were written down in those ancient times that suggest that no mere human could have composed the Torah. Could anyone in 3300 BCE have stated unequivocally, without fear of being proven wrong, that only three species of animal — camel, hare, and rock badger — chew their cud but do not have split hooves, and that only the pig family has split hooves but does not chew its cud? This had to come through Divine knowledge. How could the Torah confidently predict that if the Jews did not keep the commandments, their Sanctuary would be destroyed and they would be dispersed throughout the world? The fact that the Torah dared make these predictions indicates that only G-d could have been the force behind it.

As for the claim, advanced by some skeptical writers, that Moses composed the Torah himself: Would Moses have written so much about his ancestors' shortcomings? Would he have given laws without reasons? Would he have chosen Joshua rather than his own sons to succeed him as leader? Would he have denied his fellow tribesmen, the Levites, a permanent portion of the Holy Land? Why would he portray himself as rebuked by G-d and punished by being unable to enter the land of Canaan, or his brother as censured because of the episode of the golden calf? Similar objections can be made against any proposed human author. Why indeed would the Torah write about all the complainers, the spies whose mission had such bad results, the rebellion of Korah, the seductions by the women of Moab, which portrayed the Jewish people so negatively?

These are monuments to the authenticity of the Torah and its truthfulness, and also to its great purpose. The truth hurts, but it also wakes us up. The Torah concealed no flaw in the Jews, their ancestors, or their leaders. Compare this to books about other major religions and their founders, whether the Koran, the New Testament, or the Buddhist sutras, which relate only the praises of Muhammad, the Nazarene, and Gautama.

Other evidence provides additional hints. Rabbi Michoel Ber Weissmandel, a great Torah scholar and valiant Holocaust rescuer, discovered — without the aid of a computer — that hidden within the letters of the Torah are "codes." In sequences of letters spaced at regular intervals, words are spelled out that pertain to the section in which the sequences are found. With the aid of computer technology in recent years, his discoveries have been confirmed and expanded by independent statisticians. While debates over the codes continue, they nevertheless serve as confirmation of unusual features of the Torah that suggest an extraordinary authorship.

## ❦TORAH AND MESORAH

When people refer to the Torah, sometimes they mean the Five Books of Moses, known in Hebrew as the *Chumash* ("Five") and in scholarly writings as the Pentateuch (from a Greek word meaning "five"). These five books — *Genesis, Exodus, Leviticus, Numbers,* and *Deuteronomy* — are the foundation of the Written Torah. It tells the story of the development of the Jewish nation, from the creation of the world through the death of Moses, when the Jews were about to enter the Promised Land. They also contain the basic laws and beliefs of Judaism.

Over time, records of other events were recorded by, or under the guidance of, various prophets, kings, and teachers. These appear in the books known collectively as the Prophets (*Nevi'im*) and Writings (*Kesuvim*). They describe events from the conquest of the Land of Israel under the leadership of Joshua down to the building of the Second Temple, approximately from the thirteenth to the fifth centuries BCE. Prophets and Writings also contain philosophical concepts that amplify on the Five Books to form the foundation of Jewish theology. The three sections of the Written Torah — *Torah, Nevi'im, Kesuvim* — are collectively known by the acronym Tanach (TNCh).

More generally, the term "Torah" can refer to the entirety of our tradition that can be traced back to the time of Moses. This includes the Oral Torah, which consists of the teachings and interpretations communicated to Moses during his prophetic experiences on Sinai as an explanation of and supplement to the Written Torah. He taught these gradually over the next forty years to Joshua, the elders, and the rest of the Jewish people.

The Oral Torah was originally transmitted only "by mouth," passed from one generation to the next by direct teachings from master to disciple. This ensured that people would learn Torah from an expert and from one who was actually practicing the Torah. They would receive it with a proper explanation and would devote time to examining the Torah carefully with another person, rather than reading it casually. The requirement of oral transmission also protected the tradition from outsiders who might distort it (as indeed happened to the Tanach when Christians incorporated it into their religion as the "Old Testament"). Only when the Oral Torah was in danger of being forgotten, during the oppressive times of Roman rule when many great teachers were imprisoned or killed, did our sages decide that they had to allow the Oral Torah to be put in written form. Rabbi Yehudah HaNasi completed the final arrangement around the year 3948 (188 CE) in the form of six Orders of the Mishnah ("second" teaching). Each section represents an orderly arrangement of the laws on its particular subject. The six orders and their topics are as follows:

- *Zera'im* ("seeds"): agriculture
- *Mo'ed* ("time"): Shabbos and festivals
- *Nashim* ("women"): marriage, divorce, and phases of family life

- *Nezikin* ("damages"): civil and criminal law
- *Kedoshim* ("holy things"): Temple service and related topics
- *Taharos* ("purities"): questions of ritual purity

Explanations and commentaries on the Mishnah were compiled by successive generations of rabbis, and are known as the Gemara. Two versions of the Gemara were collected and made available, together with the Mishnah that is their subject, one in Israel and one in Babylonia where there were major academies of learning. These combined texts of Mishnah and Gemara are known as the Talmuds: the Jerusalem Talmud, compiled by Rabbi Yochanan in Israel in the 4th century CE; and the Babylonian Talmud, compiled by Ravina and Rav Ashi in Babylonia in the late 6th century CE. There are 63 tractates (topical volumes) of the Babylonian Talmud, which is the more comprehensive of the two, and the most frequently quoted. The Talmuds are unparalleled compilations of practical law, philosophical discussion, logical arguments, and stories for moral edification. It has intrigued scholars for centuries, and has remained the bread and butter of the Jewish people. Indeed, no rabbi can be considered a learned person without having demonstrated serious and in-depth study of the Talmud. All later developments in authentic Jewish law and theology rest upon Talmud as well as Tanach.[6]

The concept that the Torah comes directly from G-d applies with equal force to the Oral Law. Even though it was not written down by Moses or succeeding leaders, it was passed down in an unbroken chain of tradition until it was eventually put into writing. This chain of tradition is called *Mesorah*. It is difficult for us to imagine today that such a tradition could be faithful to its original. We live in a society that depends on written texts for its "facts," and where word of mouth is considered no more reliable than rumor. In ancient societies, however, where written materials were rare and few could read, accurate oral transmission was

---

6. For a further elaboration of the development of interpretation in Jewish history, see Appendix A, "Outline of Jewish History."

expected and demanded, and memory was developed to an extent almost unbelievable today. This has been verified by anthropologists working in preliterate societies.While the Oral Torah was not required to be transmitted *verbatim,* there is no reason to doubt that it was transmitted effectively and concisely, conveying the original meaning faithfully to each generation. Indeed, the Mishnah as we have it today bears the marks of mnemonic devices that aided in accurate transmission.

Moreover, where divergences did occasionally occur, these were also faithfully recorded, discussed, and examined. This is a testimony to the truthfulness of our sages and their intense efforts to transmit the pure essence of Divine Teaching. A famous example is the divergent opinions on certain topics of two great first-century sages, Hillel and Shammai, in their understanding of conclusions reached from the Oral Law. Their disputes are recorded and the academy of sages decided that in most cases the law would follow the (generally more lenient) interpretations of Hillel. At the same time, it is worth noting that the divergences were small in number compared to the breadth of Torah; the two schools agreed on many more things than they disagreed, and none of the disagreements affect fundamentals of belief and principle.

The Talmud states that G-d concluded his covenant with Israel for the sake of the Oral Torah.[7] G-d knew that disputes would arise, and that examination of each issue by the scholars of the day would be essential. The Written Torah often words its commandments very concisely, or only in general terms, so they would often be unclear without the details furnished by the Oral Torah. For example, the Written Torah states that one must wear *tefillin,* described in the Bible as a "sign on your arm" and "*totafos* between your eyes." Clearly, something should be worn on the arm and the forehead — but what? Only with the Oral Law do we have a description of what *tefillin* look like, what they contain, and how they are to be placed on these parts of the body. We know, too, that this tradition was not

---

7. Talmud *Gittin* 59b.

"made up" later because archaeologists have discovered *tefillin* more than two thousand years old. In the same way, objects like the *succah* and the *lulav*, the *shofar*, the *tzitzis* (fringes), and even the way to observe Yom Kippur are only known from the Oral Law.

## ≈§ THE TORAH AND THE WORLD

The Torah is the foundation of Judaism. Without it, Judaism could not exist, and Jews would have floundered as just another lost nomadic tribe of the Middle East. With it, Jews can act as G-d's people, emissaries from the Divine. The Torah is an all-inclusive blueprint for life, including a deep understanding of life's purpose and practical guidance for establishing a humane society. Nothing is beyond the scope of the Torah. Ben Bag Bag in *Pirkei Avos* summarizes the Torah's value: "Occupy yourself with it again and again, for everything is in it."[8]

If the Torah, as suggested above, is an instruction book for mastering the world, then it must contain many types of instructions. With the laws that guide a human being's relationship with others, known as *mishpatim* ("judgments"), we can successfully navigate the intricacies of relationships, whether in family, business, or politics. It has laws called *edos*, "witnesses," which testify to the existence of G-d and His presence in the world. These include laws of Shabbos and holidays, prayer, and physical symbols like *tefillin, tzitzis,* and *mezuzah,* as well as the Holy Temple, its priests, and its sacrifices. A third type are laws of purity and holiness, known as *chukim* ("statutes"). The Torah does not give specific reasons for these laws, but they enable human beings to develop self-discipline, faith, and humility. Examples are the dietary laws (*kashrus*) and not wearing a garment that has in it both wool and linen (*shatnez*).

The Torah also provides inspirational stories and role models

---

8. *Pirkei Avos* 5:26.

as it recounts the origin of the Jewish nation and its refinement through many trials and tribulations. We will mention some of these in later chapters. They enable us to raise our sights and encourage ourselves to live on a higher level.

> *Torah is compared to water:*
> *Just as water ensures the life of the world, so the Torah ensures the life of the world.*
> *Just as water is free to all, so is the Torah.*
> *Just as water descends from heaven as rain, so the Torah was given from heaven.*
> *Just as waters come down with the accompaniment of thunder, so the Torah was given with lightning and thunder.*
> *Just as water revives and refreshes, so Torah purifies and rescues a human being from evil.*
> *Just as waters flow from a higher level to lower ones, so the words of Torah abandon the haughty and stay with the humble.* [9]

## ⨳ THE CONCEPT OF CHANGE IN THE TORAH

No one has the power to change the laws of the Torah. It is a foundation of our faith that Moses was the greatest of all prophets, past and future, as is written in the Torah: "There has not arisen a prophet in Israel like Moses, whom G-d knew face to face." Moses received his revelation directly from G-d with perfect clarity, unlike other prophets whose prophecies were masked in symbolism. Indeed, one of the primary functions of the revelation at Mount Sinai was to underscore the absolute authenticity of the prophecy of Moses in the eyes of Israel, for all subsequent generations. The Rambam teaches that we must emphatically repudiate the teaching of any individual — even if

---

9. Talmud *Eruvin* 54a.

the person seems to be a prophet — who calls on us to change, modify, or abrogate any aspect of Torah law, either from the Written Torah or from the accepted oral interpretation.[10] As the Torah itself says, "You shall not add to it or detract from it" (*Deuteronomy* 4:2).

Further, Torah teachings are timeless. As it also says, "The things that are revealed belong to us and to our children forever" (*Deuteronomy* 29:28). Because it embraces the depths and heights of wisdom, for over 3000 years the Torah could be observed and cherished by Jews in all kinds of societies and situations.

The values of the Torah may not correspond to those of the surrounding society. In recent generations, many have complained that they appear to be irrelevant to our situation. With historical perspective, however, we can see that this objection has been raised many times, and has always proven to be false. Contemporary values are of human origin and are transient, while those of the Torah are Divine and eternal, rooted in an understanding of human nature that could only be provided by G-d. When King Solomon, one of the greatest geniuses of all time, considered certain commandments irrelevant, G-d said, "A thousand like Solomon will pass away, but not a single dot of the Torah will be changed."[11]

A parable: A man in a museum observed crowds gathering before a painting, admiring its beauty and design. When he looked, however, the painting appeared to be a series of dark and ugly blotches, and he couldn't understand what people liked about it. He complained that it made no sense at all. Then someone noticed that his glasses had become smeared and darkened. When he cleaned them, it completely changed his view of the painting.

Likewise, when we do not see the beauty of the Torah's logic, we should consider that it is our vision that is clouded. We can "clean our glasses" only by learning it more thoroughly and thinking more deeply.

---

10. Rambam, *Mishneh Torah, Hilchos Yesodei Torah* 9.
11. Talmud Yerushalmi, *Sanhedrin* 2:6, *Shemos Rabbah* 6:1.

# ✑ DIVERSITY AND DIVERGENCE
# WITHIN JUDAISM

Torah has been the binding force of the Jewish people for more than three thousand years. Jews have been and can be from any race, geographical territory, or national citizenship. There are two large families of Jews — those who trace their lineage to northern, central, and eastern Europe, known as Ashkenazim, and those of Mediterranean and Oriental origin, who are Sephardim. These large general groups have different customs, including variations in their prayer books, and they pronounce the Hebrew language differently. But both uphold their lineages of dedication to the Torah as Divine teaching and the law of life. (The only *religious* differences within Judaism are those of an ancient tribal lineage: Cohen [Hebrew *kohen*], Levite, and Israelite.) The *kohen* is a descendant of Aaron, who served as the officiating priest in the Tabernacle in the wilderness, and whose descendants served in the Holy Temple in Jerusalem. The *kohanim* today have the function of blessing the people in a special ceremony on holidays, and they perform the ritual of "redemption of the first-born male". If any *kohanim* are present when the Torah is read publicly, one of them will be called up for the first *aliyah* (honor of reading).

The Levites were assistants to the *kohanim* in the Temple, and are descendants of the tribe of Levi (which included other families besides that of Aaron and Moses). A Levite is normally called up for the second *aliyah* when the Torah is read. The remainder of the Jewish people are called Israelites. The specific tribal lineage of the rest of the people is not usually known, and they are not differentiated in religious functions.

There is one unifying factor among Jews of all colors of skin, all languages and cultures, namely that all Jewish souls were present at Mount Sinai at the giving of the Ten Commandments, when they recognized they would begin to receive the Torah. They all responded, "We will do and we will listen." That is why

G-d called them His "kingdom of priests and a holy nation."

In that sense all Jews are kin. A great rabbi once kept visiting a sick individual, spending time by his side until the man recovered. When he was restored to health, the man asked the rabbi, "You were very devoted to visiting me when I was sick, but I'm not sure why. Do I know you? Are we related, or are we acquaintances from somewhere?"

"Yes," the rabbi nodded. "We stood together at Mount Sinai."

Given our historic commitment to G-d and Torah, any movement that allows or actively supports intermarriage, or encourages participation in other religions, is undermining authentic Judaism. The same is true for those who hold that the Torah is obsolete, and we need only follow the guidelines of humanitarian ethics. Unfortunately, such movements exist today. They are not really cultural diversity within Judaism, but divergence from the basic commitments of Judaism itself.

Divergences have existed before — the Sadducees near the beginning of the common era, the Karaites who gained a substantial following in the 7th-10th centuries, the Frankists in the early modern period. These have virtually all disappeared (there are a few small groups who claim to be Karaites), and their beliefs and variant Judaisms have no influence today.

In modern times, the pervasive influence of Enlightenment thinking gave rise to new divergences, with names like "Reform," "Conservative," or "Reconstructionist" Judaism. These are all very recent movements of the 19th and 20th centuries. "Orthodox" is not really a denomination within Judaism, but a label that came to be applied to Jews who did not "reform," "conserve," or "reconstruct." Prior to the emergence of the new movements, there were Jews who observed the Torah, Jews who observed some of it, and Jews who observed none of it. An Orthodox Jew is one who diligently practices and works at understanding the meaning of our religion, attempting to the best of his/her ability to continue the traditions handed down from Sinai.

The early reformers of the 19th century, following in the footsteps of rationalist thinkers like Moses Mendelssohn of the previous century, wanted Judaism to be in tune with the important trends in the modern world. They also went further than Mendelssohn in adapting Jewish practices so as not to be so different from other religions, particularly liberal Christianity. As one can read in the history of 19th century Judaism, these reformers hoped that Jews would gain esteem and anti-Semitism would vanish if Jews became more open to the nations around them. Following this logic, they abandoned Hebrew schools and gave their children a strong secular education to gain a foothold in the professional world. They modeled synagogues on church architecture, introduced organs and choirs singing ("Jewish") hymns, removed the barrier between men and women in services (itself a recent Protestant innovation in Christianity), and introduced the Christian ceremony of confirmation. Once a Christian lawyer happened into one of the reformed services and did not realize he was in a synagogue until a chance remark of the "preacher" betrayed that he was speaking to Jews.[12]

Sadly, the early leaders never anticipated how far the movement would go. Rapidly, Reform Jews came to practice a religion that looked more like Christianity than Judaism except for memorializing Passover, Chanukah, and the High Holy Days instead of the non-Jewish holidays. All six of Mendelssohn's own children converted to Christianity, and others who followed in his footsteps radically changed the Judaism he had practiced.[13] Some reformers left Judaism to become active in political or humanitarian movements, for they could not justify leading a Jewish religion that was not different from any other ethical movement. Today, it is rare to find Reform Jews with a Reform lineage longer than three generations (that is, most have great-grandparents who were Orthodox). Assimilation and intermarriage rates are

---

12. Judah L. Magnes (1877-1948), address at Temple Emanuel, New York, 1910.

13. David Friedlander, Mendelssohn's disciple and successor, expressed his willingness to accept baptism into the Christian Church in Berlin, with the condition that he be allowed to deny the divinity of the Nazarene and be excused from participation in the rites of the church. The answer was a sharp rebuff. Friedlander led the movement to Germanize Jewish life, urging radical changes in the rituals, repudiating the authority of rabbis, and rejecting the Torah as the foundation of Jewish life.

higher among Reform Jews than any other Jewish group. Some Reform leaders, like Isaac Meyer Wise in America, saw even in the 19th century the extremes to which the movement was heading and bemoaned the lack of Hebrew instruction. But he could do little at that point to stem the tide.

The Conservative movement arose in protest against the extremes of Reform. While affirming that the Written Torah is of Divine origin, Conservatives hold that the Oral Torah has been determined by councils of sages, and was not given by G-d to Moses. They conclude that such councils today can revise the laws, even if such revision goes against all previous understandings. In practice, this has unfortunately led to changes for the sake of expediency. Gradually, the gap between the majority of Conservative rabbis (who often have been trained very traditionally) and their congregations widened, both in level of Jewish education and in level of observance. Today, Conservatism has accommodated to American culture far more than would have been expected at its founding 100 years ago. It is quite possible that if the founders of Conservative Judaism saw how far the movement had digressed from their original intent, they would look upon it as a branch of Reform.

Two factors are involved in these divergent movements. One is the too-easy acceptance of change. Once the idea of the eternality of Torah is abandoned, the field is wide open. While the leaders of one generation might believe that they had set firm limits to reform and revision, the next generation can see the limits in a completely different way. How much change can occur before one no longer has the original? If you have a fence on the borders of your property, and you agree to let your neighbors alter it "just a little," you have set a precedent, so that your grandchildren's inheritance may be considerably less than you intended.

Second, over the generations, people do not even realize how much has been lost. Neither Reform nor Conservative Judaism established institutions of education on the scale that would have been necessary to perpetuate themselves as their founders intended. While all of Judaism in America suffered from lack of schools before World War II, Reform and Conservative largely continued to ignore the need to provide Jewish education for their members beyond the childhood years. Frequently, they offered only after-school or elementary education. Only in recent years have some of these communities recognized the crucial importance of Jewish high schools and continuing adult education. As a result, those who grew up in these movements knew that they were Jewish and could celebrate the more obvious aspects of the Jewish holidays, but did not realize how much more there was to living a Jewish life.

Most important, the changes these movements made were not Divinely sanctioned. In Reform, this was not an issue for the members and leaders, for the ideology of the movement was that Torah was not Divine anyway, and people could abide by it or not, as they chose. Conservatives saw the error of Reform, but were not willing to maintain the stream of tradition. For three thousand years, all Torah discussions of our rabbis had been explicitly "for the sake of heaven," with a prayer that G-d would look favorably on their endeavors. Conservatives abandoned this line of tradition in favor of historical biblical studies, implying that the movement did not concern itself with devotion and dedication to the Divine Will. The approval of the surrounding culture, and particularly the world of secular academic scholarship, was more important.[14] Today, there is far more interchange, and similarity, between Reform and Conservative congregations than between either of those and the traditional Jewish communities.

The key issue in all these divergent movements is the questioning of the Torah as G-d's blueprint for the world. Every person's deepest relationship to G-d and to the Jewish people hinges on the acceptance of the Torah, written and oral, as a gift

---

14. The Conservative movement has been defined largely by the Jewish Theological Seminary (New York). In its early days, the faculty and administration were made up of very observant Jews, but they embraced secular studies wholeheartedly. The institution was put in *cherem* (excommunicated) by an organization of Orthodox rabbis who saw their approach as undermining the Divine origin of the Written Torah, despite Conservative disclaimers to the contrary. The Conservatives accepted the division and no attempt was made to heal the breach.

to us from G-d. Our understanding of this does not come from merely repeating the words, nor from a rigid and blind devotion. It develops as we do the work, to "occupy ourselves with Torah." As we learn it, our understanding deepens and the truth becomes clear.

# ►§ THE CRUCIAL IMPORTANCE OF LEARNING TORAH

The Talmud tells us that every Jew is required to learn Torah. Moses taught that it is our own unique form of wisdom and understanding, enabling us to achieve our proper status among the nations. Therefore every Jew, after this life is over, will be brought before the heavenly tribunal and asked, "Did you study Torah?" If we answer "no," we will be challenged, "Why did you neglect it? Torah study is the primary occupation of every Jew!"

A person who was a pauper will defend himself, saying, "What could I do? I had to support my family." He will be told about Hillel, who earned next to nothing, one small coin a day. Yet he spent half of it to pay the guard at the door of the House of Study to gain entrance, and used the rest to provide his family with their needs. One Friday afternoon, when he had no money, he climbed up to the roof to overhear the words of the scholars. It was winter, and snow began to fall. The next morning, he was found frozen on the skylight. Fortunately, the sages were able to revive him by the fire. "This man is truly worthy of having Shabbos profaned for his sake!" they declared.

The well-to-do businessman will not have the excuse of poverty, but he will say, "What could I do? I had to keep my business going, and had so many things to take care of, I couldn't study any more Torah than I did."

The reply to him will be, "Were you wealthier than Rabbi Elazar ben Charsum?" He had a thousand ships and owned a thousand villages, but he never knew what they looked like. He did not want to take time to inspect his properties because he preferred to spend day and night studying Torah. His own servants did not know their master. Once they saw him pass by and, thinking he was a day laborer, forced him to work. "Please let me go! I must learn!" he begged them. Eventually someone recognized him and they released him.

A sensuous person will be asked, "What stopped you from learning Torah?"

"What should I have done?" he will excuse himself. "I love life — it is full of pleasure and beauty. I was unable to control my passions, because I was given this nature. How could I spend time cooped up in some room, studying Torah?"

He will be told, "Your excuse is not acceptable. Are you more handsome than Joseph? Potiphar's wife tempted him daily, yet he overcame his evil inclination. Were you more surrounded by material temptations? He was second in command over all of Egypt, a civilization of wealth, beauty, and sensuousness. Yet he devoted himself only to G-d's will. Why couldn't you take an example from him?"[15]

We might add, in our day, that some will give the excuse, "I did not learn Torah from my parents. They were not observant, and had not learned enough to teach me." Many times, through the accidents of history, Jews have been "orphaned" from Torah, separated temporarily from their tradition. But in every time and place we have renewed our connection, cherishing our holy books and attaching ourselves to expert teachers. This is possible in our time too.

In short, we must all shift our priorities to put learning Torah at the top of our list, or it will get pushed aside by our very busy lives. "Don't say," said Hillel, "that you will study when you have time, for you may never have time."[16]

Moreover, we must study to pass on the tradition to our children. As we say in the Shema, "You shall teach these words diligently to your children." This tells us that only when we personally transmit the Torah to the next generation will they

---

15. Talmud *Yoma* 35b.
16. *Pirkei Avos* 2:5.

know it as clearly as if they had personally witnessed the giving of the Torah. Moreover, if we can teach others, we should. The Talmud says, "The one who teaches his neighbor's child Torah is considered as if he himself had begotten him."[17] In Part II, we will develop more fully the nature of Torah and its commandments.

---

17. Talmud *Sanhedrin* 19b.

# 5

—◦◦◡◦◦—

# Jews And The World

—◦◦◡◦◦—

## ❧ THE IDEA OF THE CHOSEN PEOPLE

Jews have been numerically insignificant in the world — as the Torah itself says, "the fewest of all the nations" (*Deuteronomy* 7:7), but we have compiled an admirable record, not only in terms of survival, but also with a rich history and remarkable accomplishments. Why? Because G-d selected us to be a Chosen People. G-d carefully nurtured this nation, including sometimes testing them, to blossom as His select creation. This is explained by the following parable:

A king once owned a grand and beautiful garden, which he leased to a tenant farmer. After a while, his curiosity grew as to what had been done with it, and he asked to see his old garden. He was shocked to see that it had been left to rot, with thorns and thistles running rampant. "Destroy everything!" the outraged monarch decreed.

Then, as his men were setting to work with their sickles, the king came upon a single rose. It was fragile, but its fragrance wafted gently through the air, and its beauty brightened the entire orchard. The king was smitten by its beauty and his anger disappeared. "Stop!" he ordered his men. "I don't want the garden razed after all. If it can produce so beautiful a flower as this, it should be preserved."

The meaning is this: In the past, G-d had destroyed the earth and saved only one family, that of Noah. But now, the parable tells us, G-d is willing to restore the whole earth on account of one family — now a whole people, descended from Abraham, Isaac, and Jacob — just as the whole garden was saved for the sake of that one flower. The "chosen people" is the one that has survived all the things that have befallen the world since the beginning of human history.

Nevertheless, the expression "chosen people" should never be used as an indication of elitism or haughtiness. We must be humble in recognizing that G-d uses us to serve a specific purpose, and therefore willing to accept a larger share of responsibility to G-d.

A Midrash tells us that G-d approached other nations of the world to offer them the Torah. To Edom he said, "Will you accept the Torah as the basis of your lifestyle?"

"What does the Torah say?" asked the Edomites.

"One important commandment," said G-d, "is, 'You shall not kill.' "

"Never any killing?" they responded. "But our entire existence depends on our being able to kill and conquer others. If the Torah forbids killing, we cannot accept it."

G-d then offered the Torah to the nation of Ishmael. "What does it contain?" asked the Ishmaelites.

"You shall not steal," G-d replied.

"If that is so," they said, "then we regret to decline your offer. If we cannot steal, we will starve. Take the Torah and give it to someone else."

So it went, with nation after nation refusing to accept the Torah, for they could not agree to live according to its laws. Finally, G-d approached the nation of Israel. "Will you accept My Torah?" He asked.

The Jews' famous response was, "We will do and we will hear," agreeing to obey first of all, and find out the details later.[1]

The Midrash casts a dark shadow on the other nations of ancient times. The point, however, is not to prove the superiority of the Jews. Rather, the authors of the Midrash were using a dramatic method of making the point that morality is not something one invents to agree with one's lifestyle. Rather, it comes from a Divine Source. Our ancestors understood this and, for that reason, were able to accept the Torah. The Midrash is telling us in essence that the great Revelation at Sinai, foundation of all systems of morality and worship, entailed also the notion of the Chosen People.

*Ogden Nash may have said: "How odd of G-d to choose the Jews," however, we answer: "It's not so odd; the Jews chose G-d!"*

## ◆§ THE SPECIAL MISSION OF THE CHOSEN PEOPLE

The most important task for the Jewish nation is stated in the Bible: "Now therefore, if you will obey My voice and keep My covenant, then you will be to Me a select portion above all nations, for the earth is Mine. And you shall be unto Me a kingdom of leaders (priests) and a holy nation" (*Exodus* 19:6).

Humans were created for a specific purpose: to emulate G-d's righteousness on earth (see above, Chapter 2). Yet generations of human offspring found this very difficult to do. G-d then chose to focus on one specific nation to pursue this mission. They would act as a model for the rest, a small-scale Divine experiment that could demonstrate to the rest of mankind how to behave properly. This nation is the Jews.

This mission means that the Jews who stood at Mount Sinai accepted certain responsibilities on themselves and their descendants, for all time. On an individual level, they would have to

---

1. *Rashi* and *Sifri* on *Deut.* 33:2.

(1) accept and worship G-d as the One and only all-powerful G-d; and (2) observe the 613 *mitzvos* (precepts or commandments) of the Torah, and the extensions and applications of those laws as derived by the sages of each generation. On the national level, all Jews were to create a community of people dedicated to G-d, as a model of righteousness for all nations to emulate. This would be more than a collection of individuals who purified themselves; it would mean a whole society and culture devoted to G-d.

An important concept in this mission is that of "holiness." G-d tells us that to complete our mission as the chosen people, we must first of all be a holy nation.

The term "holy" as used in the Bible means two things. First, to be holy means to be separate, removed, distinct from one's surroundings. This means that the Jews have to be a nation set apart from others with their own unique way of life, on the mundane level as well as the more obviously spiritual levels.

Second, holiness means dedication, as when a priest dedicates himself completely to his role of service to G-d. Dedication leads to perfection. By devoting ourselves to G-d's Torah and adhering to its *mitzvos,* we can live up to both aspects of holiness.

Just as the individual *kohen* (priest) dedicated himself to G-d's service and to teaching G-d's laws, so too the nation of Israel is intended to dedicate itself to spreading the word of G-d and demonstrating, by personal and collective example, what it means to bring G-d's ways into human life.

> *"All employees report to the manager's office!" The call went out over the factory's public-address system each day, ever since the owner of the company had left on an important business trip. The manager whom he had appointed to be in charge assembled everyone each morning and read aloud the instructions left behind by the boss.*
>
> *When the owner returned, he was shocked to see that workers were standing idle, machines needed repairs, and the general condition of his factory was run down. He angrily called in the manager and asked him for an explanation.*

*"I left clear instructions with you when I departed,"* said the boss. *"Didn't you follow them?"*

*"Of course,"* the manager defended himself. *"I read them to all the workers every day while you were gone."*

*"You* read *them?" cried the boss. "Now I know why there's such a mess. You recited them, but didn't bother to see that they were implemented, or attend to the morale of the workers. I didn't give you the instructions just for reading, but so you would know how to run the factory in my absence."*

*The incompetent manager is like people who study Torah and pray only out of habit, reciting words without letting the meaning affect their hearts or change their behavior.*

— the Chofetz Chaim (Israel Meir Ha-Cohen)[2]

This service is not a part-time effort. Consistency and continuity are demanded of the Jewish people. Just as the ancient Tabernacle and Holy Temple, and even our synagogues today, have a *ner tamid* (perpetual light), we too must continuously be a "light" to the nations. We must continuously act in accordance with G-d's wishes. We cannot be pious only on Yom Kippur or on a *yahrzeit* (anniversary of a relative's death), but every day of the year. Nor should we pray or perform other observances listlessly, out of habit or routine, but we should seek to live and act in an inspired way. We must make our service, every day, a matter of practical action. Lofty words and thoughts or rote repetition have little meaning by themselves.

## ✒§ AMBASSADORS TO THE WORLD

Judaism teaches that we are essentially ambassadors of G-d. We operate G-d's embassy on earth. If a government official of one country travels in another, the behavior of that person is

---

2. *Mishlei Chofetz Chaim.*

taken to be representative of the lifestyle and values of the whole people of that foreign country. So also with the Jewish people — our behavior reflects on the One Who sent us, and we have to act with awareness and sensitivity to our situation.

What is true on the positive side also applies to the negative. If a special assistant to the president makes a mistake, it is greatly magnified by the press and public. It brings disgrace not only to the special assistant, but also to the president whom he is supposed to serve. Likewise, Jews who do not live up to the standards set for us in the Bible (which is the best-selling book in the world) not only reflect poorly on themselves, but on the whole people and on the esteem in which G-d is held in the eyes of humankind.

The Maggid (storyteller) of Dubno explained the choosing of the Jewish people with a parable:

**A PARABLE:** *A fabulously wealthy landowner decided to get married. But rather than marry a woman from an affluent family, he decided his purpose would be best served by marrying a woman of poor and humble background. He ended up choosing as a wife one of his own maidservants.*

*Before the marriage he explained to her at length what her new position would entail. No longer would she be merely the cook in the kitchen with a few helpers. Now she would supervise the entire household staff, making sure everything was done to a high standard. She would have to learn to act with dignity but not arrogance. She would also have to be careful of the people she associated with and the impression she made on others.*

*In return, he promised, she would receive not only the wealth that came with being his wife, but his love and devotion. He would always treat her with the respect and deference due to a lady of her position.*

*Similarly, G-d exalted the Children of Israel above the other nations. This honor brings duties and responsibilities with it. The Jewish people are distinguished not by wealth and power, but by their obligation to serve the Master of the Universe by representing His Will on earth.* [3]

That Jews are expected to maintain a higher level than anyone else is clear from the way the media reports events in Israel. Violence and immoral behavior can be found anywhere, but when a Jew or the Jewish state commits a questionable act — not to mention a crime — it is publicized much more harshly than when another nationality does the same thing or worse.

What has set the Jewish people apart for 3000 years is their awareness of being ambassadors of G-d, His representatives on earth. Whether it was refusing to submit to decrees against religion, dying for the faith, uprooting ourselves to avoid forced conversion, practicing Judaism in hiding, or longing to return from exile, our nation as a whole has carried the banner of G-d and Torah for these centuries, a living witness to the Almighty. This has been the way we have carried this special responsibility.

# ❧ CHOSENNESS, SEPARATENESS, AND INTERMARRIAGE

Most Jews through the centuries have understood that their responsibility required them to be separate from other nations. In particular, this has meant not intermarrying with non-Jews. This is specifically stated in the Torah, regarding the other nations the Jews would encounter when they left the wilderness for the settled land of Canaan: "Neither shall you make marriages with them. Your daughter you will not give to his son; nor his daughter shall you take unto your son, for she will turn away your son from following Me. . . ." (*Deuteronomy* 7:3-4).

In our cosmopolitan society, this boundary is difficult to understand. It involves the concept of holiness which we described above, emphasizing separation as a discipline to enable

---

3. *The Parables of the Dubno Maggid.*

the Jewish people to stay in touch with their purpose. Rabbi Samson Rafael Hirsch, a great 19th century leader, wrote compellingly about this:

> It is not from hostility against members of other faiths that you should not intermarry with any non-Jews, but out of anxiety for Judaism, the sole treasure of your people. You must avoid mixed marriages on account of the obligation which G-d has laid upon you to transmit His law to your descendants and help to continue Israel's mission through them. Therefore, as long as Israel remains Israel, all marriage with non-Jews is forbidden . . . In order that the sons of Israel may not fall in love with non-Jewish girls, nor the daughters of Israel with non-Jewish youths, G-d's law has also forbidden to Israel too great intimacy with other peoples.[4]

One rabbi related the approach he took in dissuading young men who were considering intermarriage:

> *I usually meet the young man late in the evening in the synagogue and ask him to come into the main sanctuary. The atmosphere is quiet, with five hundred empty seats; the only lights are in back, and a few near the Ark. Then I say to the young man, "Open the holy Ark."*
>
> *He may ask, "Rabbi, now?" and I answer, "Yes, now."*
>
> *After he opens the Ark, I ask him to take out the Torah scroll. Again he may ask, "Me, now?" and I answer, "Yes, now." He takes it out.*
>
> *Then I tell him emphatically, "Throw the Torah on the floor. Stamp on it and spit on it!" Invariably the young man says, "Rabbi, you must be kidding."*
>
> *Then I take the Torah from him and return it to the Ark. Immediately, I say firmly to him, "By marrying out of your religion you are throwing down, stamping, and spitting on the holy Torah."*[5]

---

4. Rabbi Samson Rafael Hirsch, *Horeb.*
5. *How to Stop an Intermarriage*, p. 2.

If a person from another religious or cultural background wants to make a commitment to the great purposes of Jewish life, conversion is a possibility. Otherwise, however, we can appreciate people from other cultures but we cannot become too intimate with them. The fact is that most children of mixed marriages are raised without any Jewish identity — not only no religious identification, but without cultural identity either.[6] Contrary to popular belief, such marriages do not result in combining the best of Jewish and non-Jewish culture, but the dilution of both.

The Chief Rabbi of Britain, Lord Immanuel Jakobovits, has written in our generation,

> That this process of attrition is infinitely less dramatic than the mass slaughter of six million Jews only aggravates the situation. When Jews are lost through interfaith marriages instead of gas chambers no one weeps, protests, or demonstrates. There is no enemy to galvanize the defenders into frantic action, and no outburst of anguish to stir the conscience of survivors. This vast cancer is the painless type. Unaware of the danger signals, the patient will not even resort to a doctor for treatment until it is too late.

Intermarriage, as the Rambam wrote more than 800 years ago, is a desertion of Judaism.[7]

# ↝ JUDAISM AND OTHER RELIGIONS

Jews have, unfortunately, deserted Judaism in other ways in recent times, through participation in cults and other religions. According to one expert, an estimated 150,000 Jews are

---

6. The argument has been made that interfaith marriages will increase the Jewish population. This has not proven to be the case. In most mixed marriages, the non-Jewish spouse does not convert, and two thirds of the non-Jewish partners do not view their children as Jewish, even if the mother is Jewish. In Jewish law, the child is Jewish if the mother is Jewish, but when the partners do not honor this fact, the Jewish child may follow the lifestyle of the non-Jewish father, breaking the chain of tradition.

7. Rambam, *Mishneh Torah, Hilchos Asirei Biah,* 11.

involved in more than 3000 different cults that flourish in America today. Such a thing was virtually unheard of in previous centuries. As with intermarriage, people often justify their interest in other religions as natural to life in a cosmopolitan society with a "universalistic" outlook. But this reflects a shallow understanding of what Judaism is all about.

In fact, most Jews in cults and other religions lack deep knowledge of their own faith. Often they have grown up in situations where they or their families were ashamed of being Jewish, or felt pressure not to display their Jewishness, or did not have access to good Jewish education. The children were deprived of the knowledge of their own strength and uniqueness as part of a great people. They were unprepared for challenges to their identity and became vulnerable to outside elements.

In fact, a number of movements have particularly targeted Jews, as though persuading a Jew to join their religion is a greater victory than converting a non-Jew. This in itself testifies to the power and strength of the Jewish people, as capturing a lion is a greater achievement than trapping a weaker animal.

The only way to respond to this situation is to educate our youth to know our rich heritage. The Jewish nation, throughout its long history, was proud of its lifestyle, its Torah, its leaders, and the examples they set on the basis of Torah teachings. Despite the fact that we were constantly persecuted, vilified, and "ghettoized," Jews remained proud and confident that they had a fine and precious way of life. They celebrated Shabbos and holy days with everything they had slaved to earn during the week, and the fact that the surrounding world looked on them with disdain did not bother them in the least. They were not humiliated, because they knew their strength.

How did this situation change so that Jews became willing to consider another religion? There are two aspects to the story: one has its roots in Germany, in the early 19th century derivation of the Reform movement from Enlightenment perspectives; the other in the massive immigrations to America in the late 19th and early 20th centuries. The former we have discussed in more detail (see Chapter 4). Here we can just state that a false ideology of universalism, rejecting anything that smacked of difference from other peoples, spread rapidly in Germany, and to some extent in other western European countries. German Jewish immigrants were among the first Ashkenazim to establish communities in North America in the mid-19th century, so their power and influence played a large role in shaping American Judaism. The German Jews did not, of course, want Jews to leave Judaism for other religions, but they diluted the uniqueness of our traditions to the point that "liberal" Judaism seemed little different from liberal Christianity, humanism, or ethical culture. They also encouraged academic approaches to biblical studies and Jewish history, which influenced many generations of young Jews, unequipped to engage in deep debates, to question traditional teachings.

Immigration itself changed the face of Judaism simply because immigrants found it extremely difficult to maintain their old ways of life. Jewish communities were often small and scattered, and Jews faced intense pressure to conform to the dominant culture. Even Jews who were somewhat observant became pessimistic about their ability to maintain their way of life and pass it on to their children. Wanting to make it easier for the next generation, they often did not elect to give them the opportunity to learn in a *yeshiva,* but were content to send them to public school and offer some Jewish education in the afternoons. This was not enough to prepare their children for the onslaught that they and the ensuing generations would face. At the same time, learned rabbis were reluctant to immigrate from the strong, settled communities of Europe to face the difficulties of creating Jewish life almost from scratch in America. Thus, Jews who wanted more learning for themselves and their children found it difficult to obtain. The generations who grew up in the 1920s through the 1950s often had only a smattering of Jewish education.

The weakness within and the rapidly changing multicultural environment outside created an alarming situation. Uneducated in their own tradition, Jews learned more and more about the secular world and, inevitably, about other religions. Large numbers of American Jews had been taught by teachers who did not value the *mitzvos* and who had redefined the Jewish purpose in terms of a general universal ethic. As a result, many Jews did not hesitate to turn to other faiths when they had religious or spiritual questions.

In addition, some representatives of traditional Judaism, confronting an American culture that was in many respects shocking, adopted an extremely defensive posture. Concerned about the effects of modernity on their own children, they did not always seek out their lost brethren or invite children of "modernized" homes into their schools. Over a few decades, the gap between the traditional Jew and the nearly assimilated Jew grew rapidly.

This began to change in the 1950s. Those who had escaped or survived the Holocaust came to America and joined with their brothers and sisters who had maintained islands of tradition in America. Schools and other institutions were established, so that even Jews with absolutely no background could come and learn. The works of our great thinkers began to be translated into English, and audiotapes made it possible to hear the words of Torah-trained teachers anywhere. Now it is possible, and imperative, that our young people become aware of our great heritage.

Jews introduced the world to the concept of the One G-d. Our Jewish Bible has been studied by countless millions and served as a guide and foundation for other religions and moral systems. The religious and ethical life of Jews has become a model for high moral standards, emphasis on the close-knit family, and assistance to one's fellow man. Our philosophers and thinkers have shed light on every facet of spiritual development.

# ≈§ AREN'T ALL RELIGIONS ESSENTIALLY THE SAME?

In our universalist culture, some might argue that, yes, Judaism has a great tradition, but so do other religions, and really they all amount to the same thing, different paths to the same goal.

Unfortunately, this is one of those common misconceptions that people repeat over and over again until it sounds true. While religions have some very general similarities, a direct comparison of beliefs, practices, and ways of life shows us that religions are very different.

Polytheistic religions, where people divide their allegiance among many gods, still exist today, for example in popular Hinduism. From a Jewish point of view, this is a mistake that can lead a person down a slippery slope, where one becomes distracted from singleness of purpose and loses consciousness of higher levels of being. According to the Rambam, the original spiritual consciousness of human beings was focused on the One G-d. But over generations, people turned their attention more and more to G-d's messengers, and finally ended up worshipping nature in the form of idols.[8] This is the general tendency of human religiosity, if it is not corrected.

Respecting the many forces in the world, be they natural or spiritual, is valid. But for a Jew, focus on the Oneness of G-d is essential; it is part of our innate purpose. It is significant that today, proponents of traditional polytheistic religions often agree that there is one Creator or Source behind everything, and that the various "powers" are simply our cousins, so to speak, in the created world. In fact, this points to the strong influence of monotheism — and ultimately Judaism — on these religions. All the more should we continue to dedicate ourselves to the message of Oneness, so that the level of everyone's spirituality can be maintained.

Other religions deny that G-d is the Creator of the world, or that He takes a personal interest in creation, as in most forms of Buddhism. Moreover, in this approach, one also believes that there is no purpose or goal to human history. According to this approach, each individual is caught in his or her own attachments to the world, which causes one reincarnation after another. The only thing that makes sense is to release oneself from attachments so that one will not be reborn. One should

---

8. Rambam, *Avodah Zarah* 1:2,3.

also be concerned for others, to help them be liberated as well.

This kind of belief system has been extremely attractive for a psychologically oriented generation of people, seeking self-fulfillment and not finding it satisfaction in the material world. Buddhism is indeed a psychologically sophisticated religion. However, it is in direct contradiction to many Jewish beliefs, the most important being that G-d has a plan for the world and for all humanity. The apparent accidents that lead one to seek a spiritual path (even a Buddhist one!) are not accidents at all, nor a mechanical working out of karma from past lives, but part of G-d's mercy on His creatures. Because G-d is personal and involved in creation, we can pray to Him and develop a sense of His presence, doing small miracles daily in our lives.[9]

The religions of the West, both Christianity and Islam, adopted from Judaism the belief in a personal G-d Who also created the universe. From the Jewish viewpoint, Islam, which began in the 7th century CE, is a direct derivative of Judaism: a monotheistic religion with a few basic practices that encourage faith. However, Islam requires a person to believe in Muhammad as the final and complete prophet of G-d for everyone, and that the Koran is the perfect book of revelation, implying that Jewish (and Christian) revelations are of a lower status. The messages that Muhammad transmitted may have some truth in them, but they do not compare to the Divine revelations that distinguish Jewish history, which were experienced by a whole people.

Christianity also accepted Jewish belief in a personal Creator G-d as its basic framework, together with belief in a Divine plan for history and the ultimate resurrection of the dead. But this religion is based on the claim that Jesus, a 1st-century Galilean Jew, was the Messiah, that he was resurrected, and is himself Divine, the one and only son of G-d. Christians believe that his death atoned for the sins of all humanity and that he will reappear on earth in a "second coming." They also believe that G-d manifested in a third form, the "holy spirit" (thus making a "trinity"), which guides the Christian church. A person who

9. *Aruch HaShulchan* 219.

believes all this, according to traditional Christianity, will go to heaven after death; and those who do not will receive eternal punishment.

From a Jewish viewpoint, the belief in a "trinity" borders on polytheism; but even more importantly, the claim that Jesus was G-d is idolatry. Rambam stated in his code of laws, that one conceives G-d to be a corporeal being is a heretic and an apostate.[10] According to Judaism, no human being can be completely identified with G-d. As for the "holy spirit," this is a Jewish concept indicating a high level of inspiration that makes prophecy possible. It was never intended to mean an entity separable from G-d, let alone permanently residing in a human institution.

Christianity, like Islam, respected the revelation to Jews, and Christians even kept the Hebrew Bible to study as holy scripture (which Islam did not). But they also claimed that the revelation of Jesus had surpassed all previous revelations. Paul, a formative force in early Christianity (although he never knew Jesus alive), held that the laws of the Bible were too difficult for most people to observe and were unnecessary to gain eternal life in the time of the general resurrection. A person needed only to believe in the atoning death and resurrection of Jesus, and try to live a good life according to Jesus' example.

Jews do not believe that Jesus was the Messiah. He did not accomplish the tasks of the Messiah as predicted by the prophets of the Bible over the centuries — for example, bringing lasting peace to the world, restoring the Jewish people to their land, and ridding the land of foreign rulers. Rather, a few decades after his death, horrible wars broke out between the Jews and their Roman rulers, the Temple was destroyed, and a few decades later the Holy City, Jerusalem, was razed.

Nor has Christian history been marked by peace and love. Christianity's exclusive claims of Divine truth led to such extremes as the Crusades and the Inquisition, in which thousands of Jews and other innocent people died. In modern times,

---

10. Rambam, *Mishneh Torah, Hilchos Teshuvah* 3:7.

Christians have fought each other bitterly as the religion divided into a multitude of sects. If the Messiah had already come, the world should not be in such a sorry state, nor should the religion that the "Messiah" supposedly founded. The explanation that there will be a delayed "second coming" of the Messiah has no foundation anywhere in the Hebrew Bible. As most scholars of Christianity now agree, this belief was clearly invented by the early sect of Christians when the expected resurrection of all the dead, and other promises of the Messianic era, failed to occur.

Actually, it is not at all clear that Jesus ever intended to found a new religion. He was thoroughly Jewish and certainly focused his message on Jews. His ethical and moral statements could easily have come from the rabbinic teachers of his time. Probably he was a reformer, upholding the cause of the Galilean peasants who felt distant from the Temple and felt that the Judaism of his time did not reach them. He may have had messianic pretensions, or perhaps those were foisted on him by his followers. Later generations, disappointed that the Jews did not unite in large numbers behind the "Jesus movement," turned Christianity away from its Jewish roots and laid the foundations for centuries of anti-Semitism.

Christian anti-Semitism began quite early, is evident in writings of many of the "Church Fathers," blossomed in the Middle Ages, and came to full fruition with the Holocaust during World War II. It would take us too far afield to recount this history, but it is important for Jews to realize that anti-Semitic tendencies are still hidden within many Christian beliefs and attitudes, which may on the surface appear innocuous. Recently, liberal Christian seminaries have made attempts to correct these attitudes. Even in the Roman Catholic church, changes are evident — the Pope has officially removed the charge of "killers of Christ" which was held against the Jews for nearly two thousand years. Christians are beginning to appreciate and study the Hebrew Bible and Jewish tradition. However, some Christians (Evangelists) still are honoring Judaism only for their own purposes. One Christian tenet is that Jews must survive and return to their land in order for their "Messiah" to return!

In recent times, liberal Christianity has become strongly ethical in its emphasis, and thus seems to have similarities to Judaism, which has always emphasized man's behavior to his fellow man. Some people speak of a "Judeo-Christian civilization" based on the great values that the two religions share. However, we as Jews should remember that our tradition is the one that strove to preserve ethical behavior in the face of unethical conduct of Christians over many centuries. We have a right to be proud of that fact, proud of our record of humanity. We do not have to accept others' dilution of our rich tradition, our heroism and sacrifice for our principles, into a vague modern "Judeo-Christian" entity. We should not let our desire for good relationships with non-Jews undermine the pride we can pass on to our children.

In Judaism, the whole purpose is service of G-d according to His plan, following the ways established in the Bible as G-d's revelation. We do not worship our past leaders or embark on crusades to convert others. We are interested only in being an example to others of how to bring G-d's Divine plan to fruition on earth. This is a unique path, not like any others. But we are assured that if we follow it, we will be the agents of a future beyond our wildest dreams.

## ☙ THE MESSIAH AND THE FUTURE OF THE WORLD

I n return for allegiance to G-d, Jews were promised a future as an extraordinary nation. They would play a unique role in the history of the world, ensured of survival under Divine protection, and would eventually regain their homeland, the Land of Israel.

In addition, Jews were promised entry into the World to Come. Every Jew has a share there, with a very few exceptions, because every Jew is part of the Torah nation that has been willing to make sacrifices and special efforts to provide a role model for others. Non-Jews also can earn a share in the World to Come, on an individual rather than a national basis, by following the seven Noahide Laws (see Chapter 1).

The Jewish nation is also promised the coming of the Messiah, literally the "anointed one," like G-d's chosen leaders in Jewish history (Moses, King David). The Messiah will be a human being who will bring about universal peace and tranquility, together with respect for G-d, so that all people will follow G-d's ways. In the time of the Messiah, Jews will return to the Land of Israel, the Holy Temple will be rebuilt, and a phenomenal healing will occur of all those who are sick or handicapped.[11] Belief in the coming of the Messiah is a basic tenet of Jewish faith. As we say in the famous song, *Ani Ma-amin,* we believe that the Messiah may come at any time, and we will not despair even if there are delays.[12]

In several places, the Bible predicts the future messiah. Even as far back as the wilderness experience, hints to the Messianic era occur. Moses prophesied before his death that Israel would be dispersed throughout all the lands of the earth for having broken its covenant with G-d. The verse concludes, "Then the Lord your G-d will turn your captivity and will have compassion on you, and will return and gather you from all the people where G-d had scattered you" (*Deuteronomy* 30:3).

The Messianic era is eloquently described by our great philosopher, the Rambam: "In those days, there will be neither famine, nor war, nor jealousy, nor strife. Material goods will be in abundance, and luxuries as plentiful as the dust."[13] The nations will recognize Israel as the source of teachings of morality, ethics, and righteousness, and will seek out sages of the Jewish people to be their teachers. This is what the prophet Isaiah had in mind when he spoke the verse that we sing in synagogue at the time of taking out the Torah scrolls: "For out of Zion shall go forth the Torah, and the Word of G-d from Jerusalem" (*Isaiah* 2:3).

---

11. *Isaiah* 2:4, 11:9, 35:5-6, 42:4; *Micah* 5:2; *Amos* 9:11.

12. Rambam, *Thirteen Principles, Perush HaMishnayos,* end of Talmud *Sanhedrin.*

13. Rambam, *Mishneh Torah, Hilchos Melachim* 12:5.

The resurrection of the dead will also occur after the coming of the Messiah, and this will be a time of general healing. Exactly how this will occur is not clear; the secrets of the resurrection and the Messianic era have been compared to the secrets of creation itself! But the sages stressed that the idea of the resurrection was a very important teaching. As is written in the Talmud, "These do not have a share in the World to Come: one who says there is no resurrection of the dead to be learned out of the Bible."[14] In every prayer service, we mention this belief (in the second blessing of the *Shemoneh Esrei,* the silent prayer said while standing) as the most dramatic example of G-d's power. We can perhaps remember that a human being first comes from a tiny cell, the amazing union of sperm and egg. That certainly is a miracle. Is the resurrection of a body from a speck of bone any more miraculous?

The centrality of belief in the resurrection comes as a surprise to many Jews who have been influenced by secular thought. We did not get this belief from Christianity — the reverse is true. That is why it was so important for early Jewish Christians to convince their fellows that Jesus had been resurrected — it would have served as a proof of the beginning of the messianic era. (They were greatly disappointed, as mentioned above, that a general resurrection did not occur to confirm their religion.) Nor is there clear evidence that we picked it up in Persia, as some have claimed.[15] In general, while there have been debates about the idea, these have usually been among Jews heavily influenced by non-Jewish ideas. For example, the Greeks held that body and spirit were antithetical and no resurrection was possible; so the idea was hotly debated during the Hellenistic period of Jewish civilization. But these debates subsided, and the people followed the sages in accepting this as part of Jewish faith. The

---

14. Talmud *Sanhedrin* 90a.

15. Zoroastrianism is sometimes said to have influenced Jewish beliefs about the afterlife, particularly about "heaven" and "hell." However, mainstream Judaism rejected the extremes of dualism implied here, and particularly the idea of eternal punishment. Though there are parallels in Persian thought to the idea of a bodily resurrection, unlike Persian thought, in Judaism this concept is inseparable from the Torah concept of the unity of body and spirit. It is also clearly alluded to by the prophet Ezekiel, before the Persian period.

Rambam was thus able to write in the 13th century the following:

> I say that the resurrection is a doctrine renowned and accepted among all our people. This is acknowledged by every one of our groups and mentioned frequently in the prayers, narratives and supplications which were composed by the prophets and sages and which fill the pages of the Talmud and the Midrash. It is that the soul will return to the body after it has been separated from it. Among our nation there is no difference of opinion on this matter, no dissenting voice. We are not permitted to place any reliance on any member of our religion who does not believe in this.[16]

We are also promised Jewish survival for eternity. There remains only one nation to which the Almighty has made it known publicly, by signs and miracles, that He is the Creator of all and Ruler of all rulers, and He has promised that His chosen nation will last for eternity. G-d continues to keep His promise to Israel, showing by miracles and wonderful happenings that the covenant between Him and His people will last forever. Generations and kingdoms come and go, but as it has been said, "Just as G-d will not change, so Israel will never be destroyed."[17]

## ৵৵ ISRAEL IN THE VIEW OF THE NATIONS

The chosenness of the Jews sometimes seems to be in contradiction to the great suffering the Jewish people have experienced. As we explained earlier, sometimes G-d chastises the Jewish people, among others, to prod them into examining their ways and reforming their lives. G-d may use other peoples and nations to do this. In fact, the Torah itself states that when the Jews forsake G-d, their enemies will gain the upper hand over them. This has proven true in many significant periods in Jewish history:

---

16. *Iggeres HaRambam* (*Letters of Rambam*), *Maamar Techias Hameisim*.
17. *Sefer Malachi* of the *Trei Asar*.

- In ancient Persia, when the Jews mingled with Persians at King Achashverus's celebrations, it led to Haman's plot to destroy the nation.
- The adoption of Greek ways by Jews in Israel led to greater oppression by the Syrians, until only the revolt of the G-d-fearing Maccabees turned the tide.
- Imitating the ways of the Spanish elite led to Christian suppression and eventually exile and the Inquisition.
- Russian pogroms began in earnest after Jews attempted to assimilate into Russian society.
- The Holocaust emanated from Germany, heartland of the Enlightenment, a country that encouraged its Jews to be more German than Jewish.

These unpleasant reminders of what happened when Jews adopted non-Jewish ways are also a sign of a Divine plan. The recurring cycles of destruction and renewal remind us of the Torah's promise that punishments would occur, but a remnant would always be saved.

Yet, even though the dispersion of the Jewish people caused them great suffering, it was also for the good. The scattering among all nations facilitated the Jewish mission to the world, to proclaim the existence of one G-d and to demonstrate His teaching to others. This does not mean teaching non-Jews the 613 commandments, which only Jews need to learn, but it does mean informing them of the Noahide commandments.[18] The situation is something like that of the biblical figure Joseph who, because he was exiled from his family, was able to save everyone. He could save not only his own relatives, but all of Egypt during a long, terrible famine. Likewise, though Israel has been persecuted and degraded, the Jewish nation will ultimately restore the world to good through the Messiah, who like Joseph will benefit his own people as well.

Thus many among the other nations have recognized the greatness of the Jews and the unique place they hold in human history. The American historian Will Durant wrote, in *The Story of Philosophy*:

---

18. Talmud *Chagigah* 11 and Rambam, *Mishneh Torah, Hilchos Melachim* 8:11.

The story of the Jews since the Dispersion [*sic.*] [exile] is one of the epics of European history. Driven from their natural home by the Roman capture of Jerusalem, and scattered by flight and trade among all the nations and to all the continents; persecuted and decimated by the adherents of the great religions — Christianity and [*sic.*] Mohammedanism — which had been born of their scriptures and their memories; barred by the feudal system from owning land and by the guilds from taking part in industry; shut up within congested ghettos and narrowing pursuits, mobbed by the people and robbed by the kings; building with their finance and trade the towns and cities indispensable to civilization; outcast and excommunicated, insulted and injured; yet without any political structure, without any legal compulsion to social unity, without even a common language, *this wonderful people has maintained itself in body and soul, has preserved its racial and cultural integrity, has guarded with jealous love its oldest rituals and traditions, has patiently and resolutely awaited the day of its deliverance,* and has emerged greater in number than ever before, renowned in every field for the contributions of its geniuses, and triumphantly restored, after two thousand years of wandering, to its ancient and unforgotten home. What drama could rival the grandeur of these sufferings, the variety of these scenes, and the glory and justice of this fulfillment? What fiction could match the romance of this reality?

The noted American author, Mark Twain (who was no friend of the Jews politically), wrote the following in 1899:

If the statistics are right, the Jews constitute but one percent of the human race. It suggests a nebulous, dim puff of star dust lost in the blaze of the Milky Way. Properly, the Jew ought hardly to be heard of; but he is heard of, has always been heard of. He is as prominent on the planet as any other people, and his commercial importance is extravagantly out of proportion to the smallness of his bulk.

His contributions to the world's list of great names in literature, science, art, music, finance, medicine, and abstruse learning are also very out of proportion to the weakness of his numbers. He has made a marvelous fight in this world in all ages, and has done it with his hands tied behind him. He could be vain of himself and be excused for it. The Egyptians, the Babylonians, and the Persians rose, filled the planet with sound and splendor, then faded to dream stuff and passed away; the Greeks and Romans followed, and made a vast noise, and they are gone; other people have sprung up and held their torch high for a time but it burned out, and they sit in twilight now, or have vanished.

The Jew saw them all, beat them all, and is now what he always was, exhibiting no decadence, no infirmities of age, no weakening of his parts, no slowing of his energies, no dulling of his alert and aggressive mind. All things are mortal but the Jew; all other forces pass but he remains. What is the secret of his immortality?

In fact, there is no secret at all. If the Jews have been uniquely productive, it is because G-d made them so. Part of the mission of our people is to be a "light to the nations," and for that purpose, He made us able to be respected and honored for our achievements.

Leo Tolstoy, the Russian writer, understood more fully the religious basis of the Jewish people's endurance:

The Jew is that sacred being who brought down from Heaven the everlasting fire, and has illuminated with it the whole world. He is the religious source, spring and foundation out of which all the rest of the peoples have drawn their beliefs and their religions.

The Jew is the emblem of eternity. He who neither slaughter nor torture of thousands of years could destroy, he who neither fire nor sword nor inquisition was able to wipe off from the face of the earth, he who was the first to produce the oracles of G-d, he who has been for so long the guardian of prophecy, and who transmitted it to the rest of the world — such a nation cannot be destroyed. The Jew is everlasting as eternity itself.

After millennia of surviving against all odds, we do not want to abandon our treasure for the attractions of other religions, nor erase future generations by intermarriage. We must remain a strong people, committed to our purpose and mission, committed to our love for G-d.

# 6

## The Nature of the Jewish People

Viewing history from a large perspective, we see that Jews have an enormous responsibility. If Jews are the recipients of a great revelation and the bearers of an amazing tradition, and if Jews are deeply involved in giving birth to a greater future for humanity, then Jews have to be models of Divine teachings. It follows that the people have to create and nourish the qualities within themselves, and the institutions and leadership that will strengthen their ability to accomplish their purpose. It also means that the people as a whole have to guard themselves from being too much influenced by the world. The world as we know it today is intensely focused on the physical: physical pleasures, conquest of nature through technology, material success. In such a context, it is easy to be distracted from one's spiritual mission. Therefore, the Jewish people were warned from the beginning to be careful of the negative influences around them, and to guard the unique nature of their peoplehood.

In this chapter we will discuss some of the qualities necessary for Jewish life, the structures that nourish these qualities, and the influences of the outer environment.

# ✑ THE INNER QUALITIES
# OF THE JEWISH PEOPLE

**FAITH**

FAITH IN G-D IS AN IMPORTANT QUALITY THAT IS EMPHASIZED OVER and over again in the biblical stories. Throughout history, the nations of the world have always had difficulty in believing in a G-d Who transcends this world, whose essence cannot be captured in an image or statue. It is not so different for us today. We all too often trust other factors in our lives, putting our faith in the toil of our own hands or in the lottery, in medical technology or in healing herbs, in our school systems or our therapists. The stories of the Bible come to tell us that the whole show is being run by Someone Else.

Economically, the lessons from the Torah are quite direct. During the forty years that the Jews traveled in the desert after leaving Egypt, *mahn* (manna) fell from the heavens every morning at the command of the Almighty. Every Jew was ordered to collect a set amount per person. If he tried to collect more than necessary, the excess amount rotted. The act of gathering extra food, to try to hoard it for a future time, indicated a lack of trust in the Almighty's ability to provide food every day.

The Torah requires that in the Land of Israel, all farmers must let their land lie fallow during the year of *shemittah,* which occurs once every seven years. The Jew is promised that if he observes this faithfully, his produce during the sixth year will provide him for the seventh as well. Man's faith in G-d will give him the peace of mind to know that help will arrive and his needs will be satisfied. During that year, the wild-grown produce does not belong by right to any individual. The entire land and its products are considered free, under the legal ownership of no one but G-d. This is to acknowledge that all our earthly possessions, symbolized by our land and produce, are ultimately under G-d's rule. We should never let ourselves be deluded into thinking that we are in full control and complete ownership of anything.[1]

---

1. *Zohar, Vayikra* 5b.

A man once came to Rabbi Yisrael Salanter, a great 19th century teacher of ethics, to complain that he did not have enough funds to live comfortably. The rabbi replied, "Have complete faith in G-d. If you do, He will provide you with $1000." The man left, reassured.

However, a month later he was back. "I've been waiting quite a while for the money, and I haven't received anything yet," he protested.

"Have you maintained faith in G-d and trusted that He will give you the $1000?" asked the rabbi. The man nodded. "Well," continued the rabbi, "I have $500 here. Would you take that instead of the $1000?"

The man replied eagerly that he would. The rabbi shook his head, "This shows that you do not have complete faith in G-d, for if you truly did, you would not be willing to accept the $500 instead of the $1000 you were promised."

The point of the story is not that we should sit and wait for money to rain from heaven. Most of us would certainly want to take the $500. Rather, it is to illustrate that true faith is difficult to attain and, rather than live in faith, we are always looking for opportunities to control the situation in order to get what we want.

Likewise in other areas of life: Even when we are well provided for, we want to have things come the way we want them to come. For example, in the desert, despite all the miracles that G-d performed for the Israelites, they complained. Several times, they complained about the lack of water, even saying that they would rather have died in Egypt than die from thirst in the desert. More than once they murmured about Moses' leadership. G-d sent a fire into the midst of their camp to shake them out of their self-centered reality. However, they again complained, this time about the lack of meat in the desert. G-d sent a strong wind to blow an abundance of quails from the seaward lands. The people gathered and ate the quail so greedily that some died from gluttony.

The people's complaining and criticism were so pervasive that, at one point, Moses was ready to give up. The burden was too great. In return, G-d appointed seventy elders to assist him as spiritual leaders of the people, and gave them the spirit of prophecy also, though not on the level of Moses himself.

Still, the leaders could not completely correct the Jews' lack of faith. Their greatest sin during the wilderness period was their lack of faith in G-d's ability to bring them into the Land of Israel, which was to be the culmination of the whole process. This is called the "sin of the spies." They were only a few days' march from the promised land, and Moses appointed twelve scouts, one from each of the twelve tribes, to explore the land of Canaan and report back on the natural conditions, the inhabitants, and the civilization that existed. The twelve were reputable and trusted men in each of the tribes. After spying out the land for forty days, they returned, bringing with them huge fruits as evidence of the land's fertility. However, ten of them presented a very discouraging picture: it would be impossible for the Jews to conquer Canaan. In their view, the cities were too well fortified and the inhabitants too powerful.

Caleb and Joshua, Moses' chief disciple, disassociated themselves from this pessimistic report and counseled that the people should march on Canaan. The people, however, had lost heart and sided with the majority report. They openly rebelled, proposing the election of a new leader to take them back to Egypt. They refused to listen to the renewed pleas of Caleb and Joshua, even threatening to stone them.

At this point, G-d expressed His intention to destroy the people and form a new nation exclusively from Moses' descendants. Moses again interceded successfully on his people's behalf. But, while their destruction was averted, they were condemned to wander in the wilderness for forty years (one year for each day of the spies' trip), until all the males between the ages of 20 and 60 had died. Joshua and Caleb were the only exceptions to this decree. Then the new generation would enter the promised land to witness the fulfillment of G-d's promise.

It is worth contemplating this event a little more. The date of this tragic error, when the people accepted the report of the faithless spies, was Tishah b'Av (the ninth of the Jewish month of Av). This later became a day of repeated tragedy for Israel. On this day came the destruction of both Temples, the fall of Betar in the Bar Kochba War, the expulsion of the Jews from Spain, and the beginning of World War I, inaugurating the bloody wars of the 20th century. Seemingly, the sin of the spies paved the way for future sorrows, so that we would be constantly reminded of it. Why was this such a great evil?

Up until this point, the Israelites had adopted the attitude of *Na'aseh v'nishma*: "[First] we will do and [later] we will understand." This is a total and unequivocal expression of faith in the Almighty and His commandments. They had accepted G-d's leadership. Even though they complained of hunger or thirst, they stayed with the mission. When the ten spies delivered their pessimistic report, however, the people's outlook changed. They became hesitant and fearful. They no longer accepted G-d's guarantees of protection, and they began to question His strength and doubt His entire promise. This loss of faith was so profound that it became the root of other tragedies.[2]

The story of the sin of the spies is also a parable for us in our personal lives. We must develop the faith that G-d is leading us to our destiny, just as He was leading the Israelites into the promised land. If we do not accept the challenges that come our way, if we shrink back in fear because things appear to be difficult, we may lose our opportunity. Eventually, what G-d plans will be accomplished, perhaps in the next generation. But we may not experience the fulfillment of our hopes in our own lives because of our own fears.

In fact, over the centuries, our people have shown enormous faith. During all the numberless times of crisis that have befallen the Jewish people, their absolute faith in the Almighty has filled them with the will and ability to persevere. Without this faith, Jews would have succumbed to oppression and despair long ago. All Jews have an inheritance of faith and faithfulness from our ancestors, a treasure on which we can draw. We must remember how potent that faith is, and how potentially destructive the lack of faith, to keep ourselves on the track.

---

2. *Midrash Rabbah* 21:5

THE TORAH TELLS THE STORY OF AN ENEMY OF THE JEWISH PEOPLE, King Balak, who hired a non-Jewish prophet to help him destroy the Jews in battle by placing a curse on them. When G-d refused to allow him to deliver a curse on the people, Balaam came up with another plan. He suggested to Balak that he could entice the Jews to commit sexual immorality with women from the tribes of Moab and Midian. This, he believed, would arouse G-d's wrath against his nation and allow Balak to achieve victory. Balak followed the plan and, in part, succeeded. Twenty-four thousand Israelites perished in a plague sent by G-d as punishment for their participation in this grievous sin. Had it not been for Pinchas, the grandson of Aaron and son of Elazar who was then the High Priest, more lives would have been lost. When an Israelite and a Midianite woman flagrantly committed an act of immorality, Pinchas summarily executed them. As a reward for his zeal, G-d promised Pinchas that the priesthood would be forever retained by his descendants.

**MORALITY**

This account, so shocking to modern sensibilities, tells us how important our personal sexual morality is in protecting our spiritual sensibilities. The connection is indicated by the Torah's restrictions on contact with other peoples: the Jewish people were forbidden henceforth to avoid social interaction with the Moabites and Midianites (Moabite female converts are exempt from this ruling). One might think that a similar prohibition would be placed against the Egyptians, since they had forced us to work as slaves. However, the more severe approach toward the Moabities was that they did more than hurt us physically; they tried to destroy us spiritually. Sexual immorality not only damages our bodies, but deeply affects our souls as well.

The laws prohibiting sexual immorality are very explicit in the Written Torah. They specify specific relationships and acts that are unconscionable. Sex in general is regarded very positively in Judaism — not, as in some other religions, as essentially sinful — but it must be sanctified through religious law. G-d wants us to live a decent, morally pure life, not an animalistic one. Animals have sex drives but cannot exercise control over them. Humans can and should rise above their instincts, not acting on every impulse. This is how we exercise free will and rise above animal limitations.

At the same time, the sexual impulse is a very strong drive. Because of this, Judaism urges us to take precautions against situations that might weaken our self-control. That is why men and women (except blood relatives and spouses) are told not to stay alone together or have physical contact. For the same reason, men and women are separated by a *mechitzah* (partition) in the synagogue.[3] This enables individuals to concentrate more fully on their prayers, rather than having one's mind distracted by people of the opposite sex. This is also the basis for Judaism's strict laws regarding modesty in clothing and behavior. Modesty and restraint are regarded as hallmarks of the Jewish nation, because we are deeply concerned about sexual morality, which in turn makes possible a deeper spirituality.

In a related way, Judaism encourages individuals to choose marriage partners on the basis of many criteria, not only physical attraction. A common sense of purpose is far more important than the physical, which is often temporary. Mutual respect and related interests are pillars on which successful marriages are based, for these are the foundation of lasting love. If a couple is able to share many kinds of bonds, their marriage will survive not only the small squabbles that come from living together, but also the changes in physical form that come with age, and the swings of emotion that are part of each relationship. This also provides the structure for their children to grow up in a secure environment, the stable family life that is all too rare in secular society today. Needless to say, the ability to control sexual impulses limits the potential for marriage problems due to infidelity. The benefit comes to parents as well as children, and provides a model for generations to come.

*Pirkei Avos* teaches us, "Who is a strong man? He who conquers his 'evil impulse' [immoral passions], as it is stated, 'One who rules his spirit is better than the conqueror of a city.' " (4:1).

---

3. Talmud *Succah* 51.

The Talmud also states, "Happy are Israel when they are engaged in the study of Torah and performance of good deeds, for their evil impulse is then at their mercy, and they are not at its mercy.[4] Rabbi Shimon ben Elazar stated, 'Let me illustrate the nature of the evil impulse by means of a parable. It may be compared to a bar of iron that has been plunged into the furnace: as long as it is inside the furnace you may mold it to whatever form you wish. So it is with the evil impulse, which can be controlled with the fire of Torah.' "[5]

# ⁓§ STRUCTURES OF COMMUNAL LIFE

OF ALL THE STRUCTURES THAT NOURISH JEWISH LIFE, THE MOST important is the family. In the morning prayers, we recite a
**FAMILY** beautiful verse from the Torah, "How good are your tents, O Jacob, and your dwelling places, O Israel" (*Numbers* 24:5). This blessing alludes to the Jewish family. In fact, this blessing came out of the mouth of the non-Jewish prophet, Balaam, mentioned in the previous section. Though he wanted to curse the people, G-d produced a blessing from his mouth. This blessing made him recognize the secret of Jewish strength, and led him to suggest to Balak the method of undermining the Jewish people — through immorality that would threaten the family.

In Judaism, the family provides the individual with a sense of love and worth, passes down G-d's traditions from generation to generation, and is the bridge between the individual and the Jewish nation as a whole. The family has enabled Judaism to survive during the hardest of times, including anti-Semitic oppression, pogroms, and dire poverty.

Judaism is unique in stressing the married couple and the family from its origins. Unlike some other religions that derive from a lone male figure, Judaism has its roots in the faith of Abraham and Sarah, Isaac and Rebecca, Jacob, Rachel and Leah.

---

4. Talmud *Avodah Zarah* 5.
5. *Avos D'Rav Nosson*.

Moses, Aaron, Miriam — all were married, and marriage is considered the best state in which to develop one's spirituality down to this day. The family unit is the cornerstone of the Jewish people and its basic protective structure. A strong religious family helps all its members weather the tempests of life.

An integral part of the major holiday of Passover is the recitation of the story of the Exodus from Egypt with our children. The unusual foods and customs of the *seder* table are intended to prompt the children's questions, so that the adults can respond. This suggests that in all areas of life, Jews should satisfy the curiosity of their children by teaching them the meaning of life in light of the Torah.

Parents who raise their children well are considered the real heroes of Jewish existence, and their work can never be praised too much. Every parent is obligated to train his children in observance of the commandments, in accordance with the age and capacity of the child. It is written, "Train the child according to his way" (*Proverbs* 22:6), meaning, observe the child's *own* way and educate him or her accordingly. From the time children begin to talk and show understanding, Jewish parents teach their children short verses from the Torah that are basic to their proper spiritual development; later, gradually, they learn what these verses mean according to their level of understanding. The verses *Shema Yisrael, Hashem Elokeinu, Hashem Echad* ("Hear O Israel, the Lord is our G-d, the Lord is One), and *Torah tzivah lanu Moshe morashah kehillas Yaakov* ("Moses commanded the Torah to us; it is an inheritance of the community of Jacob") are among the first things that children are taught when they begin to speak.[6]

Parents are further required to teach their children Torah and to see to it that they receive formal instruction in Jewish religious studies. This is in fulfillment of the biblical precept, "And you shall teach them [these words of Torah] to your children," which is said in the *Shema*. No parent should be satisfied with providing only a superficial smattering of such knowledge, but

---

6. Talmud *Succah* 42.

should make every effort to give the children a quality Jewish education. It is also a great good deed to help others financially to give their children such an education. Further, the family should regularly attend the synagogue. (A child should not be brought there, however, until he is of an age that he can behave properly.)

The Jewish family's best opportunity for being together is at the Shabbos table. The meal is enhanced with singing of special Shabbos songs (*zemiros*) and discussion of stories with Jewish themes. It is wise to teach stories and sing Jewish songs, rather than draw the children's attention, in these very impressionable early years, to fairy tales or meaningless songs. The tunes and the stories will remain with them for many long years.

Sometimes in raising a child we must discipline, as when we respond at the Passover table sharply to the "wicked son" who asks, "What is all this to you?" We rebuke him, saying that if he had been in Egypt, he would not have been saved, but would have remained and died there. (Israelites who did not want to leave actually did die during the plague of darkness.) King David, although loyal and faithful to G-d, did not admonish his sons when necessary.[7] As a result, his son Avshalom rebelled against him, instigating a civil war with the loss of many lives including Avshalom himself. Later on another son, Adoniyahu, also rebelled and tried to assume the throne, but was prevented from doing so. Consequences of a too-lenient upbringing can be unpleasant events in the future of the family.

IT IS IMPOSSIBLE TO OVERESTIMATE THE IMPORTANCE OF WOMEN IN Judaism. While traditional Judaism appears on the surface to be

**WOMEN'S CRUCIAL ROLE** a male-dominated religion, it is nothing like some other religions where only men can fulfill the holiest roles. Certain *public* roles are given to men, as we will see, but this has nothing to do with the innate holiness of a person's task.

Further, women are in no way regarded as inferior to men in their natural abilities. There is no reason, in Torah thinking, to

---

7. *Rashi* in *Megillah* and Chofetz Chaim, *Mishnah Berurah* 343.

believe that a woman could not perform the functions of doctor, lawyer, politician, or virtually any profession just as capably as a man, or more so. When women do perform the same jobs as men, they should receive equal pay and benefits. However, Judaism holds that a woman should not sacrifice her family for the sake of a profession.

When a couple is blessed with the ability to have children, this is an extraordinary opportunity to expand their life mission. They must reassess their lives to consider what having children means in each parent's service of G-d. For most women, the requirements of the household take greater precedence than before she had children. Our sages were well aware of this, and assigned her many of the *mitzvos* associated with the home, such as lighting the Shabbos candles and taking off a portion of the dough (*challah*). These are not merely physical activities, but suggest her responsibility in terms of spiritual priorities for the whole household.

Because the woman is often required to be at home, the man is given many of the commandments relating to public life, such as helping to make a quorum for prayer in the synagogue, rabbinical duties, and testifying in public court. The fact that a man's *mitzvos* appear more on the spotlight does not make him in any way superior or more holy. The very essence of a child's soul depends on the mother's being Jewish, not the father's. Her religious identity and the way she lives it are crucial to the success of the entire family.

Some point to the daily blessing, "Blessed are You, G-d . . . Who did not make me a woman," as evidence that Judaism considers women inferior. This is not true. The blessing refers to the fact that men are obligated to perform more *mitzvos,* quantitatively, than women, and therefore thank G-d for the extra opportunity. Men do more *mitzvos* because women are exempt from commandments dependent on time, such as *tallis, tefillin,* and certain acts related to the holidays. The Torah did not want to force women to go to the synagogue or study hall every day, to pray at length and learn. The household is just as holy as the synagogue, and women can pray there as well. In addition, women can be more secluded from the negative influences of society, therefore keeping the family on a higher spiritual level. Indeed, their role in giving birth is considered a G-dly act of creation that puts women on a higher spiritual level to begin with. Exemption from public *mitzvos* gives the woman more time to attend to important matters, ranging from managing the household and attending to the children's development, to her own private spiritual growth.

Rabbi Moshe Feinstein, *zt'l* (the accepted Torah leader for the Jewish people in our generation), stated the principle quite clearly:

> We must know that women do not lack in levels of holiness in relation to the performance of *mitzvos*. The commandments are based on the collective holiness of the Jewish nation without differentiation between men and women. This is learned from the revelation at Sinai, at which G-d tells [the Jewish Nation], "You will be for Me a treasured nation and a holy people." This was said to the women as well as to the men. Every place that the Torah refers to the great and holy nation, women are set equal to men. Therefore women also say in the blessings, "Who has made us holy with His commandments." This applies even to those *mitzvos* from which G-d exempted women (for reason of the limited time allotted to fulfill those *mitzvos*). These exemptions were for that reason and not due to any relative unworthiness of women, G-d forbid.[8]

Women are essential partners in the maintenance of the Jewish nation.

In addition, Judaism severely condemns the exploitation of women, viewing them merely as sex objects and the stereotyping of women as a group rather than individuals. Abuse of women, whether physical, emotional, or verbal, is absolutely forbidden by the Torah.

Historically, Jewish women have proven to be the key element in the survival of the nation in our worst historical circumstances. Besides the matriarchs (Sarah, Rebecca, Rachel, and Leah) whom we discussed earlier, many other great Jewish women contributed to the survival and growth of the Jewish

---

8. Quoted in *Samson's Struggle*, from *Igros Moshe, Orach Chaim*, Vol. 4.

nation. The sages tell us that it was ultimately because of the righteous women that the people were liberated from Egypt.[9] They maintained Jewish identity and taught their children Hebrew throughout the period of slavery. When the ruthless regimen of work inflicted by their Egyptian slavemasters drove the men to such a state of despair that they felt utterly spent, there was danger that the Jewish people would, G-d forbid, cease to exist. The valiant women of the era inspired their husbands with faith and courage. They breathed into them their own indomitable spirit to live, so that even under these seemingly hopeless conditions they continued to have intimate relations in order that the Israelites should multiply. With full faith in G-d, they believed it was within His power to save the children of Israel.

When Pharaoh decreed that all male Jewish children be thrown into the Nile River, husbands separated from their wives, refusing to father any more children. In this they were following the lead of Amram, father of Miriam and Aaron, who left their mother Yocheved. Miriam confronted him, saying, "You are worse than Pharaoh. He kills only the baby boys; your decision is a refusal to give life to the girls as well." Amram saw her point, returned to Yocheved, and Moses was born.

Miriam was also one of the seven prophetesses (Sarah, Miriam, Devorah, Channah, Avigail, Huldah, and Esther).[10] She led the women in singing *Shirah,* the Song of the Sea, in praise of the Almighty after He split the Red Sea for the Jews to cross. In addition, due to her greatness the Jews were given a well of water that miraculously traveled along with them during their sojourn in the desert.

Devorah was another prominent Jewish woman who was a judge, leader, and prophetess. She inspired and successfully led the Jews in the wars against the tribes of Canaan. Her song of praise is also recorded in the Bible. Yael is mentioned in connection with the same war, a woman of distinction because of her heroism in killing the enemy general, Sisera.

---

9. Talmud *Sotah* 11b.
10. Talmud *Megillah* 14a.

Channah is known for her devotion to G-d, especially in prayer. Her complete involvement in prayer is a model for all of us. Avigail, one of David's wives, interceded to stop what could have been a terrible civil war, and Huldah, a prophetess in the time of King Josiah, restored the Torah to its greatness. Esther is the heroine of Purim, who saved her people from the death decreed by the evil prime minister of Persia.

Other women could be named. Ruth, whose love for Judaism caused her to leave everything behind and convert to Judaism, merited being the ancestress of the dynasty of David. In the time of the Maccabees, when Judaism was threatened by the Greeks and Hellenistic collaborators, the heroism of Channah and her seven sons became an inspiration to all Jews to resist any and every attempt to destroy our religion.

Much of this information is unknown to the larger public, who still see Judaism as having negative views of women. In addition, secularists often use the distinctive roles of men and women in Judaism as a kind of bait to win Jewish women over to political or religious reforms. They often distort the Torah conception of women to do so, even going so far as to claim that Jewish women are made into second-class citizens. Nothing could be further from the truth. Here are a few quotes from Tanach and Talmud to indicate the very high esteem on which our Sages regarded women.

> Man is not complete until he is united with a woman.
>
> Without a protective hedge, the vineyard is laid waste; without a wife, a man is a homeless wanderer.
>
> A good wife, whom one finds, far above rubies is her worth; the heart of her husband trusts in her. Her children rise and call her blessed.
>
> He who finds a wife finds good.
>
> A good wife, there is no end to her goodness.
>
> Home is the wife. I never call my wife "wife." I call her "home" [bayis] for she makes my home.
>
> Love your wife as you love yourself and honor her more.
>
> Be careful to honor your wife, for blessing enters the house because of her.

In conclusion, it is most appropriate to quote *Igros Moshe* written by Rabbi Moshe Feinstein. "There is no difference as to the degree of respect that a woman must show her husband and that which a man must show his wife. When a woman became a prophetess the people were as obligated to listen to her as they were to a male prophet. In many areas a woman is praised more than a man both in the Torah and in the words of our Sages."

A UNIQUE PEOPLE REQUIRES HIGH STANDARDS OF LEADERSHIP. WE have an extraordinary model in our first leader, Moses, and a special regard for all our succeeding leaders, those who passed the Torah down to us.

**LEADERSHIP**

The greatest leader the Jewish people ever had was Moses. He is one of the very few leaders referred to as the servant of G-d. This attribute is the highest praise that can be given to a human being, for it testifies to the individual's total devotion to his Master.[11] Moses' extreme devotion to G-d was in no way motivated by personal aspirations for glory. For instance, we find that after the Israelites made the golden calf, G-d wanted to destroy them and start a new nation from Moses alone. Moses, however, pleaded with the Almighty instead to preserve the Jewish people. He even went so far as to say that if G-d destroyed the Jews, then He should also erase his (Moses') name from G-d's Book (*Exodus* 32:32).

The Rambam lists, among his Thirteen Principles of Faith for a Jew, that it incumbent upon us to recognize the unsurpassed stature of Moses.[12] As the Torah states, "There arose no prophet in Israel like Moses, whom G-d knew face to face" (*Deuteronomy* 34.10). The Torah also says, "No man knows his [Moses'] burial place" (*Deuteronomy* 34.6). Our Sages explain that Moses is not enshrined in an ordinary tomb, but within the heart of every Jew.

The leader who succeeded Moses was his disciple Joshua. He served Moses with total devotion, morning to night. His ability

---

11. Commentaries on *Joshua*, including *Daas Sofrim* and *Radak*.

12. Rambam, Thirteen Principles, *Perush HaMishnayos*, end of Tractate *Sanhedrin*.

reflected Moses' greatness, so that he was said to be the moon to Moses' sun. Even before becoming leader of the Jewish nation, he showed great personal courage and integrity. Joshua was one of the twelve spies sent by Moses to scout out the land of Canaan. Upon their return, he was one of only two who refused to go along with the negative and despairing report given by ten of the spies. He spoke up to counter their disheartening words. His reward was being chosen by G-d to lead the Jewish people into the Land of Israel.

Under Joshua's tenure, G-d brought about great miracles. The most famous is when the sun stood still in the heavens, enabling Joshua to finish a battle. This was clear indication to all the people of his greatness and worthiness as Moses' successor.

Many of the qualities that Moses and Joshua possessed were admired by the people, but none was more important than their total belief in G-d. Through their personal example, they inspired others to have faith as well.[13] Any leader of the Jewish people must be one whom others will respect and want to model themselves after. He should be sincere and concerned for others, not considering himself superior to his fellows. Yet he should also be firm and unwavering in his devotion to G-d. If G-d's supremacy is challenged, or the commandments are in danger, he should react vigorously against those who rebel. In this sense, a Jewish leader must be strong and dynamic.

One example of this dynamic quality is that of Pinchas, who, as related above, killed a prominent Jew and a Midianite princess after their act of public immorality (*Numbers* 25:8). Pinchas is praised for taking the initiative in punishing those who flagrantly disobeyed G-d's laws. He was zealous not for his own benefit, but on behalf of G-d. His action spared thousands of additional Jews from the plague that had been inflicted on them because of the immorality. He also demonstrated how to act swiftly, decisively, and uncompromisingly to uphold the law. Leaders who hesitate or advocate compromise on essential matters of Torah are not following the correct example. Of course, it is a human tendency,

---

13. Reb Shlomo Mendelovitz, *Sefer Shlucha D'rachamana.*

in our desire for goodwill among people, to rationalize rather than confront the wrongdoers. But this only leads to weakness and ultimately to ignoring restrictions of the law altogether. It is not proper behavior for a Jewish leader.

The Chofetz Chaim once told a parable that explains the nature of a weak leader:

> **A PARABLE:** A man was once seen taking very expensive goods out of a store. Because he seemed to be moving in a suspicious manner, a policeman began following him. When the man noticed, he quickly ran with the goods and dumped them in the river. When the policeman was asked later whether he was sure the objects thrown into the river were stolen goods, he replied, "The way the man was so eager to get rid of them seemed proof enough to me that they weren't his."

Likewise, those who are eager to compromise Jewish laws and tradition are demonstrating that they did not truly consider the Torah theirs. They were as unattached to it as the thief to possessions that did not really belong to him.

While a Jewish leader must be uncompromising, he should never be haughty. Like all of us, he must remember that he is but dust and ashes. His bones will rest in the same soil as other men. A story is told of the Rabbi of Lublin who was asked by one of his rabbinic colleagues why he had so many followers, when he admitted he was not worthy of their honors. "What can I do if Jews flock to me?" the Rabbi of Lublin asked.

"Why don't you simply ascend the pulpit this Shabbos and announce that you do not deserve to be their rabbi?" the colleague suggested. The Rabbi decided to follow his advice. He rose and announced that he was just an ordinary Jew, and there was no reason for anyone to seek his blessings. Those present were overwhelmed by his statement. What humility their Rabbi displayed! What great piety! Word of his greatness spread and an even larger crowd than before came to ask for his blessings.

The Rabbi's friend saw that the announcement had caused a most unexpected result. He therefore suggested that the Rabbi take the opposite approach and announce that in reality he was a very great *tzaddik* (holy person). "Oh, no!" the Rabbi of Lublin exclaimed immediately. "When you wanted me to say that I am a simple Jew who does not deserve honor, I more than agreed with you. However, now you want me to lie and say that I am a saint, and that I will not do!"

The Rabbi of Lublin recognized that he held his position only by the grace of G-d, and not because of his own piety.

A leader who himself makes errors cannot easily escape the consequences of his mistakes. When he sins, others will follow his example, and the blame for the nation's downfall can be laid at his doorstep. That is why a Jewish leader must be exceptionally careful about every action he takes.

> *The power of a strong leader is indicated in the following parable:*
>
> *A wealthy merchant set out on a journey, traveling with many wagons, heavily laden with merchandise. Snow had fallen, and the caravan lost its way. The wagons made several wrong turns, and only after many unsuccessful attempts did they get back on course.*
>
> *The merchant was very distressed. One of his assistants noticed his displeasure and tried to cheer him up. "Why are you so worried?" he asked the merchant. "After all, we finally did find the right road. Besides, it often takes me quite a while and many wrong turns till I find the right path, so this is not so unusual."*
>
> *"Perhaps," replied the merchant. "But if you would go on this road, you would be traveling alone. The footprints you created in the snow would quickly become obliterated and no one would notice them a day later. But I am traveling with a lot of loaded-down wagons, and they will leave obvious tracks in the snow that will not easily go away. If I take a wrong turn, others will see the tracks and follow me along an incorrect path. I will be leading all future drivers astray, and that is what I am upset about!"*

Some of our leaders were willing to sacrifice their lives in order to be a proper example for the Jewish people. When the Jews were about to make the golden calf, an individual by the name of Chur, the son of Moses' sister Miriam, did everything in his power to prevent the mob from going ahead with their plans. He lectured them severely, warning them that their act was sacrilegious and that they would later be sorry. He argued with them in every way possible to bring them to their senses. But his opposition only aroused fury from his fellow Jews, and the people compounded their sin by killing Chur. He had made his loyalty very clear.

Chur's reward was an exceptional grandson: Bezalel, the chief craftsman of the Tabernacle (the portable sanctuary that the Jews carried in the wilderness). When the Torah speaks of Bezalel, it mentions not only his father, Uri, but lists his grandfather as well. The reason is that Bezalel received part of his merit to be chosen for such a great job from the extraordinary leadership of his grandfather Chur.

Sometimes the leadership failed in exactly following the path laid down by G-d. Aaron's oldest sons, Nadav and Avihu, offered incense on unconsecrated fire (not taken from the altar). Such an offense by priests, who were supposed to set an example for everyone else, was unpardonable. The two were punished by "fire which came from before the Lord"; they died instantly. Aaron was grief stricken, but Moses explained to him that priests were held to a very high standard of sanctity. In fact, to prevent the remaining priests (Aaron's other sons, their brothers) from becoming defiled by touching the dead bodies, Aaron's cousins, Mishael and Elzaphon, had to bury the bodies. Aaron and his two remaining sons, Elazar and Issamar, were instructed not to exhibit any mourning, thereby demonstrating their submission to G-d's will. The priests were also warned not to drink any strong liquor, as Nadav and Avihu had, before discharging their duties in the Tabernacle or instructing the people.

Our Sages explain that this dramatic example teaches another lesson. Nadav and Avihu had also previously expounded the teachings of the Torah in the presence of their own teacher, Moses. This was regarded as demonstrating lack of respect for their teacher's authority. From this it is learned that one who publicly challenges a sage who is imbued with G-d's wisdom is considered to be undermining the basis of the Torah. Of course, this does not mean one cannot raise questions. But questioning must not be done in a way that demeans or belittles the teacher or his/her subject.

The Torah states that we follow our Sages and practice the laws as they teach them, because they are a "fence" around the Torah. When we have something very precious, or something that should not be touched, we guard it by building a fence around it. No one leaves a precious diamond in the open or a live wire unprotected. Similarly, the Sages, under certain limited circumstances, decreed special laws that served to enhance the holiness of the Torah and make sure that the Torah laws themselves would not be broken. This occurred even in ancient times. For example, the Almighty said to King Solomon, "My son, now that you have been wise to enact a fence around the prohibition of carrying on Shabbos, My heart too will rejoice, for the Torah commandment of Shabbos will thereby be reinforced." King Solomon himself said, concerning a person who transgressed an ordinance of the Sages, "He who breaches the fence shall fall prey to a serpent".[14]

Rabbi Akiva was one of the greatest of our Sages, and he refused to disobey the words of the rabbis who had preceded him despite great personal tribulations. An incident happened when, because of his adherence to Torah, Rabbi Akiva was imprisoned by the Romans. While he was in jail, Rabbi Yehoshua would bring him a jug of water daily. One day, Rabbi Yehoshua was stopped by a prison warden, who cruelly spilled out half the water in the jug. Rabbi Yehoshua hurried to deliver the remaining water to Rabbi Akiva and explained what had happened. Then he saw Rabbi Akiva preparing to wash his hands.

"There is not enough water here for you to both drink and

---

14. Talmud *Eruvin* 21b on *Ecclesiastes* 10:8. These are not totally new laws. The Talmud says that there is nothing not intimated in the Torah, for all the words of the Sages were given by the Almighty to Moses at Mount Sinai, including revealing the laws that the Sages were destined to innovate (Talmud Yerushalmi, *Peah* 1:1).

wash your hands," noted Rabbi Yehoshua. "Why not use all the water for drinking?"

Rabbi Akiva shook his head. "My fellow rabbis declared that one must wash his hands before every meal. How could I go against their dictum? No, I will use the water for washing; if there is any left, I will drink. I would rather go thirsty than transgress a rabbinic prohibition."

# ◆§ THE INFLUENCES OF ENVIRONMENT

DIVINE TEACHINGS NEED AN APPROPRIATE MILIEU IN WHICH TO flourish. To explain this, we will begin with the external first: the

**PROTECTING OURSELVES**

influence of environment. Jewish teachings throughout the generations have emphasized the influence of environment on character. A verse in the 2nd century ethical text *Pirkei Avos* says, "Keep away from a bad neighbor and have no association with the wicked."[15] Centuries earlier, the first verse in Chapter 1 of *Psalms* stressed the same idea: "Happy is the man that has not walked in the counsel of the wicked, nor stood along the way of sinners, nor sat in the seat of the scornful, but his delight is in the Torah of G-d, and in His Law does he meditate day and night."

> In the medieval period, the Rambam wrote of the principle involved here:
>
> It is the very nature of man to be influenced in opinion and action by his friends and colleagues and to behave like the people around him. Therefore, we must cleave to righteous people and sit near scholars in order to learn and be influenced by their actions. We must keep away from the wicked in order not to learn from their behavior. If you live in a place where the people do not behave properly, you should move to a place where the inhabitants are righteous. If this is not possible, you should dwell alone.[16]

---

15. *Pirkei Avos* 1:7.
16. *Hilchos Dei'os* 6:1; *Pe'er HaDor*.

That is why the company one chooses is so important. If one selects the companionship of undesirable characters, their corrupt ways are bound to be a source of bad influence. If, on the other hand, one seeks the company of Torah scholars and well-mannered people, then he will gain for himself not only a good name, but also a model on which to base his own behavior.

> *If you want to know a man, ask who are his friends.*
>
> *The rotten date-tree seeks out the society of the barren tree.*
>
> *Not without reason did the raven seek out the crow, for they are both of a kind.* [17]

Throughout history, the Jewish nation has faced the challenge of adverse influence from its surroundings. One example comes from the event known as the "golden calf." A group of Egyptians who had converted left Egypt along with the Jews; they are described in the Bible as the "mixed multitude." The ancient commentaries suggest that this particular group of converts may have adopted Judaism more out of admiration of Jewish power than from belief in G-d. In any case, they were less attuned to the significance of the movement that they had joined. Consequently, when Moses did not return on schedule from Mount Sinai and the leaderless people felt lost, these converts instigated the adoption of a new man-made god.

Their ideas influenced many Jews to subscribe to a direct violation of one of the Ten Commandments. Most of the people became involved in constructing a golden calf to be an intermediary between themselves and G-d. When Moses came down from the mountain carrying the stone tablets of the Ten Commandments, he was astounded to see the disgraceful behavior of the people dancing and cavorting around the calf. He immediately broke the tablets and ordered the deaths of three thousand participants in the rebellion. The difference between the Egyptians and the Jews may have seemed small, but their influence was devastating.

---

17. *Mishlei Chachamim;* Talmud *Bava Kamma* 92b.

One might think that, after those events, Judaism would have rejected all converts. But this did not happen. Instead, our Sages devised clear procedures for conversions that would ensure, as much as is humanly possible, that the converts recognized fully the responsibility that they were undertaking. Shortly we will look at the significance of that process.

Of course, negative influences can come from many sources besides specific individuals. For example, Jewish thinkers, intent on understanding the world as deeply as possible, have often studied non-Jewish systems of thought, from Aristotelian philosophy to modern computer science. Sometimes, in that encounter, the thought-systems of non-Jewish origin have undermined Jewish practice and thought. It takes an extraordinary and highly dedicated thinker such as the Rambam to integrate insights from other systems into Judaism. All too often, the influence has been negative. When the famous 18th century German philosopher Moses Mendelssohn attempted to bring in ideas from the Enlightenment, he initiated a process that led to the break-up of Judaism.

Perhaps most important is acceptance of different lifestyles that can have an influence, even when the peoples officially stay separate. Jews have never felt that they had to completely cut themselves off from society, as do monks or some small sects. However, sometimes the draw of alien cultures has been so strong that it has been damaging. Greek culture influenced Jews in ancient times, Spanish culture in medieval times, German society and culture in modern times, with tragic effects. Judaism offers a supreme guide to life that does not need support from other lifestyles or philosophies. But that lesson needs to be repeated in every generation.

Even earning a living should not be a reason to live in a place that has no Torah or that has too many immoral people. Nor should one take a job that puts a person daily in questionable society. The Chofetz Chaim explained that, when G-d took the Jews out of Egypt, He had a choice of leading them through the land of the Philistines, with its civilized comforts but dangerous moral influence, or through the desert with physical barrenness but spiritual security. G-d chose the desert and sent them sustenance through the miracle of the manna from heaven. If the Almighty can provide a miracle for six hundred thousand for no other purpose than to protect them from a negative environment, He can surely provide support for the man who wants to refuse a job that can affect his spirituality adversely.

> *A father who wanted to help his son earn a livelihood set him up as a vendor of perfumes. The store was located in an immoral neighborhood. Some time later, the father inquired about his son's welfare. He was infuriated to learn that his son was associating with harlots, and wanted to have him punished severely. A friend of the family rebuked the father and said to him, "Of all possible professions, you chose that of a perfume dealer and set him up in a corrupt environment. Are you now surprised at his behavior?"*

Today we are witnessing intermarriage and assimilation in epidemic proportions. Worried parents ask how they can prevent their children from losing touch with Judaism completely. Socially, it is clear that the framework of our "multicultural" life pushes Jews to become integrated within the non-Jewish culture. Large numbers of young Jews attend public schools and receive little if any Jewish education; therefore, their classmates and friends are likely to be non-Jews. From birthday parties at age 5 to parties at age 15, they have plenty of opportunity to create close relationships with their non-Jewish neighbors. By the time they are ready to marry, many young people do not even expect their parents to object to a non-Jewish partner, and are surprised when their parents are unhappy about the idea! They have been taught to adapt successfully to the non-Jewish society, so why should the parents not be pleased with their success?

Dangers to Judaism do not come only from philosophy and belief systems. They are integral to the way we raise our children. Parents' sudden objections to intermarriage may ring hollow with a child, since his parents clearly have affinities with a non-Jewish lifestyle themselves. Efforts to prevent intermarriage must begin when the children are young, so that by the time a child leaves high school, he has had a sound Jewish upbringing and education. The children will know why they are Jews, what their heritage means, and how they can be part of a Divine purpose in the world.

Parents must be especially careful about sending their children to schools that have a good secular education but also must be committed to authentic Judaism and have an environment with profound influence on them. Examples of the depth of concern our leaders have shown on this issue abound throughout modern Jewish history, but one story will suffice. Rabbi Yosef Chaim Sonnenfeld, Rabbi of Jerusalem in the early 1900s, once approached the Austrian ambassador in Palestine, requesting his assistance in a certain matter. It had been brought to the attention of the rabbi that an orphan child, being raised by Orthodox foster parents, had been taken by a certain Dr. Hertzberg, who was an official of the government, and placed in the latter's new school which combined secular studies with a religious education. Rabbi Sonnenfeld respectfully requested that the ambassador intervene in getting the child out of this school and back into Rabbi Sonnenfeld's yeshivah.

The Austrian ambassador could not understand why the rabbi was so concerned. "I've been to that school and it is running a very fine program. All the religious laws are observed. Dr. Hertzberg is merely improving upon the education that your institution offers by adding secular studies. What harm is there in that?"

Rabbi Yosef Chaim asked the ambassador if he recalled the famous incident concerning Dr. Helman, tutor of the children of the Austrian defense minister during the Franco-Prussian War. One day, the minister heard his eldest son singing a French army marching song. The father was furious and insisted that his son tell him where he had learned that abominable tune. "What is wrong with a mere French song?" the son protested. "Dr. Helman taught it to us during our French classes."

The Austrian defense minister summoned the tutor and, screaming with rage, demanded of him, "How dare you teach my children a song that the enemy sings when they march to battle to kill our soldiers! You are guilty of high treason!"

In a voice filled with emotion, Rabbi Sonnenfeld concluded his plea before the Austrian ambassador. "Dr. Hertzberg's new school with its emphasis on foreign culture will, in the long run, bring death to our religion and to our young people. The purity of our Torah education must not be tampered with." The ambassador immediately arranged for the orphan child to be withdrawn from Dr. Hertzberg's school and placed, once again, in Rabbi Sonnenfeld's yeshivah.[18]

We learn from this that the subjects taught in our schools are not necessarily presented in a neutral way. This is clear from the way that anti-Semitic countries in the past taught even neutral subjects like science. The spirit, the orientation, and the approach are all important, even in the secular studies departments. If a school does not have the supervision of people committed to Torah on every level, the minds of Jewish children can be deeply affected by views that are antithetical to Torah, to Judaism, and to their own self-esteem.

THE ULTIMATE "ENVIRONMENT" FOR THE JEWISH PEOPLE IS THE Land of Israel. The bond between the Jewish people and the Land

**THE HOLY LAND OF ISRAEL**

of Israel began in the time of Abraham, when G-d promised him, "I give the land you live in to you and your offspring to come, all the Land of Canaan as an everlasting possession" (*Genesis* 17:8). In the final prophecy to Moses just before his death, the Torah states, "And the Lord said to him, 'This is the land of which I swore to Abraham, Isaac, and Jacob. I will give it to your offspring' " (*Deuteronomy* 34:4).

It was only on the soil of Israel that all the commandments of G-d could be implemented; it was only on that soil, "in that place that He will choose" (Mount Moriah in Jerusalem), that the permanent central sanctuary of the Jewish people could be built. It is only on the soil of Israel that the Children of Israel would

18. *Giants of Jewry*, Vol. II.

realize their fullest potential as a people; and it is only on that soil that G-d's promises to all the Jews could become reality — if the nation proved itself worthy by its adherence to the commandments and its loyalty to the covenant. As the people were called upon to become a "holy people," their land was to be a "holy land."

The Land of Israel was not to be defiled by the pagan practices then prevalent in that area of the world. The Jewish people were ordered to remove these pagan rites and abominations from the land. Here are some of the things the Torah said about protecting the land:

> They should not dwell in your land, lest they cause you to sin against Me (*Exodus* 23:33).
>
> Beware lest you make a covenant with the inhabitants of the land. . .lest he become a snare in your midst (*Exodus* 34:12).
>
> If you will not drive out the inhabitants of the land before you, those whom you leave shall be pricks in your eyes and thorns in your sides . . . .
>
> And it shall be, that which I intended to do to them I shall do to you (*Numbers* 33:55-56).
>
> Make no covenant with them and have no mercy on them (*Deuteronomy* 7:2).
>
> You must destroy them: the Hitti, the Emori, the Canaani. . .as the Lord your G-d commanded you, in order that they should not teach you to do according to all their abominations (*Deuteronomy* 20:17-18).

Why were these warnings so severe? Why couldn't the Jews be allowed to live peacefully alongside the former inhabitants of the land? The depravity of the Canaanites — the abominations they practiced ("even their sons and daughters they burn in fire to their gods" — *Deuteronomy* 12.31), their tolerance for incest and murder — made them unique in their wickedness. The Jews could not be allowed to live alongside such nations, for their evil ways would have influenced the Jews as well.

People sometimes ask: By what right did the Israelites conquer the land of Canaan from the other nations who had lived there for so many years? Even today, some ask what right the Jews had to settle and colonize the Land of Israel in seeming disregard of Arabs (or Palestinians) who had lived there for centuries. These questions are best answered with a parable of the Dubno Maggid:

A wealthy merchant who owned a beautiful house decided to travel abroad and settle elsewhere for awhile. He did not want to sell his familial home, but neither did he want it to decay while he was away. He solved this problem by turning over his home to a reputable young man who would have full use of the home and the surrounding land, but on one condition: Whenever the owner would return, he must not be denied any request in connection with the house. The owner must be treated with respect, as befitted a landlord. Legal documents were drawn up by a lawyer and signed by witnesses, listing all the numerous rights of the tenant and also the obligations to the landlord, the true owner of the house.

After an absence of many years, the landlord returned. He didn't really want to bother the man who was living there. In fact, he was willing to allow him to stay, so long as he didn't disturb the landlord and continued to abide by the conditions. Despite the landlord's good intentions, the tenant's response was, "You are a stranger here. You have no right to this house. It is mine and I am free to do as I please."

"Stranger?" answered the shocked owner. "Who is the stranger in this house? You seem to forget our agreement. This is my house! I built it, raised my family here, and was kind enough to allow you to live here, rent-free, so long as you cared for the property and followed my rules."

The young man saw that he couldn't persuade the old man to leave willingly, so he took the case to court. At first the judge was inclined to rule in favor of the tenant. However, when the landlord showed him the conditions of the original deed of transfer, he agreed that the law was on the side of the old man. Turning to the younger man, the judge said, "Had you fulfilled your part of the agreement and allowed him to live peacefully with you in the house, following his conditions as landlord, you may be sure that you would not have been thrown out of your home. Instead, you violated the one condition under which he ceded the property to you. You were insolent and refused to abide by the conditions set forth by the owner."

The same is true with respect to the Land of Israel. G-d is the ultimate owner, and He had set conditions on which people could live in the land. The Canaanites and other nations did not fulfill the conditions. It was only a matter of time before they were ejected. Moreover, He promised the land to Abraham and his children forever. They were the landlords who had inherited the home. When the Children of Israel returned to the land, they were like the old landlord returning. However, just as the old landlord would have allowed the tenant to stay, so Joshua set certain conditions if the Canaanites wished to remain in the land unharmed. They had to live by the laws of G-d, the ultimate owner, and give up their abominable practices. These conditions were set forth in written proclamations to the seven nations that were living in the Land of Israel when the Jews crossed the Jordan.[19]

The three conditions, which most Canaanites refused to accept, were (a) to abide by the Seven Noahide Laws, including prohibitions against idol worship and other practices, (b) to accept no positions of leadership, and (c) to be prepared to assist the ruling government of the Jews with labor and financial contributions. Had they been willing to accept these conditions, the Israelites would have made a covenant of peace with them. When they refused, the Israelites were commanded to drive them out or destroy them.

The Jew living anywhere other than the Land of Israel was considered as being "in exile," regardless of how comfortable and secure he might be there. But does it really make a difference if a Jew lives in Israel or somewhere else? The privilege of living in Israel can be compared to the good fortune of a child living happily with his father and mother. Whatever the child needs, the parents will lovingly provide. For how can a loving father refuse his child's request when the child is residing in his

---

19. Talmud Yerushalmi, *Shviis*, 6:1.

parents' home and fulfilling their wishes? However, if the son lives in a far-off country, the ties are not so close. So it is with the people of Israel in their land. When we live in the Holy Land of Israel, we know that our prayers and wishes will be fulfilled more speedily and with more clarity than anywhere else in the world.

One who was not privileged to fulfill this dream was Rabbi Chaim Krozno. He too had decided he must travel to the Holy Land. While on the voyage by ship, a terrible storm arose and his ship was forced to return. Rabbi Krozno and his fellow passengers escaped injury, but he never again had the opportunity to make the journey. He remained despondent over this for the rest of his life. When he was about to die, he asked only that his name be inscribed on his tombstone, nothing else. He felt that he had no merits because he had not been able to travel to the Land of Israel in his lifetime. This illustrates the deep attachment that our holy leaders had for the land. It was no mere nationalistic sentiment, but a deeply ingrained knowledge, that the Land of Israel offers a person a special opportunity to develop his relationship with G-d.[20]

In our daily prayers, we ask for the Jews' complete return to Israel and the restoration and rebuilding of Jerusalem and the Holy Temple. Basing his conclusion on the Torah's "And you shall take possession of the land" (*Numbers* 33:52), Nachmanides concludes that taking up residence in the land is a great mitzvah.[21] "And you shall take possession of the land and live therein, for to you have I given the land to possess it" (*Numbers* 33:53). At all times we must remember that Jews living in Israel are fulfilling G-d's wishes in a special way. However, living in the land is not an end in itself. As the Chofetz Chaim explained from the Passover Haggadah, "Had He given us the Torah and not brought us into Israel, it would have been sufficient kindness." This praise of G-d shows that Torah without Israel is possible, but the Land of Israel without Torah is incomplete.

---

20. End of the *Kuzari*.
21. Ramban on *Numbers* 33:53.

# ✎§ CONVERSION: BECOMING PART OF THE HOLY COMMUNITY

We mentioned above that, despite an early negative experience with Egyptian converts, Judaism has continued to allow non-Jews to enter into the covenant. Since Sinai, the basic definition of a Jew is one who is born of a Jewish mother[22] or one who has converted to Judaism in accordance with *halachah* (Jewish law).[23] The precise methods have been carefully designed by the Oral Torah.

Conversion to Judaism can never be a mere formality. It effects a change in the very essence of a person, changing the person at the soul level into a Jew. G-d, the Creator of all souls, gives the newly converted person a Jewish soul that connects him or her to all other Jews. Any other ceremony than the halachic one cannot have that effect, and therefore has no validity.

The laws of the conversion process are designed to promote sincere, genuine conversions and to deflect a person from converting whose reasons are extraneous to a major change in one's spiritual life. They are also intended to ensure that the person will indeed be willing to accept the Jewish religion.

The Talmud describes the procedure by which a prospective convert can become a Jew. He is first asked, "What prompted you to convert? Don't you know that Israel today is thrust down, despised, and persecuted?"[24] If the prospective convert indicates his desire to convert in spite of the above warning, the Rabbinical Court then arranges that he be taught the essential principles of Judaism. If, after the period of study, the Court finds that the prospective convert is still determined to accept completely and without reservation the whole Torah, he is ready for the last indispensable steps. If he is a male, he must undergo circumcision,

---

22. Talmud *Kiddushin* 68b.
23. *Shulchan Aruch*, *Hilchos Geirus*, *Yoreh Deah* 268.
24. Talmud *Yevamos* 47.

which is a physical manifestation of his Jewishness. The final step, required of both male and female, is immersion in a designated *mikveh* or ritual pool, for purification and sanctification. The convert emerges from the water as a new person, a Jew. He or she is a Jew in every respect, enjoying all the privileges and responsibilities of full-fledged membership, and is an integral part of the chosen people.

Jews, unlike members of some other religions, do not actively attempt to convert non-Jews. Even more, we create difficulties and roadblocks in the face of the prospective convert. In this manner, we ensure, as much as possible, that social pressures do not coerce, that ulterior motives are minimized, and that the sincere will of the convert is the only force bringing him or her to this decision.

A conversion that does not follow these procedures and laws is not valid. This includes accepting all the *mitzvos* (precepts, laws) of the whole Torah. It is, practically speaking, quite possible that converts will not have learned all the laws in detail yet, but they must still accept them in principle, committing to observe them as their knowledge grows. This is exactly what happened to the whole Jewish people at Mount Sinai, when they said, *Na'aseh v'nishma,* meaning, "We will do and we will understand [later]." They committed to the laws of G-d, knowing they had much still to learn.

Many in our modern society do not realize that Judaism is not a club or political action group based on paying dues or sharing a sentiment. It is a religious community with specific requirements and commitments, joining one people in a common mission. Genuine conversions contribute to the unity of the Jewish people; nonhalachic ones contribute to fragmentation of the people. An improper conversion does not make a person a Jew of a different denomination; it simply is invalid, and the convert remains essentially a non-Jew.

# PART TWO

# 7

# A Life of Mitzvos

## ✑ INTRODUCTION

The Talmud teaches, "G-d wanted to benefit Israel, and He therefore gave them Torah and commandments in abundance."[1] This may seem a strange notion: What benefit is it to have a long list of duties to fulfill? We can understand this by a parable. Imagine a gardener hired to clean up a garden that is totally overrun with weeds. He does not know what plants were originally there, or which ones are important to the owner. Unless he is given a list of priorities and a plan of the original garden, he might tear out plants that the owner loves, or waste time pruning plants that the owner considers to be weeds. So are the commandments to us: they reveal G-d's plan and priorities, G-d's own values. If we follow them, we can come to understand the entire world as a beautiful garden — and help make it into a Garden of Eden.

---

1. Talmud *Makkos* 23b.

The essence of the Torah is its commandments or *mitzvos*. There are 613 *mitzvos* in the Torah, of which 248 are positive precepts, and 365 are negative ones. Many of these commandments, however, deal with the laws of purity and sacrifice and were applicable only when the Temple stood in Jerusalem; the actual number relevant to Jews today is much smaller.

The commandments were given for all times, thus it is forbidden to add to or subtract from any of the Torah's commandments. Rabbinical authorities rule in order to clarify the commandments as they apply to a given situation, or to protect them from possible violation. Only a few actual new commandments were ever formulated, namely those having to do with establishment of additional holidays like Chanukah and Purim, and with the ritual washing of hands before eating bread.

Since the Torah was Divinely given, one cannot pick and choose only certain commandments to observe, according to one's own judgment. The commandments reflect the Will of G-d. The gardener cannot clean up only part of the garden and leave the rest overrun with weeds. Likewise, we are expected to learn about and observe all the commandments.

## ⮤ REASONS FOR THE COMMANDMENTS

Our sages have explained ten reasons why G-d gave us commandments, in terms of why they are beneficial for us:

1) When we keep the commandments, they help us remember and recognize the importance of G-d in our lives, and make us more willing to place complete faith in Him. Torah offers us a precise system constructed to bring us closer to our Creator. With this instruction book, we can perfect ourselves. Coming close to G-d is not easy, however. It is like traveling in new territory — if you have a map, you have a far better chance of reaching your destination. Where the journey is difficult, and

we are prone to error, it is wise to observe every signpost, marker, and instruction. Then the journey will be successful.

2) The *mitzvos* help us live a pure, decent life and curb our baser instincts. The discipline of the commandments enables us to cultivate our powers of self-control and restraint. In Judaism, the *gibor,* the person of strength and valor, is the one who conquers his selfish impulses.[2]

3) The commandments were given to provide spiritual nourishment to the Jews. Through the *mitzvos,* G-d could fulfill His altruistic purpose in creating a world: to benefit His creatures. They are for the sole good of the recipients.[3]

4) The *mitzvos* of the Torah enable us to develop a special orientation toward life known as holiness. After listing all the laws and regulations incumbent on a Jew, the Torah states, "Speak to the whole Israelite community and say to them, "You shall be holy for I, the Lord your G-d, am holy" (*Leviticus* 19:2). This call for the sanctification of Israel permeates all of Jewish law. Holiness does not lie in a saintly withdrawal from life, however, or from excessive denial of human pleasures. It consists rather in full participation in family and communal life, sharing the sorrows as well as the joys that life offers. The main point is to develop the capacity to distinguish and choose between right and wrong, the good and the bad, the true and the false. The commandments of Judaism help us do this.[4]

5) The commandments remind a Jew that he or she is a member of the Chosen Nation. The Torah was entrusted to the Children of Israel at Mount Sinai as a mark of distinction and honor. The Talmud illustrates this with a parable: A king had an orchard in which he planted all sorts of trees. He would allow no one to enter it, until his children grew up. Then he told them, "My children, I have looked after this orchard and

---

2. *Pirkei Avos.*

3. Rabbi Chaim Volozhin, *Nefesh HaChaim.*

4. See Rabbi Moshe Chaim Luzatto, *The Path of Hashem,* and Rabbi Samson Raphael Hirsch, throughout his commentary on the Torah.

never allowed anyone to enter it. Now you shall have it. Tend it as carefully as I have." The children are the nation Israel, to whom G-d said, "Before I created the world I made the Torah ready and kept it from any other nation." All these commandments were given to Israel, not to any other nation.

6) A large number of the commandments deal with the relationships human beings have to one another, and are necessary for the preservation of a harmonious society. Thus, the basis of the Torah is the maxim, "What is hateful to you, do not do to your neighbor."[5]

7) The commandments help unify the Jewish people by reminding them of their unique history. They also serve to maintain the identity of the Jewish people, by setting them apart from non-Jews. With regard to many laws, G-d states, "I am G-d, your G-d, Who set you apart from the nations" (*Leviticus* 20:24).

8) The *mitzvos* serve also as a survival mechanism, enabling Jews to remain firm in their faith even during the harshest persecutions and through periods where assimilation was a danger. Indeed, this is an indication of the Divine nature of the commandments, for they have kept the Jewish people alive for countless generations. As Moses said, "See, behold I have imparted to you laws and ordinances as the Lord my G-d has commanded me . . . for what great nation is there that has laws and ordinances as perfect as all this teaching that I set before you this day?" (*Deuteronomy* 5:8).

9) The commandments serve in a pedagogic capacity, transmitting G-d's teachings from one generation to the next. "G-d established a law in Israel, which He commanded our fathers to teach their children so that it may be known to future generations, to children yet unborn, and these would in turn repeat it to their children" (*Psalms* 78:5-6). This is of the highest importance, since it is only constant transmission that can guarantee the continuance of our faith.

---

5. Hillel, cited in Talmud *Shabbos* 31. See also Rambam, *Guide for the Perplexed.*

10) Above and beyond all the reasons we can give for G-d's commandments, there are reasons that only G-d Himself can know. Just as we cannot fully comprehend G-d and His creations, so we cannot fully comprehend the reasons for the *mitzvos*. As the prophet Isaiah stated, transmitting verbatim G-d's message: "My thoughts are not your thoughts. . .for as the heavens are higher than the earth, so are My ways higher than your ways, and My thoughts than your thoughts. . . .So shall the word that emanates from My mouth not return to Me void without accomplishing My purpose, and succeed in furthering My goal for it" (*Isaiah* 55:8-11).

## ►§ COMMANDMENTS WITH NO APPARENT RATIONALE (*CHUKIM*)

The Torah contains a number of laws called *chukim* — statutes whose reasons human beings have not been able to understand clearly. Nevertheless we accept and observe them, because they have been given to us by G-d. Not only do we owe G-d unquestioning obedience because He is our Creator, but we must have faith that G-d knows what is best for us as agents to accomplish His Divine purposes.

Among such laws are the precepts of *kashrus*, involving the permission to eat only kosher foods; the prohibition against eating blood; the laws of *shatnez*, which prohibit wearing mixtures of wool and linen; and *kilayim*, the laws against planting and cultivating certain mixtures of plants and crossbreeding or harnessing together various kinds of animals. Each of these statutes is a law for which no explanation is provided in the Torah, nor are they easy to explain by human reason. Significantly, they have to do with our relationship to the worlds "below" us, the realms of plants and animals. We must assume that, despite our ability to have "dominion" over the earth, there are aspects of our relationship to the vegetable and animal worlds that we cannot understand. We accept and observe them despite our inability to fathom their meanings, because G-d is the Master of creation.

*Rabbi Raphael Jami from Tunisia was once stopped by a fellow Jew as he was hurrying through the streets. "Excuse me, Rabbi," said the other man, "but since you are a learned individual, perhaps you could explain to me why we are forbidden to shave with a razor. There seems to be no reason for this, to my mind."*

*"Pardon me, my friend," replied Rabbi Raphael, "I'd like to answer your question, but I'm just on my way to the pharmacy to buy some medicine, and I must get it right away."*

*"But why are you making this long trip yourself?" asked the man. "Why didn't you send a messenger to buy the medicine?"*

*"Because I also want to ask the pharmacist about the effectiveness of the medicine," the rabbi replied.*

*"I'm sorry, but I don't understand," said the man. "Why must you ask the pharmacist? Surely if the doctor has prescribed that medicine he is to be relied upon, and you need not ask the pharmacist, for the doctor knows better!"*

*"Ah!" exclaimed Rabbi Raphael. "Do you hear what you have just said? You want me to accept the word of the doctor unquestioningly. Then why do you not accept G-d's 'prescriptions' as they are? Even I am just the 'pharmacist.' If the Almighty ordered us not to use blades for shaving, then He must feel that this is beneficial for us. It is our medicine to take and it works, whether we understand it or not."*

The Torah tells us to put these laws "upon and over your heart." In other words, regardless of whether or not our intellects can grasp the purposes behind these commandments, it is our duty to keep them "over and above" the emotions and desires of our hearts. There is, however, a clear benefit to us: By fulfilling these commandments to the letter, we gain self-control, purity, and complete faith in G-d.

# ঙ§ BEING A GOOD JEW

Sometimes we ask, "Why isn't it enough just to believe in G-d and have a good heart? Doesn't G-d appreciate that we try to do the best we can?" Of course, G-d appreciates our intent. But as Jews, our commitment to G-d must be not only in our beliefs, but also our behavior. The garden — which is the world — has to be tended. All books about Judaism emphasize that Judaism is a "way of life" that involves doing, not just believing. The commandments are the means by which concepts and values receive actual application to everyday life. "Study is the supreme thing, but only if it leads to fulfillment," our Sages said.[6] Action is a necessary companion to both study and belief.

The same is true of having a "good heart." Though one's intent may be good and one's belief in Judaism strong, these must be followed by action. What would we say to a person who committed murder, if he protested, "But I have a good heart, and I believe murder is wrong?" Or, to take a less extreme example, if a person believed that it was wrong to eat animal flesh, but had roast beef for dinner, we would at least be puzzled by the contradictions in his life.

Of course, if the principled vegetarian accidentally ate meat, or occasionally was overcome by a desire for a hamburger, we could understand. People are not always perfect in adherence to their beliefs. Judaism does not expect perfection, only a commitment to grow toward higher and higher levels. But we cannot use the excuse that it is useless to attempt to observe the laws, out of fear of being hypocritical. ("I can't keep it perfectly, so I won't keep it at all.") If one doesn't make some kind of beginning or partial attempt, no progress will be made. It doesn't make sense to decide to play golf someday in the future, but refuse ever to begin learning how to hold the club.

If a person tells you, "It isn't necessary to pay attention to the Torah laws, you just have to have a 'good Jewish heart,'" you're

---

6. Talmud *Kiddushin* 40b; Rambam on Mishnah *Peah* 1:1.

being asked to believe in "cardiac Judaism." But if you tell a doctor you want to exercise your heart without exercising the body, he will predict a cardiac arrest. Just as one cannot be a patriotic American while refusing to pay taxes or obey American laws, so also with Judaism. By following the Torah and its commandments, we develop not only a "good Jewish heart" but also a good Jewish person, entirely, from a good Jewish soul.

Indeed, Judaism is distinguished from all other creeds by the observance of the specific *mitzvos,* which no other religion practices. Faith is a *mitzvah,* but only one of the six hundred thirteen. The great Rabbi Saadia Gaon put it succinctly more than a thousand years ago: "Faith was never regarded by Judaism as a consecrated act on which salvation depends; it is considered of value only insofar as it leads to right action."[7]

# ▁§ TORAH AND THE POTENTIAL FOR CHANGE

If we remember the Divine source of the commandments, we will understand why not even one letter may be changed. All the commandments, including their interpretations and details of observing them, were given to Moses on the forty days he spent on Mount Sinai. He then spent the remainder of the forty years in the wilderness teaching and explicating them. But the commandments themselves were given for all time. That is why it is written, "Things that are revealed to us belong to us and to our children forever: to keep all the words of this Torah" (*Deuteronomy* 29: 28). So the Torah itself says that we cannot change it: "You shall neither add to it nor diminish from it" (*Deuteronomy* 13:1). We cannot even interpret a commandment in a way that adds a prohibition that was not included in the Torah's teachings.

The Torah states that even if a prophet wanted to change the laws in a way that subtracted from or added to the Torah, he

---

7. Rabbi Saadia Gaon, *Emunos V'Dei'os.*

would be considered a false prophet and could be sentenced to death. The Torah wants us to understand that the structure of the laws is truly eternal. Because we are human and live in a world where everything changes, this is hard to accept.

The story is told of a stranger in town whose watch had stopped, and he wanted to know the correct time. He looked up at the clock in the tower of City Hall, but had trouble seeing it. He remarked to a passerby, "Why do you have your clock so high up? Wouldn't it be better to place it within reach so it could be seen more easily?"

"Oh, we did that once," the passerby replied. "But when people would look at their watches, each one would come over and change the hands of the clock to make it fit what his watch said. No one ever knew the correct time."

The same is true about laws. If they can be changed, they will be changed, because that is our ordinary reality. The Torah's laws must be kept high and aloft, so that they will not be tampered with or adjusted to suit the whims of different people at different times. We have to adjust our "watches" — meaning, our lives — to the Divine "clock," the Torah.

"Reform" and "reconstruction" of the Torah — or the reaction on the other side, to "conserve" it — miss the point. They become a mockery of what Torah really is, namely Divine teaching. From its very beginning, American Reform Judaism rejected the concept that G-d had given the Jewish people an eternal Torah at Sinai. In the words of the 1875 Pittsburgh Platform of the Reform movement, the Bible reflected " the primitive ideas of its own age. . . .Today we accept as binding only its moral laws and maintain only such ceremonials as elevate and sanctify our lives." Who decides what laws and ceremonials are to be maintained? Many Reform Jews have come to see that this is an impossible position, and are trying to restore some elements of traditional Judaism. But if the Torah is the Divine "clock," one has to go back to reset one's watch all over again.

The attempts to reform Judaism had very severe consequences upon generations of Jewish youth. Children have been taught that Judaism is a man-made thing, the work of wise but ancient men. G-d may exist, but not in the context of an established religion, since all of the religions are man made. Thus, they have come to see Judaism as something that leads to clannishness and even bigotry. Religion, they think, should promote only ethics that are common to everyone. With this attitude, they have little reason to attend services, observe Shabbos or keep *kashrus;* by their reasoning, these things are outdated. Why should they value Judaism at all? Why not just assimilate into modern society?

One must be very careful about the teachings to which one listens. For example, the great Reb Leib Chasman found out that his students had attended a lecture by a popular Reform thinker. Shocked, he asked how they had the nerve to go and listen to heresy. They responded that they did not care about the content; they had heard that he was a good speaker, and they wanted to enjoy his style of oratory and his excellent command of the language.

Reb Leib reprimanded them, saying, "That is like a Jew who sees a synagogue in flames — can the man possibly use that flame to light Shabbos candles?"[8]

The same sort of reply must be given to those who urge that the Torah must be brought "up to date." Judaism is established to teach the age, not to let itself be taught by the age. From the very beginning, Judaism opposed the world around it. Abraham opposed idol-worship and polytheism. Moses opposed the divinity attributed to the Pharaoh in Egypt. The prophets opposed the bestial ceremonies of the Canaanites. When the Hellenists were changing the shape of the entire Mediterranean world with their highly intellectual but G-dless culture, the Jews were the only ones to stand in opposition (this is the very reason we celebrate Chanukah). Multitudes of Jews have stood up under pressures to convert to other religions, which claimed to be a higher or better revelation in their time. Now secular rationalism claims to be the new revelation or "Enlightenment." The Torah demands that we stand up to its claims as well, whether they come in the form of materialistic desires or new "Judaisms."

---

8. *Giants of Jewry,* Vol. II.

When we are tempted by the arguments about bringing Judaism "up to date," we must examine our true motives. All too often, if we are really honest with ourselves, we find that when we want to ignore a commandment, it is because we find it burdensome or simply inconvenient. In such cases, are we acting to uphold Judaism or to make our own lives easier? Judaism as it has come down to us from our ancestors is a Divine gift that is holy, and cannot be changed according to human whim.

# ᴇ₰ HALACHAH

*H*alachah is the overall term for Jewish law. It is concerned with the proper application of the commandments to every situation and circumstance. When a halachic decision is handed down, it is the authoritative decision on any specific question.

There are no areas of human behavior excluded from *halachah*. A person's eating habits, sex life, business ethics, social activities, entertainment, and artistic expression all come under the umbrella of religious law, which expresses the values and spiritual guidelines of Judaism. Fully observed, the Jewish law is a religion for all of life. Moreover, while each Jew is a unique individual, the Jewish people are an organism. Therefore, *halachah* creates a basic structure of uniformity of practice. A Jew can experience Shabbos in any country of the world and, while the food and melodies may be different, the basic form of Shabbos is preserved. Thus it is written, "There shall be one Torah and one law for you" (*Numbers* 15:16).

First and foremost, *halachah* rests on the biblical laws and commandments in the Written and Oral Torah. The Oral Torah, which was also given to Moses at Sinai, includes the finer points of the commandments, the details of the general principles contained in the Torah and the ways they are to be applied. For example, the Written Torah says that an animal needed for food is to be slaughtered "as I have commanded you" (*Deuteronomy* 6). What is the method that has been commanded? What regulations govern slaughtering? These were part of the Oral Torah that Moses received and passed down.

The Written Torah commands us to "bind them [the words] as a sign upon your hands and as frontlets between your eyes" (*Deuteronomy* 6:8). This reference to *tefillin* (phylacteries) does not give a clue as to how they were to be made, or how they were to be "bound" to oneself. The Oral Torah teaches this.

During the second century CE, circumstances developed that led the Sages to approve the writing down of the Oral Torah for the first time. The result, as we have explained, is known as the Mishnah. This in turn became the cornerstone of the Gemara, which describes the discussions and debates of the Sages as they sought to examine and apply the laws. Together the Mishnah and Gemara constitute the Talmud. Two Talmuds were compiled, one in the Land of Israel and a more extensive one in the academies of Babylonia. The Talmuds were accepted as authentic and correct by all Israel, and that is how they became authoritative in Torah law. All later codes and decisions are binding because of their derivation from the discussions in the Talmud.

The discussions and debates in the Talmuds became famous, so that we often hear there are many opinions in Judaism. Indeed, these were so confusing to the medieval Christian scholars who attempted to read the Talmud that they used it as excuse for anti-Semitism, criticizing the Jews for their convoluted reasoning. In most cases, the truth is that they were unable to understand the methods of the rabbis, who had astounding abilities to make fine distinctions and follow a demanding logic. The Sages of the Talmud are exquisite examples of how to search, with every fiber of one's intellect, for how to do the will of G-d. Therefore, when we hear about "minority" and "majority" opinions in the Talmud, we should recognize that these refer to fine points that may affect certain cases. Also, we should be aware that the famous different "schools" of Hillel and Shammai with different opinions are pre-Mishnaic. The Talmud long ago decided which of these to follow in each general case. In all the discussions of different opinions, there are no fundamental deviations from the central laws of the Written Torah.

The Babylonian Talmud, the later and more complete of the two (and usually referred to as *the* Talmud), was compiled around 600 CE. The Sages who handed down legal decisions after this came to be known according to eras:

600-700 CE: Savora'im
700-1000: Geonim
1000-1200: Rishonim
1200-1500: Acharonim.

The laws were codified in simpler and more accessible form over a thousand-year period, first by the Rambam in his famous *Mishneh Torah,* later by the Tur, and finally in the *Shulchan Aruch* by Rabbi Yosef Karo (1488-1575 CE), the work that became most widely accepted. This work is not the individual opinion of its author but a compilation of opinions found in the Talmud. It also includes the religious judicial decisions handed down by the Sages of the post-Talmudic era. In modern times, the *Mishnah Berurah* by the Chofetz Chaim (Rabbi Israel Meir Ha-Cohen) is one of the key works that provides discussion of additional issues.

*Halachah* is understood as representing not mere legal decisions, but the will of G-d expressed in the best possible human form. Through the study of *halachah* one can gain a unique closeness to G-d. Through *halachah,* all things in the world become part of G-d's ultimate purpose. Thus it is taught in the last line of the Talmud, "One who studies *halachah* every day is guaranteed a portion in the World to Come."[9]

It is not only because of historical circumstances that the laws had to be written down and interpreted. The Torah explicitly states that authoritative interpretation and teaching were to be given over to those who succeeded Moses, Aaron, and the seventy elders in leadership capacities. It says, "You shall not deviate from all that they instruct you" (*Deuteronomy* 17:11). Priests, prophets, and the Sages of the Sanhedrin inherited the mantle of leadership in ancient times. By the Mishnaic period, after the destruction of the Second Temple, the academies of those titled

---

9. Talmud *Niddah* 73.

the Rabbis ("teachers") were the only remaining carriers of this tradition. They did not invent new Torah laws, for that is forbidden. However, they had and continue to have the power to strengthen existing laws to prevent abuse of the Torah. G-d expects us to follow the *mitzvos* of the Rabbis, and their interpretations, just as much as the laws of the Written Torah. King Solomon said long ago, concerning the prohibition of transgressing an ordinance of the Sages, "And he who breaches the fence shall fall prey to a serpent" (*Ecclesiastes* 10: 8).

The rabbi known as the Aruch HaShulchan, one of the codifiers of Jewish Law, states, "There is nothing which is not intimated in the Torah. For all the words of the Sages were given by the Almighty to Moses at Sinai, and He revealed to Moses [even] that which the Sages were destined to innovate and interpret."[10]

A story that illustrates this concept concerns the great sage Hillel the Elder, who made a point of emphasizing the authenticity of the Rabbis as guardians of Jewish law: A non-Jew once came before Shammai to embrace Judaism, with the reservation that he only be required to adhere to the Written Law. Shammai rebuffed him since, according to the tenets of authentic Judaism, the Oral and Written Laws are inseparable. When the prospective proselyte appeared before Hillel, however, the great rabbi immediately began to teach him the *alef-beis* (Hebrew alphabet), asking him to return the following day for another lesson. Upon his return, Hillel reversed the letters. When the proselyte expressed amazement that only yesterday he had been instructed differently by Hillel himself, the sage answered, "Are you not relying upon me [to understand the proper sequence of letters]? Then rely on me to teach you the Torah as G-d has commanded (i.e., the Oral as well as the Written law)."[11] The lesson is, even in simple matters we depend upon our teachers (and the books they choose, and all the directions they give) for authentic teaching. How much more so, as matters become more complicated, do we need to depend on them?

In every generation, certain rabbis are accepted as religious

---

10. Cited in the Introduction to *Shulchan Aruch Choshen Mishpat*.
11. Talmud *Shabbos* 31.

leaders and authorities because of their great scholarship and piety. Their study of Bible, Talmud and the codes is outstanding, and their compassion and understanding of human beings is great as well. In their own lives, they are devoted to G-d and careful about the laws, because in matters so important, one cannot follow someone who does not "practice what he preaches." These are the kind of people of whom the Torah says, "You must observe all that they decide for you" (*Deuteronomy* 17: 10). We should seek to learn Torah only from a rabbi who exemplifies this greatness. If a person is not outstanding in piety and observance, he is not worthy of the prestige and authority of a religious leader, no matter how great his scholarship.[12]

If two factions oppose each other in a question of law, the opinion of the faction including the greatest number of recognized sages is that which must normally be followed. However, if it is well known that the smaller group is superior in wisdom and scholarship, then its opinion must be followed. If there are many Torah scholars in the community who disagree with an individual rabbi, he should yield to the opinion of the majority. However, this is true only where the majority are on the same level of wisdom and Torah knowledge as that one rabbi. One can see from these guidelines that the Torah depends on great scholarship and fine insight, and does not descend to a lower level just because of numbers. Thus, a rabbi should under no condition yield to the laity in any question of Torah law simply because large numbers of people want a certain decision. The nature of Judaism is not to be decided by majority vote.

## ~§ THE OBSERVANT
## JEW AND MODERNITY

People often ask how it is possible to be an observant Jew in today's "modern" world. The truth is, what is considered

12. Talmud *Moed Katan* 17.

modern today can easily turn old fashioned tomorrow. We do not have to be historians to realize how rapidly human beings change their fashions, hair styles, modes of entertainment, values, and interests. One could just as easily ask: How could Judaism possibly be practiced in medieval Spain or ancient Rome?

Judaism's basic laws deal with the eternal condition of human beings — our true and deep nature. There is nothing old fashioned about such admonitions as "Honor your father and your mother," or "You shall not murder." They are as valid today as when G-d gave them to Moses more than three thousand years ago. The poor and the sick are still part of the world's population, and as much in need of assistance as ever. We must still be reminded to love others as we love ourselves, and to avoid slandering or injuring our neighbors. How could one say, with modern crime statistics in the daily newspaper, that we no longer need to be told to forsake murder, robbery, and cheating? There is nothing outdated about such laws.

Nor are Jewish holidays irrelevant. As virtually everyone recognizes, they unite us and remind us that we indeed have a special purpose. By celebrating Pesach, Succos, Purim, Chanukah and other such holidays, we join with other Jews in re-creating a family, a community of solidarity. Nor is it a small matter that these and other *mitzvos* create community and encourage us to work at a relationship with G-d. With the impersonality of today's world, our need for a caring community and a personal, loving G-d has never been greater. Prayer, Shabbos observance, and communal activities nourish parts of ourselves that would otherwise go hungry.

But a Jewish holiday is not merely a commemoration of a past historical event. It is a time when the world receives Divine emanations of a specific spiritual quality relevant to that time. For example, Shavuos is not only a commemoration of the day that the Jews received the Torah on Mount Sinai; it is also a time when a person can be more receptive to the Torah, and have direct spiritual assistance in the effort to grow in Torah learning and observance. These qualities are available to anyone who opens himself to them.

Judaism has survived — and Jews have survived — because they adapted the culture around them to fit the Torah, not because they changed Judaism to fit their culture. In Israel, Babylon, Spain, Morocco, Ethiopia, Poland, Romania, Hungary, Russia, South America, Canada, not to mention all the countries of Western Europe and the regions of the United States, the Jews became respectable and law-abiding citizens, but they gave first allegiance to their religion. The basic laws and ideals of Judaism have proved sufficiently timeless and universal to be able to be sustained in many societies during many different eras of history.

The following paragraph penned by a non-Jew, the famous French philosopher Jean-Jacques Rousseau, expresses his admiration for the Jews and their laws:

> To prevent His people from fusing with foreign peoples, He gave them customs and practices which are incompatible with those of other nations; He loaded them with specific ceremonies; He encumbered them in thousands of ways to keep them incessantly in good shape and to render them always foreigners amongst other men; and all the bonds of fraternity that He placed between the members of His republic were barriers that kept them separate from their neighbors and prevented them from mingling with others. It is in this way that this strange nation, so often subjugated, so often apparently dispersed and destroyed, but always passionately attached to its code, has still been preserved up to the present day scattered among the others without mixing with them, and that its customs, its laws, and its ritual continue to exist and will last as long as the world, despite the hatred and persecution of the rest of the human race.[13]

---

13. Rousseau, *Considerations sur le gouvernement de Pologne* . . .

# 8

## Lovingkindness in Society

The Torah is a blueprint for proper behavior between human beings, between humans and the universe, and between humans and the Creator. The human world is a central concern, so many Torah laws specify how we should act toward others. These are known as *mitzvos bein adam lachaveiro,* commandments about what is expected between human beings. While many people have the image of a Torah-observant Jew as concerned with rituals, the observance of proper relations between human beings is equally if not more important. The great first-century sage Hillel summed up the essence of Judaism by stating, "What is hateful to you, do not do to others."[1] Rabbi Akiva, an outstanding leader of the Mishnaic period, taught, "The commandment, 'love your neighbor as yourself' summarizes the essence of the whole Torah."[2] The Talmud says, "Whoever aspires to piety and saintliness, let him fulfill all the

1. Talmud *Shabbos* 31.
2. Talmud Yerushalmi, *Nedarim* 9:4.

laws of *Nezikin"* — namely, the laws dealing with monetary, civil, and criminal matters.

The Torah itself insists that the love of one's fellow man cannot be separated from the love of God. "And now Israel, what does G-d require of you but to revere Him. . .and to walk in His ways" (*Deuteronomy* 10:12). The Talmud elaborates, "Just as He is gracious, so should you be gracious; just as He is merciful, you too should be merciful. Just as He is full of kindness and truth, so you too should be full of kindness and truth."[3] The first-century leader Rabbi Yochanan ben Zakkai asked his students, "What is the key to a proper approach to life?" Several students gave answers, but the one he preferred was that of Rabbi Elazar ben Arach, who said, "A good heart." "This quality," said Rabbi Yochanan, "includes all the others."[4] If one really is trying to love G-d, one must work on loving and caring for one's fellow beings.

*The Torah says, "Be perfect with the Lord your G-d." The Chofetz Chaim, one of our modern sages, pointed out that being "perfect" implies stringent adherence to commandments that are between human beings, as well as those involving one's relationship to the Creator. One who concentrates on only one type of commandment and neglects the other type is like a simple farmer who went to the big city to purchase an* esrog *(citron for the Succos holiday) for his son-in-law, who was a Torah scholar. When he returned with a beautiful* esrog *for which he had paid a large sum of money, he showed it off to his neighbor. The neighbor was impressed, and begged him to sell him half of it. The farmer agreed, cut it in half, and gave it to him.*

*When the farmer proudly presented the half* esrog *to his son-in-law, the latter was perturbed. "Why are you so upset?" asked the farmer. "I showed this to some prominent rabbis in the city, and they all agreed it was an exceptionally beautiful* esrog.*"*

---

3. Talmud *Shabbos* 133b.
4. *Pirkei Avos* 2:13; Talmud *Shabbos* 31a.

*The son-in-law sighed. "I wish you would have bought me an ordinary esrog, as long as it would be whole, rather than half of a perfect one."*

*The same is true, concluded the Chofetz Chaim, with people who place all their emphasis on one form of commandment — doing those mitzvos perfectly, perhaps, but still only fulfilling half their obligations. This is not to diminish the importance attached to performing even one mitzvah.*

One must be fulfilling the ethical precepts of the Torah in order to be fulfilling properly the laws governing one's relation to G-d. One cannot steal from someone in order to buy matzah or build a *succah*. The Talmud stresses this in the following passage:

> If someone studies Torah and Mishnah, attends to the scholars, is honest in business and speaks pleasantly to others, what do people then say about him? "Happy is the father (and teacher) who taught him Torah. . . for this man has studied the Torah — look how fine his ways are, how righteous his deeds!" But if someone studies Torah and Mishnah, attends to the scholars, but is dishonest in business and discourteous in his relations with people, what do people say about him? "Woe unto him who studied the Torah, woe unto his father (and teacher) who taught him Torah! This man studied the Torah; yet look how corrupt are his deeds, how ugly his ways."[5]

If a religious person acts in a manner that would invite the latter type of remark, he has desecrated the Divine Name, a transgression of the severest magnitude, for which it is said that even Yom Kippur cannot atone. Again, the Talmud insists, "The very first question a person is asked when he is brought to final judgment is, 'Have you dealt with integrity and faith?' "[6]

The core of the Jewish tradition is the concept that G-d created human beings in His own image. Each of us possesses within ourselves a spark of the Divine that must not be violated. Revealing that Divinity in each person is the purpose of the

5. Talmud *Yoma* 86a.
6. Talmud *Shabbos* 31.

*mitzvos bein adam lachaveiro* (the commandments between a person and his/her "friend"). When we observe these commandments, we begin to internalize the dynamics of the Torah. We become attuned to a keen sense of awareness of self, others, the universe, and, of course, G-d. By living according to Torah principles, each of us can develop into a special individual who radiates goodness through words and actions.

Our literature contains numerous accounts of Torah-inspired personalities who influenced others deeply for the good. They accomplished this not through pressure or proselytizing, but through the examples they set in their daily activities and behavior. Their lifestyles, even more than their teachings, became a profound statement of the religion by which they lived. As we discuss the ethical laws, we will consider a number of such individuals throughout the ages who exemplified greatness in ethics and morality. They stand for us, as they did for the generations before us, as examples of men and women with desirable characteristics which we can cultivate by applying Torah principles and observance of *mitzvos* in our own lives.

## ⊷§ LOVE YOUR NEIGHBOR AS YOURSELF

The Torah states, "Love your fellow man as yourself, for I am G-d, your G-d." The medieval philosopher Rambam expounds on this, "We must praise others. We must care about their money just as we care about our own money and our dignity. We can never derive honor from humiliating someone else."[7] Similarly, the founder of Chasidism, the Baal Shem Tov, used to say, "Love your fellow man as yourself. You know that you have many faults; nevertheless, you still love yourself. That is how you should feel toward your friend: Despise his faults, love him." Rabbi Eliezer, in the Mishnaic period, had already summed it up: "Let your fellow man's honor be as dear to you as your own."[8]

---

7. Rambam, *Mishneh Torah, Hilchos Dei'os* 6:3.
8. *Pirkei Avos* 2:15.

By loving our fellow human beings, we as Jews also sanctify the Will of G-d. That is why the Torah follows the phrase, "Love your fellow as yourself," with the words, "for I am G-d, your G-d." We are not nurturing love in our hearts only for ourselves, because of what we might get in return or because society will be a better place, but because G-d wants it. If we want to be connected to G-d, we must work on this in ourselves.

The Talmud states, "If your hand hurts your eye, or your teeth bite your tongue, you do not retaliate because one part of you has injured another. Take the same attitude toward your fellow man, and do not hasten to fault him."[9]

The concept of loving others as oneself is very noble. But is the commandment practical? Can it in fact be carried out? Or is it just too much to expect a person to show others the same concern he lavishes on himself? In fact, our Sages advised that if one pays attention and works on developing oneself slowly, it can be done. A famous example is one we mentioned briefly above, from the great sage Hillel, who was asked by a non-Jew to explain the whole Torah "while he was standing on one foot," meaning to summarize its main points quickly. Hillel replied, "Whatever is hateful to you, do not do to others. Now go and learn."[10]

Hillel was well aware of the fact that loving others is difficult. So his first suggestion was to avoid destructive actions against others. Refraining from acts of revenge, from verbal attacks, and from holding grudges would be examples. Once one has established a basis of self-control, one can work on more positive acts of love. Hillel made sure to add, "go and learn," signifying to the non-Jew that there would be other steps to follow.

Rabbi Yisrael Salanter, a great 19th century teacher of ethics, was known for kindness and consideration for others. Once he was washing his hands for ritual purposes, and someone noticed that he was using the exact minimum amount needed. When asked why he was being so stingy with the water, he replied, "Of course, I consider the *mitzvah* of washing before eating bread

9. Talmud Yerushalmi, *Nedarim* 9:4.
10. Talmud *Shabbos* 31.

very important. But when I use up the contents of the barrel of water, my maid has a difficult struggle to bring up a new barrel. The more water I use, the more barrels she will have to lug. To spare her unnecessary hardship, I use as little water as possible."

Rabbi Salanter also refrained from rising too early in the morning. He knew that whenever he awoke, his maid would also rise to tend to his needs, and he did not want to curtail her sleep. Once, before Pesach, when the heads of the matzah baking asked his advice as to what they should be most careful about, he replied, "Make sure that, even though speed is of utmost concern, no one shouts at the widows who work in the matzah factories."

The development of feelings of love for others is something we can all emulate, as happened with a certain young man who was wondering whether he should continue his Torah studies. It was suggested that he consult the Chofetz Chaim, one of the leading Jewish sages of the early-20th century. The young man agreed, and affirmed that he would base his final decision on his encounter with the sage. When he entered the Chofetz Chaim's house, he saw him tearfully pacing, reciting Psalms. He asked about the source of the rabbi's distress, and he was told that a stranger whose relative was ill had asked the Chofetz Chaim to pray for his recovery.

Overwhelmed by this manifestation of love for a fellow Jew who was a complete stranger, the young man realized that only the study of Torah can cultivate such powerful compassion, and he became a disciple of the Chofetz Chaim.

# ◆§ ACTS OF LOVINGKINDNESS

In addition to the general commandment to love others, the Torah emphasizes the specificity of *gemilus chasadim*, doing acts of lovingkindness. *Pirkei Avos* states, "The world stands on three things: Torah, worship of G-d, and doing kindness" (1:2). This includes many kinds of actions, such as charity, hospitality, caring for the sick, attending to the deceased, and others. In general, a person who is able to think of others before thinking of his own special interests is attuned to the spirit of *chesed*. That is why the prophet Hosea tells us that the Almighty prefers acts of kindness above all the sacrifices offered to Him (*Hosea* 6:6).

A number of activities are highlighted as prime examples of *chesed:*

1) Helping another to find a job, or lending him money to start a business. We should not wait until our help is called for, but should try to help before a person's financial situation collapses.

2) *Chesed shel emes*, final respects to the deceased and escorting the deceased (*levayas ha-mes*).

3) *Hachnasas orchim* or hospitality. Abraham, the father of the Jewish people, had this as one of his greatest virtues. His desire to be hospitable to strangers, for example, led him to sit outside his tent on a hot day, waiting for wayfarers, even though he had just circumcised himself. *Pirkei Avos* 1:4 states, "Your house should be open wide, and you should let the poor feel at home with you."

4) *Bikur cholim*, visiting the sick. The Almighty himself came to visit Abraham while he was healing from his circumcision; so we too are required to emulate Him and visit the sick. The *bikur cholim* society, dealing with the needs of those who are ill, has always been a fixture of Jewish communities. It is not only a communal obligation, but a personal one as well, to give special care to the sick. It is said that each individual who visits brings to the sick person a special portion of the Divine Presence. Even in secular times, the special devotion of Jews to this *mitzvah* has led to many Jews being involved in the healing professions.

5) *Hachnasas chasan v'kallah*, providing funds for a poor groom or bride to enable them to marry. In addition, rejoicing with the bride and groom at a wedding is a *mitzvah* of *chesed*. They are making a major change in their lives, and the support of friends and community will make the transition easier.

6) Doing favors for others, such as offering a person a ride.

7) Cheering up another person or listening to his problems.

8) The Torah states specifically that if we see someone loading or unloading an animal, we are obligated to help. This, the *Sefer HaChinuch* explains, extends to other similar *mitzvos* where someone is trying to handle a burden too heavy for him. If we see a person carrying a heavy suitcase or changing a tire, we should offer assistance.[11]

9) *Nichum aveilim*, comforting mourners. This is a great *chesed*. By calling on the mourners during the week of *shivah* (seven days of deep mourning), extending to them our sympathy and condolences, we show them that we are with them even in their sorrow.

These *mitzvos* literally bring life into the world. In Mishnaic times, a pupil of the great Rabbi Akiva suddenly fell ill. The scholars of Rabbi Akiva's academy did not visit him. The sick young man had not been especially outstanding in his studies, so they felt it was beneath their dignity to interrupt their studies to go to his house. Rabbi Akiva was outraged by their insensitive behavior. He personally went to the home of the sick pupil, waited on him, supplied him with all his needs, and took a deep interest in his treatment. After he had recovered, the student said, "My master, you have saved my life." When his students assembled shortly afterward, Rabbi Akiva began his lecture by telling them, "Be advised that not visiting the sick is equivalent to hastening their death and shedding their blood."[12]

Regarding the *mitzvah* of attending to the deceased, we have a story of Rabbi Yisrael Salanter. The rabbi was in the midst of praying the morning service, when he heard a loud argument between the heads of the town's two burial societies. A poor woman had died, and each society claimed that it was the other's obligation to bury her. Rabbi Salanter immediately removed his *tallis* (prayer shawl) and *tefillin* (phylacteries), gathered together a few students, and said they would join together in the burial of

---

11. *Shulchan Aruch, Choshen Mishpat,* 272:8; *Sefer HaChinuch* Ch. 1.

12. Talmud *Nedarim* 41.

the woman. Since neither society wanted to perform the burial, it was incumbent upon them to do so. One must drop whatever he is doing to perform this final act of *chesed* for a deceased person.

In our active concern for others, we should be on the lookout for opportunities to perform acts of kindness. In this vein, another story is told about Rabbi Salanter. One Yom Kippur evening, he arrived at the synagogue unusually late — long past *Kol Nidrei.* Later, he explained that on his way to shul he had heard a baby crying. He investigated and found that the infant was all alone in a nearby house, with no one to care for it. The parents had apparently gone to shul themselves, expecting the baby to sleep. Rabbi Salanter decided that he could not allow the baby to remain in distress. He had stayed and comforted the infant until it went back to sleep, and only then had come to shul. Though Rabbi Salanter was a widely revered Torah scholar, he did not think it beneath his dignity to care for a baby.

Rabbi Chaim Soloveitchik, the Rav of Brisk, demonstrated his compassion for others in the following way: The wood for Rav Chaim's house was supplied by the community. Once, the treasurers noted that the expense seemed to be unusually large for heating one family's home. On investigation, it was found that all the poor men in town were taking all the wood they needed from the unlocked wood bin in the rabbi's yard. The treasurers immediately had a lock put on the bin. When Rabbi Chaim heard of this, he refused to take any more wood for himself. He could not enjoy warmth, knowing that others were freezing outside. The wood bin was subsequently unlocked and left open for everyone.

A man once came to Rabbi Baruch Ber Leibowitz and asked him to pray for the recovery of his wife. Ten years later, Rabbi Baruch Ber met that person and asked him about his wife. The man answered that she was well, and then found out that throughout the entire ten years, Rabbi Leibowitz had not stopped praying for his wife's well-being.

A wealthy Jew once visited the Leipniker Rav and proposed a match between his son and the rabbi's daughter. The rich man then noticed that the rabbi looked upset. "A child in this town is dangerously ill, and I am worried about him," explained the rabbi.

"But why are you so worried about a strange child?" asked the visitor. Upon hearing this question, the rabbi decided that his daughter would not marry into this man's family. Anyone coming from a family that showed so little concern for others could not be a desirable match.

Such qualities of *chesed* we should aspire to for ourselves and encourage in our own families.[13]

## ⰘNOT EMBARRASSING OTHERS

We saw earlier how Rachel demonstrated utter selflessness by sparing her sister Leah embarrassment at the marriage their father had arranged. She might have lost her own chance to marry Jacob, but her sister's honor came first.

Another example is that of an ancient rabbi known as Mar Ukva. One of the great Sages among the Jews in Babylonia, he was occupied not only with Torah study but also with dispensing charity in his community. He wanted to ensure that no poor person should have to be embarrassed by accepting charity, so he distributed it secretly, leaving it in a crack in the door or wherever else it would be sure to be found by the needy individual. The poor person and his family never knew who left the money, and could direct their thanks only to G-d, as Mar Ukva wanted.

One day, Mar Ukva's wife came to meet him at the yeshivah, and the two went home together in the evening. On their way, Mar Ukva secretly dropped off money at several homes. At one particular house, the recipient was most curious to find out who his benefactor was, so he was standing watch at the door when they came down the road. As he approached, Mar Ukva realized someone was watching at the door, so he and his wife quickly ran away. The man began running after them, and the only place

---

13. Talmud *Yevamos* 79.

they could find to hide was a public baker's oven. Although the oven was empty and the fire was out, the bricks of the oven floor were still very hot, and Mar Ukva burned the soles of his feet. His wife's feet were not affected by the heat, so she told him to put his feet on hers. There, they stayed for awhile until they considered it safe to return home without being seen by the poor man.

Mar Ukva wondered why his wife merited to be protected from the heat, but not he. She explained, "The charity I do is of greater benefit than yours. You give a needy person money to buy food, while I provide him with a prepared meal." Both, of course, were to be greatly praised, for they went to great lengths to avoid embarrassing a poor person.

At the elegant Passover *Seder* of the great 19th century scholar Rabbi Akiva Eiger, one of his guests accidentally spilled some wine onto the tablecloth. Noticing the man's embarrassment, Rabbi Eiger discreetly shook the table so that his cup of wine also tumbled over. "Something must be wrong with the table. It's not standing properly," Rabbi Eiger commented. In that way, he immediately dissolved the guest's shame.

## ᵉ§AVOIDING EVIL SPEECH

Our love for others must extend beyond our actions to include the way we speak to and about people. Speaking negatively about another person is considered a most heinous act.[14] The Torah states, "You shall not go up and down as a talebearer among your people; neither shall you stand idly by the blood of your neighbor; I am the Lord" (*Leviticus* 19:16). The parallel commandments virtually equate slander with being an accomplice in murder!

Our Sages have said that *lashon hara,* speaking negatively about people, actually causes more harm than a physical assault on the person. Granted, a person who has been hurt physically

---

14. Talmud *Avodah Zarah* 19b; Mishnah *Eruchin* 15.

feels pain, but it usually subsides in a short while. A disparaging remark, however, can linger on to haunt the victim for years. Someone who makes a stray comment that a prospective job applicant looks untrustworthy can cost him not only his job, but other jobs as well. Word spreads very easily, especially if it seems to be a bit of juicy gossip. Speaking evil can be compared to opening a bag of feathers on a windy day. Even if one wanted to gather them all back, one could not because they have been dispersed afar by the wind.

In addition, gossip and slander hurt anyone who hears them, and they harm the speaker as well. Casual comments that we hear can affect our perception of the person talked about for a long time to come. How true is the saying, "If it were not for the listeners, slander and gossip would not exist!"

In the Torah, we read the story of the ten spies (out of twelve) who spoke ill of the Holy Land. Because of their *lashon hara* about the Land of Israel, and because the people listened and believed their negative report, the entire people was punished by not being allowed to enter the land for forty years. The adult males, except for Caleb and Joshua, all died before entering the land. A Talmudic sage pointed out that if they, who sinned only with respect to the land, were punished so severely, how much more will a person suffer who speaks evil about his fellow man.

Further, the Torah alludes to a punishment for speaking *lashon hara,* namely, an ailment called *tzaraas* whose symptoms were similar to leprosy. The person with this ailment had to be kept in quarantine apart from the rest of society. While this disease no longer occurs, the symbolism is clear: Those who speak evil about others believe they are gaining status for themselves by belittling their fellow man, in effect causing him to be shunned. The punishment is *midah k'neged midah,* "measure for measure," that the speaker of *lashon hara* must himself be isolated from society, thus experiencing the shame and loneliness of the victim of his gossip.

The great Talmudic sage Rabbi Yannai once observed a peddler striding through town chanting, "Who wants to buy the elixir of life? Who wants to buy the secret of long life?" Rabbi Yannai approached him and asked him to reveal his secret potion for a lengthy existence. The peddler refused, but Rabbi Yannai persisted. Finally, the peddler responded, "You do not need any special potions. The key to a long happy life is contained in our holy books, which state, 'Who is the man who desires life? . . . Guard your tongue from evil!' " (*Psalms* 34).

Rabbi Yannai turned to his companions and said, "I did not fully understand the meaning of the verse until now. The peddler brought it to my attention that avoiding *lashon hara* is itself a remedy for the torments of life. If one keeps away from speaking ill of others, from animosity and arguments, one has a better chance of living a calmer, more peaceful, therefore longer life. That, indeed, is the elixir of life!"

Because of the importance of this aspect of ethics, we have a number of laws concerning *lashon hara*. "You shall not go about as a talebearer," mentioned above, forbids speaking evil. "You shall not accept a false report" (*Exodus* 23:1) tells us not to accept derogatory information about others. We are not to listen to *lashon hara* or to another form known as *rechilus*, a report that someone spoke or acted against us. The prohibition against listening includes even the situation where we do not intend to believe what is said.

If we inadvertently hear *lashon hara*, we are forbidden to believe it is true. Only when it is essential to know derogatory information for a practical, constructive purpose is one permitted to listen to it. For example, if we need to correct a person under our instruction (such as one of our children), if we wish to hire a worker and are asking for a recommendation, or if we are inquiring about a marriage prospect, we may listen. But even then, we cannot accept what we hear as absolute truth; we must exercise caution.

The reason that merely listening to *lashon hara*, without believing it, is harmful, is that it encourages the speaker to continue relating derogatory information. If a speaker of *lashon hara* sees that he has an audience, he will continue to malign others. On the other hand, if his reports are met with a statement like, "I don't want to hear what I didn't see myself," or even with a look of displeasure, it may help him resist the temptation to continue.

*Rechilus,* a report that someone has spoken or acted against you, is the cause of many disputes. When we accept such a report, it is very difficult not to bear a grudge or even quarrel with the alleged defamer. This can engender hatred and enmity that is very difficult to dissolve.

The Chofetz Chaim was legendary for his efforts to avoid and prevent *lashon hara;* he wrote important books and essays on the topic. He once paid a visit to a prospective supporter of his academy. When he arrived, the man, a wealthy business-man, was in the midst of preparing a telegram to his business partner. He rose to greet the Chofetz Chaim and engaged him in a conversation. Soon the Chofetz Chaim recognized that the talk was focusing on a certain individual, and gossip might ensue. He suddenly arose and glanced at the telegram on the man's desk.

"It looks as though you had carefully thought out every single word here," he commented, "for you have rewritten this several times."

"I certainly have," said the man. "Every unnecessary word here will cost me extra money."

The Chofetz Chaim marveled at this. "If only everyone were as careful as this when choosing what to say! Don't they know that every unnecessary word they speak will cost them dearly in the World to Come?"

Once the Chofetz Chaim was traveling in a wagon with horse traders. During the trip, his companions talked on and on about horses and cattle. Then, in the middle of their conversation, one of the travelers began speaking about another dealer. The Chofetz Chaim reprimanded them for speaking and listening to *lashon hara,* and asked them to go back to discussing animals rather than people. They paid no attention. So he asked the wagon driver to stop, and he got off in the middle of the road. It pained him more to listen to evil gossip than to make the long journey on foot.

# ⌁ADMONISHING YOUR NEIGHBOR

It is easy to understand that "Love your neighbor as yourself" involves treating other human beings with great respect. More difficult is the concept that this commandment also involves telling a person when he has acted improperly. Yet, when we love a person, we want to keep him away from harm. Admonishing a friend, when it is done in an appropriate way, can lead to the same result. We can thereby help our friends avoid sorrow and save them from grave danger.

If a group of people are sitting in a rowboat and one starts drilling a hole under his seat, the others' failure to stop him will cause them all to drown. Similarly, if we see a Jew committing a transgression and we make no attempt to stop him, we also bear responsibility, not only for him but for ourselves and the whole people. Thus the Chofetz Chaim used to say, "If I knew that by falling down before a man's feet and kissing his dirty shoes, I could help him to repent, I would gladly do so. How could the cleanliness of my mouth compare to the importance of a Jew fulfilling his duty?"

The Jewish nation is compared to the Torah. Just as a Torah scroll is rendered unusable if it is missing even one letter, so too, if even a few Jews abandon their faith, it makes the nation incomplete. We are meant to be united, and we must try to persuade our brothers and sisters to join together with us. Similarly, we must never consider any Jew permanently lost.

Yet this *mitzvah* is a very delicate one. Criticizing others when we are angry, or when we have obvious benefit from getting them to change, will accomplish nothing. We must have a relationship with a person before that person will listen to us, so acceptance and patience are the first steps.

Rabbi Shimon ben Lakish, also known as Resh Lakish, started out his adult life in the company of robbers. Rabbi Yochanan once met and befriended him. Shimon ben Lakish had enormous physical strength, but Rabbi Yochanan had the depth of perception to see beyond the physical, and believed that Shimon's strength might be utilized for greatness in Torah. In a friendly manner,

Rabbi Yochanan made every effort to arouse Shimon's interest. In the end, Resh Lakish devoted his life to Torah and married Rabbi Yochanan's sister. He attained prominence as one of the greatest Talmudic scholars.[15]

The Chofetz Chaim was well aware of the delicacy of this *mitzvah*. He once arrived at an inn where he noticed at one table a Jew without a *yarmulka,* gulping down his food without reciting any blessings. The Chofetz Chaim inquired as to his identity, and was told that this was a Jew who had been forcibly taken into the Czar's army as a teenager and who had now been in the army for over twenty years. Indeed, the innkeeper warned the Chofetz Chaim not to approach the man, for he was known to be a rough sort and might turn violent at a moment's notice.

Nevertheless, the sage walked over to him. "You are Jewish?" The man looked at him suspiciously and nodded. "Is it true that you have been in the Czar's army for more than twenty years?" he asked. The man nodded again. "In that case," continued the Chofetz Chaim, "I have the greatest respect for you. You are on a much higher level than the rest of us, for you have faced much greater challenges than we, but you have still remembered that you are a Jew."

The man listened to these words in amazement. He knew this man was the greatest Jewish leader of Europe, and here he was coming not to condemn him but actually to praise him! The Chofetz Chaim then went on, "Imagine how much greater you could yet become if you also kept the *mitzvos!*" Because of these gentle, friendly words, the man became a *baal teshuvah,* one who returned to the practice of Judaism.

## ◄§ NOT SEEKING REVENGE

The Torah states that not only are we forbidden to seek revenge, but also, if given the choice to help a friend or a foe, we must help our enemy first. When you aid someone you dislike,

---

15. Talmud *Bava Metzia* 84.

your actions will have a positive effect on your feelings.

A story is told of two wagon drivers who had quarreled and become bitter enemies. The two were once walking along the same road when the animal of one of them suddenly collapsed under its burden. The other wagon driver walked on until his conscience bothered him and he asked himself, "Isn't it written in the Torah, 'If you see the animal of your enemy lying under its burden, you should help him'?" (*Exodus* 23:5). He returned and helped the other man unload. In their common effort, they began speaking to each other and were reconciled. Moreover, the other man began to think, "I thought of him as an enemy, but look how he had pity on me!" The two became close friends.

What caused friendship and love to flourish between two former enemies? One fulfilled a precept in the Torah, which at first glance might have seemed unreasonable.

The Torah states, "You shall not take vengeance nor bear any grudge against the sons of your own people" (*Leviticus* 19:18). All forms of vengeance and spite are forbidden. We are asked not only to abstain from vengeance but to do positive actions for our enemies as well. As the Torah says, "You shall love your neighbor as yourself" – without discrimination or revenge (*Leviticus* 19:18).

# ✑ GRATITUDE

G ratitude is a pillar of human society. Being grateful is a way of rewarding those who have aided him and demonstrating that one does not take help for granted.[16] Too many individuals simply expect assistance from their parents, teachers, and friends. Many also demand things from others as a matter of course and do not bother to thank them when assistance is given. If we would stop and think of all the favors we are receiving, the care and sustenance provided by parents, the wisdom imparted by teachers, the kindness shown by friends, we would better be able to change our uncaring attitudes.

---

16. Rabbi Bachaya Ibn Pekudai, *Duties of the Heart (Shaar Avodas Elokim )*.

Rabbi Levi Yitzchak of Berditchev, a Chassidic rebbe of the 19th century, made his feelings of gratitude very clear. When he arrived at a small town one evening, he found himself without lodging. He was forced to trudge from house to house seeking shelter. However, no one knew who he was, and he was turned away many times. When finally, he came to a rather run-down residence at the end of town, the rabbi was not too optimistic about being accepted there either. Nevertheless, he knocked at the door and repeated his request for a night's lodging.

"Well, I am only a poor man with few furnishings," was the reply. "But if you don't mind staying in a poor man's home, it would be an honor for me to welcome you." Rabbi Levi gladly accepted the invitation and thanked the man profusely when he left the next day.

Some years later, when Rabbi Levi Yitzchak had become known far and wide as a saintly sage, he again paid a visit to that town. The inhabitants were now aware of his identity and fame, and they gathered to compete for the honor of having the Torah leader stay with them. But Rabbi Levi shook his head. "I will stay with the poor man at the edge of town, if he will allow me," he announced. "He took me in the last time, and to him I must express my everlasting gratitude. Once someone performs a favor for you, you must never forget it."

## ⇜ HONORING ONE SPARENTS

The fifth of the Ten Commandments says, "Honor your father and mother, that your days may be prolonged upon the land that the Lord your G-d gives you" (*Exodus* 20:12). The reward for honoring parents is given both in this world and in the World to Come.[17] On first glance, it would appear that honoring one's parents is another example of gratitude. Certainly, it includes gratitude; but it is also much more.

The Ten Commandments are divided into two groups. The first

---

17. *Mishnah Peah* 1:10.

five comprise laws of relationships between humans and G-d, and the second five are laws of relationships between human beings. The dichotomy is clear cut in all but one case, namely, that the commandment to honor one's parents is in the first group. Why is this? The answer is that whoever honors his parents honors G-d, because the honor of parents indicates a willingness to accept authority beyond oneself, to honor one's heritage, and to respect the source of life. Even if one has no explicit reason to be grateful to one's parents, one is still obligated to honor them. For example, in a case where a person was given over for adoption, if he later meets his birth parents, he has obligations to honor them just as much as if he had been raised by them.

The story of Damah, a young non-Jewish man, illustrates the lengths one should go in order to practice *kibbud av va'eim* (honoring one's father and mother). Damah had a precious diamond which he kept under his pillow for its protection. One day, while his father was asleep, some businessmen came to Damah's house and asked to buy the diamond. Damah replied that he could not obtain it, for to do so would mean disturbing his father and possibly waking him. The men did not believe this excuse, and thought it was just a ploy to get a higher offer. So they offered greater and greater sums of money, but despite his own personal loss, Damah still refused. Finally the men left, and Damah had lost his chance to make a fortune. Yet, for his devotion to his father, Damah received a just reward. Within his herd was born a *parah adumah,* a completely red cow, needed by Jews for purification ceremonies in the time of the Holy Temple. Such a red cow was extremely rare, and Damah was able to sell it at a very high price.

In addition, Damah's mother had emotional problems, and used to yell and spit at him in public for no apparent reason. Although he was greatly embarrassed by her actions, he did not speak to her harshly. She was, after all, his mother, and he treated her royally despite the hardships she caused him.[18] Clearly, the Talmud tells these stories in order to say that if

---

18. Talmud *Kiddushin* 31.

Damah could show such concern for his parents, we should also.

Many stories are told of how our Sages honored their parents. One day Rabbi Avahu asked his son, Rabbi Avimi, to get him some water to drink. Rabbi Avimi returned with the water, but in the meantime his father had fallen asleep. He stood next to his father with the water in his hand until his father awoke.[19]

We should serve our parents cheerfully. If we can make their lives more pleasant, we are honoring them. On the other hand, if we serve them physically but our behavior is inappropriate, we are not really fulfilling the *mitzvah*. The Sages said, "One person can feed his father fine foods and yet incur terrible sins, while another can make his father grind millstones and yet merit great rewards."

How can this be? The Talmud tells the stories: A certain person used to serve his father fattened chickens. When his father once asked, "My son, where are these from?" the son angrily replied, "Eat, you old fogey! Eat and be quiet!" On the other hand, the story is told of a king who summoned the millers of the land to come work for him. One young man took pity on his elderly father and said, "Father, it is better that you go where I am working and grind in my place, while I go to work for the king. If the king's work involves humiliation, then I shall be humiliated and not you; if it involves lashes or suffering, I shall suffer them and not you!" He made his father grind at millstones, yet he merited Paradise![20]

A man once came to Rabbi Chaim Soloveitchik of Brisk with the following question: His father had become ill in a distant city, and he felt obligated to visit him. However, since the laws of *kibbud av va'eim* (honoring one's father and mother) do not require a person to spend his own money to honor his father, and the train trip would cost money, was he still obligated to go? Rav Chaim's sharp reply was, "True, you aren't obligated to spend your own money on a train. Walk!"

When Rabbi Leib of Kelm was a young man, he once came home very late at night from the yeshivah where he had been

19. Ibid.
20. Talmud *Kiddushin* 31.

studying. His parents were already sleeping, and he did not have a key with him. In order not to awaken them, he remained in the street all night despite the cold.

Fortunately, most of us do not have to go to such extremes most of the time to honor our parents. These stories nevertheless help us remember how important the *mitzvah* of honoring parents is, and how deeply rooted it is in Jewish tradition.

We do have to remember that we must always treat our parents with respect. We may not openly contradict our parents. Even if they become senile, physically handicapped, or mentally disturbed, we are not permitted to treat them disrespectfully.[21] It is a grave sin for someone to curse his parents or hurt them in any way. If a child cannot afford to support his needy parents, he must still show them proper respect and do everything possible to ease their burdens. Even after their death, we show them respect. That is one of the reasons for saying *Kaddish* and respecting the mourning periods (see below, Chapter 14). The link between generations is sacred, for it is one of the ways we are connected to G-d. Honoring parents is a way of affirming that link and connection.

## ৶ HUMILITY

B esides the *mitzvos* that have to do with how we treat others, we also have obligations toward ourselves. Two of the crucial traits in a person who aspires to a spiritual life are humility and integrity. Both have to do with being authentic, both in recognizing one's limitations and in expressing one's best self — the Divine spark within.

The person in Jewish tradition most honored for humility is Moses. Many people might have wanted to be appointed as leader over a whole people being chosen by G-d, but Moses declined several times before he finally agreed. He actually believed he was not worthy of the honor and that others could fill the post better than he. However, it was this very quality, humility and

---

21. Talmud Yerushalmi, *Peah* 1:1.

lack of arrogance, that G-d decided made him qualified to be the leader of Israel.

When the Almighty spoke to Moses for the first time, He did not appear on the lofty peaks of a mountain. Rather, He spoke to Moses from out of a thornbush, a seemingly insignificant creation. In that way, G-d demonstrated that even the lowliest of creations can miraculously become inflamed with Divine sparks. The lesson is that even the humblest of men can make history if he is filled with G-d's holy spirit. In addition, this demonstrated G-d's empathy with the Children of Israel, who were at that time downtrodden, suffering as lowly slaves.[22]

Similarly, the Talmud states that when G-d decided to give the Torah to the Jews, all the mountains vied with each other for the honor of being the site for the great event. Each thought itself the most fitting setting for the giving of the Torah. Only one mountain, Mount Sinai, did not make any such claim. It was a rather low mountain and felt unworthy of being chosen for greatness. Yet G-d chose this site for the transmission of the Torah, again in order to demonstrate the importance of modesty and humility.

Rabbi Akiva Eiger and Rav Yaakov of Lisa were two renowned Torah giants of the 19th century who demonstrated the quality of modesty. Once, they were traveling together to a certain town by coach. As they approached the town, they noticed a large group of Jews gathered, apparently to honor the visitors. A few people ran toward them and began pushing the coach along. Rabbi Akiva Eiger immediately assumed that the people had come to pay tribute to Rav Yaakov, so he slipped out of the coach and began pushing as well. At the same moment, Rav Yaakov came to the conclusion that the crowds had gathered to honor Rabbi Eiger, so he slipped out on the other side and began pushing. When the coach reached the crowd, the people were amazed to find the coach empty and the two Torah giants walking alongside and pushing it! Then they learned that each man had considered only the other worthy of honor. Naturally, this display of modesty by both rabbis only made the populace respect them more.

---

22. Talmud *Avodah Zarah* 20b.

P rior to the building of the Temple in Jerusalem, Jewish life revolved around the *Mishkan* or Tabernacle, which contained the Holy Ark. The Ark was constructed with a layer of gold on both the outside and the inside. This provides a lesson for every individual: Just as the Ark was golden within and without, so too should every person be righteous inwardly and outwardly. Instead of behaving one way in the glare of public life and another way in private, we should remain virtuous in all circumstances. We must practice what we preach. When we wholeheartedly mean what we say, and demonstrate this in our behavior, others will take us seriously. On the other hand, a person who puts on a display of greatness in public, then acts immorally or unjustly behind closed doors, is a hypocrite. The attempt to deceive others only leads to self-deceit as well.

The great sage, the Chofetz Chaim was renowned for never assuming a false facade. Whoever saw him knew that they were seeing his true self.

The Chofetz Chaim was especially known for avoiding *lashon hara* or slander of other people. One day the Chofetz Chaim visited a town he had never before entered. He lodged at an inn and had a lengthy conversation with the innkeeper. After over an hour of talk, the innkeeper finally asked, "Could you tell me your identity?"

The Chofetz Chaim was reluctant to give his name, for he did not want the innkeeper to go to extra trouble to serve him. He hesitated, but before he could utter a reply, the innkeeper said, "Wait — you must be the Chofetz Chaim. I have never seen you, but from what I have heard, you must be he, for we have talked for a very long time and you have not said even a hint of a bad word about anyone."

A Torah sage is indeed characterized, and can often be identified, by his great deeds and character. As we saw earlier, the Chofetz Chaim embodied the concept of brotherhood for his fellow Jews, closing his store early so that other businessmen could also prosper. If someone overpaid him, he would make every possible attempt to repay the person.

Although we must do everything possible to avoid hypocrisy, we should not use this as an excuse to avoid doing positive and worthwhile things. For example, some parents do not send their children to schools with strong Jewish curricula, arguing that because they are not religious at home, they feel it would be hypocritical to send their children to yeshivos while they are totally unobservant. (This would be like a father who refuses to hire a lifeguard to teach a child to swim because he can't swim himself.) Of course the child should receive the best Jewish education possible. The parents who give this education to their children are anything but hypocrites. They are sincere in trying to aid and satisfy their children with Jewish experiences and clear direction, even though they may have experienced obstacles to connecting with tradition in their own lives.

Another example is that people hold back from doing a *mitzvah* because they feel they cannot fulfill it completely, or might not continue to do it in the future. But this is also a misunderstanding of the idea of avoiding hypocrisy. A person is hypocritical when he does not act in accordance with firmly held beliefs. A person whose faith is still in its infancy, who has religious doubts, can still observe as much as possible in some specific areas of Judaism without being "hypocritical." By heeding the teachings of Jewish tradition, even when doubts arise, one begins the process of what will someday become a wholehearted return to G-d.

## ✍ UNITY

All people have great worth in the eyes of G-d as individuals, but a Jew counts for even more because he/she is part of the Jewish nation as a whole. That is why, when a census of Israelite men was taken in the desert, each man was required to contribute a coin of one-half shekel. Why not a whole one? The half-shekel symbolized that no individual is complete when alone. No man, and certainly no Jew, is an island. We can reach the heights of Jewish spirituality only in brotherhood, when we associate and cooperate with other Jews.[23] If we go out of our way to help others, to learn from others and to join them in positive group efforts, then we become true members of the Jewish nation. Remaining aloof, we lack in developing the fullest potential of our character.

The importance of working together with others is well illustrated in the story of a man who lost his way in a huge, dense forest and kept walking in circles. Eventually, he came upon a second person, also thrashing his way through the woods. "Can you show me the way out?" he asked.

"No, not yet," said the second man. "However, through my travels I have already found out what roads not to take. Maybe together we can find the right way." With each one offering his knowledge of the forest paths, they soon found the right way. Had they not united, each would have wandered much longer.

That is why we pray with a *minyan* (quorum). That is also why the Sages discussed legal rulings among one another, and why a Jewish court is made up of at least three men. The union of individuals makes possible a clearer direction and a greater accomplishment than does each person acting singly.

This is dramatized by the story of a father who summoned his sons to his deathbed. He handed each of them an arrow and commanded them to break the arrows. Each did so with ease. But when he gave each of them a bundle of arrows, they were unable to break any of them, despite determined efforts. "You can learn from this example that in unity there is strength," the dying father said to his children.

## ☙ THE PURSUIT OF PEACE

Aaron, the brother of Moses, has been accorded a special place of affection in the hearts of Jews. When he was alive, he was exceedingly popular; when he passed away, he was deeply

---

23. Rabbi Bachaya Ibn Pekudai, *Duties of the Heart,* Introduction.

mourned. Why? Aaron was renowned as a peacemaker, one who loved and pursued peace. He deeply desired the well-being of his fellow Jews and tried to improve their ways, not through criticism but through friendship.[24]

The Torah makes a point of stating that when Aaron died, all the congregation of Israel wept for him for thirty days, because Aaron considered it his personal mission to help settle all quarrels and do his utmost to bring peace to the congregation. Whenever he heard that two people were quarreling, he would go to one and tell him that he had recently met his friend, who had stated, "That quarrel was my fault, and I bitterly regret it." Then Aaron would go to the second person and tell him the same story. When the two would meet again, they would hug each other and forget their differences. His compassion and love of peace were indelibly stamped on the memory of the Jewish people.

Moses, too, was willing to relinquish his pride in the search for peace, even though he knew he had to maintain authority over an unruly people. When a priest named Korah led a rebellion against him, Moses himself went to search for the perpetrators and tried to placate them with words of peace. He did not wait for the rebels to come to him, but took the initiative in searching for peace without worrying about his personal honor.

If we let our pride stand in the way of peace, we are like the farmer who went every day to the barn to get milk but returned with an empty pail. "Why don't you ever bring back any milk?" his wife asked. "The only way for me to get milk," answered the farmer, "is to bend down and milk the cow, and I'd rather die than lose my pride and bend down to a cow."

Our great sages strove to emulate Aaron's trait of seeking peace. Rabbi Meir, of Talmudic times, demonstrated this by the way he settled a dispute between husband and wife. The wife was a devoted follower of his and frequently attended his Torah classes. The husband became jealous, and he insinuated that her interest was more in the rabbi than in his words. When the woman protested, her husband replied, "I will believe you only

---

24. Rav Aharon HaLevi, *Sefer HaChinuch,* in *Parashas Behar; Numbers* 20:29.

if you go to him and spit in his eye several times!"

The next time Rabbi Meir saw the woman, he noticed that she was unusually downcast. When he asked why, the woman explained the situation and told him what her husband had demanded. Rabbi Meir nodded that he understood.

At the next class, Rabbi Meir approached her and said, "There is something wrong with my eye. If you spit in it several times, perhaps it will get better." The woman was shocked, but complied, in full view of others. Word of this reached the husband, and he was satisfied that his wife was doing nothing wrong. Their quarrel was settled. Rabbi Meir was most pleased. His dignity may have suffered, but he had achieved his goal.

Once two Jews came before a rabbi and requested that he resolve their dispute. They had both purchased burial plots in the same area of the cemetery, and with the exact locations unclear, they were vying for the more beautiful spot. After listening to the claims of each, the rabbi announced his decision: "Both of you have valid claims. Therefore, I say that the more beautiful spot will go to the one who dies first." There was a long silence, and from that moment on the men stopped arguing about the burial plot.

We must use all our resources to bring about peace. "The Master of Peace desires the peace of all His creations."

# 9

---

## Your Money or Your Life

---

Acts of kindness are one aspect of a Jewish ethical life. Another important set of *mitzvos bein adam lachaveiro* (commandments between a person and his/her friend) comprises acts of justice and honesty. Many of the commandments of the Torah are intended to foster a society based on justice and righteousness. We must fight for the poor, the widowed, and the orphan. The emphasis on justice is applied not only to obvious areas such as fair trials, use of proper weights and measures, and honest business practices. It also deals with the obligations of employer and employee, and the responsibilities of society to the less fortunate. As the Torah teaches with emphasis, "Justice, *justice* shall you pursue" (*Deuteronomy* 16:20). Why, ask our Rabbis, is the word "justice" written twice? To teach us that we must practice justice at all times, toward all people, whether it be for our profit or for our loss.

# ๛ GIVING TO CHARITY

The Torah states quite emphatically and at length the prescription for charity:

> If there be among you a needy man, any one of your brethren within any of your gates in the land which the Lord your G-d gives you, you shall not harden your heart, nor shut your hand to him. You shall surely lend him sufficient for his need. You shall surely give him, and you shall not give him with ill grace. Because of this thing, the Lord your G-d will bless you in all your work and in all to which you put your hand (*Deuteronomy* 25:2-8, 10).

Clearly, there is an important positive *mitzvah* to give charitably and to lend money to help the needy. The word for charity, *tzedakah*, also means "righteousness." It is not a matter of pity on the poor, but, rather, a matter of adjusting the balance of monetary resources so that the society becomes fairer, just, and righteous.

The Rambam lists eight levels of *tzedakah*. Among them are the following:

1) The highest level of *tzedakah* is making someone self-sufficient so that he no longer has to go begging or be a financial burden on the community. This can be done by lending him money to establish himself in business, finding him a job, or taking him into one's own business.

2) The second level is giving money without knowing to whom one is giving, and without the recipient knowing from whom he is receiving. This is done by giving money through an intermediary, such as a charity collector in a synagogue.

3) The third level is when the donor knows to whom he gives but the recipient does not know from whom he receives, as in sending money anonymously.

We must develop the quality of being happy when giving *tzedakah*. We are to do it in a way that causes the recipient the least amount of embarrassment and the greatest amount of happiness at the same time. Even if we do not have money to give when we are approached, we should still comfort the poor person with words, for the Talmud says that giving comfort is even greater than giving *tzedakah*.[1] Better yet, of course, is to give both.

One should give at least one tenth of his income to *tzedakah*. This is known as *maaser*. A person must be careful to give within his means, not impoverishing himself to the point he has to depend on others. However, even a poor person has a responsibility to give *tzedakah*.

It is a custom with great merit to give charity in memory of a deceased person. The influence of this *mitzvah* has positive effects not only on the donor but also on the soul of the departed. In particular, this act signifies that their memory is still having an effect on earth.

Some of the most important forms of charity include helping poor brides and the sick, supporting children who learn Torah, and supporting adults who study Torah. When both a man and a woman request assistance, one must first give to the woman because it is more difficult for her to go collecting. The same applies when giving to help poor orphans get married — first to the orphaned bride, then to the orphaned groom.

If a poor person simply requests food to eat, we should give it immediately without asking questions. However, if he requests additional assistance or a specific amount of money, we have the right to inquire into his circumstances and determine the nature of his need.

When you pledge to give *tzedakah*, make sure to give it right away, for not fulfilling one's pledge is a very grave sin. Particularly in this case, when people in need are depending on it, it is very important.

A person should do all in his power to avoid having to ask for charity, even if this means taking a job that he may feel is beneath his dignity.

The book of *Proverbs* states that the merit of the *mitzvah* of

---

1. Talmud *Bava Basra* 9b.

charity has the power to save a person from death (*Proverbs* 10:2). "Charity lengthens the days and years of man," say our Sages.[2] The Talmud cites two incidents that support this statement:

The great sage Shmuel once observed a workman carrying boxes. Suddenly, the top box fell down, and out fell a venomous snake — a dead one. Had the snake been alive, the workman would most certainly have been bitten and died. Shmuel asked the man what he had done to deserve being saved, but he had no answer. Later, however, Shmuel discovered that when the food supply had been short, this workman had willingly given up his own portion of food to give to someone who had none.

A man known as Benjamin the Virtuous was in charge of the public charity chest. One year, when a drought plagued the town, a woman came to him and begged for help. Benjamin felt sorry for her, but there was no money left. The woman cried in desperation, "If you don't help me, a woman and her seven children will surely die." Even though he was very poor himself, Benjamin gave her money from his own pocket.

Some time later, Benjamin was seriously ill and the doctors had given up hope for his recovery. Benjamin's friends prayed fervently to the Almighty and exclaimed, "Lord of the Universe! You have said that whoever saves one life is regarded as if he saved the entire world. Should then this virtuous and kind-hearted man, who saved the lives of a woman and seven children, die in the prime of his life?" The sentence of death was annulled on high, and Benjamin lived twenty-two more years.[3]

The point of the stories is that the workman and Benjamin gave wholeheartedly without thought of reward. When they were in need, G-d responded. We cannot do the accounting for G-d, however, and figure out how much charity will give us a certain reward. We should simply remember that whenever a person is sick or in trouble, it is good to give charity on their behalf. Even better is to give charity generously before one is in need; it is like a savings account in the spiritual realm.

---

2. *Tanna D'vei Eliyahu Zuta* 1.

3. Talmud *Shabbos* 156b; *Bava Basra* 11a.

# ◈ THE GREAT MITZVAH OF REDEEMING CAPTIVES

The greatest form of *tzedakah* and one of the greatest of all *mitzvos* is known as *pidyon shevuyim*, the redemption of Jews who are captives. Even if one has bought bricks to build a synagogue, one can sell them to raise money for this *mitzvah*. According to the Rambam, it takes precedence even over supporting and clothing poor people. A captive may be suffering not only from hunger and thirst but also all kinds of indignities. He lives with mental anguish all the time, not knowing whether he will live or die, and often not knowing what is happening to those he loves.

If a person ignores the plight of a Jewish captive he has heard about, and makes no effort to redeem him, he transgresses many negative *mitzvos*: "You should not close your heart." "You should not close your hand." "You should not stand by the blood of your neighbor." "You should not have hardness in your eyes." In addition, he is failing to do positive *mitzvos* including, "Open your hand to him," "Your brother should live with you," "You shall love your neighbor as yourself," and many others.

One limitation on performing this commandment is given, namely that one should not pay an exorbitant ransom, since this would encourage non-Jews to hold Jews for ransom.[4] The Maharam of Rottenberg is noted for refusing to allow the Jewish community to ransom him from prison for this very reason.

When more than one captive is involved, the ransom of women takes precedence over that of men, unless there are special mitigating circumstances.

There are a number of notable rescues of captives in Jewish history. For example, Rabbi Yeshoshua ben Chananya, one of the great sages mentioned in the Mishnah, once was visiting a large Roman city to plead the cause of his people. He was told that

---

4. Talmud *Gittin* 45.

within the city's prison was a beautiful, black-eyed, curly-haired Jewish boy who was about to be sold as a slave to a lascivious Roman. The rabbi went to speak to the boy. He began with a verse from the prophet Isaiah, "Who gave Jacob to the looters and Israel to the robbers?" The boy responded with the second half of the verse, "It is G-d, against Whom we have sinned, refusing to follow in His ways and obey His teachings" (*Isaiah* 42:24).

When Rabbi Yehoshua heard this, he remarked, "I feel certain that this boy is destined to be a great teacher in Israel. I swear I will not leave this city until I have ransomed him, no matter what amount of money is asked." He did gather the funds to rescue the boy and brought him back to Israel where he was able to learn Torah. In time, he became the renowned Rabbi Yishmael ben Elisha, mentioned in the Mishnah as the pupil of his savior, Rabbi Yehoshua, and Rabbi Eliezer ben Hyrcanus.

Many years ago, on the day before Yom Kippur, one of the wealthy men of the city of Brisk lost his fortune and was thrown into prison by his creditors. They announced that they would not release him until they were repaid 5000 rubles. When Reb Chaim, the Rav of Brisk, heard what had happened, he became deeply concerned. When the Jews gathered in the shul to recite *Kol Nidrei* on Yom Kippur eve, the Rav suddenly ascended the pulpit.

"We cannot begin," he announced. A hush spread like a wave over the participants. "One of our men is missing tonight. He is being held captive because he could not pay 5000 rubles. How can we expect the Almighty to have mercy on us, if we do not show mercy on our brother?" The members of the congregation responded warmly, pledging large sums of money to brought in immediately after Yom Kippur. Then Reb Chaim called out to his congregation, "Now I am certain that G-d will respond to our needs, for we have responded to the needs of our brother. Let us begin *Kol Nidrei*!"

A captive need not be only a person held within the walls of a prison. If Jews are prohibited from practicing their religion and also from leaving the place where the prohibitions are in force, the rabbinical authorities may rule that they are captives. In the late 20th century, when Jews in the former Soviet Union were prevented from Torah study and also denied exit visas, many *poskim* ruled that they were captives needing redemption. This put the issue of freedom for Soviet Jews at the top of the worldwide Jewish agenda, and set in motion the processes that helped many of our brothers and sisters emigrate to Israel.

## ◈ LENDING MONEY

It is a positive commandment, incumbent upon both men and women at all times, to lend money to a fellow Jew: "You shall loan My nation money" (*Exodus* 22:24). The Torah does not specify the amount. The Talmud comments, "He who loves his neighbors and lends money to the poor when they need it, the Torah says of him, 'You call and G-d answers.' "[5]

Of course, it is very important that the individual who borrows makes sure to repay the loan. A person is called wicked when he borrows and has no intention of paying back. *Pirkei Avos* refers to such a person as having an "evil eye."[6] When a person borrows from another, it is like borrowing from G-d.

When lending money to another, it is best to do so in the presence of witnesses or upon receipt of a signed document.

The Torah forbids taking interest on a loan from another Jew. Once the Chasam Sofer lent a neighbor a large sum of money for a business venture. The man's investment went well, and he repaid the loan very quickly. To show his appreciation for the favor the Chasam Sofer had done for him, he presented him with a sparkling diamond.

The Chasam Sofer held the diamond in his hand and expressed amazement at its brilliance. He held it to the light and examined it carefully. Then he thanked the man profusely and returned it to him.

"What's wrong?" asked the man. "Does the diamond have a flaw?"

---

5. Talmud *Yevamos* 63.
6. *Pirkei Avos* 2:13.

"Not at all," said the Chasam Sofer. "It is perfect. But if I kept it, I would be flawed, for I would be taking interest for my loan."

"All right," said the man. "But I don't understand. If you intended to return the diamond, why did you examine it so carefully?"

The Chasam Sofer smiled and responded, "I looked at the stone to admire its beauty and greatness. But, ah, how much greater is the *mitzvah* of not taking interest!"

The commandment to lend money includes lending to both rich and poor,[7] but lending to a poor person takes precedence. If many people are asking for small loans, and one person asks for a large loan, it is preferable to lend small amounts to the larger number of people. One fulfills a separate *mitzvah* for each loan. However, if the large loan to a single individual will save him from financial collapse, his loan takes precedence, for his continuing to do business has the potential to provide support for many, and also saves him from being a greater burden to the community.

The amount and duration of the loan depends on one's financial capabilities as a lender. The wealthier a person is, the more money he should lend to others. Even if a person cannot lend large sums, he still must fulfill the *mitzvah* to the extent possible for him. It is common for a person to rationalize that he is not obligated to make loans because he is not wealthy. To this the Chofetz Chaim responded, "How would one react if some-one offered him a chance to buy something that was a once-in-a-lifetime opportunity to gain wealth? Would he decline, saying that this is something for the rich? Certainly not!" The implication is that doing this *mitzvah* can be a once-in-a-lifetime opportunity for spiritual riches; certainly we should do it to the best of our abilities.

Even the Torah scholar constantly engaged in study must interrupt to do the business of granting a loan, if no one else is able or willing.[8] In the Chofetz Chaim's yeshivah in Radin, the

7. Chofetz Chaim, *Ahavas Chesed* 1:1.
8. Chofetz Chaim, *Ahavas Chesed* 1:1; Talmud *Moed Katan* 10b.

students ran an interest-free loan fund. The Chofetz Chaim once asked one of his very diligent students to serve as head of the fund. The student politely refused, explaining that his desire to study Torah was so strong that he did not have time to spend on running the fund. The Chofetz Chaim took out a volume of the Talmud and showed the student the descriptions of two sages, Rabbah and Abaye, both of whom came from the family of Eli the High Priest. On that family, it was decreed that their lives would be shortened (*I Samuel* 2:3). Rabbah studied Torah and lived to the age of 40. Abaye, who devoted himself to acts of *chesed* as well as Torah study, lived to the age of 60.[9] "Through the *chesed* you perform," the Chofetz Chaim explained, "you will be rewarded with more time to study Torah."

Establishing *gemachs,* or free-loan societies, is an old Jewish custom. When Jews arrived in America from Europe, one of the first institutions to arise in each community was a Hebrew Free Loan Society. Today, there are hundreds of such organizations functioning as parts of synagogues, yeshivos, and other Jewish institutions. People donate money to the society as charity, and the society in turn lends money without interest to anyone requesting a loan. The person signs an agreement to pay back in installments as with other kinds of loans. The larger *gemachs* are almost like banks except that they are nonprofit and do not charge fees for their services. Every community should have at least one such society.

A wagon driver told the Choftetz Chaim's son the following story about his father:

> *Once, when your father was a passenger in my wagon, I asked him what I could do to earn a share in the World to Come. Your father said I should start my own gemach (free-loan fund). I laughed. "I am a poor man," I told him. But he told me that one does not need a large sum of money to start a free-loan society. If I would put aside a small amount of money every week, I would accumulate a sizable amount in a few years. I took his advice.*

---

9. Talmud *Rosh Hashanah* 18.

*The fund grew, and I began lending money to my acquaintances. Now, as the funds are repaid and the size of my capital keeps growing, I am able to lend money to an increasing number of needy people.*

The commandment to lend includes not only money, but also vessels and other utensils that can be used by another. This form of *chesed* is easy for everyone to fulfill, even a person who is not wealthy. If the item you lend will be used by the borrower to earn a livelihood, the reward for lending is even greater. Clothing *gemachs* for second-hand clothing are another organized form of *tzedakah* in many communities; furniture *gemachs* help people acquire baby furniture temporarily or loan tables and chairs for special events.

We should not refuse to lend money or articles to someone with whom we are angry. Remember, even when we do not act in accordance with G-d's wishes, and He might be "angry," He still bestows kindnesses upon us. Also, we should be certain to act friendly toward a person who wants to borrow from us, so that the person should not hesitate to borrow again.[10]

## ๙ PAYING WORKERS ON TIME

The Torah specifically obligates us to pay employees on time (*Leviticus* 9:12). Not to do so violates both a positive and a negative commandment. If you hire someone by the job (for example, a tailor, plumber, or carpenter) and he finishes the work by day, you must pay him before the upcoming sunset or at least before nightfall. If an employee is hired by the week or month, the employer must pay him before nightfall on the last day of that week or month. Even if you hire someone for only one hour, not to pay him on time is a transgression of the commandment. If you hire someone to repair something, you must pay on the day the article is returned to you.

---

10. Chofetz Chaim, *Ahavas Chesed*.

Rabbi Chaim Mendini, who lived a poor and simple life, was very meticulous about paying for any services rendered him. Once the shoemaker brought him the pair of shoes that he had repaired for him. His fee was five kopeks, but Rabbi Mendini had only a ruble, which the shoemaker could not change. "Rabbi, you can pay me tomorrow," said the shoemaker.

"Oh, no!" Rabbi Chaim protested. "The Torah says, 'Don't sleep with your worker's daily wages still in your pocket and pay them in the morning.' " He ran out to one of his neighbors and borrowed the five kopeks with which to pay the shoemaker. Although he was not required to do this since the shoemaker had agreed to wait, Rabbi Chaim nevertheless went beyond what was required.

Even if you hire a young child to do a chore — to babysit or deliver a message, for example — you must pay him on the same day he completes the chore. Because of the small sums involved, it is easy to promise a child and then forget. This is considered withholding wages even if the sum is only a few pennies.

If the employer has only part of the amount of money he owes his employee, he is obligated to pay that amount on time, even though he will be late in paying the remainder. The Rambam also explains that if the employer has already held back the wages of an employee, and thus already transgressed the commandment, he must still give the wages as soon as possible.

If you know you will not be able to pay your employee on time, you may only hire him if you tell him in advance that you will not be able to pay him on time. If the worker agrees to accept payment later, then the employer has not transgressed the prohibition.

If an employer can pay only one of two workers, he should pay the poorer of the two. If a worker is leaving on a trip and will not return until after the time he was supposed to be paid, the employer should pay him before he leaves.

To pay a worker on time is greater than giving *tzedakah* because one is giving a person a livelihood.

A Jew must always be respectful of the civil laws that protect the moral fiber of society. They help regulate relationships between human beings, encouraging truthfulness, sincerity, and kindness, while condemning immorality and deceit. It is not enough to follow laws that pertain to our relationship to G-d; we must at all times observe the laws *bein adam lachaveiro,* between man and his fellow.

Our ancestor Jacob was well known for his honesty. He made a special point of practicing it throughout his life, even in the corrupt environment of his uncle Lavan's home. When taking care of Lavan's sheep, he watched them as if they were his own and never took any for himself. Jacob was a firm believer in the statement, "Truth is the tree of life whose fruits you shall eat all your days."

Our rabbis learned from and copied this admirable trait. Rabbi Shimon ben Shetach was another great sage who demonstrated honesty in his business dealings and thereby gave religious Jews a good reputation in his day. One time, needing a donkey for his travels, he bought one from an Arab. At the time, neither he nor the seller noticed that the donkey had a small package attached to its saddle. Some time later, one of Rabbi Shimon's students found the package and opened it. He was amazed by what he found.

"It's a diamond, Rebbe!" he exclaimed. "A perfect diamond! It must be worth an enormous amount. Sell it, and you will never want for money. Imagine all the *mitzvos* you will be able to do with such riches!"

Rabbi Shimon ben Shetach shook his head. "I may be able to perform many *mitzvos* with the money, but they will never cancel the demerit I will get if I keep property that is not mine. No, I will return the diamond to the Arab, its rightful owner."

"But Rebbe," protested the student, "why not keep the diamond? The Arab will never know of his loss."

"Possibly. But G-d will know what I have done. I did not earn the diamond and so it is not mine. If one claims to be a good Jew, one must be truthful at all times." True to his word,

Rabbi Shimon returned the diamond to the Arab.

"I didn't believe that anyone could be that honest," said the Arab on receiving the diamond. "The Jews must truly have wonderful laws. Blessed be the G-d of Rabbi Shimon ben Shetach!"[11] Rabbi Shimon ben Shetach's strict adherence to the laws created a tremendous *kiddush Hashem* (sanctification of G-d's name) and can remind all of us of the importance of fulfilling G-d's laws with equal zeal.

Another story from Talmudic times of a man extremely scrupulous regarding honesty is that of Rabbi Pinchas ben Yair. Two poor men who came to seek a livelihood in his region once stopped at his house and asked him to keep a small amount of barley seeds for them. They left without reclaiming the seeds. A long period of time elapsed and still they failed to return. In their absence, Rabbi Pinchas planted the seeds separately from his own, sowed and reaped the barley year after year. He stored all the proceeds in a separate silo in the barn.

Seven years later, the two men happened to pass by Rabbi Pinchas' home and suddenly remembered the seeds they had left. "Do you happen to have the seeds?" they asked him. "If so, we'll take them along with us."

Instead of giving them a few seeds, Rabbi Pinchas led them to the barn and opened the storage bins. "It's all yours," he said to the surprised men. "Go and bring donkeys and camels, and take away your treasure." Such care for the possessions of one's fellow human being is indeed a trait to be emulated.

In modern times, a story is told of a *shochet* (ritual slaughterer of animals) who came to Rabbi Yisrael Salanter stating that he wished to change his occupation. Despite the fact that he was known as a scholarly and very pious person, he still doubted his own skills and worried whether the *shechitah* (ritual slaughtering) was done exactly according to *halachah*. When Rabbi Yisrael asked him what he intended to do instead, he replied that he would open a store and become a merchant.

"My friend, if you do that, I'm afraid you'll have even more to

___
11. Talmud Yerushalmi, *Bava Metzia* 2.

worry about. As a *shochet* you merely have to worry about slaughtering the animal properly. That you have been doing for some years. As a merchant, you will be faced with the danger of committing so many more sins connected with your work: stealing, cheating, lying, and of course, the possibility of false weights and measures.''

Many stories are told about the Chofetz Chaim's honesty and integrity. Once, in a bathhouse, the saintly Chofetz Chaim saw a person using an article that belonged to someone else. The Chofetz Chaim went over to him and whispered, ''A person who washes himself with something that does not belong to him ends up dirtier than when he started.''

He owned a small grocery store which his wife willingly took the job of managing, so that her husband could devote more time to his studies. All their customers were greatly impressed with their honesty and the high quality of their merchandise. Anything that was even partially spoiled was immediately removed from stock. All the weights and measures were accurate, and prices were set according to strict religious law. Because of the owners' integrity, the residents of Radin flocked to the store. Instead of being pleased with this success, however, the Chofetz Chaim was worried that he might be taking away business from others, so he kept the store closed in the afternoon.

The Chofetz Chaim once had to testify in a Polish court as a character witness on behalf of a student falsely accused of a crime. After he testified that the student's integrity was beyond reproach, the student's lawyer told the judge, ''I would like to give the court a glimpse of the greatness of this rabbi. A thief once stole something from him, and he pursued him, shouting, 'It is yours! I forgive you!' in order that the thief should not be guilty of sinning because of him.''

Skeptical, the judge asked the lawyer, ''Do you really believe that story?''

''I didn't personally witness it,'' replied the lawyer. ''But, Your Honor, people do not relate such stories about you and me.'' Perhaps not about us either — but such models offer us an ideal toward which we can strive.

# ~§ TELLING THE TRUTH

When a person lies, he violates the Torah prohibition, "Keep far away from a false word" (*Exodus* 23:7). The commentaries emphasize the severity of lying by equating it with idolatry. The worst form of lying, other than covering up a heinous crime, is when a person lies to cheat someone financially. Conversely, the reward for financial integrity is very great.

For example, a storekeeper is forbidden to tell a customer that an item originally cost him more than it did, in order to convince the customer of its greater value, or to suggest that he is not making much profit. He may say only, "This is my price, and I won't sell it for less."

Even when false stories do not cause anyone a loss, and are told only to make the teller appear knowledgeable or entertaining, they constitute a grave offense. Similarly, embellishing true stories with gratuitous comments that contain false information is forbidden.

The brother-in-law of Reb Simcha Zissel Ziv developed a terrible illness that caused him much pain and suffering. In the beginning, he screamed in such agony that everyone around heard it and, of course, sympathized with his suffering. Following the visit of Reb Simcha, however, he bore the pain in silence. When Reb Simcha was asked what therapy he had used, he replied, "I know of no special medication. However, when we discussed his pain and suffering, he realized that perhaps his groaning might seem to exaggerate his pain. That would be like telling a falsehood, and so he ceased moaning and groaning."

We are forbidden to promise to do someone a favor or to pledge a present if we have no intention of fulfilling the promise.[12] Even if we did not purposely intend to lie — for example, when we promise someone to do him a favor — we must be careful to fulfill the promise. If someone owes money to another, he may not tell the creditor to come and get the money on a certain day, when he

---

12. *Shulchan Aruch, Choshen Mishpat* 2:28; *Kitzur Shulchan Aruch* 63.

knows that he will still not be able to pay. Instead, he should tell the creditor the truth and ask for an extension of time.

If one pledged money for charity, he must be careful to fulfill his pledge. The consequences for not doing this can be quite severe on the person or his family.[13]

In a court case, we are not permitted to lie in order to win the dispute, even if we feel certain our claim is correct.

It is very important to teach one's children not to lie, and this means modeling the correct behavior. Our sages specifically taught that a person should never tell a child he will give him something when he really never intended to do so.[14] Keep your word to a child if at all possible. In this way, your honesty will serve as an example, and it will become the child's nature to speak the truth.

We must become accustomed to admitting, "I don't know." If a person finds it difficult to say this, he is apt to lie.[15] If we inadvertently say something untrue, we should immediately admit, "I have just told you a lie" or "No, that's not true. Let me correct what I said." Do not be embarrassed to say this; it is far better than letting the lie continue. By this means you will acquire the habit of never telling a lie.

Even our facial expressions must be honest. When we nod yes or no, the movement of the head must express the truth.[16]

If a Jew lies to a non-Jew, he not only violates the prohibition against lying, but also is causing a *chilul Hashem* or desecration of G-d's Holy Name.[17] We must remember that we are ambassadors of G-d on earth, and the way we behave affects how non-Jews will think about G-d, as well as any personal feelings they may have about us.

Among the few times it is permitted to tell an untruth are in order to save someone from harm, or to make peace between two people who are having a dispute. For example, we may tell a

---

13. Talmud *Shabbos* 32.

14. Talmud *Succah* 46b.

15. Talmud *Berachos* 4.

16. Talmud *Makkos* 23.

17. *Shulchan Aruch, Choshen Mishpat* 232.

person that a friend with whom he has quarreled is having regrets about his behavior, even if we are not certain it is true.[18]

If a person firmly resolves never to lie, it will deter him from doing wrong in other ways. Before he commits any offense, he will think to himself, "How can I do this? If I am questioned about this incident, I will be embarrassed to confess. If I deny having done it, I will have broken my resolution not to lie."

A story is told of a thief who came to a rabbi confessing that he had been involved in stealing. "But," he said to the rabbi, "I can't stop stealing. I just can't help it. I've been doing it so long, every time I have the temptation, I cannot resist."

The rabbi replied, "I understand, and I won't ask you to stop stealing. But just do one thing: Promise not to lie." The thief thought for a moment and agreed.

The next evening, he was passing by a house and saw that the side window was left open, and the house appeared to be empty. He walked over and began to climb up into the window. Then he noticed someone on the street glancing his direction. He suddenly realized that he might be questioned and, although he was good at making up stories, he remembered he had promised not to lie. He leaped down from the window and continued walking down the street.

Within a few months, the man reported to the rabbi, "I've stopped stealing, and my life is so much better. Your prescription worked — not to lie."

## ✍ RETURNING LOST OBJECTS

It is a positive commandment to return a lost object or animal and, if one avoids this *mitzvah*, one transgresses a Torah commandment. This does not apply if we find objects that are not identifiable, for example loose dollars or change. If the money is found in a wallet or sack that makes it identifiable, however, we must try to locate the owner.

---

18. Talmud *Yevamos* 64.

We must return lost objects to our enemy as well. If we are hesitant to do so because we might end up in an argument with the owner, we must still make every effort to return it — even if by a third party, if necessary — for it is said, "He who fulfills G-d's *mitzvos* will know no evil."

When we return a lost object to a non-Jew, we are making a *kiddush Hashem* (sanctification of G-d's Holy Name). It is a praiseworthy thing to do because the non-Jew will recognize that Jews are honest, and this reflects well on his opinion of the Torah as G-d's law.

The Talmud Yerushalmi relates that a Roman queen once lost some jewelry while out for a walk. Although she was fabulously wealthy, she cherished the lost necklace and bracelet more than any of her other jewelry. In an effort to regain the lost articles as soon as possible, she offered a huge reward, on condition that the jewelry was returned within thirty days. After that time, the finder would be punished by death!

A sage by the name of Rabbi Shmuel bar Susrati happened to be visiting in Rome at the time and found the queen's missing jewelry. However, instead of following the royal decree, he deliberately waited until after the thirty days had passed to return the jewelry to the queen. When he did return it, she was overjoyed to get it back. But she was puzzled by his waiting so long and asked, "Are you aware of my proclamation regarding the return of my lost jewelry?"

"Yes, Your Majesty," replied Rabbi Shmuel.

"In that case I don't understand your behavior. You stood to gain a great reward for returning the jewelry right away. Instead, by waiting until after the thirty days were up, you became liable for punishment."

"Your Majesty, allow me to explain. Had I returned the jewels as soon as I found them, people would have assumed that I did so because I wanted the reward, or because I feared your punishment. But the only reason I returned them is that in our Torah, the Lord our G-d has commanded us to return a lost article to its rightful owner."

The queen recognized that Rabbi Shmuel was an honest and

righteous man, and she said, "Blessed is the Lord, the G-d of Israel." Rabbi Shmuel bar Susrati's action created a great *kiddush Hashem*.

The Talmud Bavli relates the story of a man who was walking along, carrying some live chickens, when he realized that he was both tired and hungry. He sat down in front of a house to rest for a moment and then decided to buy something to eat. The chickens had their legs tied, and he was sure they could not wander off, so he left them in front of the house.

The man returned in a short while with his food. To his great disappointment, he could not recognize the house and yard where he had left the chickens. He wandered up and down the street, but to no avail. He returned to his poor family without the chickens they had so eagerly awaited.

Meanwhile, the wife of Rabbi Chanina ben Dosa heard cackling sounds in the yard of her house. Stepping outside, she was surprised to see some chickens. She recognized that someone must have left them there by mistake, so she brought them to her husband and asked his advice. The sage told her that they were obligated to care for the person's property until he would come to claim it.

They fed the chickens with seeds and water, but did not take the eggs. The chickens sat on their eggs and warmed them until they hatched. The chicks grew into hens and roosters and, before long, Rabbi Chanina's yard was filled with hens and roosters, cackling and crowing for their food. Rabbi Chanina realized that the burden of all these chickens was too much for him, so he sold them and bought some goats. He was able to turn the goats loose and allow them to feed themselves in the pasture.

Time passed, and the owner of the chickens happened to be in the area again. He recognized the house this time, and went in to inquire if they had ever found his chickens. "Come with me," said Rabbi Chanina, and I will show you your chickens, only they have turned into goats."

The man's gratitude to Rabbi Chanina and his wife knew no bounds. He was overwhelmed by the degree of their honesty and their fulfillment of the *mitzvah* of *hashavas aveidah,* returning lost property.[19]

> *The honesty and uprightness of Reb Aryeh Levin, a sage of 20th century Jerusalem, were legendary. As a matter of principle, he avoided borrowing money. One time, however, he was in desperate need of a loan. Since he was going to receive his monthly salary that night, he felt bold enough to ask the favor of a loan from a shopkeeper in the Machaneh Yehudah market. The shopkeeper readily loaned him the amount he requested.*
>
> *Later that day a heavy snow began to fall in Jerusalem. Reb Aryeh did not have the warm clothing and footwear needed for a long hike to the other side of the city where the storekeeper lived. When he consulted with his beloved wife Chana about what he should do, she replied, "A man must stand by his word. If you promised to return the money by this evening, you have to make the effort to repay your debt as promised."*
>
> *Reb Aryeh proceeded to trek to the far-off neighborhood of the shopkeeper. When he got to the door, he heard loud angry voices inside. The wife was yelling at the storekeeper for being foolish enough to lend money to a poor man, who would probably use the bad weather as an excuse not to repay the debt. The man replied, "Don't worry. You can trust Reb Aryeh to keep his word."*
>
> *When Reb Aryeh knocked on the door, it was a startled woman who answered, saying, "Really, Reb Aryeh! For this loan you had to walk so far in this miserable weather? Couldn't we have waited until tomorrow?"*

## ✎§ IMPARTIALITY IN JUDGMENT

In pursuit of the goal of justice, judges are commanded to be completely impartial, to remain unswayed by the identities of

---

19. Talmud *Taanis* 25.

those involved in each case, and to avoid all bribes. These rules are very strict. For example, it is forbidden for a judge to accept a gift from one of the litigants. He must refuse, even if the gift was given with no intent of swaying him, and even if he has the firm intention to judge correctly anyway.[20]

Our Sages were extremely cautious not to become judges in a court case in which they suspected they might be biased. A widow once came before Rabbi Yehoshua Kutner, crying terribly while describing how a certain person had wronged her. She pleaded with the rabbi to call that person to a rabbinical court. The rabbi apologized and explained that he could no longer get involved in this matter, since a judge had to disqualify himself if he had been bribed.

"I don't understand," replied the widow tearfully. "No one attempted to bribe you."

"There are many kinds of bribes," replied Rabbi Kutner, "including the bribe of tears. I cannot help being affected by tears, especially those of a widow like yourself."

The sage Samuel was once helped across a river by a passerby. He thanked the man and inquired as to his welfare. The latter told him that he was on his way to the local rabbinical court for a lawsuit. "I am not allowed to be your judge," replied Samuel, "since you have just helped me."

Judges are also required to be very patient in hearing out all sides of a case before passing any judgment. One such person who was extremely meticulous on this point was Rabbi Shmuel Salant, head of the rabbinical court in Jerusalem. One morning several men entered his court, assisting an obviously injured man. The victim had scars all over his face and body, and he limped noticeably. His companions said that he had been beaten by a certain man, whom they named. They demanded that the other party be brought to justice.

"I will certainly bring the assailant to justice," replied Rabbi Salant. "But first, I will send my assistant to visit the other party and see whether he is in good condition."

---

20. *Kesubos* 105.

"Why is that necessary?" the men demanded. "He should immediately be brought to trial for assault!"

Rabbi Salant was not to be rushed. "Until I see the other man, how do I know which of the two is really the victim? Perhaps the other party isn't here now because he has been too seriously injured to walk!"

Investigation revealed that the other man had indeed been the real victim in the fight, and he was the one who deserved payment of damages. Holding to the principle of not being rushed into judgment before hearing all sides had enabled Rabbi Salant to establish the truth.

# 10

――❦――

# Turning Inward: The Joy of Prayer

――❦――

## ❧ THE NATURE OF PRAYER

The other side of Jewish life is the commandments that apply to the relationship between human beings and G-d, *mitzvos bein adam lamakom*. Among these, a central one is prayer. The Torah expresses the *mitzvah* to pray simply as, "You should serve Him" (*Deuteronomy* 11:13). How does one serve G-d? our sages asked — and answered: "Through prayer." *Avodah*, the word usually translated "service," once referred to the complex system of worship at the Holy Temple in Jerusalem, with priests, sacrifices, and intricate ceremonies. This was the method of bringing human beings close to G-d. Now, the method of coming close is, simply, prayer.[1]

PRAYER IS THE PRIMARY WAY THAT WE BUILD A PERSONAL RELAtionship with the Almighty. It serves as a bulwark against our

**WHY PRAY?** existential loneliness. "Man stands bewildered, adrift in a vast universe," wrote the Chazon Ish, "and like a frightened child he calls to his father in prayer."[2] We

---

1. Talmud *Taanis* 2.
2. *Iggeres Chazon Ish*.

can learn to pour out our hearts directly before G-d, without any intermediaries.[3] No matter how important a person thinks he is, he is always welcome to communicate directly with the Creator. This is a profound way of building one's self-esteem and coming to recognize one's own purpose in life.

Although it is called service to G-d, we do not pray because G-d needs prayer.[4] G-d is Infinite and complete. But prayer gives us a chance for introspection and self-analysis, allowing us to recognize that G-d is the only One Who can and does provide us with all our needs.[5] In this way we become true "servants," humble before the Almighty and frequently thanking Him for what He grants us.

Even though prayer's great benefit rests in its effects on us, G-d does receive pleasure from our prayers. In the hour that Jews pray and praise the Lord, lifting their hearts and eyes toward heaven, the Holy One, Blessed is He, looks down on them with Divine mercy and is overjoyed to hear their voices. Like a father eager to hear his children's voices in the morning, G-d awaits our prayers and is eager to respond. Rabbi Zeira stated, "A man may have a friend who seems to love him but, as soon as he asks him a favor or needs his help, the friend turns into his enemy and rebuffs him. But the Holy One, Blessed is He, appreciates a man more when he entreats, invokes, and prays. The Lord even invites man, as it were, to pray to Him."[6]

Prayer also provides a refuge from disappointment and despair. In Mishnaic times, when Jews were often in great danger, Rabbi Yochanan and Rabbi Elazar said, "Even if a sharp sword rests upon a man's neck, he should not desist from prayer."[7] Sometimes, need or danger are brought into one's life just because G-d wants the person to come nearer to Him, so that he will pray and thus elevate and exalt his soul in sincere prayer.[8]

---

3. Talmud Yerushalmi, *Berachos* 9:1.

4. *Midrash Tehillim* 102.

5. Rav Samson Raphael Hirsch, *Horeb,* on worshipping G-d.

6. *Midrash Koheles.*

7. Talmud *Berachos* 10.

8. Rav Saadia Gaon, *Emunos V'Dei'os.*

If we do not feel we are answered, we should pray again and again, as it says in the Torah, "Hope to G-d! Be strong, let your heart take courage, and hope to G-d!"[9] As the Midrash says, every lock has a key, and every prayer is a gate to G-d that can be opened by the right approach. Happy is the person who can find the right key to every gate! But even the one who does not know how to find the proper key should not despair, but should learn from the thief. Just as the thief breaks the lock when he does not have the key, so too, we should break our hearts with humility in order to penetrate the gates of prayer.[10]

OUR SAGES HAVE DELINEATED SEVERAL KINDS OF ADDRESS TO G-D within the general category of prayer:

**TYPES OF PRAYER**

(1) **Praise:** We address G-d as Creator of heaven and earth, and declare that His Holiness and His Divine Presence exist in all parts of the universe. We acknowledge His power to do whatever He wills, and testify to His lovingkindness toward all creation.

(2) **Thanksgiving:** We thank G-d for the blessings of life and the personal blessings He grants to us: food, clothing, shelter, health, income, assistance, and our other needs. We also thank Him for what He has done for the Jewish people and the world.

(3) **Request:** Human beings have a tendency to pray in times of emergency — when they really need something. The Jewish ideal is that we should come to G-d every day with our requests, and not take our daily well-being for granted. Without G-d's constant kindness, we could not survive for a moment. And G-d wants us to ask for what we need, because then we take less for granted. Our prayers are important for peace throughout the world and especially for the Jewish people. We ask G-d to teach us to care for and pray for our fellow men, to bless us with health and happiness, and to bring us closer to Torah and Jewish ideals. We ask for the

9. Talmud *Berachos* 32b.
10. *Sanhedrin* 103a.

fulfillment of our collective ideals as well — the privilege of witnessing the return of all Jews to the Land of Israel, the coming of the Messiah, and the rebuilding of the Holy Temple.

All these types of prayer are found, woven together in a profound design, in our traditional prayer book, known as the *siddur*.

OTHER THAN THE TORAH ITSELF, THE ONE HEBREW BOOK THAT IS probably most familiar to every Jew is the *siddur*, our book of

## THE PRECIOUS SIDDUR

traditional prayers. Indeed, for many Jews, this is even more familiar than the Torah because it is so personal. The *siddur* is a priceless treasure passed down from generation to generation for more than a thousand years. It has become universal among Jews and has not been substantially changed since it was first compiled in the year 858 CE, during the Geonic period. Wherever one travels, the basic structure is essentially the same, and only a few minor differences in wording occur.

Originally, the basic blessings were composed by the *Anshei Knesses HaGedolah* (Men of the Great Assembly) in the era of the Second Temple, probably about 400 BCE. Over the centuries, other elements were added to help people bring themselves into a state of concentration and strong intent (*kavanah*) in their prayers. The prayers and blessings were considered part of the Oral Law that was not to be transcribed, so they were taught orally and memorized. However, in the ninth century CE, under the pressures of the Karaite heresy, Rav Amram Gaon saw that it was necessary to write down the prayers. The Karaites claimed that none of the traditional prayers were worthy, and that only the book of *Psalms* should be used. It appears that they encouraged the copying and distribution of *Psalms*. Jews who were not learned could be beguiled by the Karaites into ignoring the traditional prayers, especially since books were so rare in those days. If the prayers were not written down, Rav Amram Gaon ruled, they would be eclipsed and forgotten.

The word *siddur* has the same root as the word *seder* (as in

Passover *Seder*), which means "order." The prayer book arranges the prayers in a special and regular order. The table of contents of any *siddur* reveals a long list of prayers for every occasion. Those recited most often — the morning, afternoon, and evening prayers (*Shacharis, Minchah,* and *Maariv*) — are found at the beginning. Then follow the services for the Sabbath and holidays. The rest of the *siddur* is devoted to prayers for other special days, for example *Hallel,* a service of praise recited on the New Moon, Passover, Shavuos, Succos, and Chanukah. Prayers for a circumcision, for protection during travel, and blessings over meals and many other occasions can be found in the prayer book.

MOST OF THE PRAYERS ARE PHRASED IN THE COLLECTIVE "WE," emphasizing each person's membership in the Jewish nation. By

**THE LANGUAGE OF PRAYER**

learning to pray for the greater good of all, we become more deserving of a positive response to our own personal pleas.[11] By following the form of the prayer book, we also educate our desires. We learn to put our own requests in perspective, making them more intelligent and meaningful.

We usually pray in Hebrew rather than in the language of the country in which we reside. Prayer in any language is of course acceptable, and it is important that a person understand what he or she is saying.

A congregation or synagogue, however, should not deviate from praying in the sacred tongue. Our prayers link our thoughts and desires with the yearnings of Jews all over the world. By praying collectively in Hebrew, we express our desire that our prayers be "international," encompassing the entire Jewish people wherever they are. The Hebrew language unites all of us, historically, through the generations, and in all countries.[12] It ties the simplest Jew ever closer to the land of Israel where Hebrew is the spoken tongue, and it enables a Jew to feel at home in any

11. Talmud *Berachos* 30.
12. Chofetz Chaim, *Mishnah Berurah, Orach Chaim* 101.

synagogue, anywhere in the world, even if his native tongue is different from the languages which others in the congregation speak.

Historically, when a Jewish community severed its bond with the Hebrew tongue, it ultimately disappeared through assimilation and intermarriage. If one loses the ability to read and use the original Hebrew text of prayers and the Torah, one will eventually lose the understanding of Jewish concepts and values that cannot be fully conveyed in a language other than Hebrew.

Since each of us is a link to other Jews and to the generations, it is a great thing to study prayer-book Hebrew even if, for the time being, you have to pray in another language. Also, if you can begin to pray in Hebrew, do so. Don't think it is hypocritical to say some of the prayers in words you don't understand. You are educating your ear and your voice to the sounds, which will become filled with meaning later. This is also how children are taught. Adults can read the Hebrew, then study the translation, and gradually the Hebrew words will become more understandable. In any case, even when you are reading words you do not understand, you can still direct your thoughts to your Creator, our Father in heaven.

A MAN SHOULD, IF AT ALL POSSIBLE, PRAY WITH A QUORUM OF TEN adult males in a synagogue, known as a *minyan* ("number"). If

**THE CONGREGATION**

there is no synagogue where you are, one should still make an effort to pray with a *minyan* in some location. Women have the option of praying alone or in a synagogue. The importance of the *minyan* is stated in *Psalms,* where it says, "Bless G-d in full assemblies." This, our Sages explained, means ten persons who are obligated to pray at set times (i.e., men).

We should try to select a devout congregation with which to pray. The aesthetic beauty of the synagogue building is not important; what counts is how the service is conducted inside, with strong intent. The cantor should be a pious and observant Jew and a person who avoids arguments.

The significance of a *minyan* is explained in the following parable. A king was once asked to decide which of two towns deserved a certain royal privilege. Both towns sent gifts to the king to win his favor. The citizens of the first towns sent their gifts individually, at different times. As each gift arrived, the king examined it and managed to find some small fault with each one. The second town, however, sent their gifts in one shipment. When this bundle of gifts arrived, the king was at once impressed by the number of gifts and the solidarity of the people, and overlooked their individual faults. The second town, of course, won the privilege.

The meaning is clear: When we each pray separately, our flaws show more clearly. When we pray as a group, the strengths of one person make up for the weaknesses of another, and the merits of the entire group outweigh the deficiencies of the individuals.

In addition, Judaism's requirement that there be at least ten men, and the stress on daily and weekly congregational services, have meant that people choose their homes in proximity to a synagogue. At least ten families have to be within walking distance to have complete Shabbos services. This has helped counteract any tendency to scatter into isolated areas. The law thus enforces interrelationship and communal vigor: "Where there is unity there is strength."

The synagogue is referred to in traditional literature as the *beis haknesses* or house of assembly. It is a place of "gathering" for prayer. When we sit in the synagogue, G-d stands above us, for its is said, "The Eternal stands in the congregation of G-d."[13] Since many synagogues also include a place to learn Torah, the synagogue is sometimes called a *beis midrash* (house of inquiry). In addition to being a gathering place for worship, it thus promotes Jewish values. When the members are adherents of Torah, the whole congregation benefits.

Although the design of synagogue buildings can vary widely, inside every synagogue will be a Holy Ark where the scrolls of the Torah are kept. If possible, it is set on the eastern wall (in Western countries), facing toward Jerusalem, the direction toward which

---

13. Talmud *Berachos* 6a.

we pray. Next to the Ark is a *ner tamid* (eternal light) that burns continuously, reminding us of the continual light in the *Mishkan* or portable sanctuary of ancient times.

In the center is a *bimah* upon which the Torah is placed to be read. The cantor or prayer leader stands at an *amud* or platform, usually in the front. A small *menorah* or candelabrum, frequently of five branches, is usually placed on the *amud,* reminding us of the seven-branched *Menorah* in the Temple. The *ezras nashim* (women's section) follows the pattern found in the Temple. Its purpose is to prevent mixing and levity between the sexes. The *chazzan* or cantor is the emissary of the congregation to G-d, leading them in prayer, while the *shamash* or sexton attends to the many duties of organizing and maintaining the synagogue.

# ⋼ HIGHLIGHTS OF THE TRADITIONAL PRAYERS

TO BRING AN AWARENESS OF G-D INTO YOUR LIFE, IT IS A WONDERFUL practice to think of G-d the very first thing in the morning. The

**FIRST THING IN THE MORNING...**

*Shulchan Aruch* heads the entire code of Jewish law with the verse, "I have placed G-d always before me." If we think of this verse immediately on awakening, and even imagine a benevolent Divine Presence near our bed, we will have a better start for our day.

To "place G-d always before me" is a fundamental principle throughout our lives. Our Sages frequently use the comparison of the way a person acts in private versus the way he acts in the presence of a king. We can think of the ways we dress and talk in the presence of our intimate friends versus the ways we act and speak at a formal occasion. In the latter situation, we take more care with our speech and watch that our conduct be refined and correct. The Jewish ideal says that we should be careful of our words and deeds at all times, because we are always in the presence of a King, the Creator Whose Glory fills the universe.[14]

When we awaken, we immediately enter upon our "priestly" service. Here are the steps of our morning ritual:

### ■ Modeh Ani

This short prayer is recited upon awakening. It says, "I give thanks before You, Living and Everlasting King, Who has restored my soul to me in mercy; great is your faithfulness." It is a prayer of gratitude for renewing our vigor.

### ■ Netilas Yadayim (washing hands) upon awakening

When we awaken, we are like new creatures who require a purification. "They [the souls] are new every morning" (*Lamentations* 3:23). We perform this purification by washing our hands from a vessel. The Talmud bases this law on a verse in *Psalms*, "I shall wash my hands in purity and I shall march around the altar, O G-d."[15] We use a cup that is not cracked, holds at least 3.3 ounces of water, and can stand by itself. (If for some reason no such cup is available, you can use another vessel that holds enough water.)

We pour water over our hands as far up as the wrist (except for the major fast days of Yom Kippur and Tishah b'Av, when we wash only to the knuckles), as follows:

1. Pour water over each hand alternately, beginning with the right hand, three times each.

2. After washing but before drying the hands, recite the blessing, *Baruch atah . . . al netilas yadaim.*

3. Wash the face after washing *netilas yadaim.*

OTHER TIMES THAT WE WASH THE HANDS (WITHOUT A BLESSING):

❖ After using the bathroom.

❖ After cutting one's hair or nails.

❖ After touching one's shoes or a part of the body that is usually covered.

❖ After scratching one's head.

---

14. *Shulchan Aruch, Orach Chaim* 1:1.
15. Talmud *Berachos* 15.

❖ After touching insects.

❖ After being in contact with a dead body, attending a funeral, or visiting a Jewish cemetery.

❖ After taking a bath or shower or upon leaving a bath-house or *mikveh*.

■ **The Initial Prayers of *Shacharis* (the morning service)**

The morning prayers have four parts or stages:

1. A series of blessings in which we thank and praise G-d.

2. *Pesukei D'Zimrah* or "Verses of Song," mostly from the book of *Psalms* and other biblical passages. If you look in the prayer book, you will see these as the section beginning with *Baruch She'amar* ("Blessed is He Who spoke") and ending with *Yishtabach* ("May Your name be praised").

3. If you are praying with a *minyan* (quorum of ten), *half-Kaddish* comes next, followed by the congregational call to prayer known as *Barchu* ("Let us bless"), which is said by the *chazzan* or cantor with a congregational response and bow. This is followed by the blessings of *Shema* and then the *Krias Shema* (reading of the "Hear, O Israel") itself.

4. The climax is the *Amidah* or standing prayer, known on weekdays as the *Shemoneh Esrei* or Eighteen Benedictions.

Most of the prayers can be said in private or with a *minyan*. However, the *Kaddish*, the *Barchu,* and the cantor's repetition of the *Amidah* are said only if there is a *minyan*.

ONE OF THE 613 *MITZVOS* IS THE COMMANDMENT TO SAY THE *SHEMA* in the morning and in the evening. The *Shema* is made up of

**THE POWER OF THE SHEMA**

three biblical passages chosen to express our faith and allegiance to G-d and our acceptance of the *mitzvos* He gave us. In this recital, we as G-d's people fulfill one of G-d's desires, namely that we accept His leadership and proclaim His unity day and night, every day of our lives. The saying of *Shema* reinforces our sense that G-d is with us, and G-d is everywhere. It is both the primary Jewish declaration of faith and an affirmation of our obligations to G-d.

The *Shema* begins with the famous sentence, "Hear, O Israel! The Lord is our G-d, the Lord is One!" The *halachah* states that one must say this sentence, *Shema Yisrael, Ad-nai El-kenu, Ad-nai Echad,* with deep concentration. The traditional custom is to put your right hand over your eyes, to keep out distraction and intensify your inner concentration. The sentence should be said aloud, with the word *Echad* ("One") slightly elongated at the end. While saying G-d's Name, you should keep in mind that G-d was, is, and always will be the Almighty Ruler of the world, reigning over the entire universe. Rabbi Yisrael Salanter, the great 19th-century master of ethics, emphasized that in order to fulfill the commandment properly, we must not only accept G-d's dominion over the entire universe, but also over ourselves in a very personal way.

We teach our children *Krias Shema* as soon as they begin to speak, because of the all-important urgency of its message. It is one of the signatures of Jewish faith. Over the centuries, many Jews who sacrificed their lives for their religion uttered *Shema Yisrael* as they were being led to their deaths.

Remember that the *mitzvah* is to say *Shema* in the morning and evening. Normally, it is said in sequence with the other morning prayers described above. If you rise before dawn and are praying early, you should try to wait until about fifty minutes before sunrise before saying *Shema,* when there is enough daylight to recognize someone standing about six feet away. Men also observe a time limit as to how late one can fulfill the obligation of saying *Shema,* but this varies according as the length of the day changes with the season. Times are available from your local rabbi. The *Shema* of the evening is said at the *Maariv* (evening) service or any time from darkness (forty-four minutes past sunset) until you go to bed. Generally, it is a tradition also to recite the *Shema,* or at least the first paragraph of it, as part of a bedtime ritual.

THE *AMIDAH* OR *SHEMONEH ESREI* IS A VERY IMPORTANT PERSONAL prayer, recited three times a day most of the year (twice a day for

**THE AMIDAH** women, in Ashkenazic custom). Each segment of the prayer is a blessing, ending with *Baruch atah* . . . ("Blessed are You. . ."). It is said very quietly, while standing erect with both feet together. This ceremonial way of saying the prayer signifies that you are delivering a personal, private letter of request to G-d. The silent prayer is cherished above all the others, and many pages of discussion are devoted to it in the Talmud.[16]

In more formal times than ours, a letter usually began with mentioning the honorable titles of the person addressed, then a presentation of the matters at hand, then a thank-you-in-advance. This is the format of the *Shemoneh Esrei.* It begins with three blessings of praise, then thirteen requests in blessing form, then three prayers of gratitude to G-d.

The ceremony of the *Shemoneh Esrei* includes taking three steps backward and three steps forward at the beginning and end of the prayer. There is a story relating to this about Nebuchad-nezzar, when he was a Babylonian official. When a letter was being sent to the Jews, Nebuchadnezzar ran three steps to catch up with the messenger and reverse the order of the addressees, so that the title of G-d would come first, before the names of the Jewish heads of state. Because of this honor to G-d, it is said, he eventually became emperor of Babylonia and had the power to destroy the First Temple in Jerusalem. All the more so should we indicate our honor for G-d, by taking steps backward and forward as we approach the presence of the King.

We bow four times during this prayer, at the following points:
a) *Baruch atah Ad-nai* . . .(beginning of first blessing);
b) *Baruch atah Ad-nai, Magen Avraham* (end of first blessing);
c) *Modim* ("We thank you," beginning of next-to-last blessing);
d) *Baruch atah Ad-nai, HaTov Shimcha u'lecha na'eh l'hodos* (end of next-to-last blessing).

---

16. The Talmud quotes Rabbi Shimon ben Yochai as having stated, "Why did they introduce the silent prayer? In order not to shame those who confess their sins" (Talmud *Sotah* 32b).

Because of the private and intense nature of the prayer, it is best to recite it in a place where you are free of distractions and can concentrate well. Don't stand in a place where you are likely to be interrupted, or hold something in your hands (other than the prayer book). Because it is also an address to the Creator of the universe, one should be dressed appropriately.

*A pious man was traveling along the road when dusk fell. He stopped at the edge of the road in order to pray. While he was in the middle of* Shemoneh Esrei *an officer approached him and asked what he was doing. The officer seemed to be of a very high rank, but the Jew did not respond and simply continued praying.*

*After he had finished, the officer shouted at him angrily, "You fool! Why didn't you answer me on the spot? I could have killed you for your insolence!"*

*The Jew replied, "Permit me to explain my behavior. If you were standing before the king, would you have interrupted your speech to greet a friend?"*

*"Of course not," said the officer.*

*"Then you can certainly understand what I did. If you would be afraid of interrupting your speech to a mere mortal king, how much more should I be afraid of interrupting my prayers to the eternal King of kings. When I speak to G-d, I have to devote all my concentration to this. How, then, could I have interrupted my prayer to answer you?"*[17]

*Of course, the man knew that the officer's threat was exaggerated. If it had really been a question of life or death, he should certainly have interrupted his prayers.*

When a *minyan* is present, the *Shemoneh Esrei* is repeated by the cantor, and everyone answers *Amen* after each blessing. Originally, this was done for the benefit of the illiterate who could not pray by themselves. This repetition occurs at every service

---

17. Talmud *Berachos* 32b, 33.

except *Maariv* (evening prayers). Also during the repetition, a special prayer known as the *Kedushah* is recited by the congregation in unison. During this extremely important prayer, everyone stands perfectly still with feet together. When the cantor repeats the *Modim,* the congregation responds with a different prayer known as the *Modim d'Rabbanan* (thanksgiving prayer of the rabbis).

THE SERVICE IS CONCLUDED IN A NUMBER OF WAYS, DEPENDING ON the day of the week and season of the year. On Shabbos, New

**ADDITIONAL PRAYERS**

Moon, and holidays, as well as Monday and Thursday, the Torah is read if there is a *minyan.* Three men are called to the Torah on the two weekday readings, seven on Shabbos (and Shabbos Yom Tov), four on the New Moon and intermediate days of the holidays, and five on Yom Tov. Even on the two weekdays, at least ten verses from the week's Torah portion must be read. After the Torah reading on Shabbos, New Moon, and holidays, an additional service known as *Mussaf* is said, centered on an *Amidah* with a special blessing for the day.

On most weekdays *Tachanun,* a prayer requesting Divine forgiveness, is said at *Shacharis* and *Minchah.* In ancient times, people said this prayer while prostrate on the ground; now the custom is to rest one's face on one's arm as a sign of repentance (use left arm if you are right-handed and vice versa; but if you are wearing *tefillin,* use the other hand). On Shabbos, the New Moon, and holidays, or when there is a joyous occasion being celebrated in public, this prayer is not said. On Mondays and Thursdays, a longer version is recited. After these prayers, a brief series of additional prayers is said, including a full *Kaddish.* The prayers conclude with *Aleinu,* declaring our belief in the One G-d and the ultimate victory of this belief (one bows at *Vaanachnu korim,* "And we bow"); it is followed by the Song of the Day, a different psalm for each day of the week.

THE AFTERNOON PRAYER WAS INSTITUTED BY OUR ANCESTOR ISAAC.
It shows that prayer is important not only at the beginning of the

**MINCHAH AND MAARIV**
(Afternoon and Evening Prayers)

day, but in the middle of the day as well. It can be said, at the earliest, at six and one-half hours after sunrise; at the latest, till sundown. (The length of an hour is calculated by dividing the time from sunrise to sunset by twelve.) Included in the *Minchah* service are *Ashrei, Shemoneh Esrei, and Aleinu.* If a *minyan* is present, the *chazzan* repeats the *Shemoneh Esrei* with the *Kedushah* and special *Modim,* just as in the morning prayer.

The evening prayer represents the prayer instituted by our ancestor Jacob. It can be said from the time that stars appear in the sky. With a *minyan,* the prayers begin with *Barchu,* followed by the blessings of the *Shema,* the *Shema* itself, *Shemoneh Esrei* (with no cantor's repetition), and *Aleinu.*

The prayer services are our substitutes for sacrifices offered in the Temple. Each service corresponds to an offering — morning, afternoon, and additional services for special days. *Maariv,* however, does not correspond to an offering, and was not always obligatory. Nevertheless, the entire Jewish nation accepted this service as a regular obligation, and it is now binding on all men.

## ৵§ PRAYER AND CONCENTRATION

D aily prayer may seem an overwhelming obligation. Why do we have to pray every day? And if we do, how do we keep it from becoming mere rote recitation of words?

We hinted at one answer to the first question above, namely, that we should not take our daily well-being for granted; so it is good for us to thank, praise, and offer requests to G-d every day. In addition, however, we should recognize that we are carrying on a form of offering that goes back more than three thousand years. In the Tabernacle and the Holy Temple, the first two sanctuaries where Jews brought their sacrifices to G-d, two separate flames burned: the *ner tamid* or perpetual light, and the *eish tamid* or perpetual flame. These symbolize that we too must continuously keep our "flames" burning, the flame of acting in accordance with G-d's will, and the flame of prayer. We cannot wait until Yom Kippur or a relative's *yahrzeit* (anniversary of a death) to pray.

At the same time, we have to work to keep our prayer alive and fresh. Once prayer becomes a regular practice, it is easy to mumble one's way through it, without thinking of the words one is saying. We want prayer to fill us with inspiration, so we must fill it with our sincere intent.

The Talmud states, "A person who prays should picture himself as if the Almighty is in front of him, as it says, 'I place G-d always before me.' "[18] Rambam also teaches us how to concentrate during prayer:

> What is concentration? One's heart should turn from all other thoughts and he should picture himself as standing in front of G-d. Therefore, he must prepare himself a little before prayer so as to have the proper intention, and then pray slowly and with feeling. He shouldn't pray as if he must do so and doesn't want to. Therefore, he should sit a little after prayer and then leave, so it does not appear as though he is rushing out.[19]

The Sages include the commandment of prayer with those *mitzvos* that require emotional commitment. If one does not have the proper intention while praying, he does not fulfill the *mitzvah* properly. G-d said to the Jewish people, "Be careful with prayer since it is greater than sacrifices"[20] (Talmud *Berachos* 32b). Even if we have few merits on other grounds, praying sincerely can bring G-d's kindness. *Ramban* states that the Jews were not intrinsically worthy of being redeemed; but G-d accepted their prayers because of their sincerity.

> In the city of Krasna, a man announced that he would walk across the river on a tightrope if given 100 gold coins. The

---

18. Talmud *Sanhedrin* 22.

19. Rambam, *Mishneh Torah, Hilchos Tefillah* 4:16.

20. Talmud *Berachos* 32b.

famous Reb Chaim of Krasna was among the spectators who came to watch. He was amazed at what a person would do for money. Yet, as he stood watching the tightrope walker, Reb Chaim was impressed with the man's total concentration on his efforts. He was obviously not thinking about the 100 gold coins that he would get at the end, or he would have fallen into the water. Reb Chaim later told his students, "Imagine! If for 100 gold coins a man can concentrate so deeply on what he is doing, how much more should we concentrate when praying and serving G-d!"

To help us toward meaningful prayer, the Sages set forth conditions conducive to concentration. They insisted on purity of thought, sanctity of place, and respectful behavior. Thus:

a) It is forbidden to talk during prayer.

b) It is forbidden to introduce distractions during prayer.

c) It is forbidden to condone levity, playfulness, or other disrespectful practices.

d) It is forbidden to pray in the presence of someone dressed immodestly, for this is distracting.

e) One should not pray in a place that might be dangerous (e.g. on top of a roof), since the thought of possible danger is distracting.

f) Recognizing that one is standing before the King of kings during prayer should lead us to dress accordingly. Some men have the custom to put on a jacket and hat, since this is a sign of formal dressing. Some wear a special belt (known as a *gartel*) during *davening*.

g) One should not *daven* in an unclean place or in the presence of offensive odors, for these also distract one from the prayers.

h) When praying, especially during *Shemoneh Esrei,* one should not stand in front of a picture, painting, or mirror, for it would appear as if one were praying to something other than G-d.

i) When praying in a synagogue, one should face the *aron kodesh* (holy ark). Anywhere else, one faces eastward toward Jerusalem. However, if you do not know in which direction

Jerusalem lies, you should face any direction (always keeping G-d in mind while praying.)

j) Many people sway while they pray, to remind them of the awe and trembling we experienced at the time of receiving the Torah at Mount Sinai. A verse in *Psalms* reads, "All my bones shall say, 'Who is like You, O Lord?' " The famous mystical text known as the *Zohar* offers another interpretation: The soul of man is like a candle. Just as the flame of a candle flickers and wavers, so too, people sway when they pray.

We should be especially careful how we conduct ourselves in the synagogue. It is a positive commandment to be in awe of the Temple, for it is written in the Torah, "You should fear My Sanctuary" (*Leviticus* 19:30 or 26:2). Our synagogues and places of learning are called "small sanctuaries."[21] Therefore, we must behave with the utmost respect, as if we were praying in the Holy Temple itself.

---

21. Talmud *Megillah* 29.

# 11

———◦⟨⟨⟩⟩◦———

# Awakening Consciousness:
# Articles and Symbols
# of Jewish Faith

———◦⟨⟨⟩⟩◦———

Certain of the *mitzvos* given in the Torah have to do with symbols of the Jew's constant connection to G-d. These help us maintain a consciousness, which ideally should be with us at all times, of G-d's Oneness and Divine Providence over all our affairs, and of our love and awe of G-d.[1] All Jews are obligated to put *mezuzos* on their doorposts. Male Jews are to wear *tzitzis* (fringes) and to don *tefillin* (phylacteries) daily, and to wear a head covering. In addition, while one can study Torah without having a written scroll, the Torah scroll is an object of honor in every community.

---

1. There are six "constant *mitzvos*": to believe in G-d our Redeemer; to know that G-d is One; to believe in no other powers besides G-d; not to let one's heart or eyes go astray; to love G-d; and to fear (or have awe of) G-d. The articles of faith are external aids to help us concentrate on these at all times (*Sefer HaChinuch, Intro.; Chayei Adam* 1; *Mishnah Berurah, Be'er Halachah* 1).

All these objects are symbols of faith and honor to G-d, manifest in the physical world. Just as an ambassador of a foreign nation will often wear the traditional clothing of his country as a notification of his place of origin, so we have physical symbols that remind us, and others, to Whom we belong. They also help us guard our behavior. "Whoever has *tefillin* on his head, *tefillin* on his arm, *tzitzis* on his garment, and the *mezuzah* on his door is secure against committing sins." They also symbolize G-d's love for the Jewish people. "Beloved is Israel, for the Holy One, Blessed is He, surrounded them with *mitzvos*: *tefillin* on the head, *tefillin* on the arm, *tzitzis* on the garment, and *mezuzah* on his doorpost."

We will consider the *mezuzah* first, since it is obligatory on everyone, and then *tefillin* and *tzitzis,* which are obligatory only on men. Then we will discuss the Torah scroll and the *yarmulka.*

## ◄§ THE MEZUZAH

The Torah tells us, "You should write [these words] on the doorposts of your house and on your gates." This is the commandment of *mezuzah*. The Oral Law explains that the words are to be written on a scroll, which is to be attached to a doorpost. Many people think that the *mezuzah* is the case, but it merely serves to protect the scroll inside it, which is the important thing. The scroll contains two passages from the Torah; namely, two paragraphs from the *Shema.*

It is obligatory for Jewish men and women to have *mezuzos* on their doors at all times.[2] The *mezuzah* officially dedicates our dwellings to the Almighty, just as all aspects of our lives have to be sanctified. Like the flag of an embassy, it represents G-d's presence in a particular place in the world.

*Onkelos ben Kalonymus, a close relative of the emperor of Rome, was not born Jewish. Nevertheless, he was*

---

2. Talmud *Berachos* 20b.

*attracted by the beauty of Judaism and, having sampled its teachings, decided to convert. The emperor did not look kindly upon this development, considering it a threat to his own paganism. He sent group after group of soldiers after Onkelos, demanding that he return to Rome. However, Onkelos told each group about his new life in Judaism and succeeded in convincing them to convert. When his soldiers did not return, the emperor was irate. He instructed the next group of soldiers not to engage Onkelos in conversation.*

*The soldiers came to Onkelos' house, insisted that he accompany them to Rome, and began to drag him out the door. Suddenly, Onkelos insisted that they stop. He went to the doorpost of his house, raised his hand, and placed it on a small box attached there. He then removed his hand and kissed it.*

*The soldiers gazed at him in astonishment. Onkelos smiled. "Do you see the difference between your human ruler and my G-d?" he asked. "A human emperor stays inside his house, with his guards outside to watch over him. But my G-d stays at the door of the house and guards all the common people inside. This little box contains a* mezuzah, *with G-d's holy words in it, protecting the Jews who live inside the house."*

*These words had a dramatic impact upon the soldiers. They had never before heard of such a leader, such a Supreme Power. Soon they, too, converted. The emperor's command went unfulfilled.*[3]

*Onkelos the convert became one of the great personages of Jewish history. He is well known today as the author of the translation-with-commentary,* Targum Onkelos.[4]

The verses inside say that one of the rewards for this *mitzvah* is "that your days may be multiplied," the plain meaning of which

---

3. Talmud *Avodah Zarah* 11a.

4. Talmud *Megillah* 3a.

is that you will have a long life. This might literally mean long life; it can also mean that observing the commandment of *mezuzah* adds quality and significance to our lives. Certainly, it serves that purpose insofar as it reminds us of our service to G-d, which itself gives life meaning. Each time we pass a *mezuzah*, we can remember that a day is not merely a measure to mark the passage of time, but is an opportunity to sanctify our space and our time to G-d.[5] This is also suggested by what King Solomon said about the Torah, "Length of days is at its right; at its left are wealth and honor" (*Proverbs* 3:16). We place the *mezuzah* on the right side of the door as we enter, so that when we come in and see it, we are reminded that our service lends quality and meaning to our lives.

A *mezuzah* is a sacred object, and the laws concerning it should be followed carefully. Here are the basic laws:

1) The verses on its scrolls must be written by a qualified scribe (*sofer*). The text must be written in special ink, in a single column of 22 lines, on a single piece of parchment. The scribe is responsible to make sure that every letter is properly inscribed, for one incorrect letter ruins the whole *mezuzah*. The text has to be written in the proper order, with nothing added or subtracted. On the back of the parchment the word *Sha-dai* is written. The parchment is wound from left to right, so that the first word exposed when unwinding it is *Shema*. It is then placed in a protective encasement (which need not be expensive).

   It is wise to spend a little more money if necessary to get a *mezuzah* that is certain to be kosher. Buying a small *mezuzah* is risky, because it is very hard for a scribe to write every part of every letter correctly on a small parchment. One should make sure that the scribe and the seller are observant Jews, so that one can be sure the *mezuzah* was made with correct intentions and fulfills all the requirements.

2) When affixing a *mezuzah*, one says the blessing, *likvoa*

5. Rabbeinu Bechayei on the Torah; Rambam, *Mishneh Torah, Hilchos Mezuzah* 6:3.

*mezuzah*, which is to be found in the prayer book. The person affixing it must be over the age of *bar mitzvah* (13 years; or *bas mitzvah*, age 12, in case of a woman). If you are affixing more than one *mezuzah*, the blessing is said only once. However, the process of putting up the *mezuzos* should continue without interruption (including any unnecessary talk), until the last *mezuzah* is affixed.

3) The *mezuzah* must be placed on the right-hand side upon entering from the outside (regardless of whether the inhabitants are right- or left-handed), in the upper third of the doorway but more than four inches from the top. It is placed on the outermost part of the doorway so that there should be no question that the entire room is included; and it is placed at an angle with the top facing toward the inside. If it cannot be slanted, it may be attached vertically to the doorpost.

4) If there are two entrances to one room, both must have *mezuzos*, each one being placed on the right side of the usual direction of entry. If it is not clear which room leads into which, the *mezuzah* is placed on the right side of the direction into which the door opens.

5) *Mezuzos* must be placed on all our permanent dwellings (whether owned or rented) with an area of at least "4 *amos* by 4 *amos* " (an *amah* is approximately 22 inches). This includes each room in the house that is that large, with exceptions noted below. It includes children's rooms, and even a house where children might be living alone such as an orphanage dormitory. It includes garages and storage rooms (of sufficient size). However, certain rooms do not require *mezuzos*: bathrooms, bathhouses, temporary dwellings such as a *succah*, unroofed sheds, and trapdoors in the floor do not. If you have a question about some unusual space or room, consult a knowledgeable rabbi.

6) The *mezuzah* is to be treated with respect; it should not be left on the floor or in other ways abused. When you move from your house, do not remove the *mezuzah* unless the new occupants may be non-Jews.

7) Each *mezuzah* is to be examined by a scribe at least twice every seven years to ensure that the letters are still intact.

King David wrote in *Psalms* (121:8), "G-d will guard your going out and coming in, now and forever". G-d protects a person for the sake of the *mezuzah* on his doorpost, not only while he is at home but even when he is away. It symbolizes the sanctity of the Jewish home and attests to G-d's watchful care over his people. Thus the *mezuzah* guides us in the most important principles and ideals of our faith.[6]

## ᴈ§ TEFILLIN

The *Shema* contains the verse, "These words that I command you today shall be on your heart . . . And you shall bind them for a sign on your hand, and for an insignia between your eyes." This underscores the importance of the *mitzvah* of *tefillin* in Jewish ritual. When a man wears *tefillin,* he reaffirms his devotion and love for G-d and his dedication to His law. By wearing *tefillin,* the Jew affirms that in his thoughts (his head) and in his intentions, feelings, and actions (on the arm, next to the heart), he wishes to serve G-d. He also asserts his intention to remember the deliverance of his people from Egyptian servitude, which is written on the parchment of *tefillin* and is a basic foundation of a Jew.

*Tefillin* are worn by adult males during the weekday morning service. Like part of a soldier's uniform, it is considered a mark of respect to wear them, and of disrespect to appear for prayer without them. If a person does not have *tefillin* of his own, he can borrow them in order to say the blessings and the *Shema* while wearing them. One should never deliberately refuse to put them on for the prayers. The Sages said, "Whoever recites the *Shema* and deliberately refuses to put on the *tefillin* [in the weekday morning prayers] is like one who bears false witness against himself."[7]

---

6. Rambam, *Mishneh Torah, Hilchos Mezuzah.*
7. Talmud *Berachos* 14b.

There are two types of *tefillin*: for the head, placed at the hairline, and for the hand, which are put on the biceps of one's weaker arm. (If one is ambidextrous, he puts them on the left arm. If he writes with one hand but does all other work with the other, he should consult a rabbi to determine which arm to use.) Each kind of *tefillin* contains the same four portions of the Torah inscribed on parchment within. The difference is that in the head *tefillin*, each portion is in a separate compartment, while in the hand *tefillin*, all are in one compartment. The passages state a Jew's obligations to G-d.

*Tefillin* must be made in a specific manner. The boxes and the stitches around them must be in the shape of a square. There should be a Hebrew letter *shin* on the right and left sides of the box for the head tefillin; one *shin* having four lines and the other, three. This *shin* must be constructed from the same material as the box. Within the box, each portion must be surrounded by a small piece of blank parchment and tied up with animal hair, then put into the compartment. The portions must be written by a competent scribe, according to Jewish law. Since the writing can become cracked or faded, thus invalidating the *tefillin*, they must be checked by a scribe at least twice every seven years. The boxes must be sewn with sinews from a kosher animal. The binding straps must be black and made from the leather of a kosher animal.

When a young man becomes *bar mitzvah*, one of his new obligations is to put on *tefillin*. This is even more important than being called to the Torah in the synagogue. Wearing *tefillin* every day remains a lifelong duty for every Jewish male.

*Tefillin* are put on just before morning prayers, after the *tallis* (see below). They should be worn during the entire morning service. In case of a special emergency, where one is not sure that he will be able to wear them for all the prayers, he should put them on and recite *Shema*. Some traditions hold that *tefillin* are not worn during the intermediate days of a festival; a man should follow the custom of his father in that regard, or consult a knowledgeable rabbi if he does not know what his father's custom was.

The hand *tefillin* (*tefillin shel yad*) are put on first. From the time one begins putting on the *tefillin,* one is not allowed to talk or answer questions (unless it is something relevant to putting on *tefillin*), until after he has put on both the hand and the head *tefillin.* One begins by placing the box on the lower half of the biceps muscle, so that when one holds his arm next to his body, the side of the box touches his chest. Before tightening the strap, one says the prayer, "I am now about to fulfill G-d's command-ment to put on *tefillin.*" (Most prayer books also specify a longer declaration to this effect.) Then, before tightening the knot, one says the blessing *l'haniach tefillin.* The strap is wound seven times around the forearm with the black side of the straps always on the outside (not allowing them to twist). The strap is then wound once or twice around the palm of the hand so that it can be held while one puts on the head *tefillin.* The exact method varies slightly according to custom.

Immediately afterward, one puts on the *tefillin shel rosh* (head *tefillin*). They should be centered in the middle of the head, just above the hairline. It is most important that no part of the box protrudes below the hairline. Although the Torah states that the head *tefillin* are to be worn "between the eyes," the Oral Law explains that they should be centered on the head, but above the hairline. If the hairline has receded, they should be worn just above the point of the original hairline. The knot must be centered at the base of the skull, in the indentation at the back of the head. The straps are then allowed to hang in front. Here again, it is important that the straps be worn black-side out. Before tightening the straps of the head *tefillin,* one says the blessing *Baruch atah . . . asher kid'shanu . . . al mitzvas tefillin.* Then he tightens the straps and says, without any interruption, *Baruch shem k'vod malchuso l'olam va'ed.* Then one completes the windings of the hand *tefillin* according to custom. (Some do not make a blessing on the head *tefillin,* but make one on the hand *tefillin* which includes the head *tefillin* as well. Here too one should follow the custom of his father.)

The hand *tefillin* are wound three times around the middle finger, symbolizing a threefold bond of love between G-d and

Israel, like a three-tiered wedding ring. While making these windings, it is customary to repeat verses from the book of *Hosea* (2:21-22): "I will betroth you to Me forever, and I will betroth you to Me with righteousness, justice, kindness, and mercy. I will betroth you to Me with fidelity, and you shall know Hashem."

One removes the *tefillin* in reverse order, first unwinding the three coils from the finger, then taking the head *tefillin* off with the left hand, then removing the hand *tefillin*. The *tallis* is removed after the *tefillin*.

The *tefillin* are sacred articles and are to be treated with reverence. One should be careful not to drop them, and if it does happen accidentally, the person should give extra *tzedakah* (charity) that day.

The Talmud says, "He who wants to show complete acceptance of G-d's sovereignty should take care of his personal needs, wash his hands, put on *tefillin*, say the *Shema*, and then proceed with his prayers. He who does this shows he accepts G-d's sovereignty and is like one who built an altar and sacrificed an offering on it."[8] *Tefillin* should be donned with pride and dignity. Their basis in the Torah testifies to the unbroken continuity of our faith for over three thousand years. They demonstrate the strength of Jewish conviction through the ages. Even during the severest persecutions, Jews did not give up the wearing of *tefillin*.

> *During the Roman persecutions when* tefillin *were proscribed on penalty of death, a pious Jew named Elisha donned* tefillin *and went out into the street. (In those times many wore* tefillin *all day, even outside.) A government official saw him and ran after him. When he reached him, Elisha had already taken off the* tefillin *and put them in his hand. "What do you have in your hand?" the officer demanded.*
>
> *"The wings of a dove," responded Elisha. As he spread out his hand, indeed a dove flew out. Thereafter, he was called "Elisha the Person with Wings." Why, it was asked, did the* tefillin *appear as a dove? Because the*

---

8. Talmud *Berachos* 14b.

*Jewish people are compared to the gentle dove, and just as a dove's wings protect him, so do the* mitzvos *protect the Jews.* [9]

The *tefillin* are a representation of our contract with G-d. Just as a person drawing up a business contract consults the best lawyers and studies every word, down to the fine print, so a man should invest time and money in obtaining proper *tefillin.*

It is taught that whoever puts on *tefillin* regularly will enjoy a long life, for it is written, "The Lord is upon them, they shall live" (*Isaiah* 38:16).[10]

# ◈ TZITZIS (FRINGES)

The first paragraph of the *Shema* gives the commandments about *tefillin* and *mezuzah;* the third paragraph commands a practice known as *tzitzis.* Any male wearing a garment with four (or more) corners must attach *tzitzis* to each corner. This reminds him of our allegiance to G-d and the *mitzvos.* Again, a Jew wearing *tzitzis* is like a soldier in his army uniform; the fringes serve as a constant reminder that as soldiers in G-d's army we are totally subservient to His commands.

The Torah portion with this commandment states, "And when you look upon them (the *tzitzis*) you will remember all of G-d's commandments." The word *tzitzis* in Hebrew is numerically equivalent to 600. The fringes include 8 strings and 5 knots; added together, these numbers total 613, the number of biblical commandments. The connection is direct: By looking at the *tzitzis,* one is reminded of all the commandments.

The *tzitzis* are attached to a garment as follows: A hole is made in each corner. Into each four whole strings are inserted and folded in half, so that 8 strings fall from the corner. The strings are double knotted, and the longest string (in a set of *tzitzis,* one

---

9. Talmud *Shabbos* 49.
10. Talmud *Menachos* 44.

is longer than the others) is wound around the other strings, and another double knot is made. Then it is wound around the other strings 8, 11, and 13 times, each time followed by a double knot. The number of windings is symbolic: 7, 8, and 11 add up to 26, which is the numerical value of the four-letter Name of G-d; while 13 is equivalent to the word *echad* (One), signifying G-d's unity. The *tzitzis* thus symbolize the last two words of the first line of the *Shema*: *Ad-nai echad,* G-d is One!

The four *tzitzis* have a combined total of 32 threads, equal to the numerical value of the Hebrew word *lev* or heart. This teaches us that we should serve G-d with a complete heart.

## ✑ THE TALLIS (PRAYER SHAWL)

M en wear the *tallis* during weekday morning prayers. It is a four-cornered garment with *tzitzis* on its corners. While in ancient times four-cornered shawls were commonly worn by men, that fashion faded. Nevertheless, out of love for the *mitzvah* of *tzitzis,* Jewish men continued to wear a four-cornered shawl for prayer. Many men also wear a *tallis katan* (small *tallis*) as an undergarment in order that they can be fulfilling the *mitzvah* of *tzitzis* all during the day.

The *tallis* should be large enough to cover most of the wearer's body. It is worn with two corners in front and two in back. Usually, it has either black or blue stripes, but this is a custom of particular communities. Sephardim do not have stripes on their *talleisim.* The Ashkenazic custom of blue stripes is a reminder of the blue thread that was originally used as one of the strings of the *tzitzis.* (A blue thread is no longer used because the source of the appropriate dye is not certainly known. However, there has been discussion of the blue thread or *t'cheiles* in recent times because the Rebbe of a small chassidic group, after an extensive study, concluded that the source of the blue dye could be determined. These *chassidim* do have a blue string in their *tzitzis.* Others are continuing to do research.)

The *tallis* has an *atarah,* which is a band of either silver or cloth, attached to the top of the *tallis.* This identifies the top of the rectangular piece of cloth.

As one begins one's prayers, the *tallis* is put on first, before the *tefillin.* Before the *tallis* is wrapped around the head and body, the blessing *l'hisatef hatzitzis* is recited (see the prayer book). If, after putting on the *tallis* and beginning prayers, one must use the bathroom, one removes it before entering the bathroom. The blessing need not be recited again when putting it back on. The *tallis* is considered a holy object that must be treated with utmost respect.

A married man covers his head with the *tallis* at certain places in the prayer in order to inspire himself with fear and awe. In addition, it is customary in the prayers before the *Shema* to gather the four fringes of the *tzitzis* into the right hand on reading the verse, "And bring us together from the four corners of the earth." It is also customary to kiss the *tzitzis* when, during the *Shema,* the word *tzitzis* is read.

According to some customs, a man wears a *tallis* only after marriage; according to others, he wears it beginning from the time he is *bar mitzvah.*

One should not wear *tzitzis* that are torn off. If they should happen to become torn while wearing them, the garment should be immediately removed and not worn again until the *tzitzis* are replaced. (One should consult a knowledgeable rabbi if one is in doubt as to whether they are invalid.) Even when they are torn, however, the *tallis* still must be treated with respect, as it is still a sacred object.

The great Vilna Gaon, in the last moments before his death, was crying as he held his *tzitzis.* When asked what was troubling him, he remarked that once a person dies, he no longer has the obligation of wearing *tzitzis.* How hard it is to separate from the world of deeds! With such an easy commandment as *tzitzis,* a person can receive a spiritual uplift, while in the next world there would be no such way to accomplish spiritual elevation.

# ❦ THE SEFER TORAH

A *sefer Torah,* which is our holy scroll, must be written on parchment produced from a kosher animal. It must be written with a quill and with special ink whose formula is known only to experts. The sheets of parchment are sewn together with thread made from the sinews of a kosher animal. Any deviation from these rules will prevent the scroll from being a kosher Torah scroll that can be used in a public Torah reading. Because of the demanding requirements, we purchase Torah scrolls only from expert scribes with reputations for piety, holiness, and experience in this sacred work. Even if all the above rules were followed explicitly, but the scribe himself was not an observant Jew, the scroll could not be used as a *sefer Torah.*

Some of the errors that make a scroll unfit for congregational Torah reading include the following: joining two letters together, writing a word too close to the next, dividing a word by leaving too much space between the letters, failing to leave adequate space between the passages (*parshios*), making a "closed" passage open or vice versa. More obvious errors, such as a missing paragraph or a superfluous letter, also invalidate the scroll. Such a scroll is treated like a printed *Chumash* (first five books of the Bible). In some cases, the errors can be corrected and the Torah made fit for use.

If the seam connecting two sheets of parchment is severed, but the majority of the seam is still together, the Torah scroll may be used, but if the majority is severed, the seam must be repaired before the scroll may be used. If no other *sefer Torah is* available, we may read from such a damaged scroll as long as it is not completely torn.

The sanctity of a *sefer Torah* is immense. It is particularly beloved by the Jewish people because it is the Torah that has kept Israel distinct from the other nations. Even a room in someone's house in which a *sefer Torah* is kept takes on some of the sanctity of the scroll, so that, as in a synagogue, levity is forbidden and decorum must be observed. If a scroll was placed in a receptacle, and that within still another one — for example in a chest or closet — the room may now be used in a regular fashion. However, it is customary to hang curtains in front of the chest or closet where the Torah is kept as a visual sign of separation between the Torah and the home.

The Torah contains a *mitzvah* that every Jew should write a *sefer Torah* for himself. This does not necessarily mean he must literally write it, or even have a whole one written; one can fulfill the *mitzvah* by donating money toward the purchase of a *sefer Torah*. It is a custom to donate Torah scrolls to a synagogue, by way of a generous gift in the name of departed parents or friends, or in the name of martyrs who died in sanctifying G-d's name (*al kiddush Hashem*). Donors may wish to inscribe their own names and/or the names of their parents on the mantle of the Torah or on the casing.

A Torah scroll should not be kept uncovered and should not be touched with bare hands. Ashkenazim dress it in a cloth mantle; Sephardim keep it in a solid casing. Both are decorated with gold and silver ornaments, reflecting Israel's love for the Torah, like the jewels of a bride.

Those who witness a Torah scroll being desecrated, intentionally or by accident (e.g. if it is dropped accidentally), must rend their garments as is done over the death of a parent. Also, it is proper in such a case to fast and give money to charity to atone for the sin committed, even if unintentional.

*In Pshevorsk, Poland, both the synagogue and the house of study were engulfed in flames. German officers and soldiers stood there enjoying the spectacle. Many Jews were gathered behind them, their heads bowed in pain and humiliation. The rabbi of the community had been ordered to stand in the front row, himself the object of scorn and derision. Suddenly the rabbi broke away and began to run. Two more Jews ran after him. The Germans stopped laughing and shouted for them to halt, but the rabbi did not hear. Nothing could stop him, not even the flames. The three Jews disappeared into the burning building. The Germans were speechless with astonishment. A few moments later the rabbi reappeared, his clothes singed, but his face shining with a triumphant smile. His two arms held a scroll of the Torah.*

*"Jewish impudence!" the German commander yelled. The soldiers pointed their rifles at the burning synagogue, so that the two men who assisted the rabbi would not be able to come out. The Germans attacked the rabbi with the butts of their rifles, but the rabbi held onto the Torah as if he and the scroll were one and inseparable — as, in fact, they were.*

# ~§ THE KIPAH (YARMULKA)

It is the custom among Jewish men not to walk bareheaded.[11] This applies at home, in the synagogue, and outdoors. This custom is not mentioned in the Torah, but was adopted voluntarily by men to emphasize that they are servants of the Almighty. It has become a mark of Jewish piety, as if to say, "Cover your head so that the awe of Heaven be upon you."[12]

*Yarmulka* is a contraction of the Hebrew words, *yorei Malkah,* fear of the Heavenly King. When a man wears a head covering, he displays respect for G-d. He shows that he is aware of a Divine Creator above him, and he will not walk around bareheaded as if he were master of the world.

The *kipah* has for centuries been an identifying sign for Jews. Wearing one is a public proclamation of being a Jew, and being proud to show it. It also reminds us to act in ways that befit a Jew as an ambassador of G-d.

---

11. *Shulchan Aruch, Orach Chaim* 2:6.
12. Talmud *Shabbos* 156b.

# 12

Sanctifying the Body:
Food and Clothing

K ing David said, "Happy is the person who fears G-d and de-
lights very much in the precepts" (*Psalms* 112:1). Ultimately,
if we follow the teaching of fearing G-d, learning Torah, observing
the precepts in the proper way, we will see outstanding results.
The saintly Chofetz Chaim commented that the reward we will
receive in the World to Come is far greater than any pleasures we
might have in this world. But even in this world, the value of the
commandments, performed correctly and with intent, is immense.
A person can transform his life through them. This is certainly
true of the way Jewish practice affects one's daily life through
physical actions associated with eating and clothing one's body.

## ঙ§ THE ATTITUDE OF
GRATITUDE: BLESSINGS

E very benefit we derive from this world is a gift from G-d. The
Holy One, Blessed is He, feeds and sustains all creatures.

Specifically, He created produce to nourish us, trees and flowers to provide fragrance and beauty. We in turn need to express our gratitude for these kindnesses. Our Sages recognized the power of a grateful attitude in life, and established blessings or *berachos* through which we can bless G-d for every kind of pleasure. There are blessings for fruits of the tree, for vegetables that grow from the ground, and even for water that we drink. They are a beautiful and important medium for expressing our awareness that we are dependent on a Source far beyond our limited resources. "The earth is the Lord's." Once we have expressed our gratitude, we are granted the right to make use of G-d's possessions.[1]

The word *berachah* (blessing) is derived from the Hebrew word *breichah*, meaning a spring. Just as a spring flows continuously, always producing fresh supplies of water, so is G-d the Source of infinite blessing.[2] In creating a universe with inhabitants, He designed it in a way that He would be continually doing good to those inhabitants. Thus it is significant that the benedictions established by our Sages are all worded in the present tense; this shows that G-d is constantly creating things anew.

The Talmud states, in the name of Rabbi Meir, that a person should recite 100 blessings every day.[3] Why? During the days of King David, a hundred Jews were dying every day. For some time, no one knew the reason. Finally David, in his meditation and prayer, came to understand that the people were not thanking G-d sufficiently for all the beneficence He had shown them. King David instituted the recitation of 100 blessings a day to offset the deaths, and the dying ceased.

In addition, the 100 blessings acts as a counterforce to the 99 curses found in the book of *Devarim* (Deuteronomy).[4]

In speaking of the ethics of a Jew in Chapter 10, we noted that one way to develop one's consciousness and level of holiness is to refrain from speaking negatively (even when we think it is the

1. Rambam, *Mishneh Torah, Hilchos Berachos* 1:3.
2. Rav Chaim Volozhin, *Nefesh HaChayim.*
3. Talmud *Menachos* 43.
4. *Baal HaTurim.*

truth) about others. But it is not only what we refrain from saying that aids us in our spiritual development, it is also how we use our faculty of speech for positive ends. When we use our mouths and tongues to recite blessings, it symbolizes our faithfulness and trust. Even when we do not have to make a formal blessing, we can include awareness of G-d in our everyday speech. That is why it is a custom among many, and a very good one to emulate, to include such phrases as "thank G-d" (*baruch Hashem*), "with G-d's help" (*b'ezras Hashem*), and "G-d willing," (*im yirtzeh Hashem*) in their daily conversations. As it says in the Bible, "I will bless the Lord at all times; His praise shall continuously be in my mouth" (*Psalms* 24:2).

When we hear another person recite a blessing, we should answer *"Amen"* at its conclusion. The word *amen* constitutes an endorsement and affirmation that the blessing is true, that the listener believes it, or that "it should soon come to pass." The Hebrew letters of *amen* (*alef, mem, nun*) are an acronym for *Ei-l Melech Ne'eman*, "G-d the Faithful King." Just as the words of the blessing should be said with devotion and concentration, so too the *amen* should be uttered with serious intent. The Talmud states, "He who responds *amen* with great fervor will have the gates of Eden opened for him."[5] (However, one does not answer *amen* after a blessing he himself has recited, unless it is part of the formal structure of the prayer itself as in *boneh Yerushalayim* in the Grace After Meals, or in *Kaddish*.)

## ৵ BLESSINGS OVER FOOD

We recite blessings in praise of G-d and when we enjoy something, including the opportunity to do a *mitzvah*. A major category is that of blessings before eating or drinking; there are six blessings for different types of food. You can find the full text of all these blessings in a prayer book.

---

5. Talmud *Shabbos* 119b.

a. *Hamotzi* is recited over bread, rolls, and matzah made from the "five grains," namely wheat, barley, oats, rye, and spelt.

b. *Hagafen* is said on wine and grape juice.

c. *Mezonos* is recited over nonbread foods made from grains, such as cake, cookies, pretzels, pasta, and related products.

d. *Ha'eitz* is said over fruits grown on a tree. A tree is defined, in rabbinic law, as a plant whose trunk and branches remain from year to year. Some things we usually think of as fruits, such as bananas and papayas, grow from treelike plants, but their branches grow anew each year, so they are regarded as "fruits of the ground."

e. *Ha'adamah* is recited over produce grown from the ground.

f. *Shehakol* is recited over everything that does not fall into one of the previous five categories. Animal products such as meat, fish, eggs, and dairy fall into this category, as do water, candy, and juice (other than grape) extracted from fruits.

The more important a food is to human beings, the greater the precedence of its blessing. The blessing over bread therefore takes precedence over all others; then comes the blessing on wine. Therefore, when we say the blessing over bread at the beginning of a meal, we do not say the other blessings on individual foods such as the meat and vegetables. Wine is considered the beverage that "gladdens the heart of man" (*Psalms* 104:15) and takes precedence over all other beverages. It is the drink of choice for reciting *kiddush* and *havdalah* for Shabbos and holidays.

Next in importance is *mezonos*, followed in turn by *ha'eitz* and *ha'adamah*. If one makes a mistake and says *ha'adamah* on the fruit of a tree (instead of *ha'eitz*), one has still fulfilled the *mitzvah*, because trees also grow from the ground. However, the reverse is not the case; *ha'eitz* cannot count as the proper blessing for a vegetable. If one made a mistake and recited *shehakol* on any of the foods that normally require a different blessing, this still fulfills the *mitzvah*.

A special blessing of *besamim* is recited on fragrant smells from natural sources (but not on perfumes, deodorants, or cleansers!).

When one wears new clothes, or on the first days of holidays or certain other special occasions, one recites a *shehecheyanu* blessing (a short prayer of thanks for being able to experience the event). When one returns from a hazardous trip, recovers from a dangerous illness, is released from captivity, or (for a woman) recovers from childbirth, a blessing is recited known as *Birchas HaGomel.* On traveling a long distance, outside the city limits, one says *Tefillas Haderech,* the prayer of the wayfarer. There are other blessings of pleasure, such as when seeing a rainbow, the ocean, lightning, or hearing thunder for the first time in 30 days. Consult your *siddur* for these and other opportunities to recite blessings.

## ⌁§ THE CEREMONY OF EATING

In our society, eating is taken very casually. The Jewish approach, however, is that eating is a highly significant activity. Even the lightest snack is preceded by a blessing, addressing G-d by name. When a real meal is eaten, the table is regarded as an altar, and when we gather around it, we are performing a ceremonial act. "Our table is compared to that of the Altar in the Temple. We should therefore behave with due reverence at the table, just as if we were worshipping before the Altar of G-d."[6] In addition, a meal with one's family or friends can promote unity, be a platform for meaningful dialogue, and remind us of our gratitude to G-d. It can also help tame one's appetite by focusing on spiritual things.

Bread "makes the meal." (Bread is defined as being made primarily from flour and water, rather than other ingredients such as eggs, juice, or milk as is usually the case with cookies or cakes; and being baked rather than cooked as with pasta.) The ceremonial meal usually includes bread and, as we noted above, the blessing over bread supersedes all others, except for blessings on wine or desserts.

---

6. Talmud *Chagigah* 27.

Before we partake of bread, we wash hands in a ceremonial manner. This is not about cleansing the hands — that should be done with soap and water as a matter of course. The ritual of hand-washing reflects our desire to sanctify ourselves before the sacred act of eating. When the Torah says "sanctify yourself," the Talmud says that this means washing hands before the meal, just as the priests did before eating their *terumah* (sacrificial portions). This is one of the customs that remind us of the analogy between our table and the Altar. Another is dipping the bread into salt before eating the first slice.

In washing the hands, we use a cup with a smooth edge (not a pitcher) that can hold at least 3.3 ounces of water. Frequently, a much larger cup is used. One takes the cup is the right hand, fills it with water, transfers it to the left hand, and pours water twice over the right hand, from the wrist down. The same procedure is repeated to wash the left hand. Then one recites the blessing *al netilas yadaim*, dries the hands, and makes *Hamotzi* on the bread.

Many of the Jewish laws applicable to eating have been incorporated into general etiquette, but there are additional ones as well. Here are some:

a. Not to speak while eating.

b. Not to eat too quickly.

c. Not to throw or otherwise abuse food.

d. Not to sleep after a heavy meal.

e. Not to stare at another person while he or she is eating.

f. Not to leave bread or any other food lying on the floor, or thrown into a ditch or dirty place. However, it may be used for animal food.

g. If one drank without saying a blessing, one should swallow whatever is in his mouth and make a blessing on the remaining drink, if there is any.

h. If one accidentally ate without a blessing and the food is still in his mouth, he should push the food to one side of the mouth and recite the blessing.

# ☙ BLESSINGS AFTER EATING

Jews bless G-d even before eating, just for having been supplied with food. How much more so should we thank G-d after having eaten, for the amazing feat of enabling our bodies to transform the food into useful energy for us. It is said that being meticulous in reciting the blessing after eating is a good omen for having one's livelihood provided in a dignified manner.[7] The after-blessings are the following:

a. After eating at least one slice of bread, one recites *Bircas HaMazon*, the full Grace After Meals.

b. *Al Hamichyah* after eating a sufficient amount of food (the size of a large olive) made of one of the five types of grain (wheat, barley, rye, oats, spelt).

c. *Al Hagafen* after drinking at least 3.3 ounces of wine or grape juice.

d. *Al Ha'eitz* after eating the five fruits for which the Land of Israel is famous — grapes (including raisins), figs, pomegranates, olives, and dates.

e. *Borei Nefashos* over all other foods not included in any of the above.

When the full Grace After Meals is said, additional ceremony is included. A psalm is said before the recitation. Many Jews pour water over their fingers; this is known as *mayim acharonim* (after-water).[8] There is no required amount of water; one simply pours a little water over the fingertips from one utensil into another, and wipes it with a napkin. Both utensils are removed from the table before the Grace After Meals.

When three men eat together a meal with bread, they auto-

---

7. *Sefer HaChinuch, Parashas Eikev.*

8. Although the Talmud designated this as an obligatory ritual, it is now treated with leniency because its primary purpose was to rinse off a special strong salt that clung to the fingers from eating with the hands, and it was dangerous for the eyes. Today, as people no longer use salt that is dangerous, the obligation no longer applies with the same force.

matically constitute a *"zimun"* and must join together in reciting the introductory invocation to the Grace After Meals. Others at the table, including women, also join in the responses if possible. If there are at least ten men saying the Grace, the name of G-d is added to the introductory formulas. Usually an honored person is asked to lead the *zimun* — a *kohen,* scholar, rabbi, or elder. On holidays and special occasions it is customary to recite the Grace with the *zimun* over a cup of wine.

The Grace After Meals is a beautiful prayer focused around four blessings. The first comes from Moses, who in gratitude to G-d composed a blessing after the manna fell in the desert. The second was composed by Joshua after the Jews entered the Land of Israel. The third comes from the kings David and Solomon. The three blessings represent, according to our Sages, three important concepts of Judaism: the existence and providence of G-d; the holy places of Israel and the Holy Temple; and the rule of G-d through an earthly king, the kingdom of David, ancestor of the Messiah.

The fourth blessing was composed by the Sages in Yavneh, after the second war with Rome (132-135 CE). After the Romans destroyed the Second Temple (70 CE), a great Jewish community had continued to flourish in the city of Betar. When the Romans later destroyed Betar as well, they not only massacred all the inhabitants but also forbade their burial. They stacked the bodies as a fence to embarrass and degrade the Jews. Despite the length of time that it took to receive permission to bury the bodies, G-d caused a miracle to occur, and the bodies did not decay. In memory of this miracle, the sages composed a blessing to add to the Grace After Meals. The blessing states that G-d "is good and does good." Despite the horrors of the war, G-d still was acting to preserve goodness.[9]

Additions are made to the Grace After Meals for Shabbos (a paragraph beginning with *R'tzei*), holidays and the New Moon (*Yaaleh v'yavo*), in the third blessing. On Chanukah and Purim we add the *Al Hanisim* paragraph to the second blessing.

---

9. Talmud *Berachos* 48b.

# ↝ THE FOOD WE EAT

The Torah is quite explicit about the laws of *kashrus* that govern the food we eat. As we will see below, it specifies types of animals that are permitted, indicates that a particular procedure of slaughtering is to be followed, forbids the consumption of blood and certain kinds of fat, and prohibits the mixing of meat and milk. Clearly, the Torah is concerned about how we treat food, especially animal food. The precise reasons for each of the permitted and forbidden foods is not given, but the general principles are unequivocal.

Also, the Torah states, "You shall be holy to Me, for I the Lord am holy, and I have set you apart from other peoples to be Mine" (*Leviticus* 20:26). This is one of the rationales behind the system of *kashrus*. The dietary laws help keep Jews from assimilating with the non-Jews among whom they live. We cannot mingle too freely; not dining together limits the amount of socializing that can be done. As our Rabbis pointed out, "If we cannot eat with them, our children will not marry their children and Judaism will be preserved."

When we practice the laws of *kashrus,* it brings a level of consciousness into eating that is otherwise almost impossible, especially in our modern culture. We become selective about where we shop, where we dine, what and how we cook, and where our food comes from. The laws teach us to pay attention to our appetites because we cannot mix certain foods, and must wait after eating some foods before we can eat others. Certain foods require special preparation. After some practice, *kashrus* becomes second nature to us, and helps us remember that we are not like animals, but live by the law of the One Who creates life and provides all food.

As Jews, we eat but do not "consume." Consuming means to devour without attention to purpose or use. Because our food is selected, carefully slaughtered and prepared, because G-d is blessed when the slaughtering is done, and before and after the food is eaten, we make clear that food has a purpose in the Divine plan. We elevate rather than consume food, raising it to a higher plane through consciousness of purpose. The plant and animal worlds are elevated to a means of praising G-d.

In this, we are "higher than the angels." Human beings can invest something physical in nature with a spiritual purpose.[10]

## ৵§ THE LAWS OF KASHRUS

1. The Torah indicates what types of animals, fish, and fowl are kosher, and which are not, listing the prohibited birds and permitted animals. The signs that differentiate kosher land animals from nonkosher ones are given explicitly, namely, that kosher animals have true cloven hoofs and chew their cud. (It is a matter of unrefuted fact that every animal with cloven hoofs also chews the cud, with the sole exception of the pig, exactly as indicated by the Torah.)

2. The prohibited birds total 24 species. We do not know the exact meaning of the words used for the birds, but the Oral Law has clarified how to distinguish kosher from nonkosher fowl. All birds of prey are forbidden, as are all birds that pick food out of the air, without waiting for it to reach the ground. Still, it is sometimes difficult to ascertain whether an unknown bird is kosher, so we only may eat those fowl that have been traditionally accepted as such.

3. Kosher fish can be recognized by the fact that they have fins and scales, as is explicitly stated in the Torah. It has been verified that all fish with scales have fins (as the Mishnah states),[11] but that the reverse is not true — many types of fish have fins but not scales. Fish do not require slaughtering like meat and chicken.

4. Insects, creeping things, and the like are called abominations

---

10. *Lev.* 11:44; 20:7.
11. Talmud *Niddah* 51b.

as food and are thus prohibited. A few kinds of jumping creatures similar to grasshoppers were at one time permitted, but we can no longer identify the appropriate species, so we do not eat them. Leafy vegetables must be carefully checked and/or treated to ensure that we are not eating insects in our salads!

5. Animals and fowl that have died of themselves cannot be eaten. They are *treifah*, which in Hebrew means "torn." (The word *treif* has been extended in popular use to include all forbidden foods, or foods not prepared in accordance with the dietary laws.) Animals killed by other animals or by hunters are *treifah* even if the animals themselves are kosher. (The *Code of Jewish Law* discourages hunting, especially for sport, because this is in the category of cruelty to animals, a practice condemned in the Bible.)

6. Kosher species other than fish must be properly slaughtered. First of all, this requires that the animal be alive; an animal on the verge of death, or suffering from a terminal disease (there are 18 categories of these), cannot be made fit to eat by slaughtering. The animal must then be killed; one cannot take a limb from a living animal.

   Following this is a specific procedure (the Torah states, "You shall slaughter as I have commanded you" — *Deuteronomy* 12:21). The animal's neck must be severed with a proper and very sharp slaughtering knife, in such a way as to sever its esophagus and trachea (for a fowl, to sever at least one of these). This must be done swiftly and without hesitation; by the time the cut is completed, the animal is no longer conscious. The knife must be examined before it is used to ensure that it has not even the slightest dent or nick. The ritual slaughterer must not only be an observant Jew educated in the laws of *shechitah* (slaughtering), but also must not be of a nervous disposition. These laws ensure the quick, humane death of the animal, with the least amount of pain possible.

7. After a fowl or beast (as opposed to a domesticated animal) is killed, its blood is covered with earth or a similar substance.

8. Following *shechitah,* forbidden fat, known as *chelev,* must be

removed. It can be distinguished from ordinary fat because it adheres loosely to the flesh and can be readily peeled off. (This prohibition applies only to oxen, sheep, and goats.)

9. After trimming the fat, the *gid hanasheh* (sciatic nerve) must be excised. Steaks from the hindquarter of the animal are prohibited. This section of the animal is rich in blood because of the many veins attached to the sciatic nerve, which runs through this part of the animal. This prohibition is based on the biblical encounter between our ancestor Jacob and the "angel," understood as the heavenly officer representing Esau. While he was wrestling with the angel, Jacob's hip was wrenched. Therefore, to this day, the sciatic nerve portion of the animal is prohibited, as the Torah explicitly states (*Genesis* 32:33).

10. The last thing to be removed is the blood, for the Torah states over and over again that no blood whatsoever may be eaten. As a first step, a number of large veins are excised; the meat is then soaked and salted in a special kashering process. This involves rinsing the meat, then placing it in a large receptacle filled with water so as to soften it to the point at which it will absorb salt. The meat is then placed on a flat, grooved board, set on an incline so that liquid can drain off. The meat is then salted on all sides and in cavities with coarse salt (effective in absorbing the blood) and placed on the board for one hour. The meat is then thoroughly rinsed three times. After this procedure, it is considered "*kashered,*" and can be cooked and eaten. Today, when we buy packaged kosher meats from an approved butcher, these procedures have already been followed.

11. Liver, because of its different properties, requires special treatment, which is *not* done by the butcher. It must be broiled over an open fire.

12. If meat has remained unsoaked and unsalted for longer than three days, its blood has congealed to the point that it cannot be *kashered* in the normal manner. If it had been washed off with cold water, it can still be *kashered* within three days of the washing. Any meat that has been scalded before *kashering*

becomes *treif* because the blood has coagulated. If it has been frozen, the blood may have congealed; thus, the only way it is permissible is if it is broiled. In any of these cases, one should consult a knowledgeable rabbi.

13. In America today, most observant Jews buy *glatt kosher* meat. The word *glatt* is a Yiddish word meaning "smooth," and it refers to the requirement that the lungs of the animal not be damaged or scarred (which might indicate the presence of a terminal disease). Determining this requires close scrutiny after slaughtering to ascertain whether the animal is kosher. The term *glatt kosher* applies only to meat — not to fowl or any other product — and it generally means that more stringent care has been taken in the slaughtering and *kashering* process.

## ◄§ MEAT AND DAIRY

The Torah prohibits a Jew to combine meat and dairy in the following ways:

a. to cook, roast, or fry dairy and meat products together;
b. to eat milk and meat that were cooked together;
c. to derive any benefit of pleasure from such a mixture (one cannot sell it or give it as a present).

In addition to meat and dairy, there is a category of food called *pareve*. These foods are neither meat nor dairy and can be combined with either of them. This large group includes fruits, vegetables, eggs, grain, fish, sugar, most beverages except milk, and pure condiments and spices.

By rabbinic law, chicken and other fowl were given the legal status of meat with respect to the laws of mixing meat and dairy. One may eat eggs with milk even though they come from hens, which are a meat product.

Dishes, pots, and other utensils used for dairy products should not be used for meat and vice versa. Therefore the Jewish household normally has two sets of tableware, dishes, pots and pans, cleaning utensils, and tablecloths or covers. A rabbi should be consulted if things become mixed in any way. Dishes are never put directly into the sink without a dishpan or rack (unless there are separate meat and dairy kosher sinks). Usually, color-coding is used to keep things separate. Refrigerators, because they contain only cold foods, can store both meat and dairy, in separate closed containers.

After eating meat, one waits six hours before eating dairy. (Jews of German extraction have the custom of waiting only three hours, and those from Holland one hour.) After a light milk meal or a dairy snack, one can wash his hands and rinse his mouth, then eat meat. However, if one has eaten hard, aged cheese (aged over 180 days, as are certain imported Swiss cheeses), one should wait six hours before eating meat.

If a drop of milk or dairy product falls on or into a pot containing boiling hot meat, or if a meat sauce or gravy falls onto or into a pot of boiling dairy, a rabbi should be consulted. The decision will depend in part on the proportion of the amount that fell in compared to the amount of food inside the pot.

If dairy and meat utensils become mixed in such a way that they have contacted heat together (as in hot dishwater), a rabbi must be consulted. If only cold contact is involved, e.g., a meat spoon was accidentally put into a cold pudding, the utensil need only be wiped off and washed.

If two people wish to eat different types of food at the same table, a divider should be placed between them, or they should use separate place mats.

## ✑ RABBINICAL SUPERVISION

Prepared foods today go through many processes, including the use of additives and chemicals. This has made the certification of *kashrus* especially necessary today, although the need for supervision also arose occasionally in the talmudic era.[12]

---

12. Rav Yitro ben Sheshes, *Teshuvas Re'evush, Beis Yosef, Hilchos Megillah* 690.

Some of the problems involved include the use of shortening, gelatin, oils, margarines, emulsifiers, mono- and di-glycerides, polysorbate, and tartaric acid, any of which may be of animal or nonkosher origin. In addition, most countries' laws do not require that every ingredient be listed, so even when you know the source of everything on the label, it may not fill kosher requirements. Questions may arise in production due to the use of the same machinery for kosher and non-kosher products. Also, a product may have dairy ingredients that are not immediately obvious, but would make the product unusable in cooking with meat.

Eating outside the home raises other issues. In general, the owners of a restaurant or bakery should be Sabbath observers, for this is also a measure of their general reliability in matters of Jewish law and especially *kashrus*. If the owners are not Jewish or not religious, a reliable *kashrus* supervisor, known as a *mashgiach,* must be on the premises.

We would like to be trusting, but we cannot rely on blind trust. A rabbi was once in a distant land where people did not recognize him. A simple Jew, on seeing the distinguished-looking individual, thought he might be a *shochet* and asked him to slaughter a chicken for him. The rabbi declined, explaining he was not a licensed slaughterer, and explained his refusal. He asked the man, "Could you lend me $1,000?"

"If I don't know you, how can I be sure that you will repay me?" the man replied.

"Since you don't know me, how could you rely on me to slaughter your chicken according to Jewish law?" the rabbi asked in return.

## ⊷ NON-JEWISH FOODS

Our Sages prohibited the eating of a non-Jew's home-baked bread or cake, even if the ingredients are kosher. This helps prevent socializing and assimilation. If a Jew helped in the baking process, or if the product is commercially made, the prohibition does not apply.

Food cooked (rather than baked) by a non-Jew is prohibited under certain circumstances, namely foods not usually eaten raw (e.g. there is no prohibition on a baked apple); foods served at a banquet, like meat or chicken (e.g. it does not apply to tea or candy); or if the gentile cooked it in its entirety. If a Jew helped by putting on the fire or putting the food on, or if the non-Jew is only warming up the food, the prohibition does not apply.

Wine, meat or fish sent to a Jew by a non-Jew is prohibited unless packaged, sealed, or marked to ensure that it has not been tampered with. Wine or grape juice handled by a non-Jew is forbidden. This is not only to prevent assimilation, but also because wines were used in idol-worship. Kosher wines are double sealed, and often precooked at a minimum temperature, so that they can be handled by non-Jews in transport.

Milk from a farm owned by a non-Jew can be prohibited because the milk might be mixed with that from a nonkosher animal. However, if a Jew does the milking or supervises it, the milk is permissible. The same holds if a Jew owns the farm and the milking is done by non-Jews, because the Jew can supervise at any time. In modern America, many Jews follow the decision of Rav Moshe Feinstein that government regulations make it possible to use the milk produced here, where nonkosher animals are virtually never used in milk production.

There are additional prohibited foods:

1. Fruits of the Land of Israel must have been tithed.

2. The fruit of a tree cannot be used in its first three years.

3. Challah must be taken from dough if the concentration is sufficiently large (about four pounds of flour). This is considered one of the duties of a Jewish woman. Today, the custom outside of Israel is to remove from the dough a small portion, the size of an olive, and to burn it. After the kneading, dough is taken and a blessing is said, *l'hafrish challah*. If one forgets, it can be separated after the bread is baked. Items

that do not use a large concentration of dough, such as cakes, cookies, and crackers, do not require this separation.

4. According to the *Code of Jewish Law,* meat and fish should not be eaten together. One should rinse one's mouth in between meat and fish courses. However, one need not use permanently separated utensils; the forks and knives should merely be washed.

5. Food left uncovered in the street should not be eaten, nor should uncovered food be left under a bed where a person sleeps.

6. Any fish already filleted requires rabbinic certification to ensure that it came from a kosher fish.

## ⊷§ KOSHER VESSELS

When one buys metal or glass dishes or utensils from a non-Jewish manufacturer, they must be immersed in a ritual bath (*mikveh*). This applies to vessels whose purpose is to contain food directly — glassware, pots and pans, dishes, flatware and serving utensils, trays like the toaster oven tray that touches food. A tray used just for serving does not require immersion. Earthenware does not have to be immersed if it is not glazed or coated with glass. Wood does not require immersion. (A slaughtering knife is questionable, because it is used on something that is not yet food.) If any utensil was manufactured and subsequently owned by a Jew, it does not require immersion.

Immersion involves putting the entire utensil in the water in such a way that all parts are touched by the water, including the handle. One must hold it loosely in order to accomplish this. A blessing is said, *al tevilas keilim,* except in cases where it is questionable (such as a completely glazed china dish). When a utensil is made of different materials, a rabbi should be consulted.

# ⊰ CLOTHING AND PERSONAL APPEARANCE

E very Jew is obligated to care about his personal cleanliness and outward appearance, not only for hygienic reasons but also for religious purposes. The Torah says, "You shall not make yourself detestable." We may not pray or learn Torah until we have relieved ourselves and removed harmful wastes from our bodies; nor can we pray in an unclean place. Our homes should be clean and orderly, for health and sanctity.

Modesty is a requirement for Jews, and so our Sages urged proper dress, including covering the body. In particular, women are asked to pay attention to modest dress as a source of feminine honor and dignity.

A scholar should be distinguished not only by his knowledge and wisdom, but also by his dignified dress and personal appearance. His hair and clothing should be neat and not shabby; but at the same time he should not dress too expensively, in order to avoid being considered ostentatious.

There is one particular prohibition about clothing, applicable to both men and women, namely *shatnez*. This is the prohibition of a mixture of wool and linen in the same garment. The word *shatnez* is a combination of three Hebrew words meaning combing, weaving, and twisting. The prohibition, therefore, extends to any material containing wool and linen wherein they have been woven, pressed, or braided together. The stiffening fabric in collars of wool coats and jackets often results in a violation of the prohibition. When one buys a suit or coat, one should be sure to have it checked by a reliable person specifically trained to test for the presence of *shatnez*. One cannot rely on the seller's word if he states that none of his suits contain *shatnez*.

"You shall not . . . destroy the corners of your beard" (*Leviticus* 19:27). Hereby, a man is prohibited to use a razor blade or knife to shave the beard from his face. "You shall not round the corners of your head" prohibits the total removal of the sideburns. Many

Chassidic Jews leave their sideburns (*payos*) dangling and do not cut them short. The Torah also forbids tattooing and other forms of self-mutilation. However, women are permitted to pierce their ears for earrings.

# ⤳ KASHRUS AND HEALTH — PHYSICAL AND SPIRITUAL

One of the great misconceptions about *kashrus* is that the dietary laws were ancient health measures that are no longer necessary. For example, some people believed that the prohibition on pork was due to its linkage with trichinosis. They would then argue that since the cause of the disease has for the most part been eliminated by contemporary inspection procedures, pork need not be prohibited. Similarly, it was claimed that salting meat was necessary before the advent of refrigeration.

These arguments are completely false. There is no basis in Torah or history for them. We keep kosher, and have kept it for millennia, because G-d commanded us to. If there were health benefits, these were byproducts. Laws of *kashrus* are called *chukim* or mandatory statutes, to be obeyed even though we may not understand the reasons for them. Our ignorance of G-d's purposes should not lead us to believe that these *mitzvos* are unimportant. Rather, we should understand that we are the ones who lack the overall perspective on all the elements of G-d's creation.[13]

Even though we do not understand the specific reasons, it is clear that there are benefits in observing such laws. The Rambam taught that the laws of *kashrus* are to be obeyed no matter what; and in addition they clearly serve the purpose of training us to master our appetites, restrain our desires, and avoid regarding the pleasures of eating and drinking as the goal of human existence.[14]

---

13. Rav Moshe Isserles, *Mechir Yayin* on *Megillas Esther*, 6.
14. Rambam, *Guide for the Perplexed*.

The Torah is concerned with our spiritual well-being and inner purity. This includes our physical health, but it also transcends mere physicality. Therefore, when the Torah tells us to avoid certain foods, it is providing for our spiritual cleanliness. This elevated principle then may be reflected in the physical world. Thus some foods that are disgusting to most people, such as insects or the meat of diseased animals, hint to us about the spiritual purpose behind such laws. Similarly, foods from naturally vicious animals such as birds and beasts of prey remind us of the qualities of character we want to avoid, while the gentler domesticated animals remind us of more peaceable traits we might want to cultivate. On a physical level, we may well be influenced by the temperament of the things we eat. Even the fact that animal foods are hedged about with so many prohibitions reminds us of the different qualities of the animal world compared to the plant world. (Vegetarianism itself does not make a kosher kitchen, however. Consult a rabbi to find out what is necessary to be a kosher vegetarian.)

*Kashrus* reminds us to be very careful about the foods we allow to enter our bodies. We should always make sure that the food-stuffs we buy do not contain nonkosher ingredients and the meat we eat was properly prepared. A Jew considers nonkosher food a kind of spiritual poison. If you're not certain of the *kashrus* of something, do not eat it. "When in doubt, throw it out." We are doing good for ourselves on many levels — physical, moral, and spiritual — when we keep these laws.

# 13

~~~

## Life's Drama: Jewish
## Rites of Passage

~~~

In the life of every Jew are special occasions that call for celebration, as well as events that call forth anxiety, grief, or mourning. Judaism's guidelines, customs, and laws for these occasions are derived from the Torah, from the examples of our great ancestors, and from the writings of the Prophets and Sages of the Talmud. While some customs may differ from one country or even one community to another, there is a general halachic framework to which all Jews adhere.

## ✦§ THE BIRTH OF A CHILD

"The whole world rejoices when a child is born." Certainly in Jewish life, there is great rejoicing in the family and the whole community. Also, all measures are taken to preserve the life of a child. The first week after birth is regarded as the most crucial period for the child's survival and, as the Talmud teaches, all laws of Shabbos may be suspended to save a person's life. Therefore everything necessary for the infant's welfare may be done on Shabbos.[1]

The births of boys and girls are celebrated differently, but both with awe and joy. For a girl, the celebration focuses on her naming, usually at the first congregational reading of the Torah (Monday, Thursday, Rosh Chodesh, or Shabbos) after her birth. Some have the custom of waiting until the Torah reading on Shabbos. The father is called to the Torah, and the name is given in a special prayer after the reading ( ___[newborn's name]___ bas ___[name of father]___ ). A prayer of good health for the mother is made as well.[2] Frequently the family will make a celebration in honor of the baby girl, such as a *kiddush* after Shabbos services. However, it need not be done immediately after the birth.

Ashkenazim do not name the baby after someone who is living. If he is named after someone who died young, it is customary to add an additional name. Sephardim do name children in honor of living parents.

For a boy, a celebration is held in the family's home on the first Friday night, and also after the *bris milah* (circumcision). This is called *shalom zachor* ("welcome to the male child"). Following this, on the eighth day if the child is well, is a circumcision. The circumcision may be held even if the eighth day is Shabbos or Yom Tov (unless the birth was by Caesarean section, in which case it will be postponed until after Shabbos). The infant cannot be circumcised unless he is healthy, however. If he is in an incubator, or if there is a problem with jaundice, blood count, or birth weight, the circumcision will be delayed until both the doctor and the *mohel* determine that the baby is ready.

On the night before, many Jews conduct a *wachnacht* or "night of watching." Children are invited to surround the crib of the newborn and recite *Shema* and *Hamalach hago'el* (a bedtime

---

1. Before the child is born, if there has to be a decision made whether to save the mother or the fetus, the mother's life takes precedence. After the birth is complete, both are equal in terms of the decision to save a life. Mishnah *Oholos* Ch. 7.
2. Found in all prayerbooks and discussed in depth in *Igros Moshe* by Rav Moshe Feinstein.

prayer). The father spends the night studying Torah. This is a protection for the newborn before the *bris milah* and is also meant to ensure that the child starts off his life on a path of Torah.

The importance of the circumcision ceremony for boys goes back nearly four millennia to our ancestor Abraham. "G-d said to Abraham, 'And as for you, you shall keep My covenant, you and your seed after you, throughout your generations. This is My covenant which you shall keep, between Me and you and your seed after you: every male among you shall be circumcised" (*Genesis* 17: 9-10). The Torah teaches that circumcision is the way in which a Jewish man expresses his "wholehearted" faith in G-d.

It is a positive commandment for the father to circumcise his son at the age of eight days. He may appoint a representative, known as a *mohel* or expert circumciser, to do it for him. The *mohel* should be not only trained and skilled in the procedure, but also righteous and familiar with all the laws. Circumcision is a *mitzvah* of the Torah and not merely a health practice, so it should not be performed by a non-Jew or nonreligious Jew. Although a *mohel* is not a medical doctor, he is a trained specialist, with more experience in the field than most doctors or surgeons. He has special instruments specifically designed for the circumcision.

If the father is deceased or is not Jewish, the mother is obligated to make sure her son is circumcised; if a Jewish man reaches adulthood without having been circumcised, he is obligated to have the operation performed on himself.

The circumcision must be performed in the daytime, after sunrise. A special seat is designated for the prophet Elijah, who attends every *bris* to serve as protector of the infant. A couple bring the child into the room where the circumcision is to take place. The child is given to the *sandek,* who will hold the child during the *bris.* It is a great privilege to be chosen as *sandek* because of his role in this important *mitzvah,* and the position is usually given to an elder in the family or another person of honor.

The father of the child designates the *mohel* as his representative to fulfill his obligation. The *mohel* recites a special blessing before the circumcision, and the father repeats it immediately afterwards. The guests then call out in Hebrew, "Just as this child has entered the Covenant [of G-d], so too should he enter a life of Torah, marriage, and good deeds."

The blessing *Borei pri hagafen* is recited over the wine, followed by another blessing. The child is given a Jewish name ( [newborn's name] ben [name of father] ) and a few drops of wine are placed in the mouth of the baby.

It is best to have a *minyan* (ten adult Jewish males) present at the circumcision. Then there is a festive meal (*seudah*) in which everyone should partake.

> *In a* shtetl *in Europe, the father of a newborn boy was deathly ill. As the eighth day approached for the* bris milah, *some of the family felt inclined to delay the circumcision. Anticipating that the father was about to die, they wanted to give his name to the newborn son. When the rabbi heard of this, he insisted that, on the contrary, the* bris *had to be performed on the eighth day, without delay.*
>
> *People were amazed by the rabbi's ruling and asked his reason. The rabbi replied, "You know that the prophet Elijah comes to every* bris. *Let us hope that he will not only protect the newborn but also will bring a complete recovery to the father."*
>
> *The* bris *was indeed conducted on the eighth day. The newborn did well, and the father also recovered, just as the rabbi had predicted.*

The *bris milah* is a symbol and reminder to the Jew that he is spiritually different from others. This is why, at some periods in history, persecutors have attempted to prevent Jews from performing the ceremony. During the Roman period, harsh decrees threatened death to those who performed *bris milah* on their children. Nevertheless when a son was born to Rabbi Shimon ben Gamliel, the *Nasi* ("prince," i.e. chief authority) of the Jewish community in Israel, he went ahead with the performance of the commandment.

The emperor heard rumors that Rabbi Shimon had disobeyed the law, so he summoned him for a trial, to which he also had to bring his newborn son. On their way to Rome, Rabbi Shimon and his wife stopped at an inn. They met a Roman aristocratic family there, and befriended them. The wife of the aristocrat had just given birth to a boy as well, and when she heard of Rabbi Shimon's plight, she offered to exchange her son temporarily for his. Thus, when ordered to present his baby before the emperor, Rabbi Shimon displayed an uncircumcised baby. The charges against him were dismissed. On the way back home, Rabbi Shimon's wife exchanged babies with the Roman noblewoman at the inn.

Rabbi Shimon's son grew up to become the great sage Rabbi Yehudah Ha'Nasi — Judah the Prince. The son of the Roman noblewoman became Antoninus, emperor of Rome. He maintained a close friendship with Judah the Prince and was a benevolent ruler to the Jews.[3]

## ৶ REDEMPTION OF THE FIRSTBORN

In Judaism, we are frequently reminded that the first of any gift we receive belongs to G-d. The first of the produce of the land, the first fruits of a tree, and the firstborn of domestic animals all were brought to the Holy Temple in Jerusalem to be offered to G-d. With our children also, the firstborn, if a male, would have been considered like a "priest," to be dedicated to G-d for lifetime service. As Judaism developed, the firstborn males no longer actually functioned as a priestly class, but were replaced by the Levites. Still, as a reminder of the significance of the status of the firstborn, we still practice a ceremony of redemption ("buying back"), known as *pidyon ha'ben*. We redeem the baby and restore it to its parents, thereby demonstrating that it initially belonged to G-d.[4]

If either parent is a *kohen* or a *levi,* however, the child is not redeemed, since those families still occupy a place of service to G-d. The "firstborn" status is determined by the mother. If the mother has previously given birth to another child, whether the child is living or dead, there is no *pidyon ha'ben* because the boy

---

3. *Tosafos,* Talmud *Avodah Zarah* 10b.
4. *Sefer HaChinuch.*

is not her firstborn. If the boy was born through Caesarean section, no redemption is necessary, because it was not a child that "opened the womb," as the Torah says. If the mother previously had a pregnancy which terminated early, a rabbi should be consulted to determine the status of the child.

The *pidyon ha'ben* is performed after thirty days have elapsed since the birth of the son (i.e., on the 31st day). It should not be postponed unless that day was Shabbos, in which case it can be done at night after Shabbos is over. The redemption is accomplished by the father giving a *kohen* the equivalent of five shekels (96 grams) of silver. Checks, paper money, or other types of metal coins may not be used. Simultaneously, the father declares that the coins are being given in exchange for his son. The *kohen* may, if he chooses, return the money, or put it in trust for the child. The father himself should perform this ceremony and recites the blessing.

## ৵ঌ RAISING A CHILD

Many Jews have the custom not to cut a boy's hair until he is three years old. This is based on the laws of *orlah,* the fruit of a tree which cannot be used for the first three years. The human being is compared to a tree, which must be cherished and treated carefully in its early years. The ceremony of the first haircut is known in Yiddish as *upsheren* and in Hebrew as *chalakah* (smooth). It is customary to invite family and friends for a festive meal to celebrate.

Children should be educated as appropriate to their age, in the *mitzvos* of the Torah and in learning to value Torah study. Rabbi Elazar said, "A person should devote much time to raising his children and grandchildren." The Talmud states that one who leads a child to study Torah is regarded as if he himself had accepted the Torah at Sinai.[5] The father or mother who sends the child to school to study *alef-beis,* the prayer book, the Bible and

---

5. Talmud *Kiddushin* 30.

finally Talmud creates another link in the strong chain leading from Sinai to the present, and into the future of the Jewish nation. This is true of helping others' children learn as well, for "The one that teaches his neighbor's child the Torah is considered as if he himself had begotten him."[6]

*Pirkei Avos* says of the great Rabbi Yehoshua, "Happy is the one who gave birth to him."[7] Because of his mother, he became a Torah scholar, for every day that his mother was pregnant she went to the various synagogues in the city and said to the participants, "Please, pray for this child that he may grow up to be a pious, learned Jew." After he was born, she brought his cradle to the *beis midrash* so that he could listen to the sounds of Torah learning.

As parents, we are each obligated to train our children in the observance of the commandments in accordance with each child's age and ability.[8] "Train a child according to his way" (*Proverbs* 22:6) is understood to mean that education must be tailored to the child. From the time that children begin to talk and understand a little, they should be taught the verses *Shema Yisrael* and *Torah tzivah lanu Moshe*. Then they can be taught the blessings on food.[9]

## ᴥ§ BAR AND BAS MITZVAH

A girl who reaches 12 years of age is *bas mitzvah* (daughter of the commandment), and a boy who reaches 13 years of age is called *bar mitzvah* (son of the commandment). From that time, the children are obligated to the same *mitzvos* as an adult.

If children have been educated in Jewish observance, they will already know and be practicing many of the things they now are obligated to do. For a boy, however, there are some public changes. He is now counted as part of a *minyan* for prayer; he can be called

6. *Sanhedrin* 19b.

7. *Pirkei Avos* 2:11; based on Talmud Yerushalmi, *Yevamos*.

8. Talmud *Succah* 42.

9. *Shulchan Aruch, Orach Chaim* 343; *Ritva, Hilchos Berachos;* Rav Henkin, *Sefer Eidos Yisrael*.

up to the Torah; and, most importantly, he will be putting on *tefillin* every morning (see Chapter 12). For a girl, the most notable change is that she is now obligated to light Shabbos candles.

The *bar mitzvah* in the past couple of centuries has come to be celebrated as a major family occasion. The sharing of food at a meal is indeed classified as a *seudas mitzvah* (festive meal) if the boy delivers a discourse on the Torah. In many European communities prior to modern times, the celebration was still a small, semiprivate ceremony. In the 19th century, Western European and American communities enlarged upon the tradition.

Pleasant as the festivities are, it is important to retain the original emphasis on *mitzvah* (and not "bar") in *bar mitzvah*. It is completely inappropriate to make the meal in a nonkosher restaurant or to provide improper entertainment. Also, many rabbis suggest that the family donate to charity at least as much money as they spend on the *bar mitzvah* celebration to keep it in proper perspective.

There is no basis in Torah or Jewish tradition for any ceremony known as "confirmation," at or about age 16. Some Reform and Conservative communities have imported this concept from Christianity, but Jews are actually forbidden to copy ceremonies from other religions. It is sometimes argued that such a ritual is appropriate because it enables a teenager to mark the acquisition of a more serious understanding of Judaism; but it is hardly a mark of understanding to teach them the practice of other religions. Indeed, we are all growing in our maturity of understanding, from birth to death. In Judaism, the primary difference between children and adults is the extent to which they can be held accountable for their obligations.

## ๛ MARRIAGE

Every Jewish man is obligated to marry and raise a family. The fact that the obligation is on the man and not the woman is usually understood to mean that the man needs to be commanded, while the woman usually has a natural desire for a family. Clearly, both must engage in a cooperative endeavor in order to create a lasting relationship and a Jewish home!

Through marriage, each individual uses his/her talents and resources to sanctify the home to G-d; marriage has always been considered a sacred institution. From ancient times, going as far back as Abraham and Sarah, men and women together created Judaism. Rambam classifies the laws of marriage with those pertaining to holiness. Essentially, marriage is a holy covenant between a man and a woman, with G-d as Guardian of the partnership. The term used for the marriage ceremony, *kiddushin,* means sanctification, and thereby indicates the high esteem in which the institution is held. So important is the fulfillment of this commandment that the Rabbis stated, "One who does not have a mate lives without joy, without bliss, without happiness."[10]

IN MANY OBSERVANT HOMES, PARENTS OF A YOUNG MAN OR WOMAN help with the process of finding a suitable partner by inquiring

**COURTSHIP** among friends and acquaintances about potential mates before the two are introduced. However, the idea that couples are betrothed by their parents without their agreement is false. It is against Jewish law to coerce a person into marrying someone. Still, in helping men and women to meet one another, the matchmaker (*shadchan*) has long held an honored position in the Jewish community. The matchmaker can bring together people from distant communities who might not otherwise meet, and thus reduce the need for singles to socialize in uncomfortable or inappropriate situations.

Men and women from most observant families (except for very strict Chassidic homes) go out on dates to decide whether they are compatible and attracted to one another. If all goes well, they become engaged. A long process of dating (more than a few months) is discouraged, as it tends to prolong doubt and result in hurt feelings if the couple breaks up. When the decision is made, a public announcement is made of the couple's intention to wed.

---

10. Talmud *Yevamos* 62b.

Some, especially among the Chassidim, have a ceremony known as *tena'im* (written conditions of the prenuptial agreement). If the *tena'im* are not made at the time of the engagement, they are completed right before the marriage ceremony.

The Torah explicitly lists those who are forbidden to marry because of their blood relationship. In addition, a *kohen* is forbidden to marry a divorcee or convert. Some men have the custom to avoid marrying a woman whose Hebrew name is identical to that of his mother.

Weddings are not permitted during periods of communal mourning, specifically, fast days, the three weeks during the summer between the 17th of Tammuz and the 9th of Av, and 33 days of *sefirah* (counting the *Omer*) between Passover and Shavuos. (The exact days which are counted depends on the community's custom.) Weddings are rarely performed between Rosh Hashanah and Yom Kippur, because the spirit of fun that manifests at a wedding is not appropriate during this period of solemn reflection and introspection.[11]

It is customary for the groom to be called up to the Torah on the Shabbos preceding his wedding. This occasion is known as *aufruf,* a Yiddish word meaning "calling up." Friends of the bride often honor her on Shabbos afternoon with a *Shabbos kallah* ("Shabbos of the bride"), with festive food and singing.

## THE MARRIAGE CEREMONY

THE FAMILY OF THE BRIDE CUSTOMARILY PRESENTS THE GROOM with a *tallis* before the wedding. The bride goes to the *mikveh* for a ritual immersion on the eve of the wedding. (The relevant laws of *mikveh* are beyond the scope of this work.[12]) Both bride and groom fast and pray on the day before the wedding, treating it as their personal "Yom Kippur." The origin of this custom comes from the Talmud Yerushalmi, which states that a bride and groom are forgiven on the day they begin their new lives.[13] If the wedding

---

11. Rabbi Ephraim Margolis, *Mateh Efrayim.*
12. See, e.g., Rabbi Aryeh Kaplan, *Waters of Eden.*
13. Talmud Yerushalmi, *Bikurim* 3:3.

ceremony is held at night, the fast is broken when the stars appear; however, it is forbidden to fast on Rosh Chodesh, Chanukah, and certain other minor holidays.

Before the actual ceremony, the officiating rabbi ascertains that the *tena'im* and the *kesubah* (marriage contract) are in order. These documents attest to the legality of the marriage and spell out the obligations of the husband to his wife, including his obligation to support and provide for her, and stipulate what will happen in case of his death or divorce. This *kesubah* must remain in their possession as long as they are married.

As in all legal matters, two witnesses, not related to either party, must sign the documents. The groom then lifts a handkerchief to signify the completion of the marriage agreement (*kesubah*). The mothers of the bride and groom then, together, break a plate; as with the breaking of a glass under the *chupah,* it reminds us of the destruction of the Temple even at our most joyous of moments.

After the signing comes the *bedeckung,* when the groom, escorted by family or friends, covers the bride's face with her veil. This recalls the modesty of the matriarch Rebecca when she first saw her future husband, Isaac. Then the fathers bless the young couple.

A Jewish marriage is conducted under a canopy known as a *chupah,* which symbolizes the consummation of the marriage. It is usually placed outside or under an open skylight, symbolic of the blessing G-d gave to Abraham, "Your children will be as numerous as the stars of the sky." The *chasan* (groom) and *kallah* (bride) are escorted separately by the respective parents to the *chupah,* as though they were king and queen. The parents carry lighted candles, reminders of the lightning that appeared at Mount Sinai when Israel accepted the Torah.

Under the *chupah,* the bride walks around the groom seven times, symbolically binding them together. After the officiating rabbi recites the first of the Seven Marriage Blessings, the groom places a gold ring on the forefinger of the bride's right hand, and says, "Behold, you are sanctified to me with this ring in accordance with the laws of Moses and Israel." The ring must be a simple gold band without any jewels embedded in it to avoid any questions of fraud regarding the value of the ring.[14] The wedding contract is then read. The ceremony is carried out in the presence of two qualified witnesses who are Sabbath-observant and not related to either the bride or the groom.

The remainder of the Seven Blessings are recited, then the glass is broken (symbolizing that our joy cannot be complete until the Temple is rebuilt), and the bride and groom retire to a room by themselves for a short period of privacy.

The festive meal which follows the ceremony is classified as a *seudas mitzvah* (meal of a commandment). At this celebration, which always includes music and dancing, it is a great *mitzvah* to make the bride and groom feel merry and festive.[15] The Talmud teaches that one must even stop learning Torah to bring the bride to the *chupah*.[16] Just as royalty wear special garments, always have an entourage, and are praised by all, so should the bride and groom be given royal treatment.

The first seven days after the wedding are known as the Seven Days of Feasting. Festivities are continued throughout that week, including meals at which the Seven Wedding Blessings are said at the Grace After Meals.

A JEWISH MARRIAGE IS GUIDED BY LAWS THAT STRENGTHEN THE relationship between a husband and wife, particularly through

**KEEPING THE MARRIAGE HOLY**

sexual discipline. These laws are generally referred to as the "laws of family purity." For a given period of time each month (except during the woman's pregnancy), the Torah prohibits all sexual relations. At the conclusion of this period, the woman immerses herself in a *mikveh* and relations can resume. In a Jewish community, the building of a proper *mikveh* is more necessary for spiritual well-being than a synagogue, and takes priority in deciding which to build first.[17]

14. *Shulchan Aruch, Even HaEzer* 31:2.
15. Talmud *Berachos* 6b; Maharil, *Likutei Maharil.*
16. Talmud *Kesubos* 17a.
17. Rav Moshe Feinstein, *Igros Moshe.*

It is important to build a healthy relationship in all areas of the marriage, for that is the foundation of the home. The Torah refers to a wife as *eizer k'negdo* (*Genesis* 2:20), literally meaning "a helper opposed to him." This seems a most contradictory expression. Our Sages explain the term:

A man is often a poor judge of his own character. He cannot see himself objectively and sometimes fails to notice his own faults. His wife, however, can be a good judge of his true nature, for she knows him well enough to see him as he truly is. If he observes the Torah's laws and is helpful to his fellows, then her job is to be a "helper" and encourage him in his beneficial work. However, if he is abusive toward others and disrespectful of the Torah, if his service to G-d or character development is deficient, it is her task to be "opposed to him." In this she is to help him understand (respectfully and lovingly!) his faults and to encourage him to improve. A wife must be both a "helper" and one "opposed" to her husband, depending on his tendencies in different areas of his life. In either case, her major role cannot be overstated. Of course, a spouse must act with the utmost sensitivity and diplomacy in giving necessary criticism.

Fidelity is essential as the building block upon which all else depends. "You shall not commit adultery" (*Leviticus* 20:10) is a biblical commandment forbidding any relationship between a man and another man's wife. In such an offense, both the wife and the man are equally guilty. The sin is not so much against the husband of the unfaithful wife as against G-d Himself, whose precepts are being violated.

"It is because of his wife that a man's house is blessed," say our Sages. And, "Who is rich? The one who has a fine wife."[18]

## ◄§ DIVORCE

The Talmud states that when a man divorces his wife, even "the Altar sheds tears."[19] In Jewish life, divorce is regarded

---

18. Talmud *Bava Metzia* 59; *Shabbos* 25.
19. Talmud *Gittin* 90.

as a tragic last resort after all possibilities have been exhausted for reestablishing marital harmony and for rekindling the love and affection that once existed between the couple. "When every hope of healing the breach has been lost, then the law of divorce is given for the sake of peace . . . And those who divorce when they must, bring good upon themselves, not evil."[20] Thus, when a person comes to request a divorce in a Jewish court (*beis din*), the rabbis will make every effort to reconcile the couple before proceeding with the divorce.

According to Jewish law since the time of Moses, a marriage can be dissolved only by the giving of a Jewish bill of divorce, known as a *get*. Divorces granted under secular law by the civil authorities have no validity under Jewish law; a rabbinic court competent in the laws of marriage and divorce must arrange for the giving of a *get*. The contract of divorce may not be form printed — it must be written specifically for the particular man and the particular woman in order to dissolve that marriage. The scribe and the two witnesses must be pious and observant, and may not be related to the husband, the wife, or each other.

A previously married woman who has not received a valid *get* from her husband is still considered as being married to him, and is not free to remarry another man. If the husband cannot be found — for example, if he has died but the death cannot be verified, or if he has deserted her and cannot be found and compelled to give a *get* — this creates a problem for the woman, who in Jewish law is called an *agunah*. This issue becomes especially acute during wartime. It is a very tragic and unfortunate situation since the *agunah* is forbidden to marry until the matter can be resolved.

If a woman who has not received a *get* remarries, any children born from the second union are *mamzerim*, i.e. halachically illegitimate. They will not be permitted to marry any Jewish person except another *mamzer*. Children born from incestuous relationships, or other relationships specifically forbidden by the Torah, are also *mamzerim*. However, a child born out of wedlock,

20. Eliyahu Kitov, *The Jew and His Home*.

assuming the marriage of the parents would have been halachically permissible, is not classified as illegitimate under Jewish law.

A *kohen* (descendant of the priestly family of Aaron) is forbidden to marry a divorcee, a proselyte, one who is known to be involved in promiscuous or forbidden sexual relationships, or one who is herself an offspring of a forbidden marriage. Such a marriage disqualifies the *kohen* from his duties and privileges, and affects the status of his children. However, a *kohen* is permitted to marry a widow.

# ◄§ SICKNESS AND HEALING

In Jewish law and moral teachings, human life is considered of supreme value. Preserving it takes precedence over virtually all other considerations. This attitude is most eloquently summed up in a Talmudic passage about the creation of Adam: "Only a single human being was created in the world, to teach that if any person has caused a single soul of Israel to perish, Scripture regards him as if he had caused an entire world to perish. If any human being saves a single soul of Israel, the Torah regards him as if he had saved an entire world."[21] Thus the obligation to preserve life is all-encompassing.

The duty to preserve life suspends all religious precepts except the three cardinal sins: idolatry, murder, and certain sexual offenses. Even the mere *possibility* of saving human life mandates violation of all the other laws, however remote the likelihood of saving human life may be. Moreover, we are required to work to preserve the life whether it is likely to be prolonged for a matter of years or for merely a few seconds.

Rabbi Yosef Caro wrote in the *Code of Jewish Law*, "The Torah gave permission to the physician to heal; moreover, this is a religious precept and it is included in the category of saving life. If

---

21. Talmud *Sanhedrin* 37a.

the physician withholds his services, it is considered as shedding blood.''[22]

All Jews are responsible to fulfill the commandment of *bikur cholim* (visiting the sick). This *mitzvah* entails looking after the patient and attending to his or her needs. It includes also a social visit for the purpose of cheering up the patient, and offering prayers at the patient's bedside. Rabbi Akiva stressed the importance of this *mitzvah* when he stated, "He who does not visit the sick is as guilty as if he had shed blood.''[23] Rabbi Yochanan included this as one of the six kinds of deeds "the fruits of which man eats in this world, while the principal remains for him in the World to Come.''[24] *Bikur Cholim* societies exist in many communities to help provide for the needs of the sick.

## ᴥᶊ DEATH AND MOURNING

The most important principle with regard to the death of a person is that honor and respect must be given to the deceased at all times. The body is carefully washed and cleansed, then clothed in white, by a group of qualified and pious individuals known as the *chevra kadisha* (burial society). If the deceased was a male, the body is also wrapped in a *tallis* (prayer shawl) whose fringes have been made invalid, indicating that the earthly requirements are no longer incumbent on him.

Embalming is forbidden because it requires removing the blood, and the blood must be buried with the rest of the person's body. Jewish law forbids mutilating the body, therefore autopsies are not permitted unless rabbinic authorities rule it absolutely necessary. In addition, Jewish law absolutely prohibits cremation, which is a form of mutilation. The body must revert to its original state and be buried in the earth (not in an above-the-ground crypt), as it says in the Torah — *adamah* (ground). All

---

22. *Shulchan Aruch, Yoreh Deah* 336.
23. Talmud *Nedarim* 40.
24. Mishnah *Peah* 1:1.

these laws remind us that the body itself is a holy creation, made by G-d, and should not be violated even in death.

The deceased should not be left alone before burial. A person must be designated to watch over the body. So great is this duty that if the person watching has no one to relieve him, he is exempt from reading the *Shema* and all other religious obligations.

The face of the deceased is covered with a sheet as a sign of respect. Displaying the dead in an open casket is considered a dishonor. Jews are buried in simple shrouds, indicating that the rich and poor are equal before G-d; the *"kittel"* is made out of white material, signifying purity, and is sewn without pockets to symbolize that none of our earthly possessions can be taken with us after death. A man is buried in the *kittel* that he wore during his lifetime (at marriage, and by many men on Yom Kippur and on Passover). The coffin is made out of simple, unpolished wood, and flowers, a sign of life and growth, are not encouraged at Jewish funerals.

Burial should take place as soon as possible following death, unless there are mitigating circumstances. We do not bury the dead on Shabbos, Yom Kippur, or the first day of Yom Tov (Festival). Many people leave behind the request that they be buried in the holy ground of the Land of Israel, or at least with some earth taken from the Land of Israel.

When one hears the sad news of the passing of a loved one, one says a special blessing, *Baruch . . . Dayan Ha'emes* (Blessed is the true Judge). As the Talmud says, "One is obliged to utter a blessing on hearing evil tidings just as he does on hearing good tidings."[25] If one did not say it on hearing the news, one can say it at the time of tearing one's garment at the funeral. Tearing one's garment is the proper way to express grief for the dead according to *halachah* : for a deceased parent, one tears on the left side near the heart, and for all other relatives, the tear is made on the right side. One tears the jacket, or possibly the shirt (depending on custom), but does not tear the undershirt.

Torah law prohibits a *kohen* from going into a funeral chapel or

25. Talmud *Berachos* 54.

to the cemetery unless the deceased is a member of his immediate family. It is customary that one or more people say a *hesped* or eulogy at the funeral service. Mourners follow the hearse for a block or two immediately after the funeral service at the chapel or synagogue; this is known as *ha-l'vayas ha-mes* (escorting the dead) and is a sign of respect for the deceased.

A *minyan* (quorum of ten men) is needed at the burial so that the mourners can recite the *Kaddish* or mourners' prayer. *Tzidduk HaDin* is recited during the service, stating that the Almighty's actions are perfect and his ways are just. We are being asked to accept our loss in this spirit. On leaving the cemetery, or at least before entering the house, we wash our hands as a ceremony of purification.

Neighbors usually prepare the first meal for the mourners after they return from the funeral. This helps comfort the mourners, knowing that help and support are at hand. The meal includes hard-boiled eggs as a symbol that just as an egg is round, with no beginning or end, so there is no beginning or end to life.

One observes the laws of mourning for a father, mother, spouse, son, daughter, brother, or sister. If possible, it is best for a family to observe mourning together in the home where the deceased lived. The period of mourning (*shivah*) extends normally for a week, beginning immediately after the burial. During this week, the mourners do not wear shoes made of leather, they do not shave or cut their hair, and women and girls do not use cosmetics. The mourners may not go to work, and they refrain from pleasures such as bathing, putting on freshly laundered clothes, engaging in marital relations, or learning Torah other than matters dealing with mourning. The mourners sit on low stools rather than chairs, or the cushions are removed from sofas to make low places to sit. The mirrors in the house are covered, for they are associated with vanity.

On Shabbos, the public laws of mourning are suspended, but they resume immediately afterward. Shabbos is counted as one of the seven days of mourning.

It is customary to hold daily services and burn a candle in the house of mourners during the week of *shivah*. The *shivah* period ends early on the morning of the seventh day, after morning prayers. The period of time beginning with the funeral and continuing for thirty days is known as *shloshim* (which means thirty). During the *shloshim,* one does not shave, listen to music, attend weddings or participate in other joyous occasions. This concludes the mourning period observed for any deceased relatives except for a parent. The period of mourning for a parent continues until twelve months have passed.

It is a *mitzvah* to comfort the mourners, and this is usually done by making a condolence call during the week of *shivah.* This is an act of compassion that helps the mourner through his initial period of depression and loneliness. We do not utter customary greetings such as "Hello" or "Good morning" to the mourners, but rather wait for the mourner to initiate conversation. Frivolous talk should be avoided. This is an opportunity for the mourner to remember the deceased, to express grief, and to talk of spiritual matters, if he or she wishes. Of course, we should not insist on any particular topic with a mourner; the main point is to be sensitive to his or her needs. On taking leave of the mourners, we say, "May the Lord comfort you among the mourners of Zion and Jerusalem," and express the hope that they be spared knowing any more sorrow.

A son is obligated to recite the *Kaddish* prayer, in the presence of a *minyan,* for his father or mother. This includes all three daily prayer services, for eleven months. It is a sign of reverence and a comfort for the soul of the deceased. Some set up a tombstone at the end of eleven months, but there are different customs; some do it after seven or thirty days, some after a year.

The *yahrzeit* is the anniversary of the day of death according to the Jewish calendar. It is customary to light a 24-hour candle on the eve of the *yahrzeit.* Sons say *Kaddish* and lead the prayer services if possible, and all mourners give charity on this day. Some have the custom to fast, and to visit the gravesite and say prayers there. These prayers are not recited to the dead but to G-d, asking His mercy to the living, through the merits of the deceased. Many also pray that the deceased will serve as a defender on our behalf to the Almighty. It is also customary to visit the graves of deceased relatives during the month of Elul. No eating or drinking may be done at the cemetery.

*Yizkor,* a memorial prayer for the dead, is recited on Yom Kippur and the last day of every major Jewish holiday (Pesach, Shavuos, Succos). The Sages explain that the purpose of praise for the deceased is to evoke the mercies of G-d on the departed soul. When *Yizkor* is announced, those whose parents are still alive leave the synagogue out of respect for the feelings of those who are grieving.

# 14

```
———⋘◦⟡◦⋙———
```

# The Best of Days: Shabbos

```
———⋘◦⟡◦⋙———
```

Without a doubt the observance of Shabbos, or the Sabbath, should be at the center of every Jew's service to G-d. The Sabbath is mentioned over and over again in the Torah, beginning in the story of creation, where G-d Himself rested, and is repeated in every book of the Torah in one form or another.

> Remember the Sabbath day to keep it holy. Six days shall you labor and do all your work; but the seventh day is a Sabbath to the Lord your G-d. On it you shall do no manner of work. . . .for in six days the Lord made heaven and earth, the sea and all that is in them, and rested on the seventh; therefore He blessed the seventh day and hallowed it (*Exodus* 20:8-11).

> Speak also unto the Children of Israel, saying, Truly you shall keep My Sabbaths, for it is a sign between Me and you throughout your generations, that you may know that I am the Lord Who sanctifies you (*Exodus* 31:13-14).

The Hebrew word שבת, *shabbas* means to cease from work. But Shabbos is not only a day of rest. It is also a unique day of holiness, when we can cast aside our weekday cares and material pursuits, and devote ourselves to reviving our religious spirit.

Our Sages tell us that whoever enjoys Shabbos in the proper manner will enjoy material wealth, will be saved from domination by a foreign government, and will receive his reward in the World to Come.[1]

Every storekeeper or shop owner places a sign on his store entrance that describes his business. Even if he leaves for a few weeks, the sign indicates that he is still in business. But if the sign is removed, it is certain evidence that the store has closed. So with Shabbos. It is the sign between the Creator and the Jews that He is still in business, in partnership with us. It testifies for every individual Jew to his Jewishness and his belief in the covenant between G-d and His people. Even if it should happen that a Jew violates some commandment, he still has not lost his Jewishness. By observing Shabbos, he proclaims that the covenant is still active.

Because of the centrality of Shabbos, its desecration is considered one of the most serious sins against G-d. That is why our Sages said, "One who desecrates Shabbos is considered as one who denies the entire Torah."[2]

## ⊷§ PREPARING FOR SHABBOS

The Torah states, "Remember Shabbos to keep it holy" (*Exodus* 20:8). This includes remembering it during the entire week. The great Torah leader, Shammai, was known to save special foods that he acquired during the week for Shabbos. Even from Sunday, if he saw something appropriate, he would buy it and set it aside *l'kavod Shabbos,* in honor of the Sabbath. If he found something even finer later in the week, he would use the first item and save the better one for Shabbos.[3]

---

1. Talmud Shabbos 118.
2. Rambam, *Hilchos Shabbos* 30; *Yehudoi Gaon, Baal Halachos Gedolos,* edited and expanded by Rav Shimon Kara.
3. Talmud *Beitzah* 16b.

Likewise, the Midrash relates that Rav Chiya bar Abba once asked a wealthy man, "My son, why do you deserve such riches?" He replied, "I used to be a butcher. Whenever I saw a particularly nice animal, I set it aside for Shabbos." Rav Chiya responded, "It's not without reason that you have become rich. Your merit is great."

We remember Shabbos in a number of ways. We spend extra money to honor Shabbos with a special food or wine. If one does not have enough money for Shabbos, he should borrow, knowing that G-d will give him the means to repay the loan.[4]

We clean the house on Friday, making it obvious that we are making the preparations for Shabbos. We prepare enough food for three meals. We bathe, cut our nails, and if necessary cut our hair in honor of the day. (When one's time on Friday is short or when sunset is earlier, some of this can be done earlier in the week. Something should be reserved, however, to do on Friday.) One should avoid quarrels, before and during Shabbos.

Before the Shabbos candles are lit, the table should be set. Even if there are no guests planned, the house should be neat and the members of the household appropriately dressed to "greet the Shabbos queen." The table should be set with candlesticks (these can be on another nearby table), wine and wine cup, two loaves (*challos*), a knife and cover for the *challah,* and salt.

Lights should be set in the way one wants them to be for the twenty-five hours of Shabbos, for we do not operate (though we use) electricity. They can be left off or on, or set on timers. Lights that go on automatically, such as in the refrigerator or closet when the door is opened, should be unscrewed. Thermostats should be set and not moved; timers may be used to control electric appliances (such as crock-pots) and air conditioners.

We do not use the phone on Shabbos, so it is best to turn the ringers to "off" or take the phone of the hook, to avoid disturbance. We use precut paper towels, toilet tissue (or facial tissue), and aluminum foil, or prepare these things ourselves before Shabbos.

---

4. Chofetz Chaim, *Mishnah Berurah* 242, citing the *Talmud Yerushalmi.*

It is a custom (but not a requirement) to have warm food at lunch on Shabbos day. In order to provide for this, one must set up a stove-top covering (known as a *blech*), which is a tin, copper, or aluminum sheet that covers the gas or electric burners. Otherwise they would be regarded as open fires and forbidden for use. The burner is turned on (low) before Shabbos and is left burning for the entire day at the same level. The precooked food is put on the *blech* and left to remain warm. Similarly, in order to have hot water for beverages on Shabbos, one must boil the water for Shabbos, either in an electric urn or in a kettle. The kettle may be left on the *blech* along with the warm food, or the electric urn may be used, left "on" for the entire Shabbos.

## ⋖ WELCOMING SHABBOS

Shabbos is inaugurated by the woman of the house when she lights the Shabbos candles.[5] She should do so even if the husband wants to light them. However, if she is not home, the husband or another individual must light the candles.[6] Children may do so if for some reason the parents cannot. If we are away on vacation, we light candles wherever we are staying for Shabbos. Jewish students or anyone living away from home also must light candles every week. In a hospital, if lighting candles is forbidden, a woman may light an electric bulb, but a rabbi should be consulted as to whether or not one can make a blessing on these lights. Her candles should still be lit at home by someone else in the household.

At least two candles are lit to symbolize the twofold command of Shabbos: "Remember" and "keep" the Sabbath (*Deuteronomy* 5:12). Some light more candles — or one for each member of the household. The candles symbolize peace and harmony, and are a sign of blessing. That is why women often add a special prayer

---

5. Talmud *Shabbos* 31.
6. Rambam, *Mishneh Torah, Hilchos Shabbos.*

for their children when lighting the candles, praying that their children should grow up to follow in the ways of G-d.[7]

> *At the very outset of his book* The Shabbos, *Dayan Grunfeld cites an eyewitness account of a remarkable incident that took place in a packed cattle car transporting Jewish victims from their homes to a Nazi concentration camp.*
>
> *"The train dragged on with its human freight. Pressed together like cattle in the crowded trucks, the unfortunate occupants were unable even to move. The atmosphere was stifling. As the Friday afternoon wore on, the Jews in the Nazi transport sank deeper and deeper into their misery.*
>
> *"Suddenly an old Jewish woman managed with a great effort to move and open her bundle. Laboriously, she drew out two candlesticks and two* challos. *She had just prepared them for Shabbos when she was dragged from her home that morning. They were the only things she had thought worthwhile taking with her. Soon the Shabbos candles lit up the faces of the tortured Jews, and the song of* L'cha Dodi *transformed the scene. Shabbos, with its atmosphere of peace, had descended upon them all.*

It is preferable to light candles in the room where one will be eating, but if this is not possible, it is also permissible to light in the room where one will be sleeping.

Candles are lit approximately twenty minutes before sunset. (Candle-lighting calendars give a time which is 18 minutes till sunset.) Once the sun is set, one may not light the candles at all. We can make Shabbos early by lighting candles early, but not the reverse: Shabbos comes automatically with the setting of the sun.

The procedure is as follows: 1) The woman lights the candles. 2) She extinguishes the match and discards it. 3) She covers her eyes and recites the blessing, *Baruch atah Ado-nai Elo-heinu Melech*

---

7. Rabbenu Bechayei on *Exodus* 19:3. Rav Huna said, "He who lights Shabbos candles will be blessed with scholarly sons" (Talmud *Shabbos* 23b).

*ha'olam, asher kid'shanu b'mitzvosav v'tzivanu l'hadlik ner shel Shabbos.* At this point she has taken on the obligations of Shabbos and is no longer allowed to touch the candles or matches. The husband may still do work that is normally forbidden on Shabbos, if he has not yet taken on Shabbos by saying the appropriate prayers in the Friday evening service, *and* if it is not yet sunset.

## ✑ *ZACHOR*: REMEMBER THE SABBATH

After everyone has returned from synagogue Friday night, singing and ceremonial foods create a great celebration. Members of the family and guests sing *Shalom Aleichem,* a song welcoming the angels who watch over Shabbos, then *Eishes Chayil,* honoring the woman of the house and the feminine aspect of Israel, is sung. The father recites *kiddush* over wine or grape juice as soon as possible.

*Kiddush,* which is said both at night and during the day, is the ceremony that specifically fulfills the commandment to "remember the Sabbath." Women and children are obligated to this as well as men, but a person may fulfill the obligation by hearing an adult recite *kiddush.* Only after the blessings of *kiddush* are said may one eat. *Kiddush* should be recited in the place where one eats. Two complete loaves of bread (or matzos) should be on the table, and they should be covered during the recital of *kiddush.* This reminds us of the manna in the desert that was covered by a layer of dew above and beneath. Having two loaves reminds us of the double portion of manna that was gathered on Friday, while none could be gathered on Shabbos. Most often, special braided loaves known as "challah" are used, but any whole loaf or roll can serve the purpose. One person makes the blessing over the bread, having in mind that he/she is fulfilling the obligation for all those at the table.

Mealtimes on Shabbos are very leisurely, with the meal often divided into a number of courses. Discussions of Torah and singing of Shabbos songs (*zemiros*) are customary. The second meal is served after synagogue services on Saturday, with a *kiddush* at that meal also. A third meal is served at the end of the day, following afternoon services, in the hour or so before dark. Shabbos does not end until three stars would be visible in the sky, which is a minimum of 44 minutes after sunset. Many people wait a longer time to end Shabbos, to extend the honor of the day.

Just as we remember Shabbos at the beginning of the day with candle-lighting and *kiddush,* so we honor it on its departure with the special ceremony known as *havdalah,* involving the recital of several blessings. After the evening prayer service, a cup is filled with wine so that it overflows. (If wine or grape juice is not available, one may use a beverage such as beer.) A candle is lit with at least two wicks, or two candles may be held together so that the flames unite. Sweet-smelling spices are available. As the blessings are said, each person at the ceremony smells the spices and holds his or her fingers toward the light to enjoy the blessings. The light of the fire reminds us that after the first Shabbos, Adam learned how to kindle a fire and the smell of the spices symbolically makes up for the loss of the Shabbos spirit as the day departs.

Shabbos is said to be a taste of the World to Come. Honoring it means enjoying its permitted pleasures, luxuriating in rest from the demands of the week, and devoting ourselves to spiritual things like those we will enjoy in the future world.

## ⤳ *SHAMOR*: GUARD THE SABBATH

By refraining from work, Jews show the importance and significance of Shabbos in their lives. We imitate G-d Who ceased from creative activity in order to create a day of rest. Thus we devote one day a week completely to fulfilling the work of "a kingdom of priests and a holy nation," even though during the rest of the week we may have to be involved in the world. This prevents us from being enslaved to our work and secular commitments, so that Shabbos exemplifies freedom from bondage and recalls the moment in history when the Israelites were freed from Egypt. Most of all, it demonstrates our trust in the Almighty, that He will provide for us even when we abstain from material gain for one day a week.

> *The story is told of a man riding a coach down a long winding road, who passed an old man, trudging along with a heavy load on his back. "Can I offer you a lift?" asked the rider. The old man readily agreed, and took a seat in the coach, but did not remove the package from his back. After watching him for a time, the rider asked, "Why don't you set down the package you are carrying?"*
>
> *The old man shook his head. "You were nice enough to give me a lift. How can I impede your trip by putting such a heavy burden in your coach?"*
>
> *"Don't worry," smiled the rider. "The coach is bearing the weight of your burden anyway, whether it's on your back or on the floor of the coach. You may as well put it on the floor, sit back and relax, and let the horses do the work."*
>
> *Likewise, a person should have faith in G-d, trusting in His ability to bear our burden even on Shabbos. Since it is He who carries us through every other day of the week, we need not fear that we will suffer great losses if we observe Shabbos. In the long run, the person who keeps Shabbos will gain greatly from his trust in the Almighty.*

What is the work that we are forbidden to do? Our Sages derived the definitions of work from the kinds of work that were done to build the *Mishkan,* the portable sanctuary in the wilderness. Since the *Mishkan* was an encapsulation of the greatest thing that humans could make, under the direction of G-d, the component activities needed to create it constituted *melachah,* or work. And, since work is forbidden on Shabbos even for such a great thing as building the *Mishkan* in service of G-d , those are the categories of activity that are forbidden. There are 39 of them:

1. **Plowing:** any activity that improves or prepares the soil

for plant growth, such as plowing, digging, fertilizing, or cultivating soil, or clearing stones from soil.

2. **Sowing:** any activity causing a promoting plant growth, such as putting seeds into soil, pruning or grafting, watering, weeding. This includes washing one's hands over or splashing any liquid onto growing plants or grass.

3. **Reaping:** any activity severing a plant from its normal place of growth, such as plucking flowers, picking fruit or berries from trees or bushes, plucking twigs or leaves. As a result of a *gezeirah* (a "fence" — see below), this includes climbing a tree.

4. **Sheaf-making**: any activity in which natural products, grown in the ground, are gathered together in the place where they grow. Examples include piling fruit into a heap for storage, bundling sheaves of wheat together, stringing or pressing fruit together.

5. **Threshing** — any activity by which a natural, organic product is separated from its natural enclosure, such as shelling nuts (except for immediate consumption), squeezing or pressing fruits for juice.

6-8. **Winnowing, selecting, sifting** — activities by which a mixture is improved by removing its less desirable parts. Examples are sifting flour, straining liquids to remove dirt or waste, sorting out good fruit from a heap that contains both good and rotten fruit (except when sorting is done by hand for immediate consumption).

9. **Grinding** — any activity by which a natural solid is divided into small pieces in order to make better use of it. Examples: milling corn, crushing substances in a mortar, grating or dicing vegetables (except for immediate consumption). Taking medicines, except in cases of actual pain or illness, is also forbidden by a *gezeirah*.

10. **Kneading** — Activities by which small particles are combined by means of a liquid to make a dough or paste. Examples: making dough, mixing cement.

11. **Baking** — any activity by which a substance is improved

for consumption by application of heat which changes its state, such as cooking, baking, boiling, roasting, or stirring food while it is over a flame. Note: This does not limit us to cold foods on Shabbos. We may use a stove or certain cooking appliances if they are prepared properly before Shabbos, in order to keep foods warm.

12. **Shearing** – any activity that severs what grows on the outer skin of a human or animal, such as shearing wool, cutting hair or fingernails, plucking feathers. Thus we do not comb hair with a hard brush (by a *gezeirah*), since it is highly probable that hair would be removed.

13. **Bleaching** – any activity by which a garment or cloth is freed from dirt or stains. Examples are bleaching or soaking clothes, removing stains from clothes by water or other substances.

14. **Combing raw materials** – any activity by which a compact raw material is beaten into separate fibers, such as combing raw wool or beating flax stalks.

15. **Dyeing** – any activity that changes an object's color, such as painting, dyeing clothes, dissolving colors in water.

16. **Spinning** – any activity by which thread is formed from fibers, such as spinning thread, making felt, making rope.

17-19. **Weaving** – all activities involved in weaving techniques, start to finish, including knitting, weaving, embroidering, braiding, and basket-weaving.

20. **Separating into threads** – activity by which interwoven threads or strands are separated, such as unraveling any part of a knitted garment.

21. **Tying a knot** – any activity that brings into being a permanent knot or lasting connection between two objects, such as tying a permanent knot or making twine.

22. **Untying a knot** – any activity by which a permanent type of knot is untied, such as removing strands of twine. (One can tie and untie shoes with a bow, since this is intended only as a temporary connection.)

23. **Sewing** — any activity that permanently joins together the surfaces of two materials by means of a third substance, such as sewing fabrics or pasting.

24. **Tearing** — any activity that tears joined materials to facilitate rejoining, such as tearing or removing stitches for purposes of repairing.

25. **Trapping** — any activity that so restricts the movement of a nondomesticated creature that it comes under human control, such as fishing, hunting, catching a bird or insect in a net.

26. **Slaughtering** — any activity causing loss of life or blood to a living creature, such as killing an animal, insect, bird or fish, or taking a blood specimen (except when essential to save a life).

27. **Skinning** — any activity by which the skin of a dead animal is separated from its flesh, such as peeling layers of animal hide to make parchment.

28. **Tanning** — any activity by which rawhide is made more usable or durable, including all parts of the tanning process.

29. **Scraping** — any activity that smoothes roughness from the surface of a material by grinding, polishing, or the like. Examples are sanding, plastering, using solid soap, filing fingernails.

30. **Marking out** — any activity that marks lines on a surface in preparation for cutting or writing. Examples are marking a line to guide a saw, or to guide a margin for writing a *mezuzah*.

31. **Cutting to shape** — any activity by which the size or shape of an object is altered to one more suitable for human use. This includes cutting any material to a definite shape or pattern, sawing lumber, sharpening a pencil, cutting or tearing a clipping from a newspaper.

32. **Writing** — any activity that makes lasting and meaningful figures on a surface, such as writing, drawing, painting, typing, embroidering letters on a cloth. Additional *gezeiros* ("fences") include drawing with a finger on a

moist windowpane, tracing patterns in the sand, and doing anything that might lead to writing or which is usually accompanied by writing, such as playing games in which one normally must write information down.

33. **Erasing** — any activity whose effect is the production of a clean surface for writing.

34. **Building** — those activities connected with constructing, repairing, or erecting a usable structure or shelter. All building operations are included, such as hanging a door, installing a windowpane, nailing wall paneling together, leveling the ground for building, pitching a tent. *Gezeirah*: opening an umbrella.

35. **Demolishing** — those activities that prepare space for building operations by demolishing an existing structure. Included are tearing down a dwelling to make room for a new one and removing a windowpane to prepare for its replacement.

36. **Kindling a fire** — any activity that initiates or prolongs a flame or hot glow, or any similar light- and heat-producing process. Examples: lighting a fire, regulating a flame by turning it up, smoking a cigarette, switching on an electrical appliance or causing its light to switch on, driving a car.

37. **Extinguishing a fire** — any activity that terminates or diminishes a flame or hot glow, if for some productive purpose. Example: putting out a candle to improve the wick.

38. **The final hammer blow** — any activity that puts the finishing touches on, improves, or repairs an article. Example: removing hanging threads from a new suit, repairing a clock or other appliance, finishing the tears made by the perforations in a roll of toilet paper.

39. **Carrying** — any activity by which an object is transferred from an enclosed "private domain" to a "public domain" or vice versa; also, moving any object a distance of four cubits (about seven feet) within a public domain. "Private domain" here means any enclosed space not less than four

handbreadths (about three feet) in height. Usually, the domain means a house, enclosed garden, apartment, etc. "Public domain" means a street, road, or square frequented by the public, unroofed, open at both ends, and having a width of at least sixteen cubits (about 28 feet). Carrying any object from one domain to another, or from point to point within the public domain, is forbidden — objects in one's pocket like keys, wallet, or handkerchief; or objects that one must push like a child's stroller. Carrying within a private domain, however, is allowed as much as one wishes.

One may carry something from one's house into an adjoining space that is not ordinarily enclosed — for example one's backyard — if an *eruv* (boundary) has been created to enclose the area. This can be a fence, or a specially made *eruv* with wires. This transforms a public domain to a private, enclosed one. Some communities erect *eruvim,* even in sections of large cities, allowing Jews to carry outside their homes on Shabbos. However, every *eruv* must be supervised by a qualified rabbi. If there is no *eruv,* a person should be sure that nothing is in his pockets before leaving home.

In order to preserve the spirit of Shabbos and prevent its violation, the Sages enforced prohibitive categories. One of these is *gezeiros,* which is compared to a fence around the Torah. Because violating Shabbos often involves a series of steps before one violates the actual Torah commandment, the Rabbis prohibited even the first such misstep by issuing a *gezeirah.* A person cannot, for example, climb a tree on Shabbos because he might then pluck a fruit or tear a branch. Similarly, one is not allowed to ask a non-Jew to do something we are forbidden to do (except in special circumstances) since it is not in the spirit of Shabbos. We may not play musical instruments because we might forget and tune them, which would be the final hammer blow (see 38), nor may we smell flowers that are still in the ground because we might be tempted to pluck them.

In the category of *gezeirah* is a special law known as *muktzah*. This prohibits us from handling things that are not usable on Shabbos. For example, we are not allowed to move working tools such as hammers and nails, because we cannot use them, or writing utensils (pens, crayons, etc.) because we cannot write with them. These and similar objects are classified as *muktzah*. Objects have different levels of *muktzah* which determine whether they can be moved or not.

Further, our Sages have forbidden us to be involved with weekday activities on Shabbos, because they violate the spirit even if not the letter of the day. We do not discuss business activities or chores that must be taken care of during the week. For adults, playing ball even within an *eruv* is usually included in this category.

The Talmud tells the story of a pious man who strolled through his vineyard on Shabbos to inspect his property. He noticed a breach in a section of the wall, and made a mental note to repair it right after Shabbos. Then, realizing he had profaned the day's holiness by planning weekday activities, he resolved never to mend that breach. G-d then rewarded him for his devotion: a huge fruit tree grew in that breach, filling the gap and providing an abundance of fruit that provided the man with a generous income.[8]

All these laws also apply to Yom Kippur. In addition, most of them apply to the *Yamim Tovim*: Rosh Hashanah, Succos, Passover, and Shavuos. The permissible exceptions on *Yamim Tovim* which do not coincide with Shabbos include baking or cooking food that is needed for the holiday (or the immediately following Shabbos — see below), and carrying things that are needed. For example, one can push a baby's stroller on such a *Yom Tov*, or carry a prayer book or *lulav* to the synagogue. One may also light a flame from an already existing flame, or increase a flame, but one may not start a new flame by striking a match. (One may not pick fruit or vegetables, or squeeze juice from fruits to make a beverage.) If *Yom Tov* and Shabbos coincide, the laws of Shabbos are in

---

8. *Talmud Shabbos* 150a.

full effect, and the exceptions mentioned are disregarded.

If *Yom Tov* falls on a Friday (actually beginning on Thursday evening), one may cook on that day for Shabbos provided that two conditions are met: (1) The cooking must be completed to the point that the food is edible while it is still *Yom Tov,* and (2) each household must set aside *before Yom Tov* begins an *eruv tavshilin,* two samples of food cooked before *Yom Tov* (e.g., a baked roll and a cooked egg), which are kept until Shabbos and then eaten.

Why are the prohibitions of Shabbos so important? In the World to Come every Jew will be asked, "Why did you open your shop on Shabbos? Everyone who defiles the Sabbath is considered as denying the Torah itself! Is it worth it for a few additional dollars of profit to break this most valuable vessel given to the Jewish people?" The man might reply, "What could I do? The needs of a man are many, and his sustenance meager."

This response is compared to the actions of the fool who thought he could produce more cups of water from a jug by simply adding another tap. The new tap, of course, would not provide any more water, and would only empty the jug faster. Likewise, the Master of the Universe nourishes and sustains the entire world. As Jews, our weekly sustenance comes from six "faucets"; we should not fool ourselves into thinking that adding a seventh faucet, another workday, will increase our income. Rather, we are cheating ourselves, for a full observance of Shabbos is an enormous spiritual resource for the entire week.

One Shabbos, Rabbi Sonnenfeld, a great Jerusalem rabbi, was informed that a certain Jew lit a fire in his house and was cooking. Immediately he arose and ran to the man's house. When he reached the house, he started banging on the door as one would in a time of emergency. As soon as the owner opened the door, Rabbi Sonnenfeld began discussing the holiness of Shabbos. The man's wife was taken aback by the rabbi's urgent manner. "Is this the proper way for a Jew, a scholar, a rabbi, to behave?" she demanded. "How can you enter a person's house unannounced?" The rabbi replied, "When a fire is burning in a friend's house there is no time for etiquette!"

It is important to bear in mind that all the restrictions and prohibitions of Shabbos do not apply if there is a question of someone's life or limb being in jeopardy. In that case, one must do everything possible to save the life. Not only is it permissible, but one is *obligated* to do whatever one can to help the person. Once a great rabbi was seen carrying a lamp through the streets on Shabbos. When he was later asked why, he said, "There was a sick person in a certain house, and the light had gone out. This made it difficult to take proper care of the sick person. When the family sent a messenger asking what to do, I took the lamp myself and brought it to them. It is a commandment to save the life of a dangerously ill person, even if it means working on Shabbos."

# 15

---◇◦⟨⟩◦◇---

# Holy Convocations:
# The Lunar Calendar
# and Major Holidays

---◇◦⟨⟩◦◇---

T he Jewish calendar is a lunar calendar, which in a regular year
has twelve lunar months, and in a leap year thirteen. Rosh
Chodesh, the first day of the new month, is a special holiday.
Indeed, the first commandment given specifically to the Jewish
people was to take charge of time and keep a lunar calendar, "This
month will be the first month for you" (*Exodus* 12:2).

Our Sages likened the Jewish people to the moon. It is symbolic of the history of our people throughout the ages:[1] Just as
the moon is small and insignificant-looking at the beginning
of the month, so the Jewish people as a nation are at present small, and their influence seems insignificant. But just
as the moon, day after day, reveals more of itself to us, so the
Jewish religion from one year to the next reveals more of itself

---

1. *Midrash Rabbah Shemos* 12.

and becomes better understood by the other nations.[2]

Also, just as the moon is sometimes eclipsed and cannot be seen, so the Jewish people sometimes seem isolated from the mainstream of history. But as the moon shines brightly on the following night, so the Jewish people continually reappear on the world scene, and can never be destroyed.

# ⊸§ ROSH CHODESH: THE NEW MOON

The day on which the new moon appears, or the following day, is designated as Rosh Chodesh or first of the month. Some months, Rosh Chodesh is one day, and in other months two. In ancient times, the *molad,* or appearance of the moon, was announced by the Sanhedrin on the basis of testimony and examination of two witnesses who affirmed that they had seen the new moon. Rosh Chodesh was a *Yom Tov,* with its own sacrificial offering by the *kohanim* in the Temple, and special songs by the Levites.

The procedure for examining the witnesses was elaborate: All witnesses came to a special courtyard in Jerusalem where an excellent meal was served them. (This ensured that the public would continue to volunteer as witnesses.) Of the first pair of witnesses that arrived, the more distinguished of the two would be questioned first, concerning the shape and position of the new moon. Then the second witness was examined, to make sure his testimony was factually similar to that of the first. If their testimonies coincided, the court proclaimed the day of the New Moon. Other witnesses who came later were asked general questions, so that they would not be discouraged by thinking their trip was for naught.[3]

Sometimes, when it happened that the witnesses arrived too late to declare the day a New Moon, the celebration of Rosh Chodesh would be on the next day. On such occasions, the court declared that there were two days of Rosh Chodesh — the last day

---

2. *Midrash Tanchuma* 12.
3. Talmud *Rosh Hashanah* 23.

of the previous month and the first day of the new month. Now, although the calendar is calculated mathematically and we know exactly when the New Moon will appear in Jerusalem, the Sages nevertheless declared that certain months would have two days, and others only one day of Rosh Chodesh.

Today, in place of the additional offering, we say the *Mussaf* (additional) prayer service for Rosh Chodesh. Special prayers are added in the *Shemoneh Esrei* (*Yaaleh v'yavo*) and, if this is left out, a person must repeat the *Shemoneh Esrei*, unless the omission occurs during *Maariv*. In the morning, *Hallel* is recited, a series of special psalms of praise and thanksgiving. These prayers are recited right after the *Shemoneh Esrei*, while standing. The Torah is taken out on Rosh Chodesh, and four people are called up for *aliyos*.

Many people enhance the observance of Rosh Chodesh by preparing a special feast or adding something special to the meal. We are not permitted to fast. Women generally refrain from doing specialized work on Rosh Chodesh, because it is regarded as a holiday in honor of women. When the golden calf was made by the Israelite men in the desert, the women refused to donate their gold jewelry, because they did not want to participate in making an idol. Later, however, when the *Mishkan* was being built, the women eagerly volunteered their jewelry and precious mirrors.[4] Because of these acts of devotion, Rosh Chodesh was especially designated for women as a time for celebration and rest from certain kinds of labor.

Rosh Chodesh is also a day of forgiveness for all; it is referred to in the *Mussaf* service as "a time of atonement throughout their generations." Thus we can use it as a time to ask pardon for all the sins we have committed in the previous month. In this way Rosh Chodesh is similar to the High Holy Days.

On the Shabbos preceding Rosh Chodesh we "bless" the new month. This is done every month, except for the Shabbos before Rosh Hashanah, to inform the public about the inauguration of the new month and to ask for G-d's special consideration for us.

---

4. *Pirkei d'Rabbi Eliezer* 44; *Tur, Orach Chaim* 417.

Men are obligated to say *Kiddush levanah* (sanctification of the moon) once between the third and fourteenth days after the appearance of the moon. These special prayers are said standing, outside at night, when the moon is visible. It is best to say *Kiddush levanah* when the moon is shining brightly; if it is cloudy and the moon is not at all visible, the prayers are not recited. If the moon is visible but one says the prayers indoors, one still has fulfilled the *mitzvah*.

It is preferable to say *Kiddush levanah* on Saturday night right after *Maariv,* while we are still dressed in our Shabbos clothes. This is because the Holy Temple was destroyed on a Saturday night, and *Kiddush levanah* offers the opportunity to proclaim a message of hope in the face of tragedy. Thus these prayers say, "in days to come, they [Israel] are also to be renewed like her [the moon]." We also say *David, melech yisrael, chai v'kayam* (David, king of Israel, lives and endures) when blessing the waxing moon. This reminds us that the throne of David will be established forever. After making the blessing over the moon, we say *Shalom aleichem* to one another.

## ঙ§ THE CALENDAR

A lunar year has 354 days and a solar year 365, so each year an eleven-day discrepancy accumulates between the two types of calendars. The leap year, as well as changes in the number of days in each month, are necessary to intercalate the Jewish year with the solar calendar. If this were not resolved, the Jewish holidays would gradually rotate backward in the solar calendar until, for example, Pesach would be in the winter and then in the fall. The Torah makes it clear that Pesach is to be a spring holiday, so it is understood that the lunar calendar must be adjusted to align with the earth's seasons.

Our calendar was arranged in its present form over 1600 years ago. Until 359 C.E., the Sanhedrin had functioned in Israel as the supreme judicial body in Jewish life. This supreme court decided when a leap year would occur and whether certain months should have 29 or 30 days, in order to intercalate the years. Under the *Nasi* (presiding officer) named Hillel II, the calendars were permanently synchronized. An extra month (Adar II) is added seven times in nineteen years (every two or three years). Also, the months of Cheshvan and Kislev are of variable length, so that in some years they would have 29 days, in other years 30 days, to properly adjust the length of the year. The Hebrew months are either "full" or "incomplete." A full month consists of thirty days, and has one day Rosh Chodesh (except for the two variable months of Cheshvan and Kislev); an incomplete month consists of 29 days and has two days Rosh Chodesh, the first of those days being the 30th of the preceding month.

Because of the intercalation, Hebrew months overlap with the months on the secular calendar, and a Hebrew date falls on a different secular date each year. Following is a list of the months and their approximate English months, together with the holidays and fasts that occur in each month:

**Nissan** (March-April)

- 14   Eve of Passover
- 15   First Day Passover; counting of the *Omer* begins at night
- 16   Second Day Passover (outside of Israel); first day of *Omer* Intermediate Days (*Chol HaMoed;* in Israel 16-20)
- 21   Seventh Day Passover (8th day observed outside of Israel on 22 Nisan)

**Iyar** (April-May)

- 14   "Second Passover" (*Pesach Sheini*) — a commemoration
- 18   Lag B'Omer (33rd day of counting the *Omer*)

**Sivan** (May-June)

- 6   First Day of Shavuos
- 7   Second Day Shavuos (only outside of Israel)

**Tammuz** (June-July)

- 17   Fast of the 17th of Tammuz

**Av** (July-August)

- 8   Fast of Tishah B'Av

**Elul** (August-September)

> Recitation of special prayers (*Selichos*) begins preparation for the High Holy Days. Sephardim say these prayers every morning; Ashkenazim begin several days prior to Rosh Hashanah.

**Tishrei** (September-October)

  1  Rosh Hashanah (New Year)
  2  Second Day Rosh Hashanah (even in Israel)
  3  Fast of Gedaliah
  9  Yom Kippur (Day of Atonement)
 15  First Day Succos ("Tabernacles")
 16  Second Day Succos (outside of Israel)
17-21  Intermediate Days (16-21 in Israel)
 21  Hoshana Rabbah
 22  Shemini Atzeres (Eighth Day; combined with Simchas Torah in Israel)
 23  Simchas Torah (Rejoicing of the Torah, celebrated on 22 Tishrei in Israel)

**Cheshvan** (October-November)

**Kislev** (November-December)

 24  Chanukah ("Dedication" or Festival of Lights, eight days)

**Tevet** (December-January)

 10  Fast of Teves

**Shevat** (January-February)

 15  New Year for Trees

**Adar** (February-March)

  7  Birthday and Yahrzeit of Moses
 13  Fast of Esther
 14  Purim
 15  Shushan Purim (main celebration in Jerusalem and certain other cities)

**Adar II** (March-April)

> This occurs only in a leap year. In this case, the fast of Esther and Purim fall in Adar II.

The significance of knowing and teaching our children the Jewish calendar is indicated in the following story:

> *Baron Simon Wolf Rothschild was known for his strict adherence to every point of Jewish tradition. When he wanted to have a Torah scroll written, he did not turn to the scribes in his own country, for he feared they were not true Torah scholars. He brought a scribe from Russia who, he felt sure, would write his* sefer *Torah with purity and holiness. When the scribe finished his sacred task, he came to the baron to be paid.*
>
> *"Have you received any payments at all yet?" asked Baron Rothschild.*
>
> *"In April, I received ten coins. In May, your manager paid me another ten coins. The rest is still owed me."*
>
> *Exclaimed the baron, "You count according to the gentile months and not the Jewish months? At least you could count according to the weekly Torah portions! Here is the money I owe you — and I must return to you what you have written. I am disappointed that you, a scribe engaged in a most sacred profession, do not realize that the way the Torah counts time must be our way as well. The Jewish calendar, not the secular one, must be the one around which our lives revolve."*

## ◆§ HOLIDAYS IN ISRAEL AND IN THE DIASPORA

In the diaspora, the first and last days of Succos and Pesach are each two days, and Shavuos is two days, while in Israel they are each one day. Originally, for Jewish communities outside of Israel, holidays were celebrated for two days because of doubt of which of the two days was correct. This depended on which day had been proclaimed Rosh Chodesh by the Supreme Court in Jerusalem. Since it took some time for the message to reach outlying communities, by the time the messengers arrived, the day might have already passed. Therefore, they kept two days just in case of error.

This meant, in turn, that the holidays were celebrated for two days. Even though by the time of the 15th (the date of Succos or Pesach), it was known which Rosh Chodesh had been correct, the people would not want to diminish the holiday by celebrating it less extensively than Rosh Chodesh. Thus the practice of two days of holiday came to be hallowed through centuries of practice. The extra day is *Yom Tov Sheini shel galuyos,* the "second festival day of the diaspora."

The second day is celebrated as fully as the first day, except that we are permitted to bury the dead, and do what is necessary to treat an illness when it is not life threatening.

Rosh Hashanah differs from the other festivals because it falls on the first day of the month. Even in Israel during the time of the Sanhedrin, most people observed Rosh Hashanah for two days because of the possibility of doubt. After a number of confusing circumstances, and to avoid the possibility of celebrating the wrong day for Rosh Hashanah, the Sages legislated that two days of Rosh Hashanah should be observed. Rosh Hashanah is called *Yoma arichta* (an extended day).

According to *halachah,* a diaspora Jew who is only visiting Israel observes both days of the festival, even though Israelis are celebrating only one day. Conversely, an Israeli Jew on a journey in the diaspora need only observe the first day, as he would at home. However, the Israeli should not do anything that might appear as a public desecration of the second holy day being observed by the Jews around him.

Yom Kippur is the only biblical holiday that is an exception to the above practices. It is observed for only one day, both in Israel and in the diaspora.

# ⊷§ ADDITIONAL POINTS ON THE JEWISH CALENDAR

The Torah calls Nissan the first month of the year, and Tishrei the seventh month, even though the New Year, Rosh Hashanah, is the first day of Tishrei. Why? It is during Nissan that the Exodus from Egypt took place, with all its miracles which we celebrate at Passover. Nissan is also called Aviv (spring), which can be divided into two expressions, *av* or "father" and *yud-veis* or "twelve," so Aviv is the "father of the twelve (months)." This is the month of our physical and spiritual freedom, so it replaced Tishrei as the "first." It is a time of new awakening, with the growth of spring and the rebirth of the Jewish people occurring at the same season.

The Jewish day begins at sundown because, at the end of each day of creation as described in *Genesis,* the Torah says, "And it was evening, and it was morning. . ." Also in *Leviticus* it is written, "From evening to evening you shall keep your Shabbos." Thus each 24-hour period begins at sunset. The Sabbath begins 18 minutes before sunset, in order to be careful not to take a chance on violating the holy day, and continues for approximately 25 hours until nightfall (dark enough to see three stars) on Saturday.

This way of figuring the days applies to all holidays, birthdays, *yahrzeits,* and other special occasions, as well as the days counted for the laws of family purity. For example, if a baby boy is born on Tuesday night, the *bris* would be on the following Wednesday (not Tuesday), being the eighth day of his life.

The days of the week are designated according to Shabbos as the seventh day. Sunday is *yom rishon,* Monday *yom sheini,* and so on. The name Shabbos has the same root as the word "week." The Torah, when referring to the counting of seven weeks from Pesach to Shavuos, refers to it as *sheva Shabbosos,* seven Sabbaths. Moreover, the command to "Remember the Sabbath day to keep it holy" includes remembering it during the week. Thus at the end of the daily morning prayer, when a different psalm is recited for each day of the week, each is introduced by the phrase, "Today is *yom . . . l'Shabbos.*"

We use "C.E." and "B.C.E" when designating the secular year. These initials stand for "Common Era" and "Before the Common Era." We do not use B.C. and A.D. because these refer to events in the Christian calendar, the traditionally accepted date of the birth of the founder of Christianity. We also do not customarily use Christian symbols or structures to locate ourselves in space and time. Thus we would not say, "I'll meet you in front of the church," but rather, "I'll meet you at the corner of seventh and eighth Streets." We would not say, "Let's talk during Easter week," but "Let's talk the week of the 12th."[5] In Jewish legal documents and contracts, we use the Hebrew date, which is the numbering of the years from the account of creation in *Genesis,* through all the ancestors, kings, and prophets down to today. The year 2000 (counting from Rosh Hashanah of the year 1999) was 5760 on the Hebrew calendar.

# ᵉᣬTHE HIGH HOLY DAYS

Teshuvah, meaning return to G-d or repentance, is important throughout the year, but it is especially crucial during the period of time from Rosh Hashanah to Yom Kippur, known as the "Days of Awe" or "High Holy Days." The first day of the month of Tishrei, our Rosh Hashanah, is a day of judgment for all human beings, when all the deeds of the past year are scrutinized and heavenly decisions are made for the year to come. This, then, is a period of introspection, during which people can alter the decrees against them through sincere repentance. As it says in the High Holy Day prayer services, "Repentance, prayer, and charity avert the evil decree."

A month before Rosh Hashanah, at the beginning of Elul, we start blowing the *shofar* daily in the synagogue (except on Shabbos). Special prayers for forgiveness, known as *Selichos,* are

---

5. Talmud *Sanhedrin* 63b.

recited during the last several days of the month of Elul. Then, on the two days of Rosh Hashanah (1 and 2 Tishrei), we spend much of the day in the synagogue, praying that every person will be inscribed in the Book of Life for the coming year.

The literal meaning of "Rosh Hashanah" is "head of the year." According to Jewish teachings, it is the "nerve center" of the year. From it flow the decisions that influence our thoughts and our actions for the twelve months to come.

The *shofar* or ram's horn is the central *mitzvah* of the day. It is blown to proclaim G-d as the Ruler of the Universe and to herald the beginning of the Ten Days of Teshuvah, culminating in Yom Kippur. Just as kings in ancient times had trumpets and horns blown to commemorate their coronation, so too do we honor our King and Creator. The blowing of the *shofar* also reminds us of the giving of the Torah on Mount Sinai, when the *shofar*'s sound was heard; and it invokes the merit of Abraham's binding of Isaac, when a ram was substituted for Isaac's sacrifice.

Some other customs of Rosh Hashanah include the eating of special foods that are symbolic of our desire and hope for a good year. We dip a piece of apple into honey and recite, "May it be Your will . . . to renew for us a good and sweet year." We eat pomegranates with their many seeds to indicate our hope that our merits will be many in G-d's eyes, and we avoid nuts because the Hebrew word for nut has the same numerical value as the word for sin. We recite a special prayer remembering the mercy of G-d, known as *Tashlich*, near a body of water containing live fish. If possible, this is done on the afternoon of Rosh Hashanah, but it can be done any time during the Days of Awe if one does not have a body of water within walking distance.

Yom Kippur, the last of the Ten Days of Teshuvah, is the holiest day of the year, when the Book of Life is closed. All the restrictions of Shabbos are in effect because of the day's holiness, and in addition we fast and avoid sensual pleasures so that we can concentrate completely on our prayers. Beginning with the *Kol Nidrei* service just before sunset, all Jews, young and old, assemble in the synagogue to ask G-d for forgiveness. Yom Kippur means the Day of Atonement, and it is our major opportunity to repent and rectify our misdeeds in the eyes of our Creator. An important aspect of *teshuvah* deals with relationships between people. Yom Kippur atones for sins committed against G-d, but sins against people are not forgiven until the sinner has asked for forgiveness from his fellow man. Before Yom Kippur, therefore, we should ask forgiveness from anyone we have wronged. Then we can come to G-d with a humble heart to ask for mercy.

How do we do *teshuvah* or repentance? A person must do three things: (1) acknowledge that one has sinned, (2) take one's wrongdoing to heart, truly regretting what one has done; and (3) commit oneself to not repeating the misdeed. This process is very important and powerful. A person who does *teshuvah* is considered in the eyes of G-d as though he had never sinned. Our Sages tell us, furthermore, "Where those who do *teshuvah* stand, even the completely righteous cannot stand."[6] People who have done *teshuvah* have transformed themselves through hard work in a way that the person who has not sinned has never had to do.

> *Rabbi Yisrael Salanter once went to a shoemaker to have his shoes repaired. The hour was late and darkness had already descended. Noticing that the candle was burning out, the rabbi realized that the shoemaker might have trouble repairing the shoes in the dim light, and suggested that perhaps the work could wait till the next day. "Don't worry," replied the shoemaker, "I can work very well by candlelight. As long as the candle burns, it is still possible to fix the shoes."*
>
> *Rabbi Salanter immediately recognized the deep significance of the shoemaker's words. As long as the candle burned, he could repair what was broken. Likewise, as long as the spark of life still flickers in a person, that person can still repair his sinful ways. One should never despair.*

In addition, the giving of charity plays an important role. Giving to *tzedakah* before Yom Kippur helps to make peace between Jews

---

6. Talmud *Berachos* 34b.

and their Father in heaven. It is a widespread custom for synagogues to collect for charity during the afternoon service on the day before Yom Kippur.

Observing the restrictions of Yom Kippur includes fasting, avoiding washing or anointing the body, avoiding intimacy with one's spouse, and not wearing leather shoes. It is customary to have two full meals on the day before Yom Kippur, and the meal immediately preceding the fast is often like a feast. However, one should avoid foods that will make the fast difficult, such as salty foods, and one should not overindulge to the point that it could affect one's health and stamina for the all-important prayers.

The overall theme of the High Holy Days is that G-d is King. On Yom Kippur, we begin the congregational morning prayers with the word *HaMelech* (The King). Once, Rabbi Aharon of Karlin was officiating as cantor for his congregation, and when he began the *davening* with the word "*HaMelech!*" he burst into tears.

Later he explained that the word had reminded him of a story in the Talmud: During the time when the Jews lived in Israel under the dominion of the Romans, the great sage, Rabbi Yochanan ben Zakkai, appeared before the Roman general Vespasian to ask for certain privileges for the Jewish populace, addressing Vespasian as "king." Vespasian was still only a general (although he would soon receive the news of his having been made emperor). He said to Rabbi Yochanan, "If you see me as the king, why didn't you come before now?!"

Concluding his story, Rabbi Aharon explained, "Today, when I called out the word 'King,' I saw myself being asked in heaven, 'Why didn't you come before now? If you know I am the Ruler of the universe, why did you wait so long to repent?!' "

## ⊷§ THE PILGRIMAGE HOLIDAYS

T he Torah states that all Jews are obligated to go up to the *Beis HaMikdash* (Holy Temple) in Jerusalem three times a year — at Pesach (Passover), Shavuos (the Feast of Weeks), and Succos (the Feast of Booths). On Pesach we praise G-d for freeing us from slavery in Egypt; on Shavuos, for giving us the Torah that made us into the Jewish nation, and on Succos, for the Clouds of Glory that protected us during the years in the wilderness. We also thank the Almighty for the Land of Israel and her bountiful produce.

ON THE FIFTEENTH DAY (THE FULL MOON) OF NISSAN, WE CELEBRATE for eight days (seven in Israel) the liberation of our ancestors from slavery in Egypt. On each of the first two **PASSOVER** nights (one in Israel), we hold a Passover *Seder* at which we retell the story of the Exodus, and commemorate it with certain festival foods. We eat matzos instead of bread throughout the entire eight days, and refrain from all foods that might possibly contain leaven.

The three positive *mitzvos* that apply to Jewish observance of Passover today are: (1) disposing of all leavened products on the 14th of Nissan; (2) eating matzah on the first two nights of Pesach; and (3) relating the story of the Exodus from Egypt on the night(s) of the Passover *Seder*. The Rabbinic commandments for the *Seder* include eating bitter herbs (*maror*) and drinking four cups of wine, as specified in the *Haggadah* — the booklet used by *Seder* participants containing the story of Passover.

The Torah absolutely forbids a Jew to have any *chametz* (leavened grain products) in his possession during all of Passover. We clean our houses and dispose of *chametz* by removing it completely from our possession or burning it. If we store any *chametz* in our houses or shops, it must be sold to a non-Jew for the duration of the holiday. This transaction is governed by complex laws, so we give it to a rabbi to execute the sale and to buy the *chametz* back after Pesach.

Matzah is the grain product that substitutes for bread and other products during the holiday. We are commanded by the Torah to eat it on the first two nights of Pesach at the *Seder,* as part of the "reliving" of the *Seder*. This should if at all possible be *matzah shmurah* ("guarded matzah"), the flour of which has been supervised from the time of the harvesting of the wheat. If necessary, one may eat matzah made from wheat supervised only since the grinding into flour. Machine-made matzah is acceptable, but many hold that it is best to use hand-made matzah for the *mitzvah* of the first two nights at the *Seder*. Egg matzos, or any matzah made with a liquid other than water, should not be eaten unless there are mitigating circumstances such as illness, and then only with rabbinic approval.

The *Seder* follows a special order, and it is best to have a *Hagaddah* for each person to follow along with the ceremony. The word *"seder"* means order, and the ceremony proceeds in the following sequence:

| | |
|---|---|
| **KADESH:** | blessing over the wine (*kiddush*) |
| **URECHATZ:** | washing the hands before eating a vegetable, with no blessing recited over the washing |
| **KARPAS:** | eating the vegetable |
| **YACHATZ:** | breaking the middle matzah into two uneven pieces, and putting away the larger piece for the *afikoman* |
| **MAGGID:** | telling the story of Passover |
| **RACHTZAH:** | washing the hands before matzah, including a blessing over the washing |
| **MOTZI MATZOH:** | blessings over the matzah |
| **MAROR:** | eating the bitter herb |
| **KORECH:** | eating a "sandwich" of matzah, *maror,* and *charoses* |
| **SHULCHAN ORECH:** | a festive meal, normally with several courses, including meat that has been cooked with liquid (not roasted) |
| **TZAFUN:** | eating the *afikoman* |
| **BARECH:** | saying Grace After Meals |
| **HALLEL:** | singing "Hallel," including psalms and other selections from the morning holiday service |
| **NIRTZAH:** | concluding the *Seder* |

The table is set and the food prepared so that the *Seder* can begin right after nightfall, after returning from synagogue. We want the children to be able to stay up, hear the telling of the story, and eat the matzah, so we begin as soon as possible. The *Seder* plate is placed before the head of the household, displaying symbolic foods:

1) a shank bone (*zero'a*) to symbolize the Pesach offering of a lamb;
2) a roasted egg to symbolize the festival offering;
3) *maror* or bitter herb (many people have two kinds, one called *chazeres*) to represent the bitterness of slavery;
4) *charoses,* a mixture of apples and spices to sweeten the bitterness, which also represents the mortar and bricks that the slaves had to work with; and
5) *karpas* or vegetable grown in the ground, such as parsley or potato.
6) In addition, on the same or a separate platter, three matzos will be placed before the leader representing the three parts of the nation Israel: Cohen, Levi, Israelite. This *matzah* symbolizes "the bread of poverty" and the haste with which we left Egypt.

We use our best dishes at the table and "recline" on pillows, symbolizing that we are no longer enslaved and are members of spiritual royalty. In many homes, married men wear a white robe (*kittel*) at the table. During the course of the meal we have four cups of wine, symbolizing the four acts of redemption we experienced from G-d. (Grape juice is permissible if one cannot drink wine. The wine or juice must be kosher, of course.)

The most important part of the *Seder* is the telling of the story, including the bitterness of slavery and the miracles that G-d performed for us. As the *Haggadah* says, we should feel as though we were in slavery, and we were redeemed. At the story's culmination, we wash, recite blessings, and eat matzah; we then eat *maror* dipped in *charoses,* and finally eat the sandwich in order to fulfill Hillel's opinion that matzah and *maror* should be eaten together. After the festive meal is served and eaten, we eat a piece of the matzah saved for the end — the *afikoman.* Nothing may be eaten after that. In many homes, it is the custom for the children to search for the hidden *afikoman* and "ransom" it as a method of engaging them in the *Seder.* Afterwards, we say the Grace After Meals and then sing prayers and songs, celebrating our freedom with joyous praise to G-d.

BEGINNING ON THE SECOND NIGHT OF PESACH, WE FULFILL A commandment of the Torah to count seven full weeks (from the

**COUNTING THE OMER** day of the year when a barley offering was brought to the Temple). This count culminates in the holiday of Shavuos, the fiftieth day, when the new wheat offerings were marked by the bringing of baked loaves of bread to the Temple. Shavuos is the reliving of the giving of the Torah — the whole purpose of the redemption from Egypt. It is the completion of our freedom.

Each night of the *Omer* counting, one recites the blessing *Baruch atah . . . asher kid'shanu . . . al sefiras ha'omer*. Then one pronounces the numeric day of the *Omer*: "This is the . . . day of the *Omer*." After the first week, one states the number of days and weeks, for example, "This is the twenty-fourth day of the *Omer*, being three weeks and three days of the *Omer*." One must count in a language one understands.

For thirty-three days of the *Sefirah* (another term used for the days of the *Omer* Counting), it is customary to observe certain aspects of mourning to commemorate the tragic deaths of huge numbers of Rabbi Akiva's students in the second century. Different communities observe these thirty-three days at different times, and some even observe the whole fifty-day period of the *Omer* as a semimourning period. Weddings and haircuts are forbidden during this time, as are listening to music and going to entertainment events. Lag B'Omer (33rd day of the *Omer*), when the deaths of the students ended, is a day when these restrictions are lifted (or, for some communities, ended).

THE SIXTH DAY OF SIVAN, THE FIFTIETH DAY AFTER THE BEGINNING of Pesach, is the holiday of Shavuos. It is observed for two days

**SHAVUOS** (one in Israel), commemorating the giving of the Torah on Mount Sinai, and reminding us of the first-fruit offerings of the early harvest. Thus it is also called *Chag HaBikurim* (holiday of first fruits). Synagogues and homes are decorated with green branches or flowers, just as Mount Sinai was in bloom when the Torah was given to the Jewish people.

There is a custom to stay up all night the first night of Shavuos studying Torah. Special recitations include the *Akdamus* prayer of praise, and the reading of the Book of *Ruth*. This book tells the story of a woman of a different nation, Moab, who gave up royalty, honor, and wealth to join the Jewish people. She thus earned the merit to become an ancestress of the House of David and, because of her dedication, self-sacrifice, and kindness, a model for the whole Jewish people.

Ruth is also the model of the convert, and we learn from her story the honor with which a convert should be treated with honor. The Midrash tells us that when Moses heard about the special honor accorded a convert, he expressed astonishment to G-d. G-d replied, "Look at what I did for the Israelites: I took them out of Egypt, destroyed their enemies, lit their path with clouds of glory, brought them manna and fed them quail, and gave them water in the desert. Then they accepted My Torah. In contrast, this *ger* (convert) came to Me of his or her own free will and accepted the Torah, without having seen or benefited from any miracles. Shouldn't this convert be considered at least the equal of a Levite?"

The acceptance of the Torah over 3000 years ago forms the essence of the Jewish people, whether born Jewish or converted into the religion. Every Jew today can share this experience by studying the Torah and helping others to learn it. This continues the unbroken chain of connection to G-d, directly from Sinai.

ON THE FIFTEENTH OF TISHREI, FIVE DAYS AFTER YOM KIPPUR, begins the holiday of Succos begins. It lasts for seven days, and is

**SUCCOS** followed by an eighth day, Shemini Atzeres, followed by a ninth day, Simchas Torah. In Israel, Shemini Atzeres and Simchas Torah are observed on the same day (the eighth).

During the eight days of this holiday (or seven in Israel), we dwell in a *succah* or small hut, reminiscent of the temporary dwellings of the Jews in the desert wanderings, when G-d alone protected them. The cardinal principle of the festival is to forsake one's permanent home and dwell in a much more fragile place, underlining our trust in the Creator.

The *succah* must be constructed to certain specifications:

- not less than 38 inches nor more than 35 feet in height
- not smaller than 27"x27"
- walls on at least 2½ sides, of any material that can withstand normal winds
- roof made of materials of plant origin that are detached from the ground (usually tree branches, bamboo poles, or narrow wooden slats)

During the holiday, men must eat all meals, including any food made of grain, in a *succah*. Women are exempt from this, although many do it by custom. Some people sleep in the *succah*, if space permits.

Succos — called the "season of our rejoicing" — is indeed the most joyous of holidays. The farmer rejoices over his produce, the granaries are overflowing, and he is thankful. Also, we realize by leaving our houses that our life and our happiness do not depend upon the material, and it is an opportunity to achieve greater heights in our service of G-d. Thus the spiritual joy is very deep as well.

It is customary to invite guests for all holidays, but especially into our *succah*. Once Rabbi Levi Yitzchak of Berditchev was asked why he went out of his way to invite all his neighbors, including those of a lower social stratum. He answered, "In the future, in the World to Come, when all the righteous people will be invited to the great *succah* that will be constructed out of the skin of the Leviathan [an ancient sea-creature that will reappear at that time], I, Levi Yitzchak, will also wish to enter. No doubt, someone stationed at the entrance will stop me and demand angrily why I, a nobody among great personalities, have the nerve to force my way into the *succah*. I will answer, 'Please don't be angry at me. In my own *succah*, I also spent the holiday with very ordinary people and I was not at all ashamed of them.' "

Another *mitzvah* of Succos is to "take the four species," as part of the service of praising G-d. This Torah commandment involves four plants: the *lulav* or date palm, the *esrog* or citron, the *hadas* or myrtle, and the *aravos* or willow. The palm branch, three myrtle branches, and two willows are bound loosely together in a specific arrangement so that they can be held in the right hand, while the *esrog* is held in the left. A blessing is said, and the four species are brought together and "waved" in the six directions. One should receive instruction on how to do this properly. (If one cannot get all the species, one can still use whatever one can obtain, but one may not recite the blessing.)

Of the many interpretations of this *mitzvah,* one is that it represents the unity of the Jewish people. The *esrog,* which is edible and pleasant smelling, symbolizes people who do good deeds and are learned in Torah. The palm, which has no fragrance but bears sweet fruit, is like people who are learned but have few good deeds to their credit. The myrtle, which smells good but bears no edible fruit, is like those who do good deeds but are ignorant of Torah. The willow, with neither taste nor aroma, is the Jew who has neither learning nor good deeds to his credit. The Torah tells us to gather all of these, all the four types of Jews, and hold them together. As it is written in the Rosh Hashanah prayers, Israel "shall all form a single bond to do Your will with a perfect heart."

Also, additional prayers are said throughout Succos, known as the *Hoshana* prayers. A Torah scroll is taken out, and everyone who has a set of the four species joins in a procession circling counterclockwise around the *bimah* while the *Hoshana* prayers are recited. A different order is recited every morning, until the seventh day, known as Hoshana Rabbah, when all seven sets are recited and the procession goes around seven times. After this, each person takes a bundle of five willow branches and strikes the floor five times with them.

The eighth and ninth days are full *Yamim Tovim,* like the first two. Shemini Atzeres is the last day we eat in the *succah* (without the blessing, however), and we say a farewell prayer at the last meal we consume there. Simchas Torah is a day of rejoicing and dancing with the Torah. The end of the book of *Deuteronomy* and the beginning of the book of *Genesis* are read, with every man in the congregation being called up to the Torah. In this way we affirm that the Torah has truly no beginning and no end.

# 16

~~~
Days of Commemoration:
Chanukah, Purim, and Fast Days
~~~

C hanukah and Purim are joyous festivals that commemorate miraculous salvations in Jewish history. These are not mentioned in the Five Books of Moses and therefore are not sanctified to the level of Shabbos or *Yom Tov*. However, various religious observances have been instituted to reflect their special historical significance.

Most of the fast days of Judaism, except for Yom Kippur, also reflect historical events that took place in later centuries, after the Mosaic revelation. One fast, the Fast of Esther, is connected to Purim and will be treated here, in connection with that holiday. The remainder are connected to the destruction of the First and Second Holy Temples, by the Babylonians in the sixth century B.C.E and by the Romans in the first century C.E.

# ❧ THE STORY OF CHANUKAH

When the Jews returned to the Land of Israel from Babylonia after seventy years of exile, they were permitted to rebuild the Holy Temple and in general had religious freedom. Under the scribe Ezra, they were able to reestablish their homeland on a solid Torah foundation. This tranquility, however, did not last. About a century later (333 B.C.E.), Asia Minor was conquered by Alexander the Great. His policy, and that of the Greek kings who followed him, was to export Greek culture to all the societies he conquered, and to make sure that local rulers imitated this policy also.

About a hundred and fifty years after Alexander's conquest, a Syrian ruler came to power, known as Antiochus, who was determined to enforce the expansion of Greek culture. He issued many harsh decrees against the Jews in an effort to force them to abandon their religious practices and adopt Greek culture. *Bris milah* and the observance of Shabbos, Rosh Chodesh, and the holidays were all prohibited under penalty of death. Interestingly, Torah study was not discouraged, as the Greeks believed the Torah had great wisdom. But they saw that Jewish practice interfered with acceptance of Greek culture and philosophy as the height of knowledge.

Many Jews died as martyrs rather than accept pagan culture and idol worship. Others, however, chose to revolt against this oppression. This was the first time in the history of mankind that a nation fought primarily for freedom of worship. With the help of the Almighty, under the leadership of Judah Maccabee and his brothers, the Jews were victorious over their enemies despite the Syrians' military superiority.

When Antiochus died, however, his son Eopater took up the war again, determined to defeat the Jewish guerrillas. He controlled the largest army known at the time, including 100,000 veteran armored infantrymen, 2000 horsemen, and 32 trained war elephants. It was said that when the sun shone on the glittering array of honor, the reflected light dazzled the eyes of spectators for miles around.

Against this army the Maccabees fought many desperate battles. The tide seemed to be going against them in the years-long war, but in one battle, Judah's brother Elazar noticed that one of the elephants was far more elaborately decorated than the others. Elazar, believing this to be the elephant of the king, fought his way through the soldiers and drove his spear into the belly of the elephant. The animal fell, crushing its rider, who happened to be one of the top generals. But Elazar also lost his life under the elephant.

Nevertheless, Elazar's act of bravery inspired his brethren, and they fought on. They remained in grave danger until, suddenly, a messenger came, bringing news to the Syrian king of an uprising back in his own land. His son was attempting to overthrow him. Antiochus Eopater called off the battle and made peace with Judah, so that the land of Israel was again saved.

In 162 B.C.E. after a series of victories, the Jewish camp managed to recapture the Temple Mount in Jerusalem. Their first priority was to rededicate the Temple, which had been desecrated by the Greeks. When they went to light the *Menorah*, they could not find any pure olive oil, for all the crocks of oil had either been broken or opened by the Greeks. Finally, one small container of oil was found with the seal of the High Priest still intact. It contained sufficient oil to keep the *Menorah* burning for one day. Yet, through a miracle, it lasted eight days, until a fresh supply could be obtained from the territory of the Tribe of Asher, far to the northwest of Jerusalem.

Chanukah commemorates these miracles.

## ᴇ§ THE LAWS OF CHANUKAH

Chanukah begins on the 25th of Kislev.[1] On the first night one light (either an oil light or a candle) is lit, on the second night two lights, and so on until, on the eighth night, eight lights are lit.

---

1. Talmud *Shabbos* 21b.

We also celebrate with festive meals, traditionally containing at least one dish cooked in oil such as *latkes* (potato pancakes) or *sufganiot* (jelly donuts).

In setting up the *menorah,* the first candle is placed on the extreme right side and one candle each night is added to the left of the previous. Every *menorah* also has a *shamash* or service candle by which the candles are lit. It is placed somewhat differently (for example higher or lower) than the other candles so that it is clearly not one of the Chanukah lights.

When one lights, the new candle (on the left) is lit first, then one moves from left to right. Ideally, each member of the household should light Chanukah candles, but a woman can fulfill her obligation through her husband's lighting. The *menorahs* should be separate from each other to avoid confusion to the observer as to how many lights are lit.

The *menorah* should be lit right after dark (or at sunset, according to some customs) and should last at least half an hour past the time the stars have appeared. On Friday, however, one cannot light the lights after dark, so the *menorah* is lit before the Shabbos candles. On this day, there must be more oil or larger candles, so that the lights will still be burning half an hour after the stars appear (about 1½ hours after candle-lighting time).

When one lights the *menorah* on the first night, three blessings are said; on the remaining nights, only two are recited:

1) *Baruch atah . . . l'hadlik ner shel Chanukah.* (Blessed are You, Lord our G-d, Ruler of the universe, Who has commanded us to light the light of Chanukah. Sephardim leave out the word "*shel.*")

2) *Baruch atah . . . she'asah nisim la'avosenu bayamim ha'hem bazman hazeh.* (Blessed are You . . . Who did miracles for our ancestors in those days at this season.)

3) *Baruch atah . . . shehechyanu, vikimanu, v'higianu lazman hazeh* — only on the first night. (Blessed are You . . . Who gave us life, sustained us, and preserved us to [reach] this season.)

Two traditional songs, *Ha'neros hallelu* and *Ma'oz Tzur,* are then sung. The *menorah* is not moved once it is lit.

> The *kohen* is a descendant of Aaron, who served as the officiating priest in the Tabernacle in the wilderness, and whose descendants served in the Holy Temple in Jerusalem. The *kohanim* today have the function of blessing the people in a special ceremony on holidays, and they perform the ritual of "redemption of the firstborn male". If any *kohanim* are present when the Torah is read publicly, one of them will be called up for the first *aliyah* (honor of reading).
>
> The Levites were assistants to the *kohanim* in the Temple, and are descendants of the tribe of Levi (which included other families besides that of Aaron and Moses). A Levite is normally called up for the second *aliyah* when the Torah is read. The remainder of the Jewish people are called Israelites. The specific tribal lineage of the rest of the people is not usually known, and they are not differentiated in religious functions.

The point of the lighting is to publicize the miracles of Chanukah. Therefore, the *menorah* should be lit at a window facing the street for passersby to see. Additionally, a *menorah* should be lit in every public place where Jews congregate such as synagogues or wedding halls. Some have the custom of lighting in the doorway, as was done in ancient times.

In the prayers, the complete *Hallel* is said on all eight days, and the Torah is read publicly. *Al ha'nissim* ("For the miracles") is added to the *Shemoneh Esrei* and the Grace After Meals.

How is it that so much emphasis is placed on the lighting of the candles and the miracle of the oil? Why do we not focus more on the equally miraculous victories of the Maccabees? The reason is that if we were to focus on the battles, later it would be claimed that we won because we were better soldiers. The history books would stress the human side and forget that the Almighty was responsible for the victory. The miracle of the oil, however, is impossible to explain logically. This supernal element puts G-d in the center, and reminds us that all the Chanukah miracles came from G-d.

When we light the *menorah,* we can remember that the "fire" that the Jews lit when they were willing to go to war on behalf of G-d and His commandments will never be extinguished.

# ←§ THE STORY OF PURIM

The Jews who had been exiled to Babylonia soon found themselves under a new ruler, the Persians, who had taken over the Babylonian Empire. The king Cyrus had been kind to the Jews, decreeing that those who wished to return to their homeland could go back and rebuild the Temple. But his successors were not always so generous. When Ahasuerus ascended the throne, the life of the Jews even in Persia itself became much more precarious.

The story is told in *Megillas Esther,* the "scroll of Esther," commonly known as "the Megillah." King Ahasuerus made a celebration for his coronation that lasted 180 days, and a special feast for residents of the capital, Shushan, for seven more days. He invited the Jews specifically, hoping that they would join in the festivities, eat forbidden food and wine, and commit other sins. This, he thought, would prevent their G-d from protecting them, and they would decline in power. In addition, he appointed as his prime minister a man from a notoriously anti-Jewish tribe known as the Amalekites. His name was Haman, and under his influence, Ahasuerus issued a decree that every Jewish man, woman, and child be murdered by the other Persians.

The evil Haman cast lots to decide the date for the extermination of the Jews. The name of the holiday comes from this word; Purim means "lots." The date chosen was the thirteenth day of the Jewish month Adar.

However, G-d had prepared the remedy for this danger in advance. The king had killed his queen Vashti for disobedience, and his new choice for a queen was Esther, the niece of the Jewish sage Mordecai. Esther and Mordecai roused their fellow Jews to fasting and prayer. Through many twists and turns of plot, the evil decree was abolished, and the critical days were transformed "from anguish to rejoicing and from mourning to festival" (*Megillas Esther* 9:22).

Thus the fourteenth of Adar is celebrated as the day that the Jews of Persia were saved by G-d from the wicked plot to destroy them. This story is read in the *Megillah* (a parchment scroll) on the evening and morning of Purim. The festival is celebrated with much merriment, including noisemaking whenever the name of Haman is read from the scroll.

The day before Purim is one of the five fast days besides Yom Kippur. It is known as the Fast of Esther to recall that Queen Esther declared a public fast in order to seek G-d's mercy.[2] (See below on the purpose of fast days.)

Purim reminds us of the Jewish people's miraculous survival throughout history, despite persecution and exile, so that we have outlived empires and nations who appeared to be much mightier than we. As one of the prophets wrote, "Take counsel together and it shall be brought to naught! Speak the word and it shall not stand! For G-d is with us." All conspiracies against the Jews are annulled, sooner or later, by the Lord of history.

In Roman times, a philosopher from one of the academies once asked Rabbi Eliezer, "Is it not written, 'they shall build, but I will throw down'? Now all the buildings still stand upright."

Rabbi Eliezer answered, "It was not said with respect to buildings but with respect to plots and wicked counsels that your people have always contrived against us. You build up your plans and He destroys them immediately."

The philosopher admitted he was right. "It is indeed so. Every year designs are made to exterminate you, but something always intervenes and you always survive."[3]

## ⊷§ THE LAWS OF PURIM

There are four principal commandments unique to Purim: reading the Megillah, giving to charity, giving portions of food to friends, and having a Purim feast.

*Megillas Esther* is to be read twice on Purim, once in the evening after nightfall, and once more during the day after sunrise. Men, women, and children are obligated to hear the reading since

---

2. Rambam, *Mishneh Torah, Hilchos Taanis* 1.
3. Talmud *Pesachim* 87.

all were under threat of annihilation by Haman. Many attend the Megillah reading in costume.

A *minyan* should be present if at all possible. The *baal korei* or public reader recites three blessings prior to the reading: (1) *al mikra megillah;* (2) *she'asah nisim* (as for Chanukah), (3) *she-hecheyanu.* He should read word for word from the Megillah and not recite any words by heart. If he skipped a word, he must return to the place where he made the error and continue from there. It is customary that he read the list of Haman's ten sons in one breath.

The person listening to the Megillah should make an effort to hear every word. If he missed, he should say the words quietly to himself. We are not to talk at all during the Megillah, but when Haman's infamous name is mentioned, we stamp our feet and make noise in order to "blot out" his name.

*Matanos l'evyonim* (gifts to the poor) are given on Purim. Each adult is obligated to give to two needy people. Today, most people give money, but it is also permissible to give food for the Purim day feast. In general, one should give *tzedakah* freely and generously on Purim. Whereas on other days we may inquire into the nature of a person's needs, it is the custom that on Purim we give something to everyone who asks, without investigating.

We also give portions of ready-to-eat food, known as *mishloach manos,* with each person being obligated to give at least two different kinds of food to at least one friend. Customarily, we send this gift through a third-party messenger (such as a child), thus involving more people in the *mitzvah.*

On the day of Purim, usually beginning in the late afternoon, we celebrate with a feast. At this feast it is customary to serve wine, and to drink until "one cannot tell the difference between 'Blessed be Mordecai' and 'Cursed be Haman.' " In many communities, people tell funny stories or give unusual interpretations of Torah known as "Purim Torah." At this event as well as at the Megillah readings, people often dress in costume.

In the prayers, *Al ha'nissim* is added to the *Shemoneh Esrei* and the Grace After Meals, as at Chanukah. Also, Purim is customarily the time when the synagogue collects three half-dollars from each male, symbolic of the half-shekels that were collected in the times of the Holy Temple.

## ᴥ§ FAST DAYS

Besides Yom Kippur, which was discussed in Chapter 16, and the Fast of Esther mentioned above, there are four other fast days. All of them remind us of the destruction of the Temple and the loss of the Land of Israel. According to our Sages, these disasters came upon the Jewish nation because of the people's sins. With the destruction of the Temple, Jewish religious observance was weakened, and the people tended to disperse among the nations. Our fast days remind us of the potential consequences of turning away from G-d and Torah. On these days, therefore, we not only fast but also meditate on the wrongdoings that caused these destructions. In this way the fast can be the beginning of a clearing process through which we individually and communally mend our ways.

The four days are: (1) *Tzom Gedaliah,* the Fast of Gedaliah, on the third of Tishrei immediately following the two days of Rosh Hashanah; (2) *Asarah B'Teves,* the tenth of Teves; (3) *Shivah asar B'Tammuz,* the 17th of Tammuz, and (4) *Tishah B'Av,* the ninth of Av. The first three of these days are fasts from dawn to dark; the fourth is a 25-hour fast from sunset of one day to the next nightfall, like Yom Kippur.

The Fast of Gedaliah reminds us of a time when the Jewish community turned on itself with infighting. Following the destruction of the First Temple by Nebuchadnezzar of Babylon, multitudes of Jews, including almost all the Jewish leadership and skilled workmen, were forced into exile in Babylon. Nebuchadnezzar appointed Gedaliah ben Achikom to govern the remaining Jewish community. Despite his puppet status, he was a strong leader who might have been able to inaugurate negotiations to rebuild the Temple. Unfortunately, he was murdered by an assassin, hired by a different enemy king, and the Jewish community rapidly declined.

The tenth of Teves commemorates the beginning of the siege of Jerusalem by Nebuchadnezzar. This was the beginning of the end for the First Temple.

The seventeenth of Tammuz inaugurates a three-week period of mourning, which culminates in the full fast of the ninth of Av. This period reminds us of many events that bode ill for the Jewish people, going back even into the time of Moses and the generation of the desert. The seventeenth of Tammuz itself is infused with the following sorrowful events:

1) On this day, Moses descended from Mount Sinai, saw the golden calf that had been made and worshipped, and broke the Tablets of the Law.

2) In the First Temple, the daily sacrifice had to be suspended on this day due to the siege of Jerusalem.

3) Apostomus the Wicked burned the Torah and placed an idol in the Second Temple.

4) The walls of the city of Jerusalem were breached, in 70 C.E., by the Romans, leading to the destruction of the Second Temple by Titus the Wicked. (Some say this also happened to the First Temple at this time.)

The three weeks following the seventeenth of Tammuz are marked by observance of certain laws of mourning. We do not cut our hair, celebrate weddings or other social parties, play or dance to music, buy or wear outer clothing that is brand new, such as a suit or dress. When the New Moon of Av arrives, this time of mourning is intensified. During the "Nine Days" from the first through the ninth of Av, we refrain from swimming, from eating meat and drinking wine, and from laundering clothing (except for children's clothing). Court cases should be postponed if possible.

On the eighth of Av, at the approach of sunset, one sits on the floor and eats the "final meal," consisting of a piece of bread and a cooked item — usually a hard-boiled egg — dipped in ashes. At sunset, one removes one's shoes and refrains from eating for the next 25 hours. (One may wear cloth or synthetic shoes, but they should not appear to be like fine leather.) We also avoid washing, anointing, and having marital relations. Even when washing our hands in the morning, we wash only the fingers, from the knuckles to the fingertips.

As do mourners, we refrain from greeting one another on Tishah B'Av. Until afternoon of the next day, we sit only on the floor or on low stools. We do not study Torah, except for those portions dealing with mourning and the destruction of the Temple. It is a very solemn day, and we abstain from frivolity and jesting.

*Eichah* (*Lamentations*) is read publicly in the synagogue. A series of special prayers known as *Kinos* are recited on this day.

As with the seventeenth of Tammuz, a number of sorrowful events happened on this date:

1) The spies who had gone into the Land of Israel returned, and ten of them gave Moses a highly critical report. The Jewish people believed them rather than the two spies who gave a good report, and bewailed their fate. G-d then decreed that this date would indeed give them a reason to wail, and that that generation would not be allowed to enter the Land of Israel. The people were punished to the extent that they spent the next forty years in the wilderness.

2) Both the First and Second Temples were destroyed on Tishah B'Av.

3) In the Bar Kochba War (132-135 C.E.), the last stronghold, Betar, was captured and destroyed by the Romans on this day. This was nearly as devastating as the destruction of the Temple, because so many thousands of Jews were killed in that war. To compound the tragedy, the Romans denied burial to those slain in Betar. (However, by Divine miracle, the bodies did not decay until permission was given to bury them.)

4) The Temple Mount was plowed under by the Romans on this day.

5) The expulsion of the Jews from Spain took place on Tishah B'Av in 1492.

6) The outbreak of World War I occurred on Tishah B'Av in 1914.

We avoid eating and drinking on all these fasts not merely to inflict hardship on ourselves, but to awaken our thoughts to repentance. As the Mishnah states, the reason for a fast is to confess our sins, analyze our deeds, and improve our ways.[4]

We must reflect on how we as a people have helped bring these events upon ourselves, particularly on the fasts commemorating the events surrounding the destruction of our Holy Temple. The First Temple, it is said, was destroyed largely because of idolatry and other cardinal sins. However, after the exile, the Sages of the Great Assembly prayed that the lust for idol-worship be removed from the people. Thus by the time of the Second Temple, and most assuredly by the time of the Maccabees, the Jewish people had virtually eliminated idolatry from their midst. They were willing to die rather than participate in the idol-worship of the Greeks and Romans.

The sin that brought on the destruction of the Second Temple, a different sin, was the bitter hatred and animosity that Jews showed for one another. *Sinas chinam,* or "baseless hatred," is the sin that must be rooted out through our repentance on this day. It must be replaced by *ahavas chinam,* unconditional love, and we should seek peace between ourselves and all our fellow Jews.

A rabbi was once visiting a certain town, and on Tishah B'Av was informed of a bitter feud between two groups. He was asked to mediate between them. Out of consideration for the rabbi's weakness during the fast, however, the people said they assumed he would wait until after the fast day to hear the two sides. "On the contrary," responded the rabbi. "The destruction of the Temple was caused by unwarranted hatred of one Jew for another. What is more appropriate than trying to promote peace and brotherhood on this day?"

---

4. Talmud *Taanis* 15.

# APPENDIX

## Outline of Jewish History

# Outline of Jewish History:
# The Transmission of the Torah
# Through the Ages

## INTRODUCTION

The history of Israel is different from the history of any other group of people. No matter how we look at it, there is one inescapable fact of the history of the Jews: it is unique. Nowhere else do we find a nation flourishing despite losing its state, territory, and Temple. In fact, only for a few centuries during the thousands of years of Jewish history did the Jews live in a land of their own. During the greater part of their existence the Jews have been scattered among the nations and have struggled against overwhelming odds to resist total annihilation. They have been exiled, persecuted, and massacred by nation after nation. While many nations have always risen to greatness and then declined, the Jews have continued to survive. Why?

# APPENDIX

---

# Outline of Jewish History: The Transmission of the Torah Through the Ages

---

## ✍§ INTRODUCTION

The history of Israel is different from the history of any other group of people. No matter how we look at it, there is one inescapable fact of the history of the Jews: it is unique. Nowhere else do we find a nation flourishing despite losing its state, territory, and Temple. In fact, only for a few centuries during the thousands of years of Jewish history did the Jews live in a land of their own. During the greater part of their existence the Jews have been scattered among the nations and have struggled against overwhelming odds to resist total annihilation. They have been exiled, persecuted, and massacred by nation after nation. While many nations have always risen to greatness and then declined, the Jews have continued to survive. Why?

The existence of the nation of Israel alone does not depend upon the possession of territory but upon the Torah. It was Torah that brought the Jewish nation into being; it is Torah that has kept it in existence. This is the explanation of the uniqueness of Jewish history and the secret of Jewish survival.

The most remarkable aspect of Jewish history is that its entire course was accurately predicted beforehand by the Torah. The Jews were told at the very outset that they would lose their land which they did not as yet even possess. Despite the difficulties they would encounter in exile, they were told they would survive the trials among the nations until their hour of redemption arrived.

The very survival and existence of the Jew bears testimony to the truth of the Torah as a Divine revelation, "You are My witnesses, says the L-rd."[1]

Even members of other religions have recognized that the history of the Jews has proven the authenticity of the Torah. A fourth-century Church father, Jerome, once said:

"The destruction of the Holy City, the ruin of the House of G-d, the dispersion of the Chosen People into all the kingdoms of the earth, and their continued existence as a nation, notwithstanding every attempt to exterminate them or to compel them to forsake those ordinances which distinguish them to this very day from all other nations, is emphatically one of the strongest evidences we can have of the truth of the Bible."

The purpose of this chapter is to review in short the main highlights of Jewish history. Limitations of space have forced a more generalized treatment of our history. The concepts and principles that we have stated in the previous chapters give us a deeper appreciation of what has happened to Jews throughout the ages. By analyzing our past, we are better able to face our future.

The following Outline deals with the travels and travails of the Torah, the life-soul of our people. It is not intended to be comprehensive, nor does it include secular events in the Jewish or world history. When it names great figures in our national story, they are meant as *examples* of others, not to their exclusion.

---

1. *Isaiah* 43:10.

# I

# THE TORAH

The Torah consists of the Five Books of Moses:

*Genesis (Bereishis)*
*Exodus (Shemos)*
*Leviticus (Vayikra)*
*Numbers (Bamidbar)*
*Deuteronomy (Devarim)*

## (1) *Genesis (Bereishis)*

This book relates the history of creation, the story of early mankind, and the lives of our patriarchs — Abraham, Isaac, and Jacob, and matriarchs — Sarah, Rebecca, Rachel, and Leah. Then it focuses on the children of Jacob, who became the nation of Israel. *Genesis* is not to be considered merely a history book, but rather a lesson plan for life. It teaches us that the Creator of the Universe forever guides His creations. From the Book of *Genesis* we also learn of the supreme devotion of our patriarchs to the Almighty and their willingness to sacrifice everything for that devotion.[2] *Genesis* also relates G-d's punishment of the wicked, such as the Flood and the Destruction of Sodom. In addition, one learns of the great rewards bestowed by the Almighty upon those who walk in His path, as our patriarchs and matriarchs did. Their complete honesty, love of mankind, and eagerness to help other human beings stand as a perpetual lesson for all of us.

The Book of *Genesis* concludes with Joseph's brothers evidencing remorse and repentance for having sold him, Joseph helping his family during the time of famine by settling them in Egypt, and the death of Jacob and his sons.

---

2. Rambam, *Guide to the Perplexed.*

## (2) Exodus (Shemos)

This book carries forward the history begun in *Genesis* and tells of the formation of Israel as a nation. It describes the oppression and slavery in Egypt as well as the exodus and spectacular liberation of the Jewish people. It further describes the great acts performed by Moses and Aaron as messengers chosen by G-d to lead the Jews out of Egypt. It shows Moses' great character, especially his faith, persistence, modesty, and superb leadership abilities. The dramatic account of the exodus, splitting of the Red Sea, and the giving of the Ten Commandments, are among the most outstanding features of the first half of the Book of *Exodus*.

The second half of *Exodus* is replete with highly ethical concepts and laws. G-d's deep interest in human affairs is reflected by the laws that He gave to the Jewish people. It concludes with the account of the building of the *Mishkan* (Tabernacle) that was a visible resting place of G-d's Divine Presence.

## (3) Leviticus (Vayikra)

This is primarily a book of laws, most of which are concerned with holiness and purity. It discusses the laws of the *kohanim* (priests) and the bringing of the sacrifices. It defines which animals are kosher and which are nonkosher. It contains a code of holiness stressing the high moral standards required of the Jews. It also contains laws of humaneness and charity.

## (4) Numbers (Bamidbar)

The fourth book of the Torah contains a brief summary of the experiences of the Jews in the wilderness during forty years of wandering. It records the incident of the twelve spies which resulted in the Jews remaining in the desert for forty years. It speaks of the rebellion of Korah against Moses and Aaron, of Moses striking the rock, and of the wicked Bilaam and Balak. There is a clear picture of the difficulties that confronted Moses and how with the help of G-d he was able to overcome them.

## (5) Deuteronomy (Devarim)

The fifth book of the Torah is a review of all the events of the

Jewish nation recorded in the other volumes of the Torah. A major part of the Book of *Deuteronomy* consists of Moses' address to the Jewish nation as they were about to cross the Jordan River into the Land of Israel. Moses' farewell consisted of three speeches. The first is a summary of the main experiences of Israel in the desert, the second reviews the Ten Commandments and includes the declaration of G-d's Oneness, and the third stresses the duty of loyalty to G-d.

*Deuteronomy* contains a number of humane laws and ethical teachings. It speaks of events up to the death of Moses and prepares for the succession by Joshua. It contains a moving narrative of Moses' beseeching the Almighty to be allowed to enter the Promised Land. But all that was granted to him was the chance to survey the Land of Israel from atop Mount Nebo.

It is a basic premise of our faith that every word of the Torah was dictated to Moses by G-d. Although the Book of *Deuteronomy* is written as the testimony of Moses, every word was dictated by G-d as if Moses himself were addressing the people. There is a controversy regarding the writing of the last eight verses of *Deuteronomy* since they discuss the death of Moses. Some authorities maintain they were written by Moses himself, under G-d's orders. Others maintain that these verses were written by Joshua. The time span covered in the five books of the Torah is from creation until 2488 (1273 B.C.E.).

The Scriptures are sometimes referred to as *TaNaCH*. This is an acronym for the three Hebrew words *Torah, Neviim, Kesuvim. Torah* — the Five Books of Moses; *Neviiim* — Prophets; *Kesuvim* — Holy Writings.

# II

# NEVIIM (THE PROPHETS)

The Book of *Prophets* consists of eight separate books. They are:

*Joshua — Yehoshua*
*Judges — Shoftim*
*Samuel (I, II) — Shmuel*
*Kings (I, II) — Melachim*
*Isaiah — Yeshayahu*
*Jeremiah — Yirmiyahu*
*Ezekiel — Yechezkel*
*The Twelve Prophets — Trei Asar*

## NEVIIM RISHONIM — THE EARLY PROPHETS

### (1) *Joshua*: (1273 — 1245 B.C.E.) 2488 — 2516

The Book of *Joshua* narrates the conquest and settlement of the Promised Land. It is the first of the four historical books known as *Neviim Rishonim* (First Prophets), forming a continuous narrative which begins after the death of Moses and concludes with the destruction of the First Temple (*Beis HaMikdash*).

As successor to Moses, Joshua led the Jewish people during seven years of conquering *Eretz Yisrael* (Land of Israel), and seven years of dividing the land among the tribes. In the course of that time, he defeated many nations. The spectacular victories of the Jews were highlighted by obvious miracles performed by G-d. They included the fall of the walls of Jericho and the sun standing still at Gibeon. The initial setback at Ai due to the transgression of Achan and the Jews' subsequent victory there proved G-d's involvement in these developments.

The two and a half tribes who had settled on the other side of the Jordan River helped their fellow Jews conquer Canaan, and contributed to their success. The subsequent seven years saw the land apportioned among the tribes of Israel, except for the tribe of Levi. The apportionment of the land was done by a Divinely guided lottery. Cities of refuge were set aside on both sides of the Jordan River, to shelter those who commit accidental manslaughter from retribution.

We must remember that when we speak of the conquest of Israel, we are not stressing the military prowess of Joshua and the Jews, but rather (as Joshua himself emphasized) the Divine help provided for the Jews to achieve its conquest. Since the conquest came about because of G-d's direct intervention in assisting the Jews, their continued existence in the Land is contingent upon their obeying and fulfilling God's will. That is why the Book of *Joshua* begins with the words: "This book of the Torah shall not leave your mouth; you shall meditate therein day and night, in order that you may observe to do all that is written in it, for then will you succeed in all your ways and then will you prosper" (1:8). It concludes with Joshua's plea for the Jews to enter a covenant with the Almighty. Of their own free will, they committed themselves to worship only G-d and to follow His commandments.

Before his death at the age of 110, Joshua delivered two addresses to the people of Israel, urging them to remain loyal to G-d and live according to the teachings of the Torah. He was succeeded by the Elders (*Zekeinim*) including Phinehas. The Book of *Joshua* was written by Joshua himself. However, the verses dealing with Joshua's death and that of Elazar were written by Phinehas. The subsequent leaders were called the Judges.

### (2) *Judges*: (1228 – 911 B.C.E.) 2533 – 2850

During the era of the Judges there was no king. The people were basically capable of governing themselves. Most of the Judges provided the spiritual guidance. This period lasted approximately 350 years and was a unique era in Jewish history. Although on the surface it would seem that this was a turbulent time, close evaluation reveals otherwise. Most of the period passed peacefully without any strife. Even when the Jews did sin, they were quick to repent. There were only two tragic episodes about which the prophet stated, "In those days there was no king in Israel. Every man did what was just in his eyes." One episode concerned the tribe of Dan that went astray with regard to the idol of Michah. The other concerned the tragedy of the concubine of Givah that led to a civil war that caused the near annihilation of the tribe of Benjamin and the loss of tens of thousands in battle.

(As Joshua had predicted, the heathen nations remaining in the Land of Israel continually posed problems for the Jewish conquerors. Isolated from each other by Canaanite areas, many of the Jewish settlements concentrated on their local concerns and were often influenced by the immoral behavior practiced among the Canaanites whom they had been commanded to eradicate.

But Providence did not allow them to fall victim to these dangers. Recurrent attempts by the Canaanites to repossess their former dominions forcefully reminded the Jewish tribes of the necessity for national unity and their undivided loyalty to G-d.)

The Book of *Judges* conveys a clear message to the Jewish nation: We are constantly under Divine guidance. When the Jews sinned, the enemy arose and subjugated them. When Israel obeyed the law, they were successful and were able to defeat larger and more powerful enemies.

During this period, all the Judges were leaders whose authority was not automatically passed on to their sons. No one seized power over the nation through force or violent means, except for Abimelech, the son of Gideon, who was punished shortly thereafter. These great judges realized that their own power was insignificant, and that they were merely serving as messengers of the Almighty.

Among the best-known Judges of Israel in this era were the following:

    (a) Othniel ben Kenaz — the son-in-law of Caleb. He was the successor to Joshua, and, as the first Judge, led the people for forty years. He was noted for his superior Torah wisdom which he disseminated in Israel.

    (b) Ehud — He assassinated Eglon, king of the enemy country Moab, under the ruse of visiting him. After this episode, peace reigned in the land for eighty years.

    (c) Deborah — a prophetess who led the Jewish people for forty years. She and Barak, her military commander, waged a successful campaign against the Canaanites, who were led by their chief general, Sisera. After their victory, Deborah led the Jewish people in a Song of Praise to the Almighty (*Shirah*), praising G-d for all the miracles He had done for His people. When Sisera fled from the battlefield, he sought refuge in the tent of Yael. When he fell asleep she drove a stake through his temple. Deborah the Prophetess and Yael the heroine characterize the important and heroic contributions made by Jewish women throughout history.

(d) Gideon — He came from a modest background and was chosen by G-d to lead the Jews against the Midianites. He was successful both on the battlefield and in his campaign to eradicate idol worship among some of the Jewish inhabitants.

(e) Jephthah (Yiftach) — a Judge who came from humble beginnings and delivered the Jewish people from the oppression of Ammonite invaders. In fulfillment of a vow, he isolated his only daughter after the victory. This was a tragic mistake, for he should have had his vow annulled. He was a Judge for six years.

(f) Samson (Shimshon) — He warred against the Philistines, the perpetual enemy of the Jews. Delilah, a treacherous Philistine woman, caused his downfall. After he revealed that the secret source of his superior strength lay in his unshorn head (since he was a nazarite), she cut off his hair, causing him to lose his strength. He was overpowered by the Philistines, who blinded and imprisoned him. While chained to the pillars of a Philistine temple, Samson prayed to G-d for His help against the enemy. In a final surge of strength Samson pushed the pillars apart, destroying the temple along with thousands of Philistines. He judged Israel for twenty years.

The Book of *Judges* was written by the Prophet Samuel.

**(2) Samuel:** (911-837 B.C.E.) 2850-2924

*Samuel I* and *Samuel II* are in reality one book. This book continues the history of the Jews from the time of Eli the High Priest, who was the last of the Judges, through the era of King David's reign. Most of the events during this period are centered around three great personalities: Samuel, Saul, and David.

After sincere and devoted prayer, Hannah was blessed with a son whom she dedicated to the service of the Almighty and the nation of Israel. At first, Samuel assisted Eli the High Priest. Later he succeeded him as leader when Eli's sons proved unsuitable for the role and perished in battle with the Philistines.

Samuel was both a prophet and leader, and was on an extraordinarily high spiritual level. He was extremely honest in his service to the Jewish nation. He was opposed to the people's request for a king because this indicated that they did not feel sufficiently confident with self-rule under G-d's guidance. Nevertheless, at the request of the Almighty, Samuel appointed Saul, from the small tribe of Benjamin, as the first king of Israel. Saul was very righteous, handsome, and tall, yet he was extremely modest.

*Samuel I* records the events during the administration of the Prophet Samuel and King Saul. Saul made a grave mistake in not following G-d's orders to eradicate Amalek and to wait for Samuel before offering a sacrifice as commanded by G-d. He therefore lost his right to be the king, and Samuel anointed David to be the next king. Saul became jealous of David's popularity, especially after David defeated the giant, Goliath. David was forced to flee for his life. Saul was defeated in battle with the Philistines. He fell on his own sword rather than allow himself to be captured and mocked by the enemy. He was a good king who was mourned by David and the entire Jewish nation.

*Samuel II* tells of the reign of King David. He was a great warrior who expanded the territory of the kingdom. King David is considered a great servant of G-d and a great king of the Jews, who ruled for forty years. His Book of *Psalms* is one of the great treasures of the Jewish people. However, King David did make some misjudgments for which he was punished.

He suffered the agony of seeing his eldest son, Absalom, rebel against him and force him to flee from Jerusalem. Absalom was ultimately killed, but David still mourned deeply for him. King

David enlarged his kingdom and defeated his enemies. He united all the tribes of Israel into one strong nation. He wrote the Book of *Psalms* (*Tehillim*) and established Jerusalem as the capital of Israel. He was greatly saddened at not being allowed to build the *Beis HaMikdash* because of the many wars that he had conducted. Instead, his son Solomon fulfilled this task.

The first part of *Samuel I,* up to the part dealing with his own death, was written by the Prophet Samuel. The rest was written by Gad and Nathan, who were prophets during the reign of King David.

### (3) *Kings:* (837 – 423 B.C.E.) 2924-3338

*Kings I* and *Kings II* are in reality one book, and it tells the story of the kingdoms of Judah and Israel. They cover a period of over four hundred years, extending from the last days of King David to the destruction of the First Temple. This was the period of Israel's glory, division, decline, and fall. King Solomon succeeded his father David. He was extraordinarily wise. He organized a strong army and kept his country out of war for forty years. King Solomon's fame and wisdom were widespread and enhanced the reputation of the Jewish nation. He built the Holy Temple in Jerusalem and a beautiful palace, but at the same time levied heavy taxes for their construction upon the people. He was the author of *Song of Songs* (*Shir HaShirim*), *Proverbs* (*Mishlei*), and *Ecclesiastes* (*Koheles*).

After Solomon's death, his son and successor, Rehoboam, rejected the advice of his elders and accepted the advice of his youthful friends to raise the amount of the taxes. This aroused the wrath of the populace, and encouraged Yeroboam ben Nebat to lead ten of the twelve tribes in secession. The kingdom was thereafter divided into the Kingdom of Israel, consisting of ten tribes, and the Kingdom of Judah, consisting of the tribes of Judah and Benjamin. Yeroboam feared that if the Jews traveled to Jerusalem during the Jewish festivals, the people might reunite with the Kingdom of Judah. He therefore set up roadblocks and introduced idolatry as a substitute for the Holy Temple. Because he had caused the nation to abandon the cardinal principle of Judaism and accept idolatry, he is considered as one of the most wicked people in Jewish history.

The Kingdom of Israel lasted for 240 years and was led by nineteen kings, almost all of whom did not follow the ways of G-d. Idol worship was rampant within the Kingdom of Israel and succession to the throne was marked by violence. Among the most evil of the leaders were King Ahab and his wicked Queen Jezebel. It was during their reign that the Prophet Elijah (Eliyahu) sought to bring the Jewish people back to the proper path.

The last king of the Kingdom of Israel was Hosea. He was defeated by Assyria. The Jews of his kingdom were exiled to distant lands and were lost without a trace to this day. They are known as the Ten Lost Tribes of Israel.

The Kingdom of Judah, in contrast to the Kingdom of Israel, lasted for 374 years and had twenty kings. It remained faithful to the House of David and the succession of kings continued from father to son. Although most of the rulers in this kingdom were righteous, some were wicked. Among the most notorious was Athaliah, daughter of Ahab and Jezebel (of the Kingdom of Israel) and wife of King Jeroboam. She instituted a reign of terror and promoted idol worship. She tried to wipe out the line of King David, but one descendant, the baby Jehoash, was saved.

Ahaz was another wicked king of Judah. He ignored the advice of the Prophet Isaiah and sought the aid of Assyria against the Kingdom of Israel and Damascus. This eventually led to the fall of the Kingdom of Israel and Judah's domination by Assyria. Ahaz himself set up idols and practiced human sacrifice.

One of the most wicked kings of Judah was Manasseh, who reinstated idol worship, bloodshed, corruption and violence to the land. It was his actions that initiated the decay leading to the eventual destruction of the Temple and exile of the Jews. He was taken prisoner by the Assyrians and severely tortured. He subsequently repented his evil ways but was unable to stem the tide of moral corruption that he had instituted.

(It is remarkable that the Northern kingdom disappeared first; it had been much larger, stronger and richer, but Judah, tied to the Temple and the house of David, had a closer attachment to the spiritual heritage by which the Jewish people lives. Indeed, at the time of Israel's destruction, it enjoyed a period of unexcelled (if short-lived) spiritual flourishing, under King Hezekiah. Several generations later, however, it too suffered destruction — neither the labors of the pious king Joshiah nor the warnings of Jeremiah succeeded in regenerating the state.

Despite the Prophet's warnings, Judah joined an anti-Babylonian coalition of powers. Forsaken by its allies, it soon found Jerusalem besieged by the Babylonians, yet even at this moment the Prophet's call to the wealthy to release their slaves, in obedience to the Torah, was not obeyed. Unrepentant, they led Judah to its doom.

Among the great kings of the Kingdom of Judah were:

(a) Hezekiah — He reversed the trends of his wicked father, Ahaz, and was a righteous king. During his reign, Senna-cherib, king of Assyria, besieged Jerusalem. His deputy, Rabshakeh, demanded that the populace surrender and abandon the service of G-d. Through a miracle, foretold by the Prophet Isaiah, Sennacherib's army was destroyed.

(b) Josiah — Several of his predecessors had worshipped the Baal; he led the people to repent, after listening to a reading of the Torah. He subsequently destroyed the idols in his kingdom.

(c) Zedekiah — He ignored the Prophet Jeremiah's advice to surrender to Nebuchadnezzar, king of Babylonia, relying instead on a promise of aid from Egypt. As a result, Judah was defeated, and Zedekiah (the last king of Judah) was led into captivity along with his nation.

# ⊷§ GREAT PROPHETS DURING THE REIGN OF THE KINGS

The spiritual well-being of the Jews throughout the era of the kingdoms was protected by the presence of the Prophets (*Neviim*) who served as G-d's messengers to the populace and encouraged them to observe G-d's Torah.

The main message of all the prophets was that we must keep the commandments as recorded in the Torah. G-d said to His prophets, "Remember the Torah of Moses My servant, which I commanded him ... " The authority of every prophet is derived only from the Torah, therefore, no prophet can contradict a single word of the Torah, even if he effects a miracle. Any prophet who contradicts the Torah in any way is assumed to be a false prophet and is judged accordingly. The most common reason for G-d to send a prophet was to admonish the people to keep the Torah.[3]

Among the great prophets beginning with the time of Samuel were the following:

(a) Nathan — a prophet during the reign of King David. By means of a parable he showed David how his actions with regard to Bathsheba were improper. Nathan was the prophet who told David that he would not be able to build the Temple, but that his son, Solomon, would do so.

(b) Elijah — a prophet during the reigns of Ahab and Ahaziah. He rebuked Ahab for fostering idolatry, for letting the wicked queen Jezebel execute nearly all the prophets of Hashem, and for stealing Naboth's vineyard and causing his death. Elijah predicted the agonizing deaths of Ahab and Jezebel.

Elijah performed many miracles, including the revival of a dead child. Before an assembly of hundreds of thousands of Jews, Elijah proved that the "prophets" and priests of Baal were frauds, and the entire nation of Israel cried out, "Hashem, He is the G-d!" Elijah did not die but ascended to Heaven in a fiery chariot. He will return to us to herald the coming of the Messiah.

Hundreds of stories are told about the Prophet Elijah. Many unresolved questions in the *Gemara* end with the word *"teku,"* an abbreviation said to mean "Tishbi (another name for Elijah) will answer difficulties and questions in the future."

(c) Elisha — The disciple and successor of Elijah, he was a

---

3. Rambam, *Mishneh Torah, Hil. Yesodei Torah.*

prophet during the reign of every king from Ahab to Jehoash. Like his mentor, he performed many miracles. He blessed a righteous woman that she would bear a son, and when the son later died, Elisha revived him. He cured Naaman, the Syrian commander in chief, of leprosy, but refused all rewards. When Elisha's servant Geichazi did take a reward for this, Geichazi was smitten with leprosy. Even sinful kings came to Elisha for guidance and blessings.

(d) Zechariah — He prophesied during the reign of Jehoash, king of Judah. His father, the High Priest Jehoiada, saved the life of the baby Jehoash from the ruthless Athaliah. Jehoiada made Jehoash king at the age of 7. Until his death at the age of 130, Jehoiada was the king's adviser. Jehoash then found new advisers who urged him to accept deification, like the gentile monarchs, demanding that all bow down before him. The prophet Zechariah publicly rebuked him and his advisers. The followers of the king stoned the prophet to death in the courtyard of the *Beis HaMikdash,* where his blood continued to boil without stop until Nebuzaradan, general of Nebuchadnezzar's army, entered the Temple, when he conquered Jerusalem. Nebuzaradan massacred tens of thousands of innocent Jews until the blood stopped boiling.

Jehoash's punishment came soon after the killing of Zechariah. He was defeated by the enemy, tortured, and left a sick man. He was eventually killed by two of his servants, who undertook to avenge the blood of Zechariah. Because he had ordered the death of Zechariah, Jehoash was not interred with the righteous kings of Judah.

# ✺§ DESTRUCTION OF THE FIRST TEMPLE (3338-/423 B.C.E.)

Eighteen years before the destruction of the Holy Temple, King Nebuchadnezzar of Babylon annexed Judah as part of his empire and exiled King Jehoiachin to Babylon, along with many other prominent Jewish leaders. He appointed the latter's nephew, Zedekiah, as the king in his stead. When Zedekiah refused to pay tax, Nebuchadnezzar besieged Jerusalem. After an extended period of time, the walls of Jerusalem were breached. Many thousands of the inhabitants were slaughtered and the *Beis HaMikdash* was set afire. Thousands were exiled to Babylonia. Nebuchadnezzar eventually appointed Gedaliah as the governor over the remaining inhabitants in Israel. After he was assassinated, many of the remnant of the Jews lost hope and fled to Egypt.

# NEVIIM ACHARONIM — THE LATER PROPHETS

The prophets, as messengers of God, demanded more of the Jewish people than other nations expected of themselves — and this fact is reflected in the critical manner, unparalleled among the nations of the world, in which they wrote the historical chronicles of their people. Thus we must not look down upon those times — even though the nation failed to achieve spiritual perfection. Indeed, we need only remember the positive response of the people to any king that arose who was willing to restore the rule of the Torah over the land.

The task of the prophets was to remind the Jewish people of their Divine mission, in the face of the tempting but disastrous lure of paganism. Paganism pictures the world as being dominated by mysterious natural forces and gods who terrify man by the arbitrary use of their invincible power. They do not require obedience to some moral law, but only "appeasement" through sacrifices and other rites. Otherwise a follower is free to pursue the same desire for pleasure and domination which he ascribes to and idealizes in his gods. Paganism gained many Jewish followers, primarily among the ruling classes. Kings found in it a means to justify the unrestrained use of their powers and the full expression of their arbitrary whims. Ultimately, pagan influences served to undermine public respect for the law, and thus the kings frequently became the victims of intrigues and assassinations.

It was in opposition to this state of affairs that the prophets lifted their voices. They warned that the kingdoms of both Yehudah and Yisrael were, during certain historical periods, rotten to the core because they lacked righteousness, and they proclaimed that only a state ruled by the Torah could flourish. They emphasized that pagan reliance on material power was fruitless — royal glory and national survival should be sought through loyalty to the Divine law. The first need was for the Holy Land to be cleansed of the worship of pagan idols and of the evils this had bred: exhausting power politics, perversion of justice, class oppression, and immoral practices. Again and again it was emphasized that failure to adhere to the Torah would result in domination by other powers and the exile of the Jewish people.

### (1) *Isaiah*

The Book of *Isaiah* contains sixty-six chapters and is the first of the three volumes of the Major Prophets. Isaiah prophesied during the reigns of Uzziah, Yotham, Ahaz, and Hezekiah. He served as G-d's spokesman to warn the Jews of impending catastrophe if they did not repent. However, he also offered a picture of an ideal, peaceful society if the Jews did follow in the ways set down by G-d. His warnings aroused the wrath of some of the kings, and he was executed by King Manasseh.

Since Isaiah was murdered by King Manasseh, he did not have a chance to commit his prophecies to paper. This was later done by the scholarly associates of King Hezekiah, who lived on many years after his death. The prophecies of Isaiah introduce the great theme of deliverance and restoration of the Jews by the coming of the Messiah.

### (2) *Jeremiah*

Jeremiah began to prophesy in Jerusalem approximately ninety years after the death of Isaiah. More is known about his life and teachings than about any other prophet, since the Book of *Jeremiah* contains a mass of historical and biographical material. He was cruelly insulted and accused of treason by the people he loved tenderly. He was taunted and even imprisoned by the unheeding leaders of Israel during the reigns of Josiah and Zedekiah. Yet, he fearlessly persisted in his mission of rousing the people to repent.

Nebuchadnezzar had instructed his general to treat Jeremiah with consideration and kindness. But the prophet insisted on sharing the hardships and tortures that were inflicted on his people. When the Jewish captives were led away in chains, Jeremiah tried to put his neck in the chains and trudge along with his people, but the Babylonian general pulled him out of the line of march.

After the fall of Jerusalem in 3338, he was forcibly taken into Egypt by those who fled the wrath of the Babylonian conqueror.

Jeremiah also foretold the restoration of Israel in seventy years. The Book of *Jeremiah* was written by Jeremiah himself and completed by the Men of the Great Assembly.

### (3) *Ezekiel*

Ezekiel lived during the last days of the kingdom of Jerusalem, in the reign of King Zedekiah. Prior to the destruction of Jerusalem and the Temple, his prophecies were messages of doom. After the destruction, in exile, they were messages of hope and assurances of restoration. He offered moral support to the people and through the famous parable of the "revived bones" showed that the Jews would once again be reunited and revived if they acted appropriately.

Ezekiel tells us that each man possesses the potential to be good or evil, regardless of heredity, and that the individual is the master of his own destiny and is responsible for his own deeds. Ezekiel stresses that everyone can "turn over a new leaf" and look hopefully toward the future. The final chapters of *Ezekiel*, concerning the glorious future of Israel, have provided the Jewish people with great encouragement through the long years of the exile.

## (4) *Trei Asar* — The Twelve Prophets

(a) *Hosea*

(b) *Joel*

(c) *Amos*

(d) *Ovadiah*

(e) *Jonah*

(f) *Micah*

(g) *Nahum*

(h) *Habakkuk*

(i) *Zephaniah*

(j) *Haggai*

(k) *Zechariah*

(l) *Malachi*

These are often referred to as *Minor Prophets*, referring not to their greatness but to the length of the individual books. Since these twelve books were so short, they were gathered into a single collection to safeguard their preservation. Hence they count as one book in the *Tanach*. They were first published in a single scroll by the men of the Great Assembly.

### (1) *Hosea*

Chronologically, it is a question if Hosea is the first of the *Trei Asar*, but nevertheless his book is listed first. The Sages teach that Hosea was one of the greatest of all the Prophets.

### (2) *Joel*

Joel lived during a terrible plague of locusts that destroyed the produce of the fields and vineyards. The Prophet Joel discussed Divine punishment. He urged the people to repent and assured them that if they did, G-d would grant them prosperity. His prophecy was later proven to be completely accurate; the Jews prospered when they repented.

### (3) *Amos*

He denounced the brutalities and cruelties perpetrated against the Jews by various nations. He strongly insisted upon social justice and respect for the poor and downtrodden.

### (4) Obadiah

This is the shortest of all books in the *Prophets*. It predicts the destruction of Edom, who will be punished measure for measure, as they mistreated the Jews when they helped the Babylonians to bring about the downfall of Jerusalem. Obadiah was a convert from Edom who reached the highest spiritual level a person can attain. Through his perseverance and greatness in worshiping G-d, he became a prophet.

### (5) Jonah

Jonah prophesied during the reigns of Jehoram and Jehu. Told by G-d to encourage the inhabitants of Nineveh to do *teshuvah,* he tried to shirk the task by fleeing via the sea. He knew that the people would repent and thereby cast the straying Jews in a bad light. But the ship he boarded was plagued by storms, until Jonah was cast overboard. He was swallowed by a large fish, and was only spit out after he had prayed and showed his submission to the Almighty. Eventually, the inhabitants of Nineveh did repent. Jonah felt bad about the withering of the gourd (a certain plant) that had given him shade. Using the gourd as an example, G-d showed Jonah why He must have pity on His creations. The Book of *Jonah* is read on Yom Kippur for the *Minchah hafatrah* as an example of the possibility of *teshuvah*. The Book of *Jonah* teaches us that kindness of heart and readiness to repent must be found everywhere among humanity.

### (6) Micah

He set forth the perfect ideal of Judaism when he said, "What does the L-rd require of you but to do justice, to love kindness, and to walk humbly with your G-d."

### (7) Nahum

His name signifies consolation, and he cried out for justice. He spoke of the future downfall of the Assyrian Empire.

### (8) Habakkuk

He said that though it may have seemed to the Jews that

continued victories of the enemies were inconsistent with Divine justice, evil shall ultimately perish from the earth and the faithful shall prevail.

### (9) *Zephaniah*

He aimed to arouse the moral sense of the Jewish people who had adopted some of the customs of their Assyrian conquerors. This book also contains the idea that suffering has a disciplinary value.

### (10) *Haggai*

He roused the energies and aspirations of the returning exiles so they could rebuild the Temple in Jerusalem, despite the hostility of the Samaritans who interfered with their work.

### (11) *Zechariah*

He assured the Jews that G-d would restore Israel's former glory. This book also discusses the advent of the Messiah and G-d's reign of peace.

### (12) *Malachi*

Like Haggai and Zechariah, he came after the destruction of the Temple, and prophesied in Babylonia. He stressed the importance of religion in our lives and emphasized mercy and faith. The Book of *Malachi* propounds the firm belief that ultimately all wrongs will be righted. Malachi ends his words with the exhortation (3:22): "Remember the Torah of Moses My servant, which I commanded him at Horeb for all Israel, [its] decrees and [its] statutes". These words were well cherished by later generations.

The *Twelve Minor Prophets* were first published in a single scroll by the Men of the Great Assembly (*Anshei Knesses Ha-Gedolah*).

# III

# KESUVIM (THE WRITINGS)

K*esuvim* consists of the following eleven books:

*Psalms — Tehillim*
*Proverbs — Mishlei*
*Job — Iyov*
*Song of Songs — Shir Hashirim*
*Ruth — Rus*
*Lamentations — Eichah*
*Ecclesiastes — Koheles*
*Esther — Esther*
*Daniel — Daniel*
*Ezra and Nehemiah — Ezra and Nechemiah*
*Chronicles — Divrei Hayamim*

This is not the order listed in the Talmud. It was changed in most printed editions to correspond with the sequence in which the five *Megillos* are read to the congregation during the course of the year, beginning with *Nissan.*

(1) *Song of Songs — Passover*
(2) *Ruth — Shavuos*
(3) *Lamentations — Tishah B'Av*
(4) *Ecclesiastes — Succos*
(5) *Esther — Purim*

The following synopses of the books in *Kesuvim* are in the order as listed in the Talmud.

## (1) *Ruth*

The story of Naomi and Ruth is contained in *Megillas Rus* and is read on Shavuos Ruth was a Moabite princess who converted to Judaism and pledged to stay with her mother-in-law after her husband had died. Boaz, the Jewish Judge, married her, and their great-grandson was King David. Ruth showed dedication, self-sacrifice, and determination in becoming part of G-d's Chosen People. She gave up royalty, honor, and wealth to become an outstanding Jewess. That is one reason why this *Megillah* is read on Shavuos, which commemorates the receiving of the Torah and is the anniversary of David's death.

## (2) *Psalms*

The Book of *Psalms* consists of 150 chapters. Most of them were written and compiled by King David. A number, however, had been transmitted from earlier generations. The central themes of most of the psalms are the benefits of simplicity of heart, faith in the Almighty, the greatness of the Torah commandments, and joy in the service of G-d. The psalms are as varied as life itself.

## (3) *Job*

Others, however, say that Job was a contemporary of Moses and the Book of *Job* was written by Moses. The Book of *Job* deals with difficult problems of human suffering. Job is represented as a most generous man who suffers severe tragedies and must confirm his faith in the principle that G-d's ways are just. Some are of the opinion that Job lived in the time of Queen of Sheba and the Book of *Job* was written by the Men of the Great Assembly. Yet others say that the book is a parable.

## (4) *Proverbs, Ecclesiastes,* and *Song of Songs*

These were all written by King Solomon. However, toward the end of his life he was too occupied with the affairs of state to publish his writings. Therefore, this was done by the court of King Hezekiah.

a) The Book of *Proverbs* contains maxims and teachings to guide one's conduct in everyday life. At the end of the book there is the poem which describes the perfect wife, trusted by her husband, revered by her servants, and admired by everyone. She is kind to the poor and gentle to all. She is self-respecting and dignified. Her husband and children prize her as the source of their happiness. This chapter, *Eishes*

*Chayil* (Woman of Valor), is recited every Friday night.

b) The Book of *Ecclesiastes* contains twelve chapters of wise observations on the purpose of life. In this book, King Solomon counsels patience, endurance, and discretion. He examines the value of wisdom, wealth, and pleasure. He declares that wealth does not yield happiness; it is often lost before it is enjoyed. At death it is left to people who have not toiled to acquire it. *Ecclesiastes* concludes with the counsel, "Revere G-d and keep His commandments, for this is the whole duty of man."[4]

c) *The Song of Songs* is an allegory of the "love story" between G-d and His People, Israel. Rabbi Akiva, one of the great Sages of the Mishnah, declared that the *Song of Songs* is the holiest of all the sacred writings.[5]

### (5) Book of *Lamentations*

This was written by the prophet Jeremiah describing the fall of Jerusalem and the destruction of the Holy Temple. He gives an eyewitness account of the massacres in Jerusalem and the despair of its inhabitants. The Book of *Lamentations (Eichah)* is recited in the synagogue on Tishah B'Av (ninth day of *Av*), the day on which both Temples were destroyed.

### (6) Book of *Daniel*

This is made up of two parts. The first part tells of the miraculous rescue of Daniel and his three righteous friends, Hananiah, Mishael, and Azariah. All had been taken to Babylonia before the fall of Jerusalem to serve in the royal court. Daniel survived until the days of Cyrus, who authorized the return of the Jewish exiles and permitted them to rebuild the Temple. The Book of *Daniel* relates that his three friends were cast into a fiery furnace under Nebuchadnezzar's orders. Miraculously, they survived.

The latter part of the book contains the prophecies concerning the four great empires and the future deliverance of the Jews upon the coming of the Messiah.

---

4. *Ecclesiastes* 12:13.

5. *Mishnah Yadayim* 3:5.

### (7) *Megillas Esther*

This tells the story of Mordecai and Esther, who used their influence to save the Jews from a general massacre which Haman the Amalekite had plotted against them. It shows the downfall of the arrogant and the vindication of the innocent. This incident happened after the destruction of the Temple, prior to the Jews' return to Israel. *Megillas Esther* was eventually published by the Great Assembly, of which Mordecai was a member.

The holy Temple in Yerushalayim had been destroyed, and with it Jewish independence was terminated by the Babylonian army of King Nebuchadnezzar. But the blackest clouds of destruction had a silver lining. As the Talmudic Sages describe it, "God had poured out His wrath on wood and stones," but spared the nation. The people were exiled to Babylonia (Bavel) where they elevated themselves from their suffering and where they repented. Despite the initial humiliation of exile, they were gradually able to rebuild their lives in the alien environment. In fact, the Babylonian Exile was a period of purification for the Jews.

The experience in Babylonia proved to the Jews that they could preserve their identity in a foreign land without fear of eradication as long as they were loyal to the Torah. The history of that period taught the equally important lesson that Jews could not be secure if they abandoned the Torah.

### (8) The Books of *Ezra and Nehemiah*

These are actually a single book, though later on for identification purposes they are referred to as two books. A considerable part of *Ezra and Nehemiah* contains the memoirs of the two great leaders who reorganized Jewish life in Jerusalem before the rebuilding of the Second Temple. Accompanied by 1500 exiles, Ezra the Scribe arrived in Jerusalem. They helped rebuild Jewish life in the desolate city.

The Book of *Nehemiah* is written in the first person and tells of the experiences of Nehemiah, who was appointed governor of Jerusalem. The noble character of Nehemiah is vividly portrayed as he tries to restore the ruined city of Jerusalem and rebuild its walls. He aided Ezra in giving strength to the Jewish inhabitants and was responsible for the rebuilding of the Second Temple.

The Jews who had returned to *Eretz Yisrael* from the exile in Babylonia were on the brink of spiritual extinction. Intermarriage and assimilation during the exile had played havoc with the Jewish settlers. Only a miracle could avert the destruction of Jewry in Judah. The miracle occurred: A Divinely appointed agent named Ezra, a Jew from Babylonia, arrived on the scene. He pushed for mixed marriages to be dissolved and made the Torah binding upon the people. As a result of his activity, religion returned as the central force of Jewish national life.

Ezra accomplished much more — he convened the Great Assembly of all the most prominent Sages of the era. They knew that the Divine Presence would not rest upon the Second Temple as it had upon the First — after the death of the few remaining prophets, the age of prophecy would be over and God would no longer speak directly to Israel through His emissaries. The Men of the Great Assembly therefore decided which books belonged in the Bible and checked the texts; they arranged the laws of the oral Torah in a definite order, laying the first foundation for the oral Mishnah. They also fixed the text of the prayers, stimulated Torah study, and issued a great many other important regulations.

### (9) The Book of *Chronicles*

*Chronicles I* and *Chronicles II* are actually a single book. It contains a historical record dating from the creation of the world to the end of Babylonian captivity. *Chronicles* deals primarily with the story of the Kingdom of Judah. The Book of *Chronicles* demonstrates the conviction that history is not made by chance. Only those events which illustrate a Divine purpose and Providence are described. Most of the Book of *Chronicles* was written by Ezra. The rest was completed by Nehemiah.

*Kesuvim* contains Divinely inspired teachings and wisdom that have a message for all future generations. They include important historical events that were recorded to teach a lesson for all times.

# IV

# ANSHEI KNESSES HAGEDOLAH
# (THE MEN OF THE GREAT ASSEMBLY):
# 3338-3448 (423-313 B.C.E.)

"**M**oses received the Torah from Sinai and transmitted it to Joshua. Joshua transmitted it to the Elders, the Elders to the Prophets, and the Prophets transmitted it to the Men of the Great Assembly."[6] Thus, the Men of the Great Assembly were the spiritual heirs of the Prophets, and the forerunners of the Sages of the Mishnah. Ezra ushered in the era of the Great Assembly, which he headed. Of Ezra, our Sages said that he restored the Torah to Israel. In fact, the Talmud states, "Ezra was sufficiently worthy to have had the Torah given to Israel through him, had not Moses preceded him."[7]

The Great Assembly consisted of 120 of the most eminent Torah Sages of the period, including the last of the Prophets, Haggai, Zechariah, and Malachi. The *Anshei Knesses HaGedolah* engaged in the painstaking effort of safeguarding the meticulous accuracy of the transmission of the Written Law as well as the Oral Law. Concerning Ezra, the Sages observe that he was a scribe who counted every letter of the Written Law. So too, he was a scribe who accounted for all the laws of the Oral Torah.

It was the Men of the Great Assembly who recorded the prophecies of the Twelve Minor Prophets as well as the last books of *Kesuvim*. The last of the *Anshei Knesses HaGedolah* was Shimon HaTzaddik, the High Priest. He was also the first of the *Tannaim,* the authors of the Mishnah. The Great Assembly laid the foundation for the codification of the Oral Torah in a form that could be memorized by students. The final editing of the work and codification, which was done centuries later, was known as the

---

6. *Pirkei Avos* 1:1.
7. Talmud *Sanhedrin* 21b.

Mishnah. The word Mishnah means review, and one reason for this name was that it was to be reviewed over and over again, by heart. It had to be memorized because it had been prohibited to write down the Oral Torah. The word also means secondary, which denotes that the Mishnah was secondary to the Written Torah.

---

# V

# TANNAIM AND THE MISHNAH: 3448-3978 (313-218 B.C.E.)

After the era of the Men of the Great Assembly, the tradition of the Oral Law was continued by the *Tannaim* (teachers, sages). The first of the *Tannaim* was **Shimon HaTzaddik,** who was also the last of the *Anshei Knesses HaGedolah.* His righteousness made a profound impression on Alexander the Great. Thanks to this, Alexander's conquering army did not march on Jerusalem, but instead dealt justly with his Jewish subjects.

Among the famous *Tannaim* after Shimon HaTzaddik was the "pair," **Yehudah ben Tabai** and **Shimon ben Shetach.** The latter was the brother of Queen Shlomis, the wife of King Alexander Yannai and later the ruler of *Eretz Yisrael.* He and his fellow *Perushim* (the rabbis and their followers) were persecuted by Yannai, but eventually emerged triumphant. Shimon once bought a donkey from a non-Jew and later found a diamond hidden in its saddle. He insisted on returning the diamond since he had not intended to buy it. The astounded gentile said, "Blessed is the G-d of Shimon ben Shetach."

# ৵৽CHANUKAH

A new challenge to the Jewish spirit was the advent of Hellenism. (The Greek name for their land is Hellas, and

Hellenism refers to Greek culture.) This movement attracted Jews because of its many famous philosophers. In reality it was nothing more than refined paganism. Hellenism was marked by the absence of a moral standard. Decisions were left to man's own instincts and he was allowed to follow all his base desires. Judaism could never make peace with such an attitude, which is contrary to the basic principles of the Torah.

Hellenism was a great temptation. Many Jews visited the sports arenas, where unclothed Greek youths engaged in competitive sports, and Greek amusement places, where they participated in wild festivities. At first the assimilationists adopted only the more external aspects of the foreign culture, such as speaking the Greek language and participating in public festivities. But one thing led to another. Eventually they grew alienated from the Jewish way of life, behaving like the Greeks, desecrating the Shabbos, and worshipping Greek idols.

The challenge became even more acute when the Land of Israel was conquered by the Syrians. King Antiochus, the Syrian tyrant, attempted to destroy Judaism once and for all. He felt that Jewish religious practice formed an impenetrable barrier which prevented the Jews from assimilating into the Syrian Empire.

The cruel Antiochus shrewdly prohibited everything that marked the Jewish people as distinct from their neighbors. He aimed his decrees against their religious customs and observances, for he was certain that when these practices were obliterated, the Jews — as a separate entity — would disappear. His troops also violated the Jewish precepts of morality.

This religious persecution led to the martyrdom of many pious Jews, while others fled to the hills and caves. The people had been able to accept foreign political domination and material exploitation for many generations, but they would not submit to the repression of their faith.

In the end, the priestly family of the Hasmoneans, led at first by the aged priest Mattisyahu, raised the flag of rebellion. A series of victories led to the conquest of Jerusalem and the rededication of the Temple, marked by the miracle of Chanukah. Mattisyahu died soon after the struggle begain. He was succeeded by his five sons, under the leadership of Judah the Maccabee. The Maccabean struggle against the Greeks and Hellenists paved the way for an independent Jewish state.

Judah and his brothers were all righteous men, but the ambitions of the later Hasmoneans prompted them to remain at the helm of the state even after the emergency had passed, and before long, to use their position not for leadership in the service of G-d but for the pursuit of power.

The last surviving brother, Simon, was the one who finally consolidated Israel's independence after centuries under Babylonian and Syrian control. He was a humble ruler, who called himself *nasi,* not king, but his son Yochanan Hyrkanus already struck his own coins, and allowed himself to embark on imperialistic wars. The imposition of heavy taxes enabled him to maintain a standing army of mercenaries.

Yochanan's policies were unacceptable to the spiritual leaders of the nation, as well as to their devoted followers. Thus he was driven into alliance with the secularist upper classes.

The ideological foundation of this alliance was Sadduceeism. The Sadducees denied the concept of a future world and of resurrection, and the belief in a Divine providence watching over man, rewarding and punishing his actions. Moreover, they belittled or denied the Divine authority of the Oral Law. What remained for them was a set of isolated laws enumerated in the written Torah; for the rest, they felt free to pursue the worldly success they desired. It was the rich Sadducees whom Yochanan put in control of the Sanhedrin, and with whose help he ruled. The "Pharisees," on the other hand, the carriers of the living Torah tradition, and their adherents, who made up the bulk of the common people, came to withdraw from active participation in the government. Under the circumstances they were content to keep alive among the people the true spirit of Judaism — a love of G-d pervading all aspects of a man's life and expressing itself in the devoted fulfillment of His laws.

Yochanan's son Aristobulus adopted the title of king and, to protect his authority against a suspected challenge, imprisoned his family. He died after a year of reign and was succeeded by his brother. The long reign of Alexander Jannai, witnessed the first open clash with the Pharisees: A demonstration of public discontent led the king to embark on a terrible campaign of repression and execution which claimed 50,000 victims in six years. He ordered the death of nearly all the great rabbis. His brother-in-law Shimon ben Shetach went into hiding.

After Alexander's death the process of governmental deterioration was arrested, with the accession of his pious widow, Shlomis Alexandra. Her brother, Shimon ben Shetach, leader of the Pharisees, filled the Sanhedrin with the upholders of Jewish traditions. But the breathing spell was only temporary; when the queen passed away, her sons, jealous of one another, unleashed a disastrous civil war, which was to be the undoing of the Hasmonean monarchy. Both contenders appealed to Pompey, the Roman general, who had just then arrived in Damascus. A third delegation, representing the people, asked for the establishment of a republic devoted to a peaceful life according to the traditions of Judaism. Rome was glad to intervene — and it did not leave until it had destroyed the Palestinian Jewish community.

By the year 63 B.C.E. Pompey had established one of the princes, Hyrkanus, on the throne — but at a price: Hyrkanus had to give up the royal title, pay tribute to Rome, and cede the coastal area to the Roman province of Syria. Perhaps most important, however, was that, under the settlement arranged, the effective power in the country fell into the hands of an Edomite, Antipater, Hyrkanus's adviser, who had largely been responsible for the civil war. The rebellions provoked by his oppressive policies and his subservience to the Romans only served to tighten the tyrannical grip which he and the Romans had on the country. In the year 40 B.C.E., to counter a particularly powerful popular uprising, the Roman Senate finally appointed Antipater's son, Herod, king of the Jews; by 37 B.C.E. Herod succeeded in suppressing the uprising and in cruelly "pacifying" his kingdom.

The Hasmoneans paid dearly for their sins: Their political ambitions, quarrels, and forced conversions of pagans were the direct cause for the accession to their throne of this brutal half-pagan, who consolidated his rule by murdering the surviving members of the Hasmonean dynasty, including his own wife. Altogether, Herod carried to perfection the policies of his less forthright predecessors. He flattered the Romans, on whose favor his rule depended, bribing them with the sums he extorted from his subjects. Toward these, he acted with extreme cruelty. That he did not succeed in destroying the national spirit was due to the devoted labors of the leaders of the Sanhedrin, Hillel and Shammai.

**Hillel,** a direct descendant of King David, was born in Babylonia and came to the Land of Israel. He was renowned for his patient, gentle nature. He once agreed to teach someone the Torah "on one foot" by imparting to him the rule of *v'ahavta l'rei'acha kamacha* (love your fellow as yourself). **Shammai** was also an exceptional scholar, though of a stricter nature. Their followers later formed what became known as *Beis Hillel* and *Beis Shammai,* the academies of Hillel and Shammai. The arguments between Beis Hillel and Beis Shammai found in the *Gemara* do not involve personal quarrels, but rather attempts on both sides to find the true meaning of the Torah's laws. Sharply though they may have disagreed in matters of law and interpretations, there was always love and mutual respect between them.

The Sanhedrin had been robbed of its governmental functions; but for the people at large it remained the authority deciding all questions of conduct. Owing to the disturbed times, however, doubts had arisen about some of the legal traditions. Sent by Providence, Hillel and Shammai appeared on the scene at this crucial moment, clarified the teachings of the Law, founded great schools of Torah study, and powerfully stimulated the pursuit of learning among the people.

Their work was of immense significance. The political life of the time was dominated by the blood-spattered and apparently invincible tyranny of Herod; it seemed to prove that only crude power counted. Yet Hillel and Shammai asserted that the blessed kingdom of Heaven could be established on this earth through obedience to G-d's Law; that it would prove infinitely stronger than the power of evil; and that it would ultimately overcome it. Thus they encouraged the people to concentrate all its energies upon the Torah, reminding them that this alone was of significance for the future of the nation. Sustained by the Law, the Jewish people would survive, no matter what political and material developments lay in store for it.

Hillel and Shammai were no innovators; they were solely concerned with strengthening the hold which Torah had upon the Jewish people.

# ✥THE DESTRUCTION

It was the struggle between the descendants of the Maccabees that had led to the intervention of Rome in Judean politics and its eventual domination of Judah. Discontent with Roman harshness led to the rise of forces favoring rebellion, including the Zealots. This disunity again harmed the Jews. When the rebellion broke out, Jewish forces at first defeated the mighty Roman armies under Cestius. However, the lack of harmony within the Jewish camp eventually enabled the Romans under Vespasian and Titus to triumph. The Jews at Masada decided to commit mass suicide rather than submit to the Romans.

The Romans laid seige around Jerusalem on the tenth of Teves: On the seventeenth of Tammuz, the Roman army breached the walls of the city and the Temple was destroyed three weeks later on the ninth day of Av in the year 3828 or 3870 (68 or 70 C.E.). The greatest Sage of the time, Rabbi Akiva, was one of his followers. Our Sages teach us that it was the baseless hatred of one Jew for another that caused the destruction of the Second Temple.

Years later, Emperor Hadrian of Rome promised to help the Jews rebuild the Temple but reneged on his promise. This enraged the remaining populace in Judea, and led to a revolt. The military leader of the revolt, Bar Kochba, was a man of strength and charisma. Bar Kochba was initially successful in defeating Roman armies with great displays of valor. However, Bar Kochba lost G-d's favor by impulsively killing the holy Rabbi Elazar of Modi'in, whom he suspected of being a traitor. His fortress at Betar fell to the Romans, while Bar Kochba himself was killed by a snake.

The defeated Jews were severely punished by the Romans, and ultimately ten of the most sainted rabbis, known as the *Asarah Harugei Malchus,* the Ten Martyrs, including Rabbi Akiva, were very cruelly put to death. After this, Israel, under Roman oppression, began to decline as the center of Jewish life.

This period of Jewish history was a time of severe testing. It came during the first century of the Common Era, when the Temple was burned by the Romans and the state destroyed. Here was a catastrophe which surely should have sounded the death knell of the Jews.

## ✌§ SURVIVAL

How was it that the Jews did not disappear from the face of the earth? Their homeland was gone, and all appearance of Jewish life had been stripped away. Henceforth, wherever the Jews resided, they were an insignificant minority of the population. Nevertheless, they not only survived but often flourished. Why? How could they have so successfully confounded the odds?

The answer is that the national identity of the Jews was radically different from that of other peoples. The Romans did not destroy the heart and the backbone of Jewry when they conquered Judah. What was vital to the preservation of the Jewish people was the Torah, and that remained intact despite the Roman legions.

Hashem had given the land and its rule to the Jews only for the specific purpose of demonstrating the application of the Law to all phases of life. Thus, when the nation forsook the Law and imitated other nations who relied on man's power, *Eretz Yisrael* and its rule were taken away from the Jews. The Jewish nation then returned to the spiritual foundations of its national existence.

**RABBAN YOCHANAN BEN ZAKKAI** was among the greatest of the *Tannaim.* He was the youngest of Hillel's students and lived during the Roman siege of Jerusalem.[8] Through a ruse, he spread news of his death and was carried out of the besieged city in

---

8. Talmud *Succah* 28.

a coffin, in order to meet with the Roman commander Vespasian. Rabban Yochanan persuaded the Roman to spare the Torah stronghold of Yavneh and its sages from destruction. At Yavneh, he founded a yeshivah and gathered all the great scholars who had survived in order to establish the new spiritual capital of the nation. These Sages, with their Torah learning, brought renewed vitality, vigor, and hope to the stricken remnant.

**ONKELOS** was a nephew of the emperor Titus who converted to Judaism and was able to write, with Divine spirit, a translation of the Torah.[9]

**RABBI NACHUM ISH GAMZO** was a *Tanna* renowned for his faith. He was called *"Gamzo"* because he was in the habit of saying *"Gamzo L'Tovah."* (This too will be for the good.)[10]

**RABBI AKIVA** was an illiterate shepherd who first embraced Torah learning at the age of 40. His wife, who came from a wealthy family, was willing to be disinherited in order to marry this potential scholar.[11] Eventually, he became one of the great leaders of his generation and amassed 24,000 students. The Romans caught him teaching Torah and tortured him to death. He died with the word *Shema* on his lips.[12]

**RABBI SHIMON BAR YOCHAI** and his son fled from Roman persecution and was forced to live in a cave for thirteen years. They miraculously found nourishment in the cave from a carob tree that grew there and a small well of water that suddenly appeared.[13] He was the author of the *Zohar*.

# ❧ THE MISHNAH

RABBI YEHUDAH HANASI was the most eminent Torah master of the last generation of *Tannaim*. He was a descendant of

9. Talmud *Gittin* 56b.
10. Talmud *Taanis* 21.
11. Talmud *Kesubos* 62b.
12. Talmud *Berachos* 61b.
13. Talmud *Shabbos* 33.

the House of David and a direct sixth-generation descendant of Hillel. Among all of the *Tannaim,* Rabbi Yehudah alone was known as *Rabbeinu HaKadosh,* our saintly teacher, because of his profound piety.[14]

While there was a prohibition against committing the Oral Law to writing, there was a tradition that if the Oral Torah would ever be in danger of being forgotten during a time of danger, then this prohibition could be waived.

Due to the incessant persecution and relentless oppression to which the Jewish people had fallen victim since the Roman Empire took control of *Eretz Yisrael,* the Torah was slowly being forgotten in Israel. Rabbi Yehudah HaNasi therefore undertook the task of compiling, editing, and redacting the vast array of codifications that had been transmitted by the Torah masters of previous generations. This unique labor of love, which called for vast erudition, profound scholarship, and phenomenal diligence, earned for Rabbi Yehudah HaNasi an altogether unique place in Jewish history, for the Oral Law was preserved for posterity through the Mishnah.

In compiling his work, Rabbi Yehudah made use of the earlier collection of the Oral Law, condensing it and deciding among various disputed questions. The Sages of his time all concurred with his decisions and ratified his edition. However, even rejected opinions were included in the text, so that they should be recognized as such and not be revived in later generations.[15]

Thus, the Mishnah emerged, not as a new body of knowledge, but rather as a culmination of centuries of oral transmission of the *Torah Shebe'al Peh,* the Oral Law, which traced its roots to the unbroken chain of Torah transmission, which began with Moses at Mt. Sinai.

The Mishnah is divided into six "orders", or sections, comprising sixty-three tractates. The six orders are:

(1) *Zeraim*: "Seeds," dealing with agriculture and the fruits of the field.

---

14. Talmud *Shabbos* 118b.
15. Mishnah *Ediyos* 1:5.

(2) *Moed*: "Festival," relating to laws of various holidays.

(3) *Nashim*: "Women," dealing with the laws of marriage, divorce, etc.

(4) *Nezikin*: "Damages," dealing with civil and criminal law.

(5) *Kedoshim*: "Holy Things," relating to laws of sacrifices and sacred things.

(6) *Taharos*: "Purities," pertaining to ritual purity and impurity.

---

## VI

# THE AMORAIM OF THE GEMARA: 3979-4236 (219-476)

# AND THE RABBANAN SEVORAI: 4236-4349 (476-589)

The *Amoraim* were the successors of the *Tannaim* and are known as the chief interpreters of the Mishnah. Their discussions and teachings, known as the *Gemara*, were collected and appended to the Mishnah; together they are known as the Talmud. There are two such works, the *Talmud Yerushalmi* and the *Talmud Bavli*. The *Amoraim* were the Sages who, continuing the chain of Torah tradition, explained and elaborated on the teachings of the *Tannaim* who had preceded them. They undertook the task of explaining the teachings to their generations in such a manner that the Torah would continue to guide the daily lives of the people on every level.

The greatest of the *Amoraim* in *Eretz Yisrael* was **Rabbi Yochanan,** who restored the central academy in Teveryah (Tiberias). However, with the official adoption of Christianity by the Roman Empire (which ruled *Eretz Yisrael*), times became difficult for the Jewish community. Largely in order to strengthen their own position, the leaders of the new religion embarked upon a campaign of severe repression against the Jews which, added to the general difficulties of life, brought about the practical collapse of Jewry in *Eretz Yisrael*. The deliberations of the *Amoraim* were brought to an abrupt close and collected in the *Talmud Yerushalmi,* which, as a result, remained rather fragmentary. The chain of ordination, too, came to an end. It was completed about 4110 (350 C.E.).

At the same time that the *Talmud Yerushalmi* was being compiled, the *Amoraim* in Babylonia were creating their own Talmud. The political and social conditions in Babylonia were better than in *Eretz Yisrael.* Consequently, the Babylonian Talmud contains more material and was more carefully edited than the Jerusalem Talmud. For most of the Amoraic period there were two main yeshivos in Babylonia, where the Sages of the Talmud studied. The great Torah academies of Nehardea and Sura (later Pumbedisa) were founded by **Rav** and **Shmuel** respectively. The temporal leader of the Jewish community was called the *Resh Galusa* (Exilarch). Among the other great Sages of this era were **Rav Huna, Resh Lakish, Rav Ammi, Abaye, Rava,** and **Hillel II** (who arranged the Jewish calendar).

The *Gemara* consists of discussions or commentaries relating to the Mishnah, and it developed orally for some 300 years following the editing of the Mishnah. Finally, when it came into danger of being forgotten and lost, **Rav Ashi** together with his school in Babylonia, along with his colleague **Ravina,** undertook to collect all of the discussions and set them in order. After Rav Ashi's death, his son continued the work until it was completed.[16]

The period of the *Amoraim* was not one of prophetic revelation nor of open Divine intervention in human affairs; however, it was one of the most productive and influential in Jewish history. The deliberations of the *Amoraim* provide the basis for halachic analysis and the clarification of the principles upon which the laws of the Mishnah are based. The recorded discussions of the *Amoraim,* together with the Mishnah, compromise the Talmud, which remains the primary work of Jewish learning to this day.

---

16. Talmud *Bava Metzia* 86.

The Babylonian Talmud established which opinions are conclusive, provided underlying principles for the laws, and offered homilies and stories to enhance the discussion and serve as the basis for many moral and ethical principles. It was accepted by all Israel as the final binding authority in all questions of religion and law. All subsequent codifications of Torah law are legitimate only insofar as they are based on the Talmud. To oppose even a single teaching of the Talmud is to oppose G-d and His Torah.[17]

It was just then that a wave of persecutions began to sweep across Babylonian Jewry; thus, by producing the Talmud, the Amoraim saved the body of the Divine traditions, to serve as an unshakable and inexhaustible foundation for all later Jewish life.

There was a total of forty generations spanning almost 1,800 years from Moshe Rabbeinu until the final completion of the Talmud.

The leaders of the generation following the completion of the Talmud were known as the *Savoraim*. They continued the scholarly academies in Sura and Pumbedisa in Babylonia, and labored devotedly to put final touches on the Talmud, even after it was essentially completed. Though they did not add any new laws to those already in the Talmud, they preserved and protected the sanctity of the Talmud and passed it down intact to later generations. They did this despite the hardships imposed upon them by the fanatical rulers who closed most of the places of Torah learning. The period of the *Savora'im* lasted until 589 C.E.

Since they did not add to or delete from the content of the Gemara, but supplied explanations and interpretations, they were called *Savoraim* (Expounders). Another reason they were called *Savoraim* was because they sought to understand the Mishnah and Gemara through logical argument (*sevarah*).

Among the first generation of *Savoraim* (and the last of the *Amoraim*) were Ravina, Rav Huna, the *reish galusa* (head of the Jews in exile), and Mar Zutra, who was executed by the Persians.

---

17. Rambam, *Introduction to Mishneh Torah.*

# VII

# GEONIM, RISHONIM, AND ACHARONIM

## (1) *Geonim*: 4349-4800 (589-1040)

Mohammed had cruelly suppressed the Jews living on the Arabian peninsula, because they would not accept his leadership and his religious teachings, despite the fact that some of his basic beliefs (like monotheism) and practical laws (like the prohibition of pork) were taken from Judaism. When the Jews refused to join him, he turned against them to show a clear break from Judaism, from which he had borrowed so much.

On the other hand, Mohammed's successors, in their endeavor to reach the entire civilized world, were on good terms with the Jews, who they felt would be of great use to them. With the conquest of Babylonia by the Arabs (651), Babylonian Jewry's spiritual centers began to flourish once more. The ease of communication within the Arab world had a positive result for the Jews, for it unified them and had them all relying on the religious academies in Babylon. Thus, the academies became the heart of world Jewry.

Following the *Savoraim* came the period of the *Geonim*, which lasted for almost 500 years. The *Geonim* were the disciples and spiritual successors of the Rabbanan Savorai and headed the great academies of Sura and Pumbedisa in Babylonia. They continued the transmission of the *Torah Shebe'al Peh* and replied to halachic inquiries. All Jewish communities relied on the religious leadership of Babylonia, sending their questions to the *Geonim* for response. They turned to the *Geonim* for clear Talmudic interpretation and application. Virtually no important action could be taken without their approval, for the legacy of Torah authority had passed down to them.

The halachic decisions of the *Geonim* were accepted as binding not only in Babylonia, but throughout the rest of the Diaspora as well. During this period, approximately ninety-five *Geonim* wrote many thousands of Responsa to Jewish communities in all corners of the globe.

The *Geonim* resided in Babylonia. Most of their work was written in Aramaic, since that was the language spoken by the majority of Babylonian Jews. They received requests to clarify difficulties both in the Talmud and in Halachah. The Responsa were later compiled in books. These were called the *Teshuvos HaGeonim,* which were commentaries on the Talmud as well as legal decisions that were relative to the times.

Among the *Geonim* were **Rav Amram Gaon,** who was the first to compile all of the prayers into what became known as the *Siddur;* **Rav Saadia Gaon,** renowned for his numerous philosophical writings and teachings [he was in the forefront of the fight against the Karaites whose acceptance of only the Written Law threatened to undermine and destroy rabbinic authority and the perpetuation of the Oral Law]; **Rav Sherira Gaon,** who compiled a history of the *Mesorah* order; and **Rav Hai Gaon,** the last and one of the greatest of the *Geonim.*

As the great center of Torah learning in Babylonia waned, an event occurred that led to the emergence of vibrant Torah centers in North Africa, the Middle East, and Europe. Four renowned sages were traveling together on a ship to collect money for a worthwhile cause. They were captured by pirates and were to be sold as slaves. One of these captives, **Rabbi Shemaryahu,** was brought to Alexandria, Egypt, where he was redeemed by the Jewish community there. **Rabbi Chushiel** was redeemed by the Jews in Tunisia, where he founded one of the great yeshivos of that period. The third was **Rabbi Moshe ben Chanoch,** and the fourth is unknown.

Rabbi Moshe ben Chanoch and his son Rabbi Chanoch were taken to Cordova in Spain, where the Jewish community bought their freedom. Having been robbed of all their possessions and left only with their tattered clothes, Rabbi Moshe and his son were thought to be simple, uneducated Jews. They entered the *beis midrash* of Rabbi Nassan, the rabbi and *dayan* (judge) of Cordova, who was lecturing in the academy, and stood inconspicuously on the side. During the discussion following the lecture, Rabbi Moshe made several comments and remarks which clarified the very intricate and involved topic being discussed. This indicated his vast knowledge and ability as a Talmudic scholar, one even greater than Rabbi Nassan. Besides being a great Torah scholar, Rabbi Nassan was also a man of extraordinary modesty and humility. He rose from his seat, walked over to the place where the raggedly dressed stranger was standing, bowed before him and exclaimed that inasmuch as Rabbi Moshe was a much greater sage than himself, he deserved to be the head of the yeshivah and the rabbi and *dayan* of the community.

Chasdai ibn Shaprut, leader of the Jewish community in Cordova, heard of this incident and acquiesced to the wishes of Rabbi Nassan. He appointed Rabbi Moshe head of the yeshivah as well as rabbi and *dayan* of Cordova. This great man and his son soon attracted students from all over the continent, and within a few years the yeshivah of Cordova could be favorably compared with the famous Babylonian academies of previous generations. Thus, Spain emerged as a new and outstanding center of Torah learning.

Although it is questionable who the fourth captive scholar was, some historians believe that it was Rabbi Nassan HaBavli. He was brought to Narvonne, France, where he later established a great yeshivah.

The involuntary dispersion of these eminent Torah scholars served as a bridge spreading Torah from East to West. This was very significant in stimulating the development of new self-sufficient Torah centers within each of these far-flung communities. It was from these Torah centers that the next generation of Torah scholars, known as the *Rishonim,* emanated.

The four captive sages seem to be people who coincidentally experienced personal catastrophe, tragically separated from their families. Upon closer scrutiny of the entire picture, however, one realizes that their captivity was not merely a random happening. It was all part of a Divine plan to spread Judaism to new areas and develop new centers of Torah learning.

With the closing of the great Babylonian academies, there

ceased to be any formally acknowledged center of Torah authority. Until that time, the academies of Babylonia were the direct spiritual heirs and successors of the academies of the *Talmud Bavli*. With the conclusion of the *Geonic* period, this centralization of Torah authorities ended.

## (2) *Rishonim*: 4800-5275 (1040-1515)

With the closing of the great academies and the subsequent decline of the Jewish communities in Babylonia, the Jews were dispersed throughout the world. They suffered tremendous persecution such as Crusades, Inquisitions, blood libels, massacres, severe restrictions, burning of their holy books, and constant exiles from various places in Europe.

Nevertheless, spiritual leadership continued with the era of the *Rishonim*. The Jew had been a homeless wanderer across the face of the earth, finding temporary resting places, but was soon driven out by merciless persecution. Pressured to forsake his religion and offered enticements to embrace the officially sanctioned religion, the Jew resisted both. The strength and courage of Jews during these centuries of bitterness has evoked admiration and astonishment from the intellectual non-Jewish world. As noted above, the fourth-century Church father, Jerome, admitted: "The destruction of the Holy City, the ruin of the House of God, the dispersion of the Chosen People into all the kingdoms of the earth, and their continued existence as a nation, notwithstanding every attempt to exterminate them or to compel them to forsake those ordinances which distinguish them to this very day from all other nations, is emphatically one of the strongest proofs we can have of the truth of the Bible."

The Jews who continued to cling to Judaism despite all threats did so because God and His Torah were more precious to them than all else, including life. The Jewish people rallied around their faith, their Torah and *mitzvos,* and faced the hostile world with undaunted courage.

The effect of these persecutions was to consign the Jews to lives of poverty, isolated from the cultural and social life of the Christian world. Instead of producing despair, this situation led them to an even more intense devotion to the learning of Torah. As opportunities for social interaction with the outside world diminished, Jews were freed to concentrate on more intensive learning. Jews were able to reach great spiritual heights during this difficult time due mostly to the leadership of the rabbis.

The following paragraphs offer biographical information and perspectives on the lives of the *Rishonim*. These were the great Torah Sages who flourished from the end of the Geonic period (10th century) until the 15th century. These great Sages led the Jewish people during those turbulent and persecution-filled years in Europe and the Mediterranean countries. The *Rishonim* were entrusted with Israel's most priceless heritage and most sacred trust: transmitting the Torah throughout the world.

(a) **Rabbeinu Gershom** from Mayence, lived ca. 965-1040. He was called *"Me'or HaGolah"* (Light of the Exile). He wrote a commentary on the Talmud and issued many *takanos* (amendments), the most famous of which prohibit polygamy, opening another person's mail, and coercing a wife to accept a divorce.

(b) **Rav Yitzchak Alfasi — Rif** (1013-1103) fled from North Africa to Spain in 1088. He compiled a noted halachic code on the Talmud.

(c) **Rashi — Rabbi Shlomo Yitzchaki** lived in France from 1040-1105. He was an outstanding figure of the highly developed Jewish center in France and Germany. Modestly he considered himself just a wine dealer of Troyes. In fact he was a saint and sage of towering stature. He composed commentaries on the Pentateuch and most of the other books of the Bible, as well as a very concise commentary on the Talmud. For all later generations these became the indispensable keys to the meaning of the Torah, both Written and Oral. *Rashi,* moreover, carried on a widespread correspondence and composed prayers for various occasions. The academy which he founded and headed produced many of the men who were to inspire and to lead Jewish life in France and Germany, the Tosafists.

(d) **Tosafists** — The *Baalei Tosafos* were approximately two hundred Sages in France and Germany who commented on and debated the principles of Talmudic scholarship. Using *Rashi* as the basic commentary, they used encyclopedic knowledge, profound analysis, and deep logic to explore and clarify the meaning and application of the Talmud. *Tosafos* means additions; the Tosafists were so called because they added to the existing commentaries.

Among the greatest Tosafists were *Rashi's* grandsons, *Rabbeinu Tam, Rashbam,* and others. *Rabbeinu Tam* was considered the greatest authority of his time. He called various rabbinical assemblies to deal with problems of Jewish communal life, which were mainly the result of Christian oppression. Blood libels and massacres perpetrated by the Crusaders saddened his days, and inspired many of his prayer compositions. He was an outstanding representative of the method of analytical Talmud study and he also composed many responsa.

(e) **Maharam of Rothenburg** (1220-1293) wrote many halachic responsa. He was imprisoned by the government, which wanted to use him to extort an exorbitant ransom from the Jewish community. The Maharam, fearing that this could lead to a wave of kidnappings, refused to have the Jewish community pay his ransom, and died in prison.

The Jews of Spain (called *Sephardim*) established a Golden Age in which Jewish religious and cultural contributions reached great heights. Among the Rishonim in Spain were:

(a) **Rav Yehudah HaLevi** (1075-1141) was a distinguished poet and doctor who wrote the great philosophical work, *Kuzari.*

(b) **Rav Moshe ben Maimon — Rambam** (1135-1204). Having been forced to flee from Spain, owing to Moslem persecution of Jews, the *Rambam* became (after years of wandering), the Egyptian court physician. He was the leading Jewish personality in the Moslem world and gave guidance and protection to his brethren; but his undying significance rests on his writings (Talmudic, communal, and medical).

His monumental *Yad Hachazakah*, also known as *Mishnah Torah*, is a magnificently organized compendium of all areas of Torah law. His major philosophical work was *Moreh Nevuchim*, "Guide for the Perplexed," which expounded the philosophy of Judaism and comments extensively on Scripture. He also wrote a commentary to the Mishnah and such other writings as the encouraging *Iggeres Teiman* to the threatened Jewish community in Yemen, and he codified the Thirteen Principles of Faith.

(c) **Rav Moshe ben Nachman — Ramban** (1194-1270). As leader of Spanish Jewry, he gained wide fame at an early age through his scholarship in Bible and Talmud, *Kabbalah* and philosophy. He composed works on Talmud and the *Rif*, as well as a classic commentary on the Chumash. Forced by the king of Aragon to enter into a public religious disputation with the apostate Fra Pablo, he triumphed. The Church fathers wanted to condemn him to prison or death for his victory but the king, out of respect, exiled him to Palestine. Leadership of Spanish Jewry was taken over by his disciple **Rabbi Solomon ben Aderes** (*Rashba*).

(d) **Rosh — Rabbeinu Asher** (1250-1327), who wrote a comprehensive commentary-halachic code extracted from the entire Talmud. When the famous Rabbi Meir of Rothenburg was imprisoned by the German emperor, his son-in-law and disciple, the *Rosh,* left Germany for Spain, where he assumed leadership of Spanish Jewry. He composed hundreds of responsa and above all, a concise extract of legal decisions from the Talmud, as had the *Rif* before him, but drawing on the conclusions of the *Baalei Tosafos* of France and Germany. He helped to bring to Spanish Jewry something of the austere and heroic spirit of German Jewry.

(e) **Don Yitzchak Abarbanel** (1437-1509). Rabbi Yitzchak, of Davidic descent, was the last in the long line of great Jewish statesmen-scholars in Spain. Due to his extraordinary abilities, he served as treasurer of Spain and exerted great efforts to halt the expulsion of the Jews in 1492. Failing in this he went into exile with his people, where he was finally able to complete his monumental commentaries on most books of the Bible, the Haggadah, and others, and to compose a number of philosophical works. At the same time he rendered valuable services to the rulers of Portugal and, later, Venice, which enabled him to be of assistance to his brethren in exile.

**(f) Tur – Rabbi Jacob ben Asher** (1269-1343). The *Rosh* had followed up the work of the *Rif* by composing a digest of Talmudic discussion and law. His son now followed up the work of the *Rambam* by arranging these decisions in a new systematic code called the *Arba Turim,* or Four Rows. He included the opinions of earlier scholars but, in contrast to Maimonides, omitted those laws which were not applicable during the time of exile. His system of arrangement was later adopted by Rabbi Joseph Karo in the *"Shulchan Aruch."*

Numerous codes of Jewish Law were compiled by leading rabbis during the era of the *Rishonim.* These were based on the Talmud and the decisions of the *Geonim.* The *Rif* wrote a halachic condensation of the Talmud which in turn led to codes composed by the *Rambam* and *Tur.* Later on, the most widely accepted work was the *Shulchan Aruch,* written by Rav Yosef Karo, who based his work on the earlier Codes mentioned above.

**(g) Rabbi Joseph Karo** (1488-1575). Exiled from Spain and, later, Portugal, he wandered to Turkey and Palestine, where a group of outstanding scholars was gathering – devoting itself to Talmudic studies and profound kabbalistic thought – longing for the early redemption of Israel. When they made an attempt to renew the ancient chain of ordination, Rabbi Joseph was one of the first to be thus ordained. A saintly and scholarly personality of extraordinary stature, who had many great disciples, he composed kabbalistic writings as well as commentaries on the *Rambam's* and *Tur's* codifications of Jewish Laws – and, above all, built upon them, a new code.

Rav Joseph Karo called his halachic code *Shulchan Aruch* (The Prepared Table), for it was through this digest that the vast body of *Halachah* became accessible to every Jew. The *Shulchan Aruch* became the definitive code of halachic authority which served as a unifying force for Jews everywhere.

The *Shulchan Aruch* was not the personal opinion of its author, but a compilation of opinions found in the works of the *Rishonim,* which had gained the widest acceptance. Because of the near-universal acceptance of the *Shulchan Aruch,* its decisions are considered binding, unless otherwise indicated by the leading authorities of succeeding generations.

Since the *Shulchan Aruch* was the standard of Torah law, it became the subject of many commentaries that expounded, and occasionally disputed, its opinions.

The *Rema,* Rabbi Moshe Isserles of Cracow, Poland, was one of the most illustrious Torah personalities of Eastern Europe. He wrote a gloss on the *Shulchan Aruch* which included halachic decisions, opinions, and customs of Ashkenazic Jewry. This commentary complemented the *Shulchan Aruch,* whose author was of Sephardic origin. It was incorporated within the *Shulchan Aruch,* which assured the work's acceptance by all factions of the Torah community, thereby allowing it to emerge as a truly universal code of Torah law.

# ACHARONIM

The period of the *Acharonim* was a time of both persecution and peace. The Jews were among the most important contributors to general culture and civilization, and at the same time produced a wealth of supreme works elucidating Jewish law, philosophy, and Torah study.

In the history of Western Europe this period was called the Renaissance. For the Jews began with the dispersion of their

Spanish brethren across the continent. Just as persecution in Russia at the end of the 19th century was the impetus for waves of Jews to migrate to *Eretz Yisrael* and America, so too the expulsion from Spain was a major cause for the sprouting of Jewish centers all over Europe.

The Renaissance was a bridge between the medieval era and the modern era. Perhaps its most important feature (apart from humanism, which did not apply to the Jews) was the advent of printing. Yet the Renaissance opened with an Italian edict forbidding the printing of the Talmud and other Jewish books. When the ban was lifted (about ten years later) the *Shulchan Aruch* and many other important books were published.

Just as the *Amoraim* elucidated and clarified the Mishnah, so too the works of the *Acharonim* explained the works of the *Rishonim*. When the *Shulchan Aruch* began to gain widespread recognition, there were many *Acharonim* who devoted their time and energy to the task of interpreting the words of the *Shulchan Aruch* and the *Rema,* to clarify any ambiguities. Many commentaries to the *Shulchan Aruch* were almost universally accepted. The *Shulchan Aruch* thus became the definitive code of halachic authority, and served as a unifying force for Jews everywhere. Ashkenazic Jews followed the rulings of the Rema, while Sephardic Jews followed the rulings of Rabbi Joseph Karo.

Even during the Renaissance, the Jews were exiled from one country to another. Just when they started to feel secure and acclimated in their surroundings, they were either persecuted or forced to leave the country.

Some noted *Acharonim* were the **Maharshal,** the **Tosafos Yomtov,** and the **Shach.**

(a) **Maharshal — Rabbi Solomon Luria** (1510-1573). With the expulsion from Spain, the center of Jewish life shifted to Poland, where many Jews had migrated from countries of oppression and where a great spiritual leader now arose: the *Maharshal.* By the force of his powerful personality, he established high standards of communal life; his many responsa, even to far-off localities, spread the correct understanding of the Law; and his great academy in Lublin produced many outstanding scholars. His Talmud commentary, *Yam Shel Shlomoh,* based on close analysis and careful consideration of different versions, was completed only on several tractates.

(b) **Tosafos Yomtov – Rabbi Yomtov Lipmann Heller** (1579-1654). As Rabbi of the famous community of Prague, Rabbi Yomtov, at the age of 38, composed a monumental commentary on the *Mishnah* which explained it in the light of the Talmudic discussions. He also wrote other Talmudic and philosophical works. During the Thirty Years' War, he strove to bring about a fair and proportionate distribution of the financial burdens which fell upon the community. As a result he made some enemies, who denounced him for treason. Sentenced to death, he was imprisoned for some time and then expelled from Austrian territory. Enthusiastically received by the Jews of Poland, he continued his efforts to bring about communal justice (e.g. stopped "sales" of the Rabbinical office).

(c) **Shach – Rabbi Shabsai HaCohen** (1622-1663). Famous from his earliest youth for his knowledge and understanding of Talmudic learning, the *Shach* composed many important works – above all a primary commentary on the *Shulchan Aruch*. The Cossack uprising of 1648 caused the death of thousands of Polish Jews; many others had to flee abroad, where they were forced to remain even after peace was restored. The *Shach* found a refuge as Rabbi of Holleschau; but the suffering he had experienced (reflected in the *Selichos,* penitential prayer, he composed) caused his early death.

Other famous Torah personalities of this era included the following:

(a) **Rabbi Yehudah Loew – Maharal of Prague** (1512-1609) was a great Kabbalist who wrote commentaries on the Torah and Talmud. His profound philosophical works on a broad array of Torah subjects became the basis of Chassidic and Mussar thought to this day. His works continue to be studied intensively and are as influential as ever.

**(b) Rabbi Yonasan Eybeshutz** (1690-1764) was the founder and head of a famous yeshivah at Prague and later Chief Rabbi of the three congregations of Altona, Wandsbeck, and Hamburg, well-known centers of Jewish life and learning. He wrote a brilliant commentary on the *Shulchan Aruch* and a book of sermons, *Yaaros Devash*. His life was saddened by charges that he was secretly connected with the heretical followers of Sabbetai Zvi, the false messiah.

**(c) Rabbi Yaakov Emden** (1697-1776) was a great Torah sage and authority on halachah. During the sway of the false messiah, Sabbetai Zvi, Rabbi Yaakov Emden was one of the leading fighters for authentic Jewish belief.

**(d) Rabbi Eliyahu of Vilna — the Vilna Gaon** (1720-1797) — was a towering leader of Polish and world Jewry. He possessed incredible brilliance and already delivered halachic discourses at the young age of 7. He devoted night and day to the study of Torah, never wasting a single moment. Though he never accepted any official rabbinic position, he was, nonetheless, the recognized Torah leader of his generation. Rabbi Chaim of Volozhin, his outstanding disciple, established the prototype yeshivah.

Among other noted *Acharonim* are the **Maharsha,** and **Pnei Yehoshua.**

The expulsions, Inquisition, massacres and the Black Plague drove the Jewish communities further east into Poland and Russia, in an attempt to escape persecution. The early Jewish settlers were welcomed in Poland, and were able to establish themselves as merchants.

The Hebrew year of 5408-5409 (1648), known as *Tach V'tat* (Hebrew for 408-409), was a bloody one for the Jewish people. Bogdan Chmielnicki, a ruthless Ukrainian murderer, led his hordes of villainous brigands, known as Cossacks, in an uprising against their Polish overlords. The Jewish communities proved to be convenient targets too, just as they were in the First Crusade.

They quickly fell victim to the Cossack horsemen and their Tatar cohorts. A reign of terror gripped the Jews of Eastern Europe: Poland, Russia, and Lithuania. Over 100,000 innocent victims — men, women and children — were slaughtered *al kiddush Hashem* — as martyrs, in sanctification of Hashem's Name. The bloodthirsty Cossacks knew no pity. Jewish blood flowed freely through the communities of Poland and the Ukraines.

The dreadful year of *Tach V'Tat* passed, but the devastation was not quickly forgotten. An ocean of suffering and pain, misery and poverty, swept over our nation, from which it would not recover for many generations to come. To commemorate the terrible fate of so many thousands of innocent Jewish victims, special fast days and prayers were established.

**RABBI ISRAEL BAAL SHEM TOV – THE BESHT** (1700-1760). The massacres of 1648 had dealt a severe blow to Polish Jewry. Life was hard for the common Jew; he found little opportunity for Torah-study, and there arose the danger that he might thus lose contact with God's teachings. Hence the importance of the "Besht," the founder of Chassidism. Moved from his earliest youth by the awareness that one should see and serve God in everything, he spent years in the lonely Carpathian Mountains to reflect on the greatness of God and His teachings, and then taught these lofty ideas to the people around him. Drawing on the teachings of *Kabbalah,* he showed them the deeper meaning of human life, as Divine service, and of the Torah as the connection between man and God. He stressed joyful prayer and observance of the commandments, under the guidance of learned and saintly personalities.

In the year 1740 (*Lag B'Omer* of 5500), Rabbi Yisrael announced to his brother-in-law, Rabbi Gershon, that the time had come for him to reveal himself to the world. The Baal Shem Tov settled in Mezhibuz, where his greatness in Torah learning and piety were revealed to all. He established a *beis midrash* there with a few illustrious disciples, and his fame began to grow. He attracted masses of people from near and far. People stricken by illness came to him requesting that he pray for them, for he was considered a saintly man. Torah scholars were interested in the Baal Shem Tov's Torah teachings, and they, too, came to speak to him. The

Baal Shem Tov derived most of his Torah thoughts from the Kabbalah found in the holy *Zohar* and from the teachings of the Arizal, who also delved into the Kabbalah and lived in Tzefas two hundred years before him.

One of the principles of Judaism is serving Hashem with joy. *Mesillas Yesharim,* a classic *mussar* work written by Rabbi Moshe Chaim Luzzato, says the following: "Chassidism (great piety) does not depend upon self-denial or upon punishing oneself. One important aspect in serving Hashem is for a person's heart to be very joyous that he is privileged to be a servant to Hashem and able to study the Holy Torah and keep its *mitzvos.*" The great Kabbalist, the Ari HaKadosh (ibid. Chapter 27), constantly taught his students the importance of joy in serving Hashem. When he was asked how he reached his spiritual level, he answered, "Through joy."

The Baal Shem Tov began teaching the people that they must stop punishing their bodies and torturing themselves with fasting and other harsh means. He used to say, "Through joy, one can reach great heights and achievements, while sadness, which in itself may not be a sin, can bring a man to many serious sins." The Baal Shem Tov said that *simchah* had the power to dispel unfavorable decrees.

The word *chassid* refers to one who is pious and righteous beyond the exact requirement of the law. This applies to commandments between man and Hashem, but especially to *mitzvos* between man and his fellow man. The Talmud teaches, "One who wishes to be a *chassid* should be especially careful not to harm or hurt his fellow man."

The thing that prevents someone from achieving this piety is haughtiness. If a person is only aware of himself, then he truly cannot be a complete person. If you rearrange the letters of the Hebrew word *ani* (I), it can also spell *ayin,* which means nothing. A haughty person is worthless.

Similarly, every Jew must be viewed as a part of the Jewish nation as a whole. Just as the whole body suffers when any part of it is hurt, so every Jew suffers whenever his fellow Jew sins or experiences misfortune.

In keeping with the belief that Hashem is everywhere and close to everyone, He is also easy to reach. All that one needs in order to communicate with Him are sincere prayers. As *Psalms* teaches, "Hashem is close to all who call upon Him in truth." Even the most ignorant can be sincere and genuine in their prayers to Hashem.

Rabbi Israel aimed to strengthen Jewish life by giving to every Jew the clear and heart-stirring consciousness of his mission in the Divine universe. Chassidism drew on the teachings of the Kabbalah but, rather than popularize them, it taught the ordinary *chassid* to attach himself to the *tzaddik* who was guided by these doctrines and expressed the spirit of the Torah in his life and his teachings.

The Baal Shem Tov appeared on the scene during a dark and dreary period of Jewish history. Over a relatively short time, his followers had grown into a great Chassidic movement which transcended boundaries of countries. His legacy revitalized many Jewish communities and is still a vital force in the Jewish world, more than two hundred years after his death. To this day, Chassidism has remained a strong and influential force in the life of the Jewish people.

Rabbi Yaakov Yosef of Polno'oh, known as "the Toldos," recorded most of the teachings of the Baal Shem Tov. His major work, the *Toldos Yaakov Yosef*, which appeared in 1780, was the first book ever to expound the teachings of the Baal Shem Tov. Another great disciple was Rabbi Pinchas Koretzer. He was originally opposed to *Chassidus*, but later joined it.

When the Baal Shem Tov passed away, Rabbi Dov Ber of Mezeritch, commonly known as "the Maggid," or the Great Maggid, was unanimously chosen to take his place as the leader of the Chassidic movement. Many of the greatest minds flocked to his court. He, in turn, sent out his disciples to spread the word of *Chassidus*.

Rabbi Menachem Mendel of Vitebsk, born in 1730, was only 9 years old when he met the Baal Shem Tov. Years later, he became a disciple of the Maggid of Mezeritch, where he rose above all the other disciples. After the Maggid's death, the group wanted to elect him as leader of the Chassidic movement. He refused the position, and from that time on, *Chassidus* no longer had a single leader. Rabbi Menachem Mendel organized a large-scale immigration to the Land of Israel. His group totaled about three hundred people who braved the elements and the dangerous journey in order to settle in the Holy Land.

**RABBI SHNEUR ZALMAN OF LIADI** — The Baal HaTanya (1747-1812). An enthusiastic follower of the "Great *Maggid*," the *Baal HaTanya* was an extraordinary Talmudic scholar, who composed a practical digest of the *Shulchan Aruch*, taking into account later scholars. He was also deeply versed in *Kabbalah* and built upon it the *Tanya*, his profound work on man's nature and duties which provided the basis for a new and major branch in Chassidism (Chabad/Lubavitch). He was a saintly and scholarly personality who attempted to pacify the Vilna Gaon and others who were afraid that Chassidism might develop into a Messianic sect; but he failed and was indeed twice imprisoned as a result of denunciation by misguided opponents.

Since the time of the Baal Shem Tov, there have been scores of important Chassidic dynasties and hundreds, if not thousands, of very great Chassidic rebbes. There is no way we can mention even a fraction of them. The Nazi Holocaust almost succeeded in destroying the movement's leaders and followers — but the relatively few rebbes who survived threw themselves into the task of rebuilding after the war, and their success has been phenomenal. Due to the limitations of space, we offer only one example of such a leader.

**GERER REBBE – RABBI ABRAHAM MORDECAI ALTER** (1866-1948). Was an outstanding Chassidic leader during the last century. Aware of the challenge of the secular industrial civilization of modern Poland, he made Gerer Chassidism a dynamic popular movement with a powerful appeal to Jewish youth, stimulated the founding of Torah-study groups, and of a press expressing the Torah-viewpoint on the communal problems of the day. Through his extensive correspondence with his adherents, his influence stretched to all parts of the Jewish world. Particularly devoted to the rise of Torah-true Jewry in Palestine, he mustered great moral and practical support for it.

The Gerer Rebbe, elderly and frail, was spirited out of Nazi-occupied Europe miraculously. He came to Jerusalem and soon learned that nearly all of his hundreds of thousands of *chassidim* had been murdered by the Nazis. He ignored his poor health and began to lay the groundwork for the future rebirth. He died during the Arab siege of Jerusalem and had to be buried in the courtyard of his *shul*. He was succeeded in turn by his three surviving sons. They built Ger into a large, thriving movement in Israel and America. It is one of the largest in the world.

This story is typical of such movements as Satmar, Lubavitch, Bobov, Belz, Vizhnitz and Skver.

# ﴾THE AGE OF ENLIGHTENMENT

Throughout the ages, the Jewish people had to be careful not to allow neighboring cultures to steer them away from Judaism. From the time they lived as slaves in Egypt, and on through the years that they lived in *Eretz Yisrael* with heathen Canaanite neighbors, through the periods of Hellenist and Roman influence, Jews have always had to struggle to remain faithful to Hashem and not let themselves be influenced by the majority surrounding them.

From the Middle Ages onwards, however, there was a natural barrier to assimilation between Jews and their Christian neighbors. Anti-Semitism was so fierce that it kept the Jews isolated, frequently in ghettos, and made them more firm in their faith. Forced conversions executed by the followers of Islam, the Crusades, the Inquisition, and subsequent expulsions from England, France, Spain, and Germany all left their indelible marks upon the Jewish people. Pogroms and blood libels occurred often enough to reinforce the separation between Jews and their Christian neighbors.

It was during the Age of Enlightenment (*Haskalah*) that Jews were blinded by the promises of "liberty, equality, and fraternity." They believed that by becoming like the nations around them, they would gain esteem and anti-Semitism would vanish. Some Jews were misguided and believed it was good to be assimilated with the rest of the world, lest the nations deny them the respect and especially the equality they coveted. This was the cry of the German Jewish Enlightenment.

Such Jews preached that the laws and encumbrances of Judaism interfered with the new awakening of the "era of brotherhood" which would integrate all mankind and abolish forever all prejudices and hatreds. Moses Mendelssohn, a German-Jewish philosopher, was the role model for the founders of Reform Judaism, which denied the validity of the Torah's commandments. Some secularists even went further and preached actual conversion to a liberal form of Christianity. In fact, four of Mendelssohn's six children converted to Christianity, as did many of the children of "enlightened" Jews.

Jews began to feel inferior. "What will the nations say?" was a source of great worry to the assimilationists, as it was to the Hellenists in ancient days. By obliterating their Jewishness, they felt that the nations would learn to love them. It was a terrible mistake; some of the worst pogroms were unleashed in the cities where the Jews were like their neighbors in every respect. Also, the Holocaust began in Germany where Jewish assimilation was most complete.

David Friedlander, a disciple of Mendelssohn and his immediate successor, led the Reform movement toward Jewish assimilation and the Germanization of Jewish life. He exerted the full weight of his influence to introduce radical changes in the rituals of Judaism, repudiating the authority of the rabbis and rejecting the Torah which had guided Jewish religious conduct throughout the centuries. He expressed his willingness to accept baptism and be converted to Christianity. Friedlander addressed an anonymous letter to the chief consistorial councilor in Berlin, in which he applied for admission into the Christian Church, on the condition that he would be free to deny the divinity of the Nazarene and be excused from participating in the rites of the Church. The answer was a sharp rebuff. The Church would have nothing to do with straddlers who "halt between two opinions."

The Age of Enlightenment thrust reason before religion. Reformers introduced a new concept of "Bible criticism" which sought to question the authenticity of the Bible. By doing so, they tried to give more validity to those who were discarding the precepts of the Torah.

Two prominent German Bible critics attacked the basic belief of Judaism and its Torah. Interestingly enough, they were comparatively lenient with the New Testament and had very little criticism of it. The anti-Semites jumped on the bandwagon of the Bible critics and used their works as further "proof" that Judaism was a fraud.

Famous rabbis of that era include:

**RABBI AKIVA EIGER** (1761-1837). It was during this difficult period that Rabbi Akiva Eiger was born in Hungary in 1761. He devoted all of his time and energy to the study of Torah. His growing fame as a *gaon* (scholar) attracted students from near and far to his yeshivah in Posen. He was a great halachic authority who was approached with questions from rabbis all over the world.

Rabbi Akiva Eiger was a militant fighter against the inroads of the Reformers and assimilationists. In 1807, when the government was about to prohibit the study of the Talmud, Rabbi Akiva Eiger wrote a letter explaining the importance of the moral and spiritual value of the Talmud. His disciple, Rabbi Shlomo Plessener, wrote *Edus LeYisrael* which, together with Rabbi Akiva Eiger's letter, impressed the authorities to such an extent that they granted permission for the further study of the Talmud.

**MALBIM – RABBI MEIR LEIBUSH MALBIM** (1809-1879). Rabbi of Bucharest, Koenigsberg and other large communities, the *Malbim* was also invited to become Chief Rabbi of New York, belonging, as he did, to the great leaders of his age. He declined. He realized the challenge of the modern environment to the traditional Jewish ways and met it both in the discharge of his communal duties (suffering much from assimilationist opponents to whom he refused to give way) and in his brilliant writings on *Halachah* and, above all, on the Bible. His monumental commentary demonstrates his philosophical clarity, his familiarity with the whole

Talmudic literature, and his understanding of the spirit and structure of the Hebrew language.

**CHASAM SOFER — RABBI MOSHE SOFER** (1763-1839). The *Chasam Sofer*, Rabbi of Pressburg, was author of a great number of works, above all of thousands of important responsa, commentaries on various tractates of the Talmud and on the *Chumash*, etc. Son-in-law of Rabbi Akiva Eiger, he (and the many distinguished disciples of his yeshivah) led the fight against the Reform in Hungary and succeeded in establishing the independence and communal unity of Torah-true Jewry in that country.

**RABBI SAMSON RAPHAEL HIRSCH** (1808-1888). At a time when the Reform had won over most of Western European Jewry, he eloquently explained the eternal meaning of the Torah and that, instead of adapting it to changing cultural and social forces, we should make it our guide in the modern world, evaluating modern intellectual ideas and social forces in the light of *Torah* (*Torah im Derech Eretz*). His brilliant writings, the *The Nineteen Letters*, his Pentateuch and Psalm commentaries, *Choreb* (on the meaning of the commandments), etc. made a profound impression on his time. In his community in Frankfort he succeeded in applying his teachings in practice, above all by founding a school which prepared its youth for a Jewish life in the modern world, through teaching Torah as well as secular subjects in the light of Torah principles.

**RABBI YISRAEL SALANTER** (1810-1883) was among the great Torah scholars and leaders of this period. He was the father of the *Mussar* movement which stresses self-examination and improvement. He stressed that one should always look for and develop the best within the Jewish nation. He stressed the importance of *"bein adam lechaveiro* — the relationship between man and his fellow Jew."

Rabbi Yisrael Salanter advocated the study of *Mesillas Yesharim* (by Rabbi Moshe Luzzatto) and *Chovos HaLevavos* (by Rabbi Bachaya ibn Pakudai). The *Mussar* movement provided a positive alternative to the Haskalah.

**RABBI ISAAC BLASER** (1836-1907).

Chassidism had discharged three important functions for Polish

Jewry: It had stimulated a more conscious observance of the Law, it had thereby erected a dam against the disruptive influence of modern secularism, and it created masses of Jews who were loyal to and enthusiastic about Judaism. In Lithuania this was the work of the *Mussar* movement, initiated by Rabbi Israel Salanter (1810-1883), which stressed self-analysis and self-improvement as the foundation of proper Torah-observance. Rabbi Israel's disciple, Rabbi Isaac Blaser, Rabbi of St. Petersburg, was largely responsible for the development of *Mussar:* He collected and published Rabbi Israel's writings (in *Or Yisrael*), and directed the *Kollel* in Kovno, which became the prototype of the *Mussar* yeshivah, combining Talmudic study and moralistic self-improvement. He emigrated to Palestine in later years.

**RABBI SIMCHA ZISSEL ZIV** (1824-1898), another of Reb Yisrael's most distinguished disciples, founded and led the leading *Mussar* yeshivah, the famed Talmud Torah of Kelm. He was known as the Alter (Elder) of Kelm. Never a large institution, it concentrated on a small number of highly distinguished, mature scholars. Most of the leading *Mussar* figures were disciples of the Alter and his successors.

**RABBI CHAIM SOLOVEITCHIK** (1853-1919), Rabbi of Brisk (Brest-Litovsk), was one of the heads of the Yeshivah of Volozhin until the government closed it, Rabbi Chaim "Brisker" was a commanding figure in the Jewish world. His *Chiddushei Rabbeinu Chaim* (on the *Rambam's Mishneh Torah*) demonstrated his method of Talmudic analysis which became characteristic of the famous Lithuanian yeshivos in general and was spread by his disciples all over the world. His scholarship and saintliness gained for him undisputed communal authority, and he exercised it in order to solve the pressing educational and social problems of the age. At a time when the ease of communications made it feasible, and the common problems made it vital, he helped establish Agudath Israel (1912) to bring about a worldwide organization of the Jewish people under the banner of the Torah, for the solution of all national problems in the spirit of Torah.

# ᴖᶳ WAR AND CATASTOPHE

World War I broke out on Tishah B'Av of 1914, and it had catastrophic effects on the Jewish people. The course of battle surged across Poland and Russia, and forced almost two million Jews to become refugees. The community structures were destroyed — in many cases never to be restored — and most of the famous yeshivos were disbanded for years. The Communist revolution cut three million Jews off from Torah observance. The upheavals of the war led to the emergence of Hitler and the Holocaust.

Nevertheless, between World War I and II, Torah life was rebuilt in Eastern Europe, although it never recovered fully. Two of the leaders of the yeshivah world were the Chofetz Chaim and Rabbi Chaim Ozer Grodzenski.

**CHOFETZ CHAIM – RABBI ISRAEL MEIR HACOHEN** (1838-1933). The Chofetz Chaim attained worldwide eminence through his works on the legal and moral teachings of the Torah, on *Halachah* and *Mussar* (notably his *Mishnah Berurah* and *Chofetz Chaim*). In his own person, saintly perfection and scholarly wisdom were united in such a manner that he became the spiritual leader of 20th-century Torah-true Jewry, and his lowly house in the little town of Radin (where he had his yeshivah) the source of communal inspiration. The Chofetz Chayim devoted all his powers to attain the carrying out of the teachings of the Torah not only among individuals but also in the public life of the Jewish nation (thus he, too, was one of the leaders of Agudath Israel from its creation until his death).

**RABBI CHAIM OZER GRODZENSKI** (1863-1940). Head of the Vilna Rabbinical Court, he was one of the leading authorities on Jewish Law and an outstanding figure in Jewish life. His responsa to questions of law, which came to him from all parts of the Jewish world, are collected in *Achiezer,* and, with the Chofetz Chaim and the Gerer Rebbe, among others, he shared the spiritual leadership of Agudath Israel. He also took a decisive part in guiding Torah-true Jewry as a whole, in protecting and stimulating its educational activities, and in organizing it for the solution of the

Jewish problems of the time, in Palestine as well as in the countries of dispersion. With his powers already ebbing, he devoted his last strength to attempts to save the yeshivos of Poland and Lithuania uprooted by the war.

**RABBI ELCHONON WASSERMAN** (1875-1940). Already long before the outbreak of the last war, Rabbi Elchonon, an outstanding disciple of the Chofetz Chaim, head of the yeshivah in Baranovich and a leader of Torah Jewry, raised his voice again and again, in a number of penetrating and challenging warnings to the Jewish people, pointing to the crisis about to engulf it. He pointed to its consequences — intolerable human pain and suffering — and he called for reflection and a return to the service of G-d, so that we may bring close the speedy establishment of His kingdom. Unwilling to leave his people in their hour of suffering, he himself fell a victim to the catastrophe he had predicted at the hands of the Nazis.

There were a great many accepted authorities, both among the commentators to the *Shulchan Aruch,* and among the writers of responsa. These apply Torah law to individual cases, and often set binding precedents. Over the years, various compilations of these later opinions were published. Among the famous ones were: *Kitzur Shulchan Aruch,* assembled by Rabbi Shlomo Ganzfried, and the *Aruch HaShulchan* by Rabbi Yechiel Michel Epstein. Both of these works are summaries of the *Shulchan Aruch.* An authoritive and popular commentary on the *Shulchan Aruch Orach Chaim,* called the *Mishnah Berurah,* was written by the saintly Chofetz Chaim.

More recently, volumes of responsa were written on more modern-day questions by the late great Torah leader, Rabbi Moshe Feinstein, and other authorities.

# ❧ ISRAEL'S UNIQUE ROLE

From the beginning of our history as a people we were assigned a unique role in world affairs. "You shall be unto Me a nation of priests, a holy people" (*Shemos* 18:16). Israel's very existence is defined by these words. The Jews were to live not only for themselves, but were to be G-d's model nation for mankind. They boldly proclaimed the creed of One Creator in the face of the polytheistic notions of the entire world around them.

When we study history, we find, repeatedly, how great nations such as Egypt, Assyria, Babylonia, Persia, Greece, and Rome built up vast empires, but still collapsed one after another. They are now only a memory. In contrast, Israel passed through many crises — its land overrun by invaders; its independence lost; its population taken captive — yet the Jewish nation survived, whereas the other peoples perished. Why?

The answer is very simple. The Nation of Israel, alone among all nations, is not characterized solely by possession of territory or political status, nor by language or culture, but only by its G-d-given Torah. It was the Torah which brought the Israelite nation into being in the first place, and the Jewish people survived only due to their continued adherence to the Divine teachings. This is the explanation of the uniqueness of Jewish history and the secret of Jewish survival. As Rav Saadya Gaon expressed it, "Our nation is a nation only by reason of its Torah."

Rabbi Samson Raphael Hirsch, in his book of essays called *The Nineteen Letters*, summed it up as follows: "Other states, everywhere, in all the glory of human power and arrogance, disappeared from the face of the earth, while Israel, though devoid of might and splendor, lived on because of its loyalty to G-d and His Law. Could Israel, then, refuse to acknowledge the All-One as its G-d, or to accept His Torah as its sole mission on earth?"